of

BIBLE TRUTHS

Illustrations

of

BIBLE TRUTHS

Compiled by
Ruth Peters

AMG

PUBLISHERS
Chattanooga, TN 37422

ILLUSTRATIONS OF BIBLE TRUTHS

ISBN 0-89957-229-4

Printed in the United States of America
03 02 01   -R- 6 5 4 3 2

*To Mrs. Ruth Peters who has volunteered ten years
of her retirement to serve as the librarian
at AMG International.*

Contents

Admonition

1. Building a Noble Character

In a great cathedral in Europe, there is a window made by an apprentice out of the bits of stained glass that were thrown away as worthless refuse when the other windows were made; this is the most beautiful window of all. You can build a noble character for yourself, in spite of all the hurts and injuries done consciously or unconsciously by others, with the fragments of the broken hopes, joys and the lost opportunities that lie strewn about your feet. No matter how badly others have hurt and marred you, they cannot prevent you from building a beautiful character for yourself; conversely, others by their best work cannot cause you to build a beautiful character. The fine character of your father or mother is not yours; you've got to build your own.

2. Christian Liberty

As in the natural body, so in the mystical body of Christ, the Church, a large measure of liberty is granted to each member. But this liberty may not pass the bounds by which another member would be injured or suffer loss. My liberty to stretch out my arms depends on how close I am to the other fellow. As Paul says in Galatians 5:13, "For brethren, ye have been called unto liberty; only use not liberty for an occasion to the flesh, but by love serve one another."

3. Fruit Needs Light

Some time ago we noticed that a tree planted at the sunny end of a house had large and beautiful blossoms. It was a feast to the eyes; but what an amazing difference in some of the branches trained round the corner of the house where they got much less sun. The blossoms were starved and drooping, and there was little promise of fruit. They had the same root and stem in common, but while one part of the tree was in the full glorious light, the other branches were in the shade.

Our character is affected in the same way by insufficient enlightenment. The dark places produce unfruitful branches: strange weaknesses, distortions, immaturities, indirection, failures in practical life and conduct. "The fruit of the Spirit is love, joy, peace, long-suffering, gentleness, goodness, faith, meekness, temperance" (Gal. 5:22, 23). If we are to bear all manner of precious fruit, each in its rightful season, we must trustfully and joyfully lay open our whole soul to the full expanse of God's light shining in the face of Jesus Christ.

1

4. No Spiritual Blind Spot

Cricketers talk a great deal about visual imperfection, for sooner or later the bowler finds the blind spot, the batsman misjudges the ball, and his sport comes to an end. The devil plays for the blind spot, and if there is such a defect in our spiritual vision, sooner or later it gets us into trouble. The blind spot in the natural eye is a necessary, unavoidable, physiological defect of which the brightest and most skillful athlete cannot rid himself. However, morally and religiously no part of our nature need be dark, and we may successfully defend ourselves in every assault. If for any subtle, selfish reason we harbor some bias of the mind, some prejudice that warps the judgment, some neglect of charity, some inertia that obstructs conviction, some deviation of aim, some deflection in action, we lay ourselves open to grievous losses and sorrows. "But if we walk in the light, as he [God] is in the light, we have fellowship one with another" (1 John 1:7). If we don't have fellowship with other believers, there is a dark spot in our spiritual vision. But the Christian whose heart is full of light enjoys the company of those of like precious faith, "and the blood of Jesus Christ his Son cleanseth us from all sin." It is our privilege to walk in the full light, to have our whole soul instructed and illuminated.

5. Faithful in This World

The student in the lower grades who is always idly dreaming of the time when he will be a senior, and thus neglects his present studies, will never be prepared to take his place with any distinction in his senior year. If we scholars in the larger school of life are so fascinated by revelations of the unseen world that we lose interest in the present one, we will never be prepared for its highest enjoyment.

6. A Good Reason for Politeness

"My boy," said a father to his son, "treat everybody with politeness, even those who are rude to you; remember, you show courtesy to others, not because they are gentlemen, but because you are one."

7. Perils of Conscience

It is essential that we should exercise conscience, but let us not forget that in this matter, as in all others, privilege is linked with responsibility. Of course, we may attribute unworthy motives to authoritarian churches that proclaim the right to dictate to the individual what is right and what is wrong. We may say, as many have said, that they adopt this standpoint for their own ends to acquire power and control. But that is not a satisfactory explanation, and it is an unworthy charge. Their action is generally based on the danger of individual judgment and the peril of the individual conscience, because this privilege that we all claim does have it perils. It is so perilous, indeed, that while we pay lip service to its sanctity and sacredness, we are compelled to curtail its freedom. There is no community that can or dare base its life upon the freedom of each individual's conscience. It would result in chaos. Jesus Christ allows us a certain freedom. Freedom is the basis of joy, but if it oversteps the bounds of moral responsibility it is too perilous.

8. Conscience Must Be Tested

Not every coin that bears the exact stamp is a genuine coin. Very often, the counterfeit, the base and worthless coin, bears the right stamp also. It isn't the impression that matters so much as the nature of the metal. Many an action that bears the impression of a good conscience is condemned before God as perilous, injurious, and destructive in its issues. The coin must be tested on the touchstone to discover if it rings true. Conscience must be tested on the touchstone of Christian principle and the Spirit of the Master. It is not enough to say, "It seems right to me." We must ask how does this action, this line of conduct, ring on the touchstone of Christian principle? Not what we think but what Christ thinks, what the Master thinks, matters most.

9. Conscience Like a Pet Dog

Speaking of conscience, E. L. Allen said, "Honestly, what use do we make of our God-given reason? I know what use I make of it. I use it chiefly to provide reasons for what I want to do without admitting it is for pursuing some personal ambition. A man may have his conscience so well disciplined and trained that, instead of blazing a trail before him, it is like a pet dog which just trots obediently at his heels and never so much as barks! 'If therefore the light that is in thee be darkness, how great is that darkness!' "

10. Shut the Door

A man went inside a telephone booth and dialed the number of a friend. When the connection was made, the friend kept saying, "I can't hear you; speak louder; I can't hear you." All he cold hear was the roar of traffic in the background. "Shut the door so I can hear," he said to the caller. In order to hear God's voice speaking to you, you've got to shut the door to the outside world so that its enticements won't distract you. Doing this could change your whole life. Then when you go back into the crowd, you'll not only be able to listen to what the world has to say, but you'll have something to say to the world that you've personally heard from God.

11. The Right to Pursue

Someone cursed Benjamin Franklin, charging that the Constitution of the United States was a farce. "Where is all the success that it guarantees us?" he sneered. Franklin, smiling, answered, "My friend, the Constitution guarantees only the right to the pursuit of happiness." Psalm 34:14 tells us to not only seek peace but pursue it.

Attitude

12. Roses among Thorns

Benjamin Franklin once said, "The sentence which has most influenced my life is, 'Some persons grumble because God placed thorns among roses. Why not thank God because He placed roses among thorns?' I first read it when but a mere lad. Since that day it has occupied a front room in my life and has given it an optimistic trend." To be meek is to have a disposition to see the roses among the thorns, rather than to complain about the thorns among the roses. Which do you see? Your answer will help you to judge whether you possess that meekness of which our Savior spoke.

13. Seeing the Beautiful

A lady, paying an early morning visit to a neighbor, was ushered into a rather untidy room for which her hostess profusely apologized, but her visitor smilingly replied, "I had eyes for nothing but these lovely roses," pointing to a vase of beauties which occupied a prominent place on the table. Just as the eye sees what it looks for, so the soul that is itself beautiful finds all that is best and noblest and most worthy of praise in the men and women.

14. A Healthy Inner Eye

After referring to Himself as the light and life of men, our Lord goes on to say that, for the apprehension of light, a corresponding and appropriate organ is required. This organ is the eye. The eye that receives light for the whole body gives light to the whole body—the light in which all its activities are carried on—and may therefore be called the lamp or candle of the body. But the amount of light received and distributed depends on the power and accuracy of the eye that receives it. The organ may be diseased. It may prevent the access of the light or pervert it so that we do not see things as they are, or even in extreme cases do not see them at all. If this solitary candle is put out, how profound must be the darkness in which we walk! If it is obscured or distorted, how radical and misleading must be the errors into which it betrays us. It is of the utmost importance, therefore, that we should keep the one organ which receives and imparts light—the light of all our seeing, all our working, all our progress—in a healthy condition.

In all this we have been dealing only with the application of the passage of Luke 11:33-36. For while speaking of the eye of the body, it is obvious that it was the eye of the soul that our Lord had in mind. The spiritual part in us has its perceptive faculty as does the physical part, and it is even more important that the spiritual candle should be lifted to its due place and kept burning brightly than that the physical candle should be placed on the lampstand and not hidden in a cellar or under a bushel basket.

If then we turn from the physical to the spiritual application of the passage, what is it that our Lord is teaching us in these words? I believe He is saying that a healthy, trained, unprejudiced understanding is required for the due apprehension and appreciation of spiritual truth, and that the health and power of the understanding by which we receive and impart the truth depends mainly on the establishing of right attitudes toward the hearing and sifting of God's Word as revealed in the Scriptures. A desire to know and follow the truth at whatever cost is a prerequisite to "seeing" the truth.

15. A Good Relationship Made the Difference

A girl who received a book from a young man, read it and said, "What a tiresome book!" The young man said, "Did you notice who wrote it?" She looked at the front page and saw that her lover was the author. She began to read it again, and at the end she said, "I never read a greater book." What made the difference? Her relationship to the writer. Look at God. Is He good or evil? It all depends on whether you are single in heart or evil in heart. If you look at Jesus, you may see Him either as a deceiver or as a Savior. What makes the difference? Your attitude, your eye.

16. Drive or Drought

When you lose hope of doing better, you lose everything that makes life worth living. A great artist was once asked, "What's the best picture you've ever painted?" "The next one," he replied confidently. But another artist was heard to lament, "Too bad I failed," though he was at the very height of his glory. "Why do you say that?" asked a friend of his in astonishment. "Because I've lost any hope of improvement," he said. He was right; the person who has stopped hoping has truly failed.

17. The Discouraged Christian

Many times the Christian wishes for death in the face of difficulties and trials. He is like the poor man carrying a load of sticks who, when he became tired, sat down on a bank, and laying his sticks on the ground said, "I am sick and tired of this. I wish death would come to relieve me." Instantly, Death slipped up and said, "Here am I; what do you want of me?" "I want you to help me put this bundle of sticks on my back again," said the astonished pilgrim. We are all prone to think that our load of sticks is heavier—

that our road more difficult and our enemies more daring than any other Christian's.

18. Wrong Attitude

Many of us Christians are like the little girl who started fighting with a friend. Her mother who heard about the quarrel talked with her little girl about it trying to show her she was wrong and her need of asking God's forgiveness. Accordingly, when the little one kneeled down to pray, she humbly asked, "O God, please forgive me for getting angry and quarreling with Charlotte." So far so good. But the wrong disposition was still there, for the child went on, "And make Charlotte come to me and ask my forgiveness. O Lord, give her no rest until she is sorry and comes and tells me so!"

19. Expecting Evil

Don't be like the woman who one day felt unusually well. "How are you, lady?" someone asked. "Today I am quite well, but tomorrow I am sure I am going to suffer again," she sighed. It is a terrible thing to expect evil that may never come your way. The expectation of evil kills many more than the evil itself.

Bible

20. The Infallible Chart

A ship's mate once challenged a chaplain with the question, "How is it that you are always talking to my men about Jesus Christ? Did you ever see Him?" "No, I never did." "Then how can you tell a man to trust in someone you have never seen? I can't see any sense in that." "Well," replied the chaplain, "when you head for a place of refuge in a storm, what sense is there in telling your men to let go the anchor when they cannot see the ground? On what principle do you trust your ship and your life to ground you have never seen and never can see?" "Oh," said the mate, "we go by our chart." "Exactly," replied the chaplain, holding up his Bible, "and I, too, go by a chart, and it is an infallible one, while yours is not. It tells me of the only sure ground of my salvation—the atoning work of Christ upon the cross. My faith, like your anchor, takes hold of this unseen but real ground, and so rides out the storm of life in peace and safety."

21. A New Heart

A certain prisoner, most cunning and brutal, was singularly repulsive even in comparison with other prisoners. He had been known for his daring and for the utter absence of all feeling when committing acts of violence. The chaplain had spoken to him several times but had not succeeded even in getting an answer. The man was sullenly set against all instruction. At last he expressed a desire for a certain book, but as it was not in the library the chaplain pointed to the Bible which was placed in his cell, saying, "Did you ever read that Book?" He gave no answer but looked at the good man as if he would kill him. The question was kindly repeated, with the assurance that he would find it well worth reading. "Mister," said the convict, "you would not ask me such a question if you knew who I am. What have I to do with a book of that sort?" The chaplain answered, "I know all about you and that's why I think the Bible is the book for you." "It would do me no good," he cried. "I am past all feeling." Doubling up his fist, he struck the iron door of the cell and said, "My heart is as hard as that iron; there is nothing in any book that will ever touch me."

"Well," said the chaplain, "you want a new heart. Did you ever read the covenant of grace?" To which the man answered sullenly by inquiring what he meant by such talk. His friend replied, "Listen to these words: 'A new heart also will I give you, and a new spirit will I put within you' " (Ezek. 36:26). The words struck the man with amazement. He asked to have the passage found for him in the Bible. He read the words again and again; and when the chaplain came back to him the next day, the wild beast was tamed. "Oh, sir," he said, "I never dreamed of such a promise! I never believed it possible that God would speak in such a way to men. If He gives me a new heart, it will be a miracle of mercy; and yet I think He is going to work that miracle upon me, for the very hope of a new nature is beginning to touch me as I never was touched before."

22. *Misuse of Scripture*

A man who was fond of having his own way at home made sure that he got it by constantly reminding his wife that the Bible said she was to obey her husband. He made this an excuse for passing off on her any tasks he found too distasteful for himself. She became a virtual slave to his comfort and that of his relatives. He conveniently overlooked the biblical admonition to husbands to give "honour unto the wife, as unto the weaker vessel." His feeling was that God had made him lord and master in his own home and he was exploiting this prerogative to the fullest. We do not invoke Him and His Word to serve our own ends.

23. *Converted Convict*

A convict, dying of a loathsome disease in the Arizona State Prison at Florence, was given a New Testament one day by a visiting prison worker. He started to read it and became so convicted of sin that he hurled it the length of the cell. When the Book landed on the floor, it fell open to the First Epistle of John. A verse boldly outlined in red caught the angry convict's eye. He stooped down to look at it, and this is what he read: "The blood of Jesus Christ his Son cleanseth us from all sin." That message brought him to his knees, crying out to God for forgiveness, for cleansing, for healing. He became a new man in Christ Jesus. He started a Bible class for the convicts, and in time secured an unconditional pardon from the Governor of Arizona. The governor's pardon freed him from prison, but the pardon the Lord gave brought him purity of spirit, soul, and body, and through him brought many others into the Kingdom.

24. *The Law of Moses*

An unbeliever of acute mind sought an acquaintance with the truth of the Bible and began to read the Book of Genesis. When he had reached the Ten Commandments, he said to a friend, "I will tell you what I used to think. I supposed that Moses was the leader of a horde of bandits; that, having a strong mind, he acquired great influence over superstition, that the exhibition was supernatural. I have been looking into the nature of that law. I have been trying to see whether I can add anything to it or take anything from it, so as to make it better. Sir, I cannot. It is perfect.

"The first commandment directs us to make the Creator the object of our supreme love and reverence. That is right. If He be our Creator, Preserver, and Supreme Benefactor, we ought to treat Him and none other as such. The second forbids idolatry—that certainly is right. The third forbids profanity. The fourth fixes a time for religious worship. If there be a God, He surely ought to be worshiped. It is suitable that there should be an outward homage, significant of our inward regard. If God be worshiped, it is proper that some time should be set apart for that purpose when all may worship harmoniously and without interruption. One day in seven is certainly not too much, and I do not know that it is too little. The fifth defines the peculiar duties arising from family relations. Injuries to our neighbor are then classified by the moral law. They are divided into offenses against life, chastity, property, and character; and I notice that the greatest offense in each class is expressly forbidden. Thus the greatest injury to life is murder; to chastity, adultery; to property, theft; to character, perjury. Now, the greater offense must include the less of the same kind. Murder must include every injury to life; adultery, every injury

to purity; and so of the rest. This moral code is then closed and perfected by a command forbidding every improper desire in regard to our neighbors. I have been thinking, where did Moses get the Law?

"I have read history. The Egyptians and the adjacent nations were idolaters; so were the Greeks and Romans; the wisest and best Greeks or Romans never gave a code of morals like this. Where did Moses get that law which surpasses the wisdom and philosophy of the most enlightened ages? He lived at a period comparatively barbarous; but he has given a law in which the learning and sagacity of all subsequent time can detect no flaw. Where did he get it? He could not have soared so far above his age as to have devised it himself. I am satisfied where he obtained it. It came down from heaven. I am convinced of the truth of the religion of the Bible."

25. The Holy Spirit as Teacher

A young woman who was soundly converted immediately began to read her Bible. One who disbelieved the Scriptures and took delight in ridiculing them asked her, "Why do you spend so much time reading a book like that?" "Because it's the Word of God," replied the girl. "Nonsense! Who told you that?" scornfully asked the unbeliever. After a moment's silence the girl asked, "Who told you there's a sun in the sky?" "Nobody," replied the scoffer; "I don't need anybody to tell me. The sun tells me." "Yes," said the girl in triumph, "and that's the way God tells me about His Word. I feel His warmth and sense His presence as I read His wonderful word!"

26. Dig into the Word

The Gospel hidden in mystery should arouse our best and most active faculties. That is why we are commanded to search the Scripture, not simply to read it. It is the great repository of all the truths and mysteries of our faith. It is a rich mine that we ought to dig into and shall never exhaust. Just as gold and diamonds and most other precious stones and metals lie concealed in the depths of the earth, so the most valued things of revelation are concealed by the great Creator and Redeemer from the common view of the world. Only as this mystery stimulates us to dig into the Word shall we unearth the treasures that God has there for us.

27. The Truthful Barometer

A young farmer in North Dakota brought home a fancy barometer for which he paid $24.65. In the following days he watched it avidly as it predicted the weather. On one of the walls of his home it hung in an honored place. But the day came when for three days it predicted "storm" while the sky was turquoise and clear. So he took it off the wall and back to town where he demanded his money back. Returning home, he and his wife became alarmed when they saw evidence of a storm ten miles out.

When they turned in their yard, their home had blown away. The furniture was up in the apple trees, and the bathtub three blocks away in a pasture. But the grandmother had believed the barometer, and when a dark cloud appeared she took the two small children and went to the shelter in the old storm cellar, long unused, and they were saved.

28. God's Eye Salve

By the aid of that most perfect scientific instrument, the ophthalmoscope, with its condensing mirror and myriad of little lenses, the ophthalmologist can look into a person's eye and not only determine approximately the necessary strength of glass required to give perfect vision, but also the existence of tumors pressing on the brain tissue, the condition of the general nervous system, the presence of disease in various organs, and the richness of the blood current as they are clearly traced on the sensitive plate of nature's camera.

What the ophthalmoscope is to the ophthalmologist, revelation from Scripture is to our higher nature—a test and criticism of supreme value. One of the ways by which we can prevent the darkening of our spiritual eyesight is to look daily at the Word of God so that the Word may become the mirror to which we are exposed. "The Word of God is quick, and powerful, and sharper than any two-edged sword, piercing even to the dividing asunder of soul and spirit, and of the joints and marrow, and is a discerner of thoughts and intents of the heart" (Heb. 4:12). If we wish to see clearly, we must test and purge our vision. Here is the radical cure for spiritual cataracts and color blindness. To see truly we must see life in God's light. After the dust and fog and mirage of a day that we have lived in our town or city, it is a wonderful restorative to cleanse the eyes with the eye salve of the Word of God.

29. Glorious Conversion

In the spring of A.D. 372, a young man in great distress of mind flung himself on the ground and burst into tears. The sins of his youth weighed heavily on his soul. Overhearing a chance conversation from a neighboring house, he was led to read the thirteenth chapter of Romans, and as a result was gloriously converted. In the language of Gaussen, "Jesus had conquered, and the grand career of Augustine, the holiest of the fathers, then commenced. A passage of God's Word had kindled that glorious luminary, which was to enlighten the Church for ten centuries . . . even to this present day. After thirty-one years of revolt, combats and misery—faith, life and eternal peace came to this erring soul; a new day, an eternal day, came upon it."

30. Sunshine and Dust

A young girl after sweeping the room, went to the window shade and hastily drew it down, saying, "It makes the room so dusty to have the sunshine coming in." She foolishly imagined that it was the sunshine which made the dust whereas it only revealed it.

31. Must You See to Believe?

A skeptical young man confronted an old Quaker with the statement that he did not believe the Bible. The Quaker said, "Dost thou believe in France?" "Yes, though I have not seen it, I have seen others that have; besides there is plenty of corroborative evidence that such a country exists." "Then you will not believe anything you or others have not seen?" "No, to be sure I won't." "Did you ever see your own brains?" "No." "Ever see anybody that did?" "No." "Do you then believe you have any?"

32. Good Advice

A young theological student came to Spurgeon to tell him that the Bible contained some verses which he could not understand and about which he was very much worried. To this the great English preacher replied, "Young man, allow me to give you a word of advice. You must expect God to know some things which you do not understand."

33. Your Book Is Good

A Brahmin said to a missionary: "We are finding you out. You are not as good as your Book. If you were as good as your Book, you could conquer India for Christ in five years." Scripture reveals the truth and sheds light on our short-comings.

34. *The Converted Skeptic*

Two unbelievers once sat in a railroad train discussing Christ's wonderful life. Even non-Christians cannot escape thinking of Christ. One said, "I think an interesting romance could be written about Him." The other replied, "You are just the man to write it. Set forth the correct view of His life and character. Tear down the prevailing sentiment as to His divinity and paint Him as He was—a man among men." The suggestion was acted upon and the romance was written. The man who made the suggestion was Colonel Ingersoll; the author was General Lew Wallace, and the book was *Ben Hur*. In the process of constructing it, General Wallace found himself facing the unaccountable Man. The more he studied His life and character, the more profoundly he was convinced that He was more than a man among men; until at length, like the centurion under the cross, he was constrained to cry, "Verily, this was the Son of God." That's exactly the testimony of John the Baptist. He says, "The one coming after me, has been before me, because he was first compared with me." He was and is God. When that is accepted, then there is no difficulty in understanding either His character or His miraculous works.

Christk

The Foundation

35. Focus on Christ

When we seek to win others to Christ, we must never think we possess any power in ourselves or lead others to believe we do through any air of superiority or lightness as we proclaim the gospel. We would do well to heed the advice of Dr. Payson, who said, "Paint Jesus Christ upon your canvas, and then hold Him up to the people; but hold Him up so that not even your little finger can be seen."

36. Nothing But Christ

Alexander Maclaren stated: "Paul felt that, if he was to give the Corinthians what they needed, he must refuse to give them what they wanted, and while he crossed their wishes he was consulting their necessities. . . . In the message of Christ and Him crucified, there lies the satisfaction of all that is legitimate in those desires that at first sight it seems to thwart. Paul determined to know nothing but Jesus, and to know everything in Jesus, and Jesus in everything. Do not begin your building at the second floor windows. Put in your foundations first and be sure that they are well laid. Let the sacrifice of Christ in its application to the individual and his sins be ever the basis of all that you say. Then, when that foundation is laid, exhibit to your heart's content the application of Christianity and its social aspects. But be sure that the beginning of them all is the work of Christ for the individual sinful soul, and the acceptance of that work by personal faith."

37. Good Foundation Necessary

Tourists stand in wondering admiration before some of the palaces of the old world that have endured for more than a thousand years without a crack or seam. The Pantheon at Rome stands just as it did well over two thousand years ago. This would be impossible had not its foundations been right. The Rialto Bridge that spans the Grand Canal in Venice was erected in A.D. 1588. It has stood as it now stands for over four centuries, but that bridge rests on twelve thousand piles driven deeply into the soil. What is true of buildings is also true of life. God cannot and will not build the Christian virtues into your life, or fill you with the Holy Spirit for His service, until the proper foundation of receiving Christ and Him crucified as your Savior and Lord has been laid.

38. First Consideration

An architect is a master builder. He conceives of a building in its totality. However, he realizes that his first consideration must be the ground on which it is to stand; it must have a solid foundation. Of course, no one can live in a house that consists only of its foundation. A superstructure is needed. But without a proper foundation the superstructure will not stand.

His Deity

39. The Brightness of His Glory

Jesus Christ, by His constant designation as the Son, must not be considered as belonging within time and space. Take as an illustration the sun and its rays. Does the radiance of the sun proceed from the substance of the sun itself or from some other source? We all know that it proceeds from the substance itself. Yet, though the radiance proceeds from the sun itself, we cannot say that it is later in point of time than the existence of that body, since the sun has never appeared without its rays. It is for this reason, says Chrysostom, that Paul calls Christ "brightness" (Heb. 1:3), setting forth thereby His being and His eternity from God. The fact that Jesus Christ, the Word, is presented as a separate personality from God the Father does not mean that He is less eternal, less infinite, and therefore less God and less responsible for the creation of the world, than God the Father.

40. Christ, the God-Man

A professor of theology once asked his students to get a sheet of paper and divide it into three columns. In the first column they were to write every passage where Christ is spoken of as God-Man; in the second column all the passages where Christ is spoken of as God alone; and in the third, all the passages where Christ is spoken of as man alone. The papers were badly balanced. The first and second columns filled right up, but as to the third column, no one found a passage speaking of Christ as man alone. There just is no such passage.

41. Christ, the Mirror of Deity

In the Rospigliosi Palace in Rome is Guido Reni's famous fresco, "The Aurora," a work unequalled in that period for nobility of line and poetry of color. It is painted on a lofty ceiling, and as you stand on the pavement and look up at it, your neck stiffens, your head grows dizzy, and the figures become hazy and indistinct. Therefore the owner of the palace has placed a broad mirror near the floor. In it the picture is reflected and you can sit down before it and study the wonderful work in comfort. Jesus Christ does just that for us when we try to get some notion of God. He is the mirror of Deity. He is the express image of God's person.

42. The Creator before the Creature

When you say to a child, "Give me a glass," he knows what you are talking about. The word "glass" is associated in his mind with an object. Philosophers like Kant tell us that before we have the phenomenon, i.e., that which can be seen or felt by the senses, we have the *noumenon*, i.e., that which is conceived of by intellectual intuition. In other words, the object's image is first formed in the mind, and then it is produced as an object. We see a table. It is beautiful. We admire it, but more than that, we accept the fact that behind that object there was a concept in the mind of someone. Or consider the Empire State Building. Before it was erected, it took form in the mind of an architect who transferred his thoughts to paper as a blueprint. Only then could the building be put up for everybody to see. John tells us that Jesus Christ existed before the beginning of the world. The Creator was before the creature.

43. A Difficult Question

A Jewish soldier had been attending services where he heard of the character and teaching of the Lord Jesus Christ. He went to his rabbi and said, "Rabbi, the Christians say that the 'Christ' has already come, while we claim He is yet to come." "Yes," assented the rabbi. "Well," asked the young soldier, "when our Christ comes, what more than Jesus Christ can we expect?" What, indeed, since Jesus Christ was fully God?

44. Glory with the Father

To recognize all that lies within another person, you must possess as much or more. A layman cannot possibly appreciate all the qualities and recognize all the abilities of a medical doctor. It takes a medical doctor of equal stature to recognize them. That is why, before a person is permitted to practice medicine, he is submitted to a professional state examination. In a similar way, only God the Father could recognize and appreciate all that was in God the Son. Jesus Christ could not find that recognition while here on earth among men and will never be fully recognized and appreciated by mortal man.

45. Immanuel, God with Us

Count Zinzendorf, the founder of the Moravians, was converted in an art gallery in Dusseldorf while contemplating a painting of Christ on the cross which had the inscription, "I did this for thee. What hast thou done for me?" This picture had been painted by an artist three hundred years before. When he had finished his first sketch of the face of the Redeemer, this artist called in his landlady's little daughter and asked her who she thought it was. The girl looked at it and said, "It is a good man." The painter knew that he had failed. He destroyed the first sketch and, after praying for greater skill, finished a second. Again he called the little girl in and asked her to tell him whom she thought the face represented. This time the girl said that she thought it looked like a great sufferer. Again the painter knew that he had failed, and again he destroyed the sketch he had made. After meditation and prayer, he made a third sketch. When it was finished, he called the girl in a third time and asked her who it was. Looking at the portrait, the girl exclaimed, "It is the Lord!" That alone makes the coming of Christ meaningful to the world—not that a good man came, not that a wise teacher came, not that a great sufferer came, but that God came—Immanuel, God with us.

46. *The Incomprehensible Christ*

In a company of literary gentlemen, Daniel Webster was asked if he could comprehend how Jesus Christ could be both God and man. "No, sir," he replied, and added, "I should be ashamed to acknowledge Him as my Savior if I could comprehend Him. If I could comprehend Him, He could be no greater than myself. Such is my sense of sin, and consciousness of my inability to save myself, that I feel I need a superhuman Savior, one so great and glorious that I cannot comprehend Him."

47. *Jesus Christ Is God*

"I know men," said Napoleon in exile on the island of St. Helena to Count Montholon, "I know men, and I tell you that Jesus was not a man! The religion of Christ is a mystery, which subsists by its own force, and proceeds from a mind which is not a human mind. We find in it a marked individuality which originated a train of words and actions unknown before. Jesus is not a philosopher, for His proofs are miracles, and from the first His disciples adored Him. Alexander, Caesar, Charlemagne, and myself founded empires but on what foundation did we rest the creation of our genius? Upon force. Jesus Christ founded an empire upon love, and at this hour millions of men would die for Him. I die before my time, and my body will be given back to the earth, to become food for worms. Such is the fate of him who has been called the great Napoleon. What an abyss between my deep misery and the eternal kingdom of Christ, which is proclaimed, loved, and adored, and is extending over the whole earth!" And turning to General Bertrand, the Emperor added, "If you do not perceive that Jesus Christ was God, I did wrong to appoint you general!"

48. *One with the Father*

A Chinese Christian woman was preaching Christ to the scholar of a market town. He heard her courteously and after a little while said, "Madam, you speak well, but why do you dwell on Jesus Christ? Let Him alone. Instead of Jesus Christ, tell us about God." Whereupon she replied, "What, sir, should we know about God if it were not for Jesus Christ?" How true, and this is precisely the meaning of the second clause of John 1:18.

His Power

49. Christ Comes to Puerto Rico

At a meeting where someone attacked missionary work, a Jewish gentleman asked if he might say a few words. "A few years ago," he began, "my bank sent me to make some studies of a place in Puerto Rico. It was the worst, the dirtiest city imaginable. It was a real hell. Two years ago I went back to that same city—it was entirely new. The change was unbelievable. The houses, the streets were all so clean. The taverns had gone out of existence! What had happened, I wondered. Did they elect a new mayor? Was the place invaded by new educators? No. A Christian missionary had come to work among them and teach them about Christ. I went and found this missionary and gave him a generous gift for his work. I saw with my own eyes what Christ can do in just a short time."

50. Christ, the Master Builder

Agostino d'Antonio, a sculptor of Florence, wrought diligently but unsuccessfully on a large piece of marble. "I can do nothing with it," he finally said. Other sculptors tried their hand at it, but they too gave up the task. The stone lay on a rub-bish heap for forty years. Out strolling one day, Michelangelo saw the stone and its latent possibilities and ordered it brought to his studio. He began to work upon it, and ultimately his vision and work were crowned with success. From that seemingly worthless stone he carved one of the world's master-pieces of sculpture—David! The secret lay in Michelangelo, not in the stone. Look at life—your own with all its disappointments, and the lives of others with all that God has accomplished in them or all that He is able to accomplish. Expect Him to produce a masterpiece because you know the quality of the work of the Master Builder, Christ.

51. Held by Christ

A minister traveling on a train in Europe was the sole occupant of a compartment, save for a young man reading a newspaper. The youth was also a Christian, but so weak was his faith, and so many were his temptations, that he told the minister he did not think he would be able to stand life a week longer. The minister took from his pocket a Bible and a penknife and said, "See, I will make this penknife stand up on the cover of this Bible, in spite of the rocking of the train." The young man, thinking that this was some conjuring trick, watched the proceeding with interest, saying, "I am afraid that it will not be very easy to do that , sir." "But," said the minister, "I am doing it." "Oh, but you are holding it," retorted his fellow passenger. "Why of course. Did you ever hear of a penknife standing up on its end without being held up?" "I see," was the young man's comment. "I see you mean to teach me that I cannot stand unless Christ holds me. Thank you for reminding me of that."

52. The Source of Life

It is said that Tennyson was walking one day in a beautiful flower garden when a friend said to him, "Mr. Tennyson, you speak so often of Jesus Christ. Will you tell me what Christ really means to your life?" Tennyson stooped and pointing to a beautiful yellow flower said, "What the sun is to the flower, Jesus Christ is to my soul."

53. Weakness Becomes Strength

In front of the great Cathedral of Amiens stands a statue of Jesus Christ, and on either side His twelve apostles. Below them are written their greatest virtues, in contrast to their greatest vices. In Peter's case, his outstanding quality is his courage, but below it you see a figure of Peter fleeing from a leopard, representing his cowardice. Then beneath that you see the same figure sitting on a leopard and riding forth to conquest. The sculptor wished to teach us that by contact with the Lord Jesus Christ that very thing which is a man's weakness can be transfigured into his strength; that very thing from which he fled can become the glorious chariot on which he rides forward, conquering and to conquer.

His Uniqueness

54. A Baby with a Message

A six-year-old tiptoed softly up to the little low crib where one of this world's very latest hopes was lying throned and swathed in the coverlets that love had sewn for its coming. Big brother's face was gravely intent, his eyes bright and shining. He stooped far over and gazed down at that wrinkled, peevish bit of a face. "Now, baby brother," he whispered into one tiny red ear half hid by the clustering black hair, "tell me about God before you forget." The brother thought that the tiny baby had a message from God. There was one Baby who did. He was born in Bethlehem. But His existence did not begin at the time of His physical birth. He had a message for us from God the Father. It is found in the old familiar words of John 3:16. "For God so loved the world, that he gave his only begotten Son, that whosoever believeth in him should not perish, but have everlasting life."

55. A Birthday Never Forgotten

How many people celebrate your birth? When a prince is born, there is usually a big national celebration. But when a child is born into a poor family, little or no celebration may take place. Yet, children of humble origin have often become national heroes whose birthdays continue to be celebrated long after their deaths. However, there is only one Person whose birthday is still celebrated nearly 2,000 years after the event—and He was born in a stable!

56. Christ—No Social Reformer

A Brahmin once said to a Christian missionary in India, "There are many things which Christianity and Hinduism have in common. But one thing Christianity has that is not found in Hinduism." "What is that?" asked the missionary. The Brahmin's answer was, "We do not have a Savior." He was right. Christianity is different in that Christ did not come as a social or economic reformer but as a Savior of individuals. God came to earth, not to change the adverse conditions under which men live but to change the sinful hearts responsible for such evil in the world.

57. The Light of the World

As George Matheson said, "Christ has illuminated the world, not by what He did, but by what He was; His life is the Light of Men. We speak of a man's life-work; the work of Jesus was His life itself. . . . It is good to be told that the pure in heart shall see God, but the vision of heaven in a pure man's face outweighs it all. They tell us that the Easter morning has revealed His glory; rather would I say that His glory has revealed the Easter morning. It is not resurrection that has made Christ; it is Christ that has made resurrection. To those who have seen His beauty, even Olivet

can add no certainty; the light of immortality is as bright on His Cross as on His Crown. 'I am the resurrection' are His own words about Himself—not 'I teach,' not 'I cause,' not 'I predict,' but 'I am.' "

58. Napoleon's Perception of Christ

It was Napoleon who said, "Everything in Christ astonishes me. His spirit overawes me, and His will confounds me. His ideas and His sentiments, the truth which He announces, His manner of convincing are not explained either by human observation or the nature of things. His birth and the history of His life; the profundity of His doctrine, which grapples the mightiest difficulties, and which is of those difficulties the most admirable solution; His Gospel; His apparition; His empire; His march across the ages and the realms—everything is for me a prodigy, a mystery insoluble, which plunges me into a reverie from which I cannot escape—a mystery which is there before my eyes, a mystery which I can neither deny nor explain. Here I see nothing human. The nearer I approach, the more carefully I examine. Everything is above me. Everything remains grand—of a grandeur which overpowers. His religion is a revelation from an Intelligence which certainly is not that of man."

59. Only One Door

Charles H. Spurgeon made a penetrating observation when he said there were many rooms in the ark but only one door. Similarly, there is only one door in the ark of our salvation, and that is Christ.

60. The Only Victor

A general may defeat all his enemies on the battlefield yet be unable to defeat his critics at home. He may be able to control the men under him and yet be unable to control himself. He may be victor in the eyes of men, yet defeated in the estimation of God. And he may congratulate himself that no one has been able to stand up against him, yet he will go down at last before man's final enemy, death.

Thus, all men's victories are partial in this life. Even the victory over sin and evil that the regenerated believer has in Christ is at best incomplete. Only one Man has ever conquered sin and death completely and defeated all His enemies.

61. Think about It

Do you know for sure what's going to happen to you after you die? The prospect of that should make you think. It made Peter Waldo anxious for the first time when, at a party, a friend of his suddenly keeled over and died. He went home and looked through his library of history books, scientific books, and philosophical books, trying to find something about death. But they told him nothing. Finally he turned to the Bible. There he found information that couldn't be found elsewhere—basic truths that were given by Christ Himself,

who had experienced death and conquered it. He told what it is and what would happen to the righteous and the unrighteous after death occurs. This is a subject that vitally concerns everyone. Christ is the only one who ever rose from the dead of His own volition and by His own power. That's why His revelation about what happens after death appeared believable to Waldo. Peter Waldo became a noted Christian reformer, founder of the Waldensian Church of Europe.

62. A Unique Person

An unbeliever once asked a Christian, "If I told you that this child was born without the intervention of a human father, would you believe it?" After a little thought the Christian replied, "Yes, if he were able to grow up and live like Christ." In other words, Christ's sinless life, His death and resurrection make the virgin birth believable.

The Mediator

63. The Advocate

A great minister who was noted for his Christlike spirit as well as for his consecrated ability, dreamed that he had died and stood at the gate of heaven knocking for admission. He gave his name, only to be told that his name did not appear upon the books. Finally, at his earnest entreaty, he was bidden to enter and was told he would have the privilege of appearing before the Judge of all the earth, and if he could stand His test he might abide in heaven forever. Standing before the throne, he gave his name, and the following questions were put to him: "Have you led a righteous life?" He said, "No." "Have you always been kind and gentle?" Again he replied in the negative. "Have you always been forgiving to those who have been around you?" "No, I have miserably failed there." "Have you always been honest and just?" He answered, "I fear not."

As question after question was put to him by the Judge, his case seemed more and more hopeless. The last question was asked him, and to that, too, he was obliged to give the same negative reply. Just when he seemed to be in despair, the brightness about the throne became brighter, and suddenly he heard a beautiful voice—the most beautiful to which his ears had ever listened. It was sweeter than a mother's voice; it was more beautiful than all the music of heaven; it filled all the arches of the skies and thrilled the soul of this man as he stood before the Judge trembling and about to fall. The speaker said, "My Father, I know this man. It is true that he was weak in many ways, but he stood for Me in the world, and I take his place before Thee." Just as the last words of this sentence were spoken, the dream was over and the man awoke; he had his lesson, and it is a lesson for us all.

64. Christ Feels Our Suffering

Plato was right when he said that no one has a right to become a doc-tor who has always been healthy. Christ suffered, and therefore He can understand our suffering. He did not deserve to suffer for He was sinless. But God was glorified through His suffering, which was not really for Himself but for us, for our sin.

65. Jesus Christ, the Communicator

An unbeliever once asked a preacher why John called Jesus Christ "the Word." It seemed a strange appellation to him. The preacher answered, "It seems to me that as our words are the means that permit us to communicate with others, John used it to show that Jesus Christ is the only means whereby God chose to communicate with man." Jesus Christ, then, is God's speech or discourse to man.

66. Only One Mediator

When Alexander the Great visited Diogenes the cynic, he asked what he could do for Diogenes. The cynic answered that there was only one thing which Alexander could do for Diogenes, and that was to abstain from standing between him and the sun. There are many great and mighty people who like to stand between God and man, but they only obscure man's vision of God. Only Jesus Christ, God incarnate, can bring God as the regenerating and transforming Spirit into our experience.

The Provider

67. *Christ the Provider*

Once a great king visited a town to lay the foundation stone of a new hospital. Thousands of school children greeted him and sang for him. Soon after the king passed a group of children, a teacher saw a little girl crying. She asked, "Why are you crying? Did you not see the king?" The little girl sobbed out, "Yes, teacher, but the king did not see me." How different the Lord Jesus Christ is from earthly kings. Not only does He give life to each one, but He is also personally interested in and personally maintains each life.

68. *Depend on the Control Center*

A beautiful illustration of our dependence on a solidly established base while we are moving at a distance, is the journey of Apollo 11 to the moon. A space station in Houston, Texas, was the seat of command. The three spacemen dared not disregard it as they circled around the moon and as two of them landed on its surface. Thus Paul tells the Corinthians that any work they undertake must be based on the firmness, the absoluteness, the dependability of the Lord Jesus Christ. He arose. He did what He said He was going to do. He told us that we shall rise. That is our control center. We can depend on it. We dare not disregard it. It is a matter of life and death.

As I was viewing this feat of man at the time Neil Armstrong was landing on the moon, I was impressed by the remark made by one news commentator, "These men cannot remain on the moon. They must follow instructions. They do not have only themselves to think of but also the entire project." Think of that, Christian, when you are tempted to act independently of the control center, Christ the Lord. You have not only yourself to think of, but also Christ and His Kingdom.

69. *He Lives*

A Japanese nobleman who came to America visited a Sunday school to study its function. The superintendent asked him to say a few words to those present. Now this visitor was a Confucianist, and he began by saying that the teachings of Confucius and Christ are just about the same. There are very few differences, he said, and therefore he regarded Christians as brothers. When he had finished, a distinguished merchant, a member of the Sunday school, rose to his feet. Of course, he recognized the moral teachings of Confucius, he said, but added the following: "There is, however, a basic and vital difference between Confucius and the Lord Jesus Christ. Confucius is dead and remains in his grave until Jesus Christ will raise him. But the tomb of Christ is empty. He lives and He will not see death again. He is in our midst this hour of our Sunday school."

70. His Invisible Presence

A little girl came home from Sunday school in much perplexity. "Mama," she said, "our teacher said today that we must come to Jesus if we want to be saved, but how can we come to Him when we cannot see Him?" "Did you not ask me to get you a drink of water last night?" said the mother. "Yes, Mama." "Did you see me when you asked me?" "No, but I knew that you would hear me and get it for me." "Well, that is just the way to come to Jesus. We cannot see Him, but we know that He is near and hears every word we say, and that He will give us what we need." As we try to see Jesus by faith, He will become real to us. Only through Him can we get a vision of God.

71. Hope for the World

Some years ago several congressmen, who were devout Christians, were taking a walk one evening. Their conversation drifted to the subject of religion and the state of the world. They were not enthusiastic about the outlook and were just about to agree that the whole world was on the toboggan when they chanced to pass a little chapel. From within came the words of a familiar hymn:

There is a fountain filled with blood
Drawn from Immanuel's veins;
And sinners plunged beneath that flood,
Lose all their guilty stains.

As his face lighted up, one said to the others, "As long as people get together and sing that song, there is hope for the world, after all."

72. Joy in Christ

A certain king instructed his gardener to plant six trees and place statues beneath them representing prosperity, beauty, victory, strength, duty, and joy. These trees were to show to the world that the king had tried to make his reign fruitful. They were also to typify the statues beneath them. The gardener planted six palm trees. When the king came out to inspect the work and looked at the statue of joy, he said, "I surely thought you would typify joy with some flowering tree like the tulip or magnolia. How can the stately palm symbolize joy?" "Those flowering trees," said the gardener, "get their nourishment from open sources. They live in pleasant forests or orchards with hosts of other like trees. But I found this palm tree in a sandy waste. Its roots had found some hidden spring creeping along far beneath the burning surface. Then, thought I, highest joy has a foundation unseen of men and a source they cannot comprehend." Do you realize that if the light of Jesus Christ is within your heart it can be the only place in which joy is found, and yet it will be sufficient. You do not need the company of others in order to experience the joy that the light of Christ brings. A palm tree does not need the company of other trees to flourish and bring forth fruit.

73. The Position of the Observer

In a great cathedral there is a statue of Christ. As one enters the cathedral and stands before that statue, he is appalled at the ugliness and repulsiveness of the sculptor's representation of Christ. He wonders whether that is what Christ really looked like. He is keenly disappointed. But then, as he comes closer to the statue, he can see an inscription on it which reads: "Kneel down and look up." He kneels down and looks up, and lo everything about it is different. The repulsiveness is replaced by a wonderful attractiveness. The face of Christ is not ugly any more. What makes the difference? It is the position of the observer. If he stands up and looks at the statue, there is no beauty to it, but if he kneels down and looks up, he sees the face of the gentle, loving Savior.

His Rejection

74. The Humble Christ

It is related how the need of the West Indian slaves was presented to the Moravians. The Moravians were told that it was impossible to reach the slave population because they were so separated from the ruling classes. Undaunted, two Moravian missionaries offered themselves as candidates. They said, "We will go and be slaves on the plantations and work and toil if need be under the lash, to get right beside the poor slaves and instruct them."

They left their homes, went to the West Indies, went to work on the plantations as slaves and by the side of slaves, to get close to the hearts of slaves. The slaves heard them, and their hearts were touched, because the missionaries had humbled themselves to their condition. That was grand; it was glorious. Yet Christ's example was more glorious, for He stepped down from heaven to earth to get close to our side. He Himself came beside us that we might feel the throbbings of His bosom, be encircled in the embrace of His loving arms, be drawn to Him, and hear Him whisper in our ears, "God is full of grace and truth."

75. Light Dispels Darkness

No one switches on a flashlight in an area flooded by direct sunlight. We put on the light in order to dispel darkness. It is the darkness that makes the light necessary. God from eternity knew that men would choose darkness rather than light, and therefore He had to bring His light in Jesus Christ to shine in the midst of darkness.

76. No Mistake in Judgment

A young man who graduated from West Point said that so much tension and anxiety built up with regard to final examinations that the best scholar in his class fainted at the first question asked him. He felt that his standing in his chosen profession was at stake, that his future position depended on the manner in which he acquitted himself.

If the loss or gain of a little worldly distinction could so move a man, what will be the feeling of the soul when it stands alone at the bar of God? West Point honors are but for the little moment of time here, but the results of this final examination are for eternity. There are often mistakes made in worldly judgment, but there will be no mistakes made at the judgment seat of Christ.

77. Not Welcome

A young nobleman had been absent for such a long time from his extensive estate and numerous tenants that he was a stranger to them. Having returned home, he was out hunting and wandered from his party. Lost and thoroughly drenched by the rain, he sought shelter and relief in the cottages of some of his tenants, but they did not recognize him as the lord of the manor and shut their doors in his face. Knocking at the cottage of a poor widow, he heard the invitation, "Come in, thou blessed of the Lord." She gave him a suit of dry, though coarse, clothing and spread before him the best food she could provide. He went away promising to return for his own clothes. The next day he appeared with his retinue and stopped before the poor widow's door. She discovered in the young lord her unknown guest. He thanked her for her kindness shown to a stranger. She gave as a reason for her hospitality the fact that her own boy was away at sea and might be in need of shelter. When Christ came, He was surrounded by the world He had made. Yet Christ had nowhere to lay His head, for "He came unto his own, and his own received him not."

78. The Right Doctor

A young foreign nobleman came across the English Channel to consult the great English physician, Dr. Forbes Winslow. "Doctor," he said, "I do not know what is the matter with me. I cannot sleep—I am troubled night and day on account of my sins." "Oh," said the doctor, "you are seeking the help of the wrong physician," and instead of his Materia Medica, he took down his Bible and read from the 53rd chapter of Isaiah: "But he was wounded for our transgressions, he was bruised for our iniquities: the chastisement of our peace was upon him; and with his stripes we are healed." He knelt in prayer with the nobleman, who went back to his home rejoicing in salvation.

79. The Savior's Grief

Evangelist Gypsy Smith said that once, when a group of gypsies were forced to cross a swollen stream, a great number of men were drowned. One young man made a desperate attempt to save his mother who kept clinging to him. Several times he pushed her away, saying, "Let go, Mother, and I can save you." But she would not heed him and was lost. At the funeral, the son stood by his mother's grave and said over and over, "How hard I tried to save you, Mother, but you wouldn't let me!" These are the tragic words that we shall hear Jesus Christ say to many in eternity one day, "How hard I tried to save you, but you wouldn't let me. Your will was the great hindrance."

The Savior

80. Christ the Savior

A native of interior China wanted to become a Christian but couldn't understand how Christianity was superior to Confucianism and Buddhism. One morning he came to the missionary in a happy mood saying, "I dreamed last night, and now I understand. I dreamed I had fallen into a deep pit where I lay helpless and despairing. Confucius came and said, 'Let me give you advice, my friend; if you get out of your trouble, never get in again.' Buddha came and said, 'If you can climb up to where I can reach you, I will help you.' Then Christ came. He climbed down into the pit and carried me out." It takes the Savior of man to do that. Only a Savior would stoop so low as to save a sinful soul like yours and mine.

81. Christ the Way

On a dark and stormy night, a child was lost in the streets of a large city. A policeman found him crying in distress, and gathering enough from his story to locate the home, gave him directions after this manner. "Just go down this street half a mile, turn and cross the big iron bridge, then turn to your right and follow the river down a little way, and you'll see where you are." The poor child, only half comprehending, chilled and bewildered by the storm, turned about blindly, when another voice spoke in a kindly tone, "Just come with me." The little hand was clasped in a stronger one, the corner of a warm coat was thrown over the shoulders of the shivering child, and the way home was made easy. The first man had told the way; the second man became the way. This is exactly what the Lord Jesus Christ has been for us. From eternity He has told us that He is the Way. He has to become our Light also, to lead us to the Way.

82. The Cleansing Blood of Christ

A woman came to a minister one day carrying a container of wet sand. "Do you see what this is, sir?" she asked. "Yes," was the reply, "it is wet sand." "But do you know what it means?" "I do not know exactly what you mean by it, woman; what is it?" "Well, sir," she said, "that's me; and the multitude of the sins that constantly dirty my heart cannot be numbered." Then she exclaimed, "Oh, wretched creature that I am! How can such a wretch as I ever be saved and keep clean from the influences of the world?" "Where did you get the sand?" asked the minister. "At the beach." "Go back, then, to the beach. Take a spade with you; dig, dig, and raise a great mound; shovel it up as high as you can, then leave it there. Take your stand by the seashore, and watch the effect of the waves upon the heap of the sand." "Sir," she exclaimed, "I see what you mean—the blood, the blood, the blood of Christ, it would wash it all away and would keep washing any new dark stains away."

83. God Speaks to Man

Have you ever had difficulty in making yourself understood by a young child? Just try answering some of his questions: "What's the sky made of? Why did Grandma have to die? Where did God come from?" It can be quite a problem. The difference between your mental ability and the child's is not as great as that between the mental ability of God, the Creator, and you, His creature. What method did He use to communicate with man? Did He send a great cataclysm of nature to awe us into submission? No, He sent a little Baby to be born in Bethlehem. Of course, babies are born every day, but this was a very special Baby. He was God in the flesh.

84. Help for the Bankrupt!

"Deposit this in my name" means "deposit it in my account." Or "draw this in my name" means "draw this from my account." Isn't that what would happen if I were to write out a check for you? You would take it and present it to the bank. You would cash it. But the money would come out of my account be-cause my name was signed on the check. You would have to believe that I had money in the bank and the money could become yours; otherwise you would never have presented the check to be cashed. Thus, through faith in my name, you would have made my account yours in the amount that I had made available to you.

That's exactly the transaction that takes place between God and man. He has the resources which we need. He is Life and Light. Especially do we need these, in a spiritual sense, for our spiritual existence. They are made available to us in the measure that we need them, because we ourselves are bankrupt. Our name isn't worth anything at the source of Life and Light, but the Lord Jesus Christ has available what we need.

85. Practical Help

A traveler passing by and seeing a man fallen into a deep pit began to wonder aloud how he fell in. The poor man in his utter misery shouted, "If you are a friend, stop asking how I fell in but help me out!" The Lord Jesus Christ wants to impart His life to us. We may in our foolishness want a full explanation from Him as to why He permitted us to fall in the first place, but John 3:16 tells us that the most important and urgent thing is our salvation from sin and death.

86. Christ Lived among Men

A missionary visiting a poor hut in a refugee district was challenged by a suffering woman: "You tell us that you are interested in us and want to help us. But it's very easy for you to simply come to see us in our poverty-stricken home. The question is, are you ready to bring your family from the clean and comfortable home in which they live, in order to live in our district with all its poverty and suffering and sin? Would you do that in order to lift us up?" That is exactly what Christ did. "And the Word became flesh, and dwelt among us" (John 1:16).

Christianity

87. Christianity—A Religion of Light

The religion of the Lord Jesus Christ is a religion of light. One of the most splendid descriptions of our Heavenly Father is in the words of John: "God is light, and in him is no darkness at all" (1 John 1:5). James says, "Every good gift and every perfect gift is from above, and cometh down from the Father of lights" (James 1:17). Note James' descriptive name for God, "The Father of light." And the Lord Jesus declares that those who seek to do the will of God are the "children of light" (John 12:36). Our Savior never said a more splendid thing about Himself than when He uttered that sublime declaration, "I am the light of the world" (John 8:12; 9:5). Everywhere in the Scriptures, light is used as an emblem of the righteous character of those who are the true children of God. Yes, the religion of the Lord Jesus Christ is a religion of light.

88. Power of Indwelling Christ

A Buddhist monk in Ceylon, who was acquainted with both Christianity and Buddhism, was once asked what he thought was the great difference between the two.

He replied, "There is much that is good in each of them, and probably in all religions. But what seems to me to be the greatest difference is that you Christians know what is right and have power to do it, while we Buddhists know what is right but have not any such power." This is true, because no other religion has as its founder God, who became man, and in becoming man incarnated the grace and the truth of God. When Christ, then, becomes our life, we will be full of grace and truth. It is not our grace and truth but His, for He dwells within.

89. Look at Christ

Suppose you were the president of a club. A rich man comes and applies to you for membership. However, for the most part your club is made up of poor people and those who belong to the laboring classes. What would you do? Would you be flattered that a rich man wanted to join and accept him without question? Of course, it would provide a marvelous opportunity to enrich your treasury. Unfortunately, some church leaders are also opportunists. Their bad example leads some men to conclude that Christianity is a religion of opportunism. But don't look at church leaders; in fact, don't look at any person—look at Christ.

90. No Practical Use

Someone gave a sundial to a group of people in the jungle. They regarded it as a fetish and wanted to keep it holy, so they built a house over it to keep it safe. This of course, kept the sun away from it. They had rendered it useless by trying to protect it. They honored the sundial, but they made it of no practical use. That's how many people regard Christianity. It has become something they have enclosed within the beautiful walls and stained glass windows of cathedrals. But, far worse, they also wall off their Christianity from their own individual daily lives. They genuflect to a statue or kiss an icon of a saint, but they fail to follow the teachings of the people these symbolize.

Church

91. Too Many Cathedrals

An elderly woman was being conducted through a great cathedral in Europe. The guide spoke of its beauty of design, calling attention to the statues and paintings. The woman was unimpressed. At the conclusion of the tour she asked the guide, "How many souls have been saved here this year? How many people have drawn near to God here?" "My dear lady," said the embarrassed guide, "this is a cathedral, not a chapel." That's the trouble. Unfortunately we have too many cathedrals and too few chapels where the warmth of the Spirit of God is felt, conducive to a spiritual life that enhances our knowledge of God.

92. The Devil's Property

A Finnish infidel once bequeathed his farm to the devil. The will was studied by the courts, and it was decided that the way to carry out the provisions would be to leave the farm untouched by human hands. In a few years it was overgrown with brush, the buildings had tumbled down, and the whole farm presented a scene of desolation and ugliness. That's the way property looks when Satan owns it. Also churches left desolate are the result of Satan's work.

93. No Schisms in the Body

The word "schism" is a transliteration from the Greek *schisma*, which literally means "a tear in a garment or a crack in a stone." A torn garment is useless; it fails to accomplish its purpose of covering the body. A cracked stone endangers the whole structure that rests upon it. Paul writes that no member of the body should behave in such a way as to render the whole body useless. The way to avoid such schism is for the members of the body to help each other, since they are capable of recognizing one another's strengths and weaknesses.

94. Let the Other Do It

There is an incipient danger in thinking, since there are so many belonging to the Church, "Why not let George do it?" An eastern story tells of four brothers who decided to have a feast. As wine was rather expensive, they agreed that each one should bring an equal quantity and add it to the common stock. One of the brothers thought he might escape making his contribution by bringing water instead of wine. "It won't be noticed in the common wine jar," he reasoned. But when, at the feast, the wine was poured out, it turned out not to be wine at all but plain water. All four

31

brothers had thought alike. Each one had said, "Let the other do it."

95. The Wolves and the Dogs

Have you heard the fable of the wolves and the dogs? It seems the wolves were afraid of the dogs for they were many and strong, so they sent out a spy to observe them. On his return the scout said, "It is true the dogs are many, but there are not many who can harm us. There are dogs of so many kinds one can hardly count them, and, as they came marching on, I observed that they were all snapping right and left at one another. I could see clearly, though they all hate us wolves, each dog hates every other dog with all his heart." How we need to take to heart the words of Paul to the Galatians: "For all the law is fulfilled in one word, even in this; Thou shalt love thy neighbor as thyself. But if ye bite and devour one another, take heed that ye be not consumed one of another" (Gal. 5:14, 15).

96. The Church Where God Wasn't Welcome

There was a dear black saint of God who happened to enter a fashionable church. After the service he approached the preacher and told him that he wanted very much to join the church. The pastor knew that his consent to such a request would certainly not meet with the approval of the official board of the church and of the congregation. At the same time he did not want to appear cruel and harsh. So he said to this man, "John, go home and pray for two weeks for the Lord to guide you definitely whether He wants you to join this church." Accordingly, humble John took the advice and went home. When the two weeks were up, he came again to the church, and after the service the preacher said to him, "John, what was the guidance of God?" "Sir," John replied, "God told me that He has been trying to get in here for the past fifteen years and He hasn't succeeded, so I had better give up trying where God cannot find entrance."

97. Church Attendance

A Christian once said to his minister, "I can worship God and enter into the Holy of Holies just as easily in my garden as I can in a church pew." Later on the two men were sitting before a fireplace in which the embers glowed cheerily. Silently the minister went to the fireplace, took the tongs, and lifted a single glowing coal from the fire and placed it alone on the hearth. Soon it became black ash. The church-neglecting Christian said, "Ah, you need not say a word. I understand what you mean. I cannot worship alone any more than I can live alone. I'll be in my place at the church next Sunday." The environment of the church is basic to Christian growth, providing it's the right kind of church. Ask yourself two questions before joining: Is Christ preeminent there? Is the Holy Spirit at work?

98. Ichabod

A flourishing church was once reduced to complete ineffectuality. Sunday school had customarily been held in the afternoon. But the pastor and others in the church wanted to change it to the morning hour. They knew that the Sunday school superintendent was strongly opposed to this. Rather than face the matter openly with him, they met in secret and voted to change the hour. When he learned of it, his feelings were deeply hurt. Angry words were exchanged. People in the church began to take sides, and soon a sizable faction moved out. Bitterness quenched the work of the Spirit, and what was once a deeply spiritual and soul-winning church became a poorly attended one. Lacking support, the edifice itself became shabby and unattractive, reflecting outwardly the destructive result of jealousy that led to strife and divisions.

99. The Decaying Church

The building is not really the Church. God's people are. Yet the Church today spends more money for buildings than for anything else. When an artist was asked to paint a picture of a decaying church, to everyone's astonishment, instead of putting on canvas an old, tottering ruin, the artist painted a stately edifice of modern grandeur. Through the open portals could be seen the richly carved pulpit, the magnificent organ, and the beautiful stained glass windows. To one side was an elaborately designed offering plate for foreign missions —covered by a cobweb!

100. Permission to Bury a Baptist

Don't be like that bishop of whom I heard. It seems a Baptist family had a death in the family while their minister was out of town. They asked a minister of another denomination to conduct the funeral service. He said he would have to check with the bishop, so he wired him, "Can I bury a Baptist?" The bishop wired back, "Sure, bury all the Baptists you can!"

101. Unity Not Uniformity

That divisions exist in the body of Christ is apparent to everyone. The spirit of exclusive denominationalism is evidence of it. Denominations need not be schismatic; they need not cause the entire body of Christ to accomplish less than God intended it. All born-again believers are members of the same body, with God-created differences. We are not uniform, but we need not fight each other on that account; we are to care for all the members of Christ's body equally. Isolationism kills the effectiveness of the body of Christ. Paul says in Romans 14:1, "Him that is weak in the faith receive ye, but not to doubtful disputations."

102. A Sympathetic Body

In our physical bodies a toothache makes the whole body react in sympathy; the cessation of that ache makes the whole body give a sigh of relief. Why can't it be that way in the Church? Is it because we're so blind to the close and sympathetic union that Scripture enjoins between the members, that we allow the folly of selfishness to take the place of the wisdom of unselfishness?

103. The Church—an Organism

Seminary graduates are needed, and God can use them mightily, but Christ's body is not to be served only by those who have 20-20 vision, but also by some myopic Christians who have to wear glasses. Is it any wonder that after two thousand years the Christian gospel is still unknown to three out of every four people in the world? It's because the Church has become an organization devoted to uniformity instead of realizing that it should be an organism, a body that has a diversity of organs with varied gifts to serve the unified body of Christ. A lack of committed believers with no college education is just as deadly to the progress of the Church as a lack of seminary graduates.

104. Every Member Valuable

The eye is placed in the upper area of the head, so that by virtue of its position it's easy for it to entertain a high opinion of itself. The human hand drops down at the side of the body, so that it's natural for the eye to look down upon it in both a literal and figurative sense.

But the hand knows how to speak up and defend its usefulness. Suddenly a fly alights on the eye. Instantly and instinctively the hand elevates itself and brushes the fly away, saying, "Who said, Eye, that you don't need me?" The hand goes on to plow the ground, sow the seed, and reap the harvest. It mills the wheat into flour and kneads the dough to make bread. Then it turns to the eye and says, "You, Eye, would have died long ago if it hadn't been for my labor for you. Without the food I've earned, you'd have become sightless and starved to death. You can't do without me any more than I can do without you." Paul rightly says, "The eye cannot say unto the hand, I have no need of thee" (1 Cor. 12:21).

105. Blended for Harmony

The body is a delicate instrument which needs to be looked after with great care. Yet many of us don't value it as we should or take sufficient care of it. God has made each of us a living musical instrument, so to speak, capable of showing forth His praise. Each of us is like a harp of a thousand strings on which the most varied and beautiful music may be played. Every part of our body is skillfully constructed and admirably adapted to do its proper work. God has tempered or blended every organ to produce a harmonious whole. But this instrument is exceedingly liable to go wrong. The least thing spoils it and makes it unfit for its work. Unless it's properly treated we can't use it to the best advantage to glorify or show forth the perfect nature of God, its Architect and Creator. This is also true of the body of Christ, His Church. We are His members, diverse in our make-up and performance but duty-bound to blend our differences to produce harmonious music and praise that will attract the world instead of repelling it. Just as we wouldn't listen very long to an orchestra whose instruments were out of tune, neither will the world listen to Christians who sound forth the gospel against a background of divisions and quarrels.

106. Harmony in the Church

As one member of the human body harmonizes its function with the other members, we must harmonize our individual functions in the Church with those of others. There is beauty in variety, even as there is a spiritual uplift from music that harmonizes a variety of instruments and voices. We must never get out of tune by harping on the one gift we consider ours. No one of us can act independently as a member of the body. We have to cooperate with other members if we are to be of any use to the body of Christ as a whole.

107. The Church's One Foundation

Paul calls himself a wise architect because the foundation he laid was not different from the one eternally laid. How foolish an architect would be if he refused to follow the laws of nature and civil engineering which are actually the laws of God. You, too, are unwise if you diverge from the Church's one Foundation, "Jesus Christ, and Him crucified," laid down by God from the beginning.

108. The Perfect Church

I think that I shall never see
A church that's all it ought to be:
A church whose members never stray
Beyond the strait and narrow way;
A church that has no empty pews,
Whose pastor never has the blues,
A church whose deacons always deak,
And none is proud, and all are meek;
Where gossips never peddle lies,
Or make complaints or criticize;
Where all are always sweet and kind,
And all to others' faults are blind.
Such perfect churches there may be,
But none of them are known to me.
But still, we'll work, and pray, and plan
To make our own the best we can.

—Author Unknown

109. The Lord's Trumpet

In the Old Testament, under God's command, trumpets were used to call the princes and the congregation together, to announce the journeying of the camps, and as an alarm or notification device.

Trumpets were also blown in the days of Israel's "gladness," "set feasts," and over their sacrifices in the beginning of their months (Num. 10:1-6, 10). I believe that it is in this sense of gladness for the Church of Jesus Christ that this last trumpet will be blown. Can there be any more joyous event than this, when the dead in Christ shall be raised incorruptible, and living believers shall be similarly changed? The Lord's trumpet will call all believers, dead and living, to join Him in possessing a glorious resurrection body.

110. The Discontented Member

Hubert Brooke comments: "A selfish existence in one, who is in membership with many others, is a contradiction of terms, and must mean loss to all the rest, and misery to the idle member." May not this explain the restless discontent of many who are really united to Christ? They are not subject to the Head; they are not using His gifts for the common profit; they keep for themselves what is given for all. In short, they are disobedient and dishonest, and therefore discontented and missing the joy of the Lord.

111. Spirit of Christ Makes Us Like-minded

An eminent preacher says, "I was walking in a beautiful grove where the trees were wide apart and the trunks were straight and rugged. But, as they ascended higher, the branches came closer together, and still higher the twigs and branches interlaced. I said to myself: Our churches resemble these trees. The trunks near the earth stand stiffly and rudely apart; the more nearly they ascend toward heaven, the closer they come together until they form one beautiful canopy, under which men enjoy both shelter and happiness. Those who have the Spirit of Christ will be like-minded."

112. Just Keep Praising the Lord

A rural brother, considered a bit old-fashioned, visited a great city temple. As the eloquent minister drove home some great truth, the ruralite shouted, "Praise the Lord!" Whereupon an usher touched him on the arm and whispered, "Be quiet. "You can't 'praise the Lord' in this church." God pity both preacher and church!

113. Strength in Unity

If the body is ill, the head hurts, the body temperature is elevated, the heart races, the lungs labor, the skin flushes or cools as needed. The kidneys work overtime to filter out infection; the brain directs each organ and each function of the body to cooperate in throwing off the enemy and restoring the organism to health. This cooperation, this united effort against outside forces that invade the body, is an illustration of how the separate members of the Body of Christ ought to unite to work against threatening forces of evil.

114. *Where Is the Piccolo?*

It is a great discovery to know what we can do well; doing it well is the only way the whole body of Christ can function. Don't be like that member of an orchestra who played the piccolo. Amid the thunder of the organ, and the roll of the drums, the player on the piccolo said to himself, "In all this din, my little instrument doesn't matter," and he ceased to play. Suddenly the great conductor threw up his arms, and all was still. "Where is the piccolo?" he cried. God listens for our share in His orchestra no matter how small that share may be.

115. *Sad but True*

An old deacon was once asked about the state of his church. He replied, "We are in sad straits; the church is slipping back, getting worse all the time; but, thank the Lord, none of the other churches in our neighborhood is doing any better."

Commitment

116. A Stumbling Block

A missionary society was deeply impressed by the courageous devotion of David Livingstone who worked single-handedly for God in Africa. The society wrote to Livingstone: "Have you found a good road to where you are? If so, we want to send other men to join you." Livingstone replied, "If you have men who will come only if there is a good road, I don't want them. I want men who will come if there is no road at all."

117. Thy Will at Any Cost

In 1925, Betty Stam said: "Lord, I give up my own purposes and plans, all my own desires, hopes, and ambitions, and accept Thy will for my life. I give myself, my life, my all utterly to Thee, to be Thine forever. I hand over to Thy keeping all of my friendships; all the people whom I love are to take second place in my heart. Fill me and seal me with Thy Holy Spirit. Work out Thy whole will in my life, at any cost, now and forever. To me to live is Christ. Amen." Nine years later on December 8, 1934, Betty and her husband, John Stam, calmly and bravely laid down their lives for Christ when they were martyred by Chinese Communists.

118. Humble Commitment

Sophie, the scrub woman, was a Christian. One of the gentlemen in the large building where she worked said to her, "Say, Sophie, I understand that you are a Christian." "Yes, sir, I am a child of the King," was her immediate reply. "Oh! So you must be a princess, since God is your King." "I sure am." "Well, if God is your Father, and you are a princess and a child of the King, do you not think that it is beneath your dignity to be found here in New York City scrubbing these dirty steps?" Not being daunted Sophie replied, "There is no humiliation whatsoever. You see, I am not scrubbing these steps for my boss, Mr. Brown. I am scrubbing them for Jesus Christ, my Savior!"

119. Dying to Self

A wealthy university graduate chose to live frugally in a single room, cooking his own meals. As a result he was able to give two million dollars to foreign missions. In explanation of his choice he wrote these words: "Gladly would I make the floor my bed, a box my chair, and another box my table, rather than men should perish for want of knowledge of Christ." I am not suggesting that all Christians are called upon to forfeit the normal comforts of life; only, when God calls them to a life of sacrifice, they be willing to leave all and follow Him.

120. Christian Manliness

The history of missions is full of examples of Christian manliness. We think of Dr. Paul Carlson who served as a medical missionary in the Congo. He compassionately sought to heal the most loathsome of tropical diseases as he preached Christ as the only cure for sin. For several years he worked in the midst of increasing political ferment, preaching and living the gospel in which he so wholeheartedly believed. Even when he was arrested, he continued to treat the wounds of the rebels who had captured him. Under sentence of death, he bore himself heroically and died boosting another missionary over the wall to safety. The prevailing attitude of missionaries everywhere seems to be summed up in the words of one mission board secretary who commented, "It shows merely that we must go back."

121. Fresh Warriors

"Baptized for the dead" (1 Cor. 15:29) does not mean that living believers could be baptized in place of those who had died unbaptized. What Paul was actually seeking to convey here is that only those who were willing to be identified with the dead in martyrdom for Christ's sake, as well as with Christ in His death and resurrection, could be described as "those baptized for the dead."

But why does Paul use the words "for the dead?" Let us examine this phrase carefully. The first word, "for," is *huper* in Greek, which basically means "over" or " above." The literal translation of this phrase would be "baptized over the dead"; that is to say admitted publicly into the visible Church of Christ, as if the dead bodies of those who were similarly admitted into the Church before them and had died for Christ were lying beneath their feet. Metaphorically, it means in the prospect of death and as a continuance of the testimony of those who have heroically died for the faith.

Compare what happens on a battlefield. It is strewed with the bodies of those who fought and perished nobly; but the contest is still raging, and fresh combatants are continually pressing into the action. These, as they come up, may be said to be initiated into the battle over the bodies of those who have bled and died before them. Now this world is a spiritual battlefield. The contest between sin and righteousness, which commenced so soon after the fall, has been waging from generation to generation. It is waging still, and it will continue till sin and Satan are overpowered, and death is swallowed up in victory. Many, in bygone ages engaged in this warfare, have fallen on the battlefield, fighting the good fight of faith.

Fresh combatants, however, at the summons of the great Captain of our salvation are continually pressing forward to occupy the places of the slain and bravely maintain the contest. These, by the rite of baptism, were admitted to the position they now occupy as constituted Christian soldiers. With reference either to the past or the future—the deaths which have already occurred or their own death most certainly to occur—it may be said that they are either "baptized over the dead" or "baptized in the prospect of death." In this way the meaning of the expression becomes clear.

122. Courageous Christian

Chrysostom, the ancient Church Father, was a beautiful example of true Christian courage. When he stood before the Roman Emperor, he was threatened with banishment if he still remained a Christian. Chrysostom replied, "You cannot, for the world is my Father's house; you cannot banish me."

"But I will slay you," said the Emperor.

"No, but you cannot," said the noble champion of the faith again, "for my life is hid with Christ in God."

"I will take away thy treasures." "No, but you cannot," was the retort; "in the first place, I have nothing you know anything about. My treasure is in heaven, and my heart is there."

"But I will drive you away from man, and you shall have no friend left." "No, and that you cannot," once more said the faithful witness, "for I have a Friend in heaven from whom you shall not separate me. I defy you; there is nothing you can do to hurt me."

123. Value of Popularity

The gatekeeper at the railroad station demanded that everybody present his ticket before going through the gate to the train. From those who could not find their tickets readily there was much grumbling and swearing. One watching the scene said to the gatekeeper, "You don't seem to be very popular with the crowd." He cast his eyes upward to the floor above, where the superintendent's office was, and said, "I don't care anything about being popular with this crowd; all I care about is to be popular with my superior."

124. A Willing Sacrifice

"How much is your salary?" a Muslim asked a mission school teacher who had once followed the crescent instead of the cross. "Five dollars a week," was the answer. "Why, you could get ten times that in a government school!" "Yes, but I do not teach for money; I teach for God." "Well—are those all the clothes the missionaries provide? Don't you have a robe also?" The humble teacher looked down at his cotton shirt and trousers. "No, these are sufficient," he replied. The Muslim shook his head. "I never thought there was anything to this Jesus religion," he observed thoughtfully, "but there must be if a man will give up his robe and his lawful wage for it." Could it be that the gospel is impeded because we are more concerned about food and clothing than reaching others with the gospel of the grace of God? This is what Christ meant when He said, "Woe unto you that are full!"

125. Willing to Suffer

A converted native was to be baptized in a river. The missionary took a long spear with him into the swift current to steady himself. Inadvertently he stabbed the foot of the convert beneath the water. The man neither spoke nor moved. After the ceremony when the accident was discovered, the convert was asked why he had kept silent. "I thought it was part of the ceremony," he replied. In a way he was right. Baptism should be an external expression of willingness to suffer for the Lord Jesus Christ in whose Name the believer is baptized.

126. Take This Poor Indian Too

An incident is related of a missionary who came into contact with a proud and powerful Indian chief. The chief, trembling under conviction of sin, approached the missionary and offered his belt of wampum as atonement. "No!" said the missionary, "Christ cannot ac-

cept a sacrifice like that." The Indian departed, but soon returned offering his valuable rifle and the most beautiful skins he had taken in hunting. "No!" was the reply, "Christ cannot accept those either." Again the Indian went away, only to return with a conscience more troubled than ever. This time he offered his wigwam, together with his wife and child—everything for peace and pardon. "No," was the reply even to this, "Christ cannot accept such a sacrifice." At this the chief seemed utterly oppressed; but suddenly he somehow sensed the deficiency, for, lifting up tearful eyes, he cried out, "Here, Lord, take this poor Indian too!" That is the only condition for fellowship with Christ.

127. A Committed Servant

One of the greatest servants of Christ was Dr. Temple in England. A young clergyman who was being sent by Dr. Temple to a very difficult parish turned to him and said, "Dr. Temple, why do you send me there? Don't you know how difficult it is? It'll kill me if I go there." You know what Dr. Temple's reply was? "Well, you and I do not mind a little thing like that, do we? If what God has set for us to accomplish will require our lives, we should be willing to give our lives."

Compassion

128. He Gave His Coat

A young man named John saw some ragged boys and invited them to Sunday school. One boy said he would go, but he had no coat. John gave him his coat and went in with him. Years afterward, a teacher of a Bible class told the story. A man in his class said, "I was that boy, and Dr. John G. Patton, one of the most famous missionaries of the ages, gave me his coat."

129. Burdened for the Lost

The St. Bernard dogs in the Alps who seek out travelers lost in a storm take their mission very seriously. One of these dogs returned late one afternoon, wearied from fighting his way through the drifts. He went to his kennel, lay down in a corner, and acted thoroughly despondent, despite the efforts of his master to encourage him. Was he sick? Well, no—not in body, but in heart. He had failed to find anyone to help and had come back ashamed. It is such sorrow of heart, resulting in outbursts of tears on behalf of others, that should characterize the Christian.

130. An Overcoat of Love

I've been on both ends of this experience—the receiving and the giving. I remember when I first came to the United States from a warm climate. It was cold and I had no overcoat. How grateful I was to that servant of Christ, Melvin Wampler, who took off his coat and placed it on my shoulders. He went without so that I could be warm. In a similar manner I have often endeavored to do this for others. Believe me, however, there is more joy in giving and going without, than receiving and possessing.

131. Helping Your Brother

"Bear ye one another's burdens, and so fulfill the law of Christ" (Gal. 6:2). Concerning this passage, an eloquent preacher of the past wrote: "Many persons are caught with the most superficial contradiction. In the second verse it says, 'Bear ye one another's burdens'; and in the fifth it says, 'Every man shall bear his own burden.' As if both of them could not be true! As if a man carrying a burden for which he is especially responsible might not have it lightened somewhat by one who walked by his side and helped him! As if a little child carrying a heavily laden basket—which it was his task and business to carry, and which he had to take care of—might not be helped by another child walking by his side and taking hold of the handle. Might it not be said to one of them, 'This is your burden, and you must see to it'; and to the other, 'Help him with his burden.' To bear one another's burdens does not mean to take them from one another's shoulders, but to help each other to carry them."

132. Be Such a Brother

A well-to-do businessman gave a fine car to his brother. One day when the brother went to the place he'd parked the car, he saw a ragged boy looking the car over with great interest. Instead of saying, "Get away from that car, kid," he smiled at the youngster. The boy was the first to speak. "Is that car yours, Mister?" "Yes, it is," was the reply. "What did it cost?" was the next question. "Nothing," said the man. The boy looked at him curiously and said, "You don't look like the kind of guy who would steal a car." The owner laughed and said, "No, it was a present from my brother." The boy seemed incredulous. "Do you mean to say he gave it to you as a present, and it didn't cost you anything?" "That's right." Then the boy said the most surprising thing of all: "I sure do wish I could be such a brother as yours." One might have expected him to say, "How I wish I could have such a brother as yours." The man asked him what he meant, and he explained: "I'll tell you. My youngest brother had polio and he can't walk to see all the shops in town and enjoy the toys, at least by seeing them in the windows. How I wish I had a car like this to take him around. Our father died, and we won't get any presents this Christmas. But at least I can walk along the streets and enjoy the shop windows; my brother can't even do this. That's why I'd like to be a brother like your brother."

133. More Than Sympathy

Queen Victoria was a close friend of Principal and Mrs. Tullock, of St. Andrews. Prince Albert died and Victoria was left alone. Just at the same time, Principal Tullock died and Mrs. Tullock was left alone. Quite unexpectedly, Queen Victoria came to call on Mrs. Tullock when she was resting on a couch in her room. The Queen stepped forward. "My dear," she said, "don't rise. I am not coming to you today as a queen to a subject, but as one woman to another who has lost her husband." She put herself in her friend's place. That is what God did for us. That is what we should do for others.

134. Bridge Builders

The word "pontiff," used to designate the highest religious order of the Roman Catholic Church, namely the Pope, has an interesting history. This was the name which, in the old pagan religion of ancient Rome, was given to the chief priests. The pontiffs were those who were invested with pontifical power. The name as it was first applied meant "the makers of bridges." Why it was used to designate a religious order we hardly know. Perhaps those old Roman pontiffs were specially employed in consecrating those mighty instruments of earthly peace and civilization, the great roads and bridges by which the old Romans tamed and subdued the world. But in a moral and spiritual sense we ought all to be makers of bridges. Pontiff or no pontiff, minister or no minister, every Christian who walks in his Master's steps ought to make it his special business to throw bridges across those moral rents and fissures which divide us one from the other. Across these various gulfs and chasms let every one lend a helping hand to build such bridges as best we can. There cannot be a more truly pontifical work.

135. He Gave What He Had

Martin of Tours was a man in whom faith and works combined to make him a true Christian. One day he met a beggar who asked for alms. Martin didn't have any money, but he saw that the beggar was freezing, so he gave him what he had. He took off his soldier's overcoat, old and faded as it was, cut it in half, and wrapped half around the beggar. During the night Martin had a dream. He saw heaven opened, and Christ wearing half an overcoat. One of the angels asked, "Lord, why are you wearing that shabby old coat?" Christ answered, "Because my servant gave it to me." It was only a dream, but it illustrates the truth that Christ taught, that whatever we do for others in His name, He accepts as a gift to Him.

136. Hold My Hand

A young man was on the border of nervous collapse as he lay on the operating table. Among the nurses, he noticed one watching him intently. He thought he knew her and called her to him. "Yes," she said, "We have met before." Then he whispered, "Would you mind holding my hand?" She gripped it and he lay calmly waiting for the operation. What a strong thing sentiment is! It can conquer a man's fears even in the face of life's most serious crises.

137. In Honor Preferring One Another

During a spelling contest in which the prize was a fine Bible, the contestants were finally reduced to two—Betty, the daughter of a poor, hard-working widow, and Susan, the daughter of a well-to-do farmer. The sympathy of the school was with the poor girl. Finally Susan misspelled a word, and Betty won the coveted prize. Going home, Susan's mother said to her daughter, "Couldn't you have spelled that word?" "Yes, Mother." "Then why didn't you do it?" "Well, you know Betty is quite poor, and she doesn't get many presents. She wanted the Bible very much, and she tried so hard for it that I thought I'd let her have it." "What made you do that, Susie?" "My Sunday school lesson, Mother, which said, 'in honor preferring one another." So I thought I'd try it, and I'm glad I did." A few days later, Susan received as a birthday present a beautiful Bible, and on the flyleaf was written the text, "In honor preferring one another" (Rom. 12:10).

138. Legally Right, Morally Wrong

Each of us has certain legal rights in life. It is our privilege to insist that we enjoy every one of them. But in so doing we may commit moral wrong which would be injurious, not only to others, but also to ourselves and thus rob us of that most essential peace of heart. One of the apartments owned by a Christian landlord is rented by a widow with four children. Month after month, as a result of the hard work of that poor widow, the rent is paid. But suddenly she gets sick and is unable to pay the rent. The landlord has every legal right to call upon the authorities to evict this woman and her children from the apartment. His act would be legally right but morally wrong, i.e., right according to the letter, but wrong according to the spirit. If he shows kindness to this woman and her children and allows them to stay on in the apartment in spite of the fact they are not able to pay rent, he is showing the Christian quality of compassion. It is wiser to be willing to allow our legal rights to be trampled on, rather than by claiming them, to be morally in the wrong.

139. Love Your Enemies

During one of Mr. McKinley's congressional campaigns he was followed from place to place by a reporter for a paper of the opposite political party. The reporter was one of those shrewd, persistent fellows who are always at work, quick to see an opportunity, and skilled in making the most of it. While Mr. McKinley was annoyed by the misrepresentation to which he was almost daily subjected, he could not help admiring the skill and tenacity with which he was assailed. His admiration, too, was not unmixed with compassion—the reporter was ill, poorly clad, and had an annoying cough. One night Mr. McKinley took a closed carriage to a nearby town at which it had been announced he would speak. The weather was wretchedly raw and cold. He had not gone far when he heard that cough and knew that the reporter was riding with the driver in the exposed seat. McKinley called to the driver to stop so he could get out. "Get down off that seat, young man," he said. The reporter obeyed, thinking the time for the major's vengeance had come. "Here," said Mr. McKinley, taking off his overcoat, "You put on this overcoat and get into the carriage." "But Major McKinley," said the reporter, "I guess you don't know who I am. I have been with you the whole campaign, giving it to you every time you spoke, and I am going over tonight to rip you to pieces if I can." "I know," said

Mr. McKinley, "but you put on this coat, and get inside and get warm, so that you can do a good job."

140. Warmth of Sympathy

Henry Ward Beecher, while walking down a street, passed a newsboy shivering in the cold. Being moved with compassion toward him, the great preacher bought up all his newspapers, and when he handed over the money to him, he said, "Surely you are cold?" "I was," replied the lad with a gulp, "till you passed, sir."

Complaining

141. *Which Did God Believe?*

A large family sat around the table for breakfast one morning. As the custom was, the father returned thanks, blessing God for the food. Immediately afterward, however, as was his bad habit, he began to grumble about hard times, the poor quality of the food he was forced to eat, the way it was cooked, and much more. His little daughter interrupted him saying, "Father, do you suppose God heard what you said a little while ago?" "Certainly," replied the father with the confident air of an instructor. "And did He hear what you said about the bacon and the coffee?" "Of course," the father replied, but not as confidently as before. Then his little girl asked him again, "Then, Father, which did God believe?"

142. *He Grows Men, Not Peaches*

A young man who was trying to establish himself as a peach grower had worked hard and invested all his money in a peach orchard. It blossomed wonderfully but then came a killing frost. He didn't go to church the next Sunday, nor the next, nor the next. His minister went to see him to discover the reason. The young fellow exclaimed, "I'm not coming any more. Do you think I can worship a God who cares for me so little that He would let a frost kill all my peaches?" The old minister looked at him a few moments in silence, then said kindly, "God loves you better than He does your peaches. He knows that while peaches do better without frosts, it is impossible to grow the best men without frosts. His object is to grow men, not peaches." We are sometimes so concerned about our material possessions that we fail to realize that setting our hearts upon them can stunt our spiritual development. God often has to open our eyes to life's real values by taking from us its lesser ones.

143. *Stop Complaining*

Robert Hall, the great Baptist preacher, used to be subject to occasions of great physical pain, in the course of which he would roll on the ground in sheer agony. When the pain was over, the first words he used to say were, "I hope I didn't complain." How much more effective our witness for Christ would be if we didn't complain so much about our trials of faith.

144. Submit, Do Not Grumble

Unfortunately, even among Christians there are those who are chronic grumblers. A woman of this type grumbled at everything and everybody. But at last the preacher thought he had found something about which she could make no complaint—the lady's crop of potatoes was certainly the finest for miles around. "Ah, for once you must be pleased," he said with a beaming smile as he met her in the village street. "Everyone is saying how splendid your potatoes are this year." The lady glared at him as she answered, "They're not so poor. But where's the bad ones for the pigs?" If the mouth is given to grumbling, then the heart is lacking in submissiveness to God.

145. The Chronic Complainer

A certain father was a chronic growler. He was sitting with his family in the presence of a guest in the parlor one day when the question of food came up. One of the children, a little girl, was telling the guest very cleverly what food each member of the family liked best. Finally it came to the father's turn to be described. "And what do I like, Nancy?" he asked laughingly. "You," said the little girl slowly, "well, you like most anything we haven't got."

Criticism

146. Quick to Criticize

A man came up to Moody once and criticized him for the way he went about winning souls. Moody listened courteously and then asked, "How would you do it?" The man, taken aback, mumbled that he didn't do it. "Well," said Moody, "I prefer the way I do it to the way you don't do it."

147. Aiming Your Cannon

An officer on the battlefield aimed his cannon toward what he thought was the distant enemy. Just before he fired, the commander, looking through his field glasses, shouted, "Your aim seems perfect, but stop! They are not the enemy; they are our own people." Did you ever think that when you aim criticism at God's people so thoughtlessly, you are actually aiming your cannon at the Lord of your brethren?

148. Can't Dispute Facts

What does the criticism of others do to our inner self? Take the case of Col. George Washington Goethals. While contending with the manifold problems of geography and climate in the building of the Panama Canal, he had to endure the carping criticism of countless busybodies back home who freely predicted he would never complete his task. But he pressed steadily forward in his work and said nothing. "Aren't you going to answer your critics?" a subordinate inquired. "In time," Goethals replied. "How?" The great engineer smiled. "With the canal," he said.

149. A Mirrored Image

The story is told of a man and an angel who were walking along together. The man was complaining about his neighbors. "I never saw such a wretched set of people," he said, "as are in this village. They are mean, greedy, selfish, and careless of the needs of others. Worst of all, they are forever speaking evil of one another." "Is it really so?" asked the angel. "It is, indeed," said the man. "Why, only look at this fellow coming toward us! I know his face, though I cannot remember his name. See his little shark-like, cruel eyes, darting here and there like a ferret's, and the lines of hardness about his mouth! The very droop of his shoulders is mean and cringing, and he slinks along instead of walking." "It is very clever of you to see all this," said the angel, "but there is one thing that you did not perceive—that is a mirror we are approaching."

150. Allow Differences

Many years ago in Germany, so the story goes, there lived a shoemaker who had a habit of speaking harshly of all his neighbors who didn't think quite as he did about religion. The pastor of the parish in which he lived heard of this and felt he must give him a lesson. So he went to the shoemaker one morning and said, "Will you please take my measurements for a pair of boots?"

"With pleasure, sir," answered the shoemaker. "Please take off your boot." The clergyman did so, and the shoemaker measured his foot from toe to heel and over the instep, and wrote it all down in his notebook.

As he was writing up his measurements, the pastor said, "My son also needs a pair of boots."

"I'll be glad to make them, too. When can I take his measurements?"

"Oh, that's not necessary," said the pastor. "The lad is only twelve, but you can make my boots and his from the same last."

The shoemaker looked at him with a puzzled smile and said, "That would never do. They would never fit such a young boy."

"I tell you," insisted the pastor, "to make my son's on the same last."

"No, sir, I can't do it," protested the shoemaker. He began to wonder if the pastor was losing his wits.

"Well, then, shoemaker," said the clergyman, "you accept the fact that every pair of boots must be made on their own last, if they are to fit. Yet you think that God wants to form all Christians exactly according to your own last, of the same measure and growth in spiritual matters as yourself. That won't do either, you know."

The shoemaker got the point and said, "Thank you for your sermon. I'll try to remember it and judge my neighbors less harshly in the future."

151. The Spiritual Skeleton

An old fable tells of a man cursed with the power of seeing other human beings, not in the beauty of flesh and blood, but as skeletons gaunt and grisly. Some saints seem to have taken upon themselves this curse. Do you feel that you are the only one who is right with the Lord—that everybody else is a spiritual skeleton because he is not of the same denominational stripe or has not the same scruples of conscience as you? Take him or her into your circle of believers as Paul did, as long as they are calling upon the name of the Lord Jesus Christ.

152. Unjust Criticism

A Texas paper comments on the criticisms concerning a preacher: "The preacher has a great time. If his hair is grey he is too old; if he is a young man he hasn't had enough experience. If he has ten children he has too many; if he has none he is not setting a good example. If his wife sings in the choir she is presuming; if she doesn't she isn't interested in her husband's work. If a preacher reads from notes he is a bore; if he speaks extemporaneously he isn't deep enough. If he stays at home in his study, he does not mix enough with his people; if he is seen around on the streets, he ought to be home getting out a good sermon. If he calls at the homes of the wealthy, he is an aristocrat; if he calls on the poor family, then he is playing to the grandstand. Whatever he does, someone could have told him to do better." Pity the poor preacher, and for that matter every leader who has critical followers. Let us have confidence in our spiritual leaders, not blind confidence, but confidence that stems from personal persuasion that they are doing the best that they can under the circumstances.

153. Misjudged

There was a man who seemed stingy to everybody who knew him. He would be very scrupulous about how he spent even a nickel or a dime, so that he was greatly ridiculed. Finally it became known that he had an invalid wife and an invalid child for whom he cared, and they needed the very last penny that he could save to keep them alive. The criticism of outsiders now turned to admiration for him. Because we are unable to know everything about a man, we cannot possibly judge him rightly.

154. A Poor Example

A father, who attended church with his little boy, found fault with everything in the service. As he walked home, he criticized the minister, the sermon, the choir, and everything in general. The boy, who had noticed what his father put in the offering plate, said, "Well, Dad, what can you expect for a quarter?"

155. Remember Those Dogs

A certain unbeliever, a blacksmith, was in the habit when anyone came into his shop of telling some wrong a Christian brother, deacon or minister had done, and saying, "That is one of these fine Christians we hear so much about!" An old gentleman, an eminent Christian, one day went into the shop. The unbeliever soon began talking about what some Christians had done. The old deacon stood a few minutes and listened, and then quietly asked the unbeliever if he had read the story in the Bible about the rich man and Lazarus. "Yes, many a time; and what of it?" "Well, you remember about the dogs; how they came and licked the sores of Lazarus? Now," said the deacon, "do you know, you just remind me of those dogs—content to merely lick the Christian's sores."

Death

156. Face to Face

Men inspired by the Bible have called death by many names—the destroyer, the last enemy, the angel who summons our souls, a deep dark river. But here is Paul's picture of death from the believer's perspective—a man gazing at first into a metal mirror, seeing only baffling reflections and the fantastic shapes of half-facts, who suddenly wheels around and then sees things as they really are. He sees his fellows as they are; he sees the Savior as He is, in all His beauty—that is death for the Christian. No more peering through the mists of human ignorance to try to discern the face of the Savior; but clear, immediate, direct vision—face to face. We shall see Him as He is, and be forever like Him.

157. Just an Empty Shell

Two little birds had a nest in the bushes in the back part of a garden. Five-year-old Amy found the nest. It had four speckled eggs in it. One day, after she had been away for some time, she ran into the garden to take a look at the pretty eggs. To her dismay she found only broken shells. "Oh," she cried, "the beautiful eggs are all spoiled and broken!" "No, Amy," said her brother, "they are not spoiled. The best part of them has taken wings and flown away." So it is with death. The body left behind is only an empty shell, while the soul, the better part, has taken wings and flown away.

158. Prepare for Your Finals

Every time a certain little boy went to a playmate's house he found the child's grandmother reading her Bible. Finally his curiosity got the better of him. "Why do you suppose your grandmother reads the Bible so much?" he asked. "I'm not sure," said his friend, "but I think it's because she's cramming for her finals." Your finals may be closer than you think. There's only one book that can prepare you for them—that's the Bible, the written Word of God.

159. Suffering for a Good Cause

When the Marquis of Montrose was sentenced to death, the judge ordered that his head and limbs should be severed from his body and hanged in the Tolbooth in Endinburgh and in other public towns in the kingdom. The Marquis heard this sentence with a grim smile of pride and in defiance he cried, "I wish I had flesh enough to be sent to every city in Christendom, as a testimony to the cause for which I suffer!"

160. New Estimate of Death

Christ has brought a new attitude toward death. He has invested it with a beauty, a peacefulness and a glory unknown before. This is what caused a Greek by the name of Aristeides to marvel, when trying to explain to one of his friends the reasons for the extraordinary success of Christianity. In a letter written about A.D. 125, he said: "If any righteous man among the Christians passes from this world, they rejoice and offer thanks to God, and they escort his body with songs and thanksgiving as if he were setting out from one place to another nearby." Those believers who are gone before are not lost, not separated from us permanently; they are only waiting in another place nearby for us to join them again.

161. Burial Causes No Grief

Did you ever see a farmer weep as he placed seed in the ground and covered it with the freshly turned earth? Of course not, for that sort of burial causes no grief. The farmer knows that the buried seed will spring up into luxuriant vegetation in due course. Human burial is quite a different matter. It arouses far deeper emotions because of our attachment to the precious form laid in the grave. But for Christians this grief is tempered by the knowledge that those who die in the Lord are safe with Him, and that one day we will be reunited with them, not only in our spirits but in new and glorious bodies that will spring from the grave at our Lord's coming.

"So also is the resurrection of the dead," says Paul, referring again to his analogy of the seed. "It is sown in corruption; it is raised in incorruption" (1 Cor. 15:42)

162. The Seed—Then the Plant

You sow a seed by putting it into the ground. It must first die, and then it rewards you with a living plant. How does this take place? Can you or anyone else fully explain this philosophically, rationally? Do you refuse to eat the fruit of this seed until you know in minutest detail how it grows into a plant? Hardly. You accept the generating power of nature. When you sow wheat, you expect the same kind of plant to come up. But that plant does not contain every particle of matter that was in the seed. It contains the identity of the seed, but not the entire actual seed as it was put into the ground. Yet the plant resulting from that seed will produce seeds corresponding to that original seed, made of different and yet identical material particles. The plant in reality is that same seed which was placed in the ground, in different form. So will it be with your resurrection body. It will be the same body in the sense that it is your own body—yet no longer in the seed, so to speak, but the plant. When your soul leaves your body at death, that spiritless body is good for nothing but burial in the ground. There it can die and return to dust; and through death it will live again by God's power.

163. Glory Revealed

A minister was once called into the room of a dear saint of God who was suffering much pain. He had often visited her, and in spite of pain, found her greatly rejoicing. This time, however, he was told that she was in trouble and wished to see the minister urgently. Wondering what the trouble could be and how the devil might be tempting her, the minister rushed to her bedside. She said, "I cannot pray any more. As soon as I begin, my prayers are all turned into hallelujahs. I would have esteemed it a privilege if God had permitted me to spend my remaining days in supplications for my friends; but as soon as I open my mouth, it is all glory, glory, glory!" The minister could not but congratulate her on being drafted into the employment of the celestial choir before her time. She lived for two weeks in a gust of praise, and so she died.

164. On the Way Home

At the funeral of a minister, a little child was seen skipping lightheartedly through the cemetery at dusk. Someone asked, "Aren't you afraid of this place?" "Oh no," she replied, "I only cross through here to get home." Death for the Christian is only a "crossing-through to get home." It is not ultimate and final death.

165. A Joyful Meeting

A young woman who lay dying sought to console her father who was overcome with grief. "Dad," she said, "don't be so broken up. If I had received an offer of marriage from someone who was all you could desire for me, and whose station in life was far superior to mine, but who wanted to take me to live in a remote part of the world, don't you think you could have borne the separation, knowing all the advantages it would bring to me? But I am now being promoted to a situation incomparably beyond anything that could have happened to me in this world. Then why this reluctance to let me go? Our next meeting will be in far more wonderful circumstances, joyful, and everlasting."

166. A Re-created Body

While it is literally true that our bodies shall live again, Scripture does not require us to believe that God has to take exactly the same particles of all the physical substances of which our bodies are made and put them together again like a jigsaw puzzle. Let's not be like that woman who blithely stated that she did not believe in the resurrection of the body, because as the result of an accident she had left one leg in England, and she fully expected to die in the United States. If you expect the same atoms to be brought together again, how would you expect this to happen in the case of a man eaten by cannibals? His flesh would have been digested and become part of the bodies of those very ones who dined upon him. In the resurrection, would their bodies be robbed of the necessary particles to reconstitute the man they had devoured? Do you see to what ridiculous extremes we would be led by an insistence that God work in accordance with what we believe must happen? Of course, nothing is impossible with God. I would not find it difficult to believe that God is able to gather every fragment of bone, flesh, muscle, and sinew that made up our earthly bodies, to make up our glorified resurrection bodies. Men might conceive this impossible, but God can do it. The only reason I declare that it is not going to be so is that God's Word reveals that it will be otherwise (1 Cor. 15:37). He, an omnipotent God who created our bodies in the first place, can re-create them at the resurrection.

167. Is Our Resurrection Impossible?

Will our bodies one day be raised from the dead or not? How can we know? Impossible, says one group. Before you make such a flat declaration, look at that unattractive insect upon the blade of grass. In just a few short days you will find that insect floating in the air, a beautiful gossamer creature with wings that rival the rainbow. Look at the dry root in the dark, cold winter. When spring comes, out of that root will blossom forth a profusion of beautiful blossoms. Look at the egg, an inert and earthbound shape. Yet in it lies the eagle that can wing and soar above all other birds, or the tiny hummingbird that remains poised in mid-air before some flower, defying the pull of gravity. The doctrine of the resurrection is not inconsistent with the analogies of nature or the experience of our common history.

168. Plant Corresponds to Seed

In 1 Corinthians 15:36–38, we see that a seed must die in the ground before God causes it to spring up into a plant; that this plant will be consistent with the nature of the seed planted, yet different in form and function. To emphasize this difference between the seed and the plant is similar to the difference between the body that is laid in the grave and the body that will one day be resurrected, Paul says in verse thirty-seven, "And that which thou sowest, thou sowest not that body that shall be, but bare grain, it may chance of wheat, or of some other grain." The analogy is that of your dead body to a seed and of your resurrection body to the plant. There is nothing in Scripture that requires you to believe that the body you put into the ground is the selfsame body that will rise in the resurrection. Paul says that, with bodies as with plants, you don't bury that which is to be in the same form that it will eventually assume. A bare grain of wheat will produce a plant bearing many grains, but you don't sow the whole plant. You sow a seed and you get a corresponding plant.

169. It Is True

Death, like its master, Satan, stealthily watches to take its victims as a thief in the night. Quite often he gives no warning. Be prepared, therefore, to meet this enemy at any time. Professor J. H. Huxley was a well-known agnostic. His nurse revealed that in the last moments of his life, as he lay dying, the great skeptic suddenly looked up as at some sight invisible to mortal eyes, and, staring a while, whispered, "So it is true."

170. Alive Forever

The famed evangelist, Dwight L. Moody, once remarked in a sermon: "Some day you will read in the papers that D. L. Moody of East Northfield is dead. Don't you believe a word of it. At that moment I shall be more alive than now. I shall have gone up higher, that is all—out of this old clay tenement into a house that is immortal; a body that death cannot touch, that sin cannot taint, a body fashioned like unto His glorious body. That which is born of the flesh may die. That which is born of the spirit will live forever."

171. A Lesson from a Silver Cup

A servant who had received a silver cup from his master acciden-

tally dropped it into a vat of acid. The servant was dumbfounded when he saw the whole cup disappear. He immediately went to a fellow servant and told him that the silver cup was lost forever. "It can't be recovered. You can't even see it." The master, an educated man, came on the scene. He infused salt water into the acid, which precipitated the silver from the solution. Then by melting it and hammering the metal he restored the cup to its original shape. A skeptic who saw this was so struck by its analogy to the resurrection, which he had rejected as impossible, that he now believed it most credible.

172. A Body Fit for Heaven

What do we know about the germination of seeds? Keep a grain of wheat in your pocket all your life and it will never change. But place it in a congenial environment, a furrow of earth, and it will sprout into a living sheaf of grain. Every kind of life requires its particular corresponding environment in order to achieve its full and predestined potential. You would really be just as foolish to expect your body, as now constituted, to be able to live in the world to come, as a farmer would be if he expected to produce a harvest of wheat by keeping bare grains stored in his pocket.

173. A Divine Display of Power

"Thou foolish one, that which thou sowest..." (1 Cor. 15:36). The

Greek verb is *speireis*, "you sow all the time." This is a common every-day experience. You accept it because you see it happening all the time. How true it is that there are many wonders in the world that you would not have believed by report, if you had not come across them by experience and observation. Had you lived fifty years ago, would you have believed that a picture could be taken by Telstar, a photographic communication satellite in the sky, which would then send back a clear picture on your television screen? In fact, would you have believed television? In the air there are only video waves, but on the television screen you see a person, an actual scene. Everything is wonderful until you are used to it; the resurrection of the body owes the incredible portion of its marvel to the fact of your never having observed it. After the resurrection we shall regard it as a divine display of power as familiar to us as creation and providence are now.

174. Are You Ready to Die?

One day when Luther was a young man, he was walking with a friend named Alexis. Suddenly a bolt of lightning struck his friend and killed him instantly. From that moment on a radical change took place in Luther's life. Your life will also change if you think seriously that one day it will end, perhaps suddenly and soon. After that you will have to give an account of it to God. Are you ready for it?

175. Nature Hints at the Resurrection

An illustration of what one may learn from nature, if he only has eyes to see, is the example of a man who looked into his tropical aquarium one day and saw on the surface a tiny creature, seemingly half fish and half snake, not an inch long, writhing in what seemed its death agony. With convulsive efforts it bent head to tail, now on this side, now on that, springing in circles with a force truly remarkable in a creature so small. "I was stretching out my hands to remove it," said the aquarium owner, "so that it would not sink and die and pollute the tank, when in the twinkling of an eye its skin split from end to end, and there sprang out a delicate fly with slender black legs and pale lavender wings. Balancing itself for one instant on its discarded skin, it preened its gossamer wings and then flew out of an open window. The impression made upon me was deep and overpowering. I learned that nature was everywhere hinting at the truth of the resurrection."

176. The Foolish Question

A little boy drove his mother to distraction with questions one day. Finally she sent him packing off upstairs to bed. Later feeling troubled, she tiptoed into his room, knelt beside his bed, and told him she was sorry she had been cross with him, adding, "Now, dear, if you want to ask one more question before you go to sleep, I'll try to answer it."

Quick as a wink the youngster blurted out, "Mommy, how high is up?" Some theological questioning is just about as foolish. That's exactly what Paul calls the man who asks these questions about the resurrection body, "Thou fool." The Greek word here is *aphrōn*, which comes from the negative prefix *a*, "without," and the noun *phrēn*, "mind." You are a man without sense, without reason, Paul says, if you think there can be an explanation in detail of all observable facts and the conclusions to be drawn from them.

Discernment

177. I Would Rather Have You

A little girl had been told many times by a childless old couple that if she would come and live with them, they would get her everything she wanted—a pony and cart, a piano, and the like. One day when the couple had been particularly urgent, her father said, "Don't you think you had better go with them?" The little girl looked at him in alarm and cried, "Why, Daddy, don't you want me?" "Yes," he replied, "but I can't give you very much, and they will give you everything nice." "But I wouldn't have you!" she said as she snuggled up to him.

178. Where Art Thou?

In speaking on the text, "Adam, where art thou?" (Gen. 3:9) a preacher said, "I make three divisions to this text. First: Every man's got to be somewhere. Second: Some men are where they ought not to be. Third: They that are where they ought not to be are going to find themselves where they do not want to be." If we want to find out what sin is by experience, we shall find ourselves where we do not want to be; but if we seek to discern it by a sanctified, God-honoring reflection, then we shall never taste to find out, because we shall know the results beforehand. Remember Adam? He found himself where he did not want to be after he had tasted of the forbidden fruit. Oh, for wisdom to know the forbidden trees!

179. Plea for Mercy

Plutarch tells us that the Rhodians appealed to the Romans for help, and one suggested that they should plead the good things which they had done for Rome. This was a plea difficult to make strong enough, very apt to be disputed, and not likely to influence so great a people as the Romans, who would not readily consider themselves to be debtors to such a puny state as Rhodes. The Rhodians, however, were wiser than their counselor and took up another line of argument which was abundantly successful. They pleaded the favors which in former times the Romans had bestowed upon them, and urged these as the reason the great nation should not cast off a needy people for whom they had already done so much.

180. When Entertaining, Know the Angel

So many are like the traveler who came tired and exhausted to the door of a Christian and asked to stay overnight. When the Christian showed some unwillingness, the traveler started quoting Scripture and telling the Christian not to forget that he might have the opportunity of entertaining an angel unawares. "Yes," said the Christian, "but I don't believe that an angel from heaven would smell of liquor."

181. The Lord's Will

A little boy about eight or nine, who liked to have his own way, was told by his father, "Philip, you ought not to want your own way." He dropped his head as if he had been given a big problem to solve. After thinking a while he said, "Father, if I choose the will of the Lord and go His way because I want to, don't I still have my own way?"

182. Spiritual Warfare

Every time you look at your wallet or your paycheck, humanly speaking, the temptation arises, "How can this improve my way of life? How much more can I buy with it? Can I buy a better home, perhaps, or use it to live a cut above the common standard?" It is part of our Adamic nature to want more pleasure, more comfort, more things. During World War II, posters everywhere queried the driver, "Is this trip necessary?" We are in a spiritual warfare, and we should analyze every purchase with the question, "Is this expenditure necessary?" Our Lord says, "Look at the material substances of life and say, 'How can this be used in order to influence people for Christ?' "

183. The Discerning Artist

A poet and an artist each examined a painting by Poussin representing the healing of the two blind men of Jericho. The artist asked, "What seems to you the most remarkable thing in this painting?" The poet replied, "Everything in the painting is excellently given— the form of Christ, the grouping of the individuals, the expression in the faces of the leading character, everything." The artist seemed to find the most significant touch elsewhere. Pointing to the steps of a house in the corner of the picture, he said, "Do you see that discarded cane lying there?" "Yes, but what does that signify?" "Why, my friend, on those steps the blind man sat with the cane in his hand. But when he heard Christ had come, he was so sure that he would be healed that he let his cane lie there, since he would need it no more, and hastened to the Lord as if he could already see."

184. More Discerning?

In South America there is a tribe of Indians that interprets the past and future quite differently from us. We look at the past as being behind us and the future as lying ahead of us. We may laugh at this tribe as being less advanced than we, but they place the past in the future, and the future in the past. Instinctively they are more discerning than we. Look at their logic: what they've experienced and lived through they place before them to teach them. The sufferings of the past become the lessons of the future. We've known this, but often we haven't practiced it. They look at the future as lying behind them because it is entirely unknown; it's something that follows rather than precedes them.

185. Trifles Make Perfection

A friend once saw Michelangelo at work on one of his statues. Some time later he saw the statue and seeing so little done said, "Have you been doing nothing since I saw you last?" "By no means," replied the sculptor. "I have retouched this part and polished that; I have softened this feature and brought out that muscle; I have given more expression to this lip, and more energy to this limb." "Well, well," said the friend, "all these are trifles." "It may be so," replied Michelangelo, "but recollect that trifles make perfection, and that perfection is no trifle."

186. Death Isn't the End

Cicero, a Roman orator and politician who lived before Christ, said: "I am persuaded that my friends who have departed this life have not ceased to exist. In reality only their present condition can be called life. I adopt this faith not only because logic demands it but also because my respect for the most noble and distinguished philosophers bids me do so. I consider this world a place for nature but never

foreordained to be my home forever. My departure from this world I never deem as an expulsion from my dwelling place but rather as the departure from my hotel." Even a pre-Christian era Roman knew that death doesn't end all.

187. Recognize Authority

If you recognize the responsibilities of your position and your exact relationship to the one who is above you, you will be wise. It is not always the ruler of a country who is the most intelligent man in that country. Nor is the principal of a school smarter than the teachers under him. The same holds true of students and teachers. Many times teachers are so wrong in their philosophy of life. Recognize realities even while you recognize the deficiencies of others, for the Scriptures teach us that those who are over us are placed there by God for some purpose.

188. Our Spiritual State Versus Temporal State

A beggar on the street sits asking for alms. Along comes a person who throws a quarter into the outstretched hand, and as he does, he is thinking, "You deserve what you are going through, but I'll help you anyway." Then comes another man who has no more to give than the first one, but says, "God certainly loves you, and your need gives me the opportunity of being a giver. I am not any better than you are, but I recognize it is more blessed to give than to receive. God's favor upon you may be as great as it is upon me. Our spiritual state cannot be measured by our temporal state of affairs."

189. Don't Abuse Power

There was a king whose officers, in the midst of battle, decided to go and take food that was desperately needed from some homes in the area. When they came back with it, the king asked, "Did you pay them for what you took?" They said, "No, the king doesn't have to pay." He said, "Go back and pay them for everything that you took." A king who arbitrarily takes things from people is hated, but a ruler who pays for everything he needs and that people are willing to give up, is the one who is loved. Anyone who uses his power to take away, is abusing his power.

190. Healthy Fear

A young soldier of evident breeding and culture had one peculiarity. He would never drink alcoholic beverages with the others. One day the major asked him to take a message to the express agent in town. "Where shall I find him, sir?" he asked. "Just go into Casey's saloon and sit down. He'll show up in the course of the afternoon." The soldier drew back and said, "Beg pardon, sir, but can't I meet him some place else?" "Why, what's the matter with Casey's? Are you afraid to go there?" "Yes, sir, because drink was what made me enlist and leave my family in the first place. I was drunk and didn't know what I was

doing." "You may go," said the major curtly. "I'll find a more accommodating and less cowardly man."

From then on this soldier carried a reputation for cowardice because he was realistic enough to avoid danger he knew he was too weak to face. However, the opinion of the battery changed one day when he was one of the seven chosen to fire a cannon salute to a visiting general. One bag of powder failed to discharge, and the sergeant ordered it pulled out. As it fell to the ground, the men were horrified to see that one corner of it ignited. For a breathless moment no one moved. Then this soldier flung himself upon it and with his bare hands smothered the deadly spark. From then on he was the hero of the company. You may depend upon it; the man who is afraid of doing wrong will be brave enough when the occasion calls for it.

191. Natural Laws

The laws of nature are the expression of the will of God. God works within the world order in a living way. We may say that the world has two levels: a higher and a lower, a permanent and a temporary, a spiritual and a material. Man belongs to both orders, and he is subject to the laws of both. The same chemical elements that are in him are also in the material world around him. Therefore, he is subject to the operation of material forces such as gravitation, lightning, earthquakes, and such phenomena. In the administration of these natural laws there is absolute impartiality. The sun is completely impartial concerning whom it shines on, and the rain on whom it falls. Nature plays no favorites.

192. Who Owns the World?

World ownership, as Frederick F. Shannon observes, is a matter of spiritual capacity. The true owner of the world is the soul capable of appreciating it. Individual response to the eternal love and wisdom is owning it. As an illustration, consider a magnificent organ. Who owns it—the person who made it or the one who paid for it? The organist himself? In reality the person who holds an indisputable title-deed to that organ is the man most capable of enjoying the music. As Shannon says, "God leases the universe to all who can pay for it by the invisible coin of appreciation. Deity hangs a sign in the window of every star, on the leaf of every tree, on the face of every flower, on the peaks of history, on the souls of immortal men and women—and that sign reads: "For Rent! The only rental fee is the capacity to enjoy."

193. Practical Christianity

Christianity must be practical. Two children were afraid they would be late for school. One said, "Let's kneel down and pray to God that He may help us not to be late." The other child offered a more practical solution: "No, let's run and pray at the same time."

194. He Knows the Shepherd

At a reception, a famous actor was asked to give a recitation. An old preacher suggested the Twenty-third Psalm. He did it with great oratorical skill and sat down to prolonged applause. Then he turned to the old preacher and asked him to recite the Psalm also. In a weak and trembling voice, the kindly man uttered the same simple verses. But no one applauded this time. People began surreptitiously to wipe away their tears. The actor rose again, "Ladies and gentlemen," he said, "I communicated with your ears and your eyes. I know the words. But my old friend here communicated with your hearts. He knows the Shepherd." Do you know Him?

195. Character or Reputation

A busybody is often interested in telling only half the truth. It's true that Christ kept company with publicans and sinners, not because He loved and practiced their sin but so that He could influence and win them. A defamatory article about a Christian appeared in a newspaper. It was really terrible. "You must sue him," a friend said. "No," was the answer. "I shall try to set him straight. I'm afraid if I sue him I shall do something that is improper. I learned early in life, and from long experience, that man's character can only be harmed by himself. The first step for me to win my detractor is to overcome my own passion for vengeance." Reputation is what other people think and say of you, but character is what you yourself decide it shall be. If you belong to Christ, then your decision is to be like Him—and by His grace you can be.

196. The Good Employer

A business man, who had a thousand workers in his employ, was once asked by a preacher, "How are you getting on with your men?" "Oh," he said, "I have no trouble." And that was at a time when there was great trouble in the labor market. "But haven't you had any strikes?" "Oh, no," he said, "I never had any trouble." "What plan do you pursue?" "All my men," he said, "know every year how matters stand. Every little while I call them together and say, 'Now, boys, last year I made so much—this year I made less; so you see I can't pay you as much as I did last year. Now, I want to know what you think I ought to have as a percentage out of this establishment, and what wages I ought to give you. You know I put all my energy into this business, risked everything and put all my fortune into it. What do you really think I ought to have and you ought to have?' By the time we come out of that consultation, we are unanimous; there has never been an exception. When we prosper, we all prosper together; when we suffer, we all suffer together; my men and I share all our problems together."

197. Nothing to Lose

An unbeliever once approached a consistent born-again believer and

began to ridicule him. "Listen to me, my friend," said the Christian. "On my instrument I have two chords—joy of faith in Christ and hope of eternal joy in heaven. You have only one—hope of joy in this life."

"What do you mean by that?"

"Let me explain. I want to be on the safe side. Suppose that after death there is really nothing, and both of us are destined to disappear into nothingness. Who do you think is getting more satisfaction out of life right now—you with your empty philosophy or I with my faith in Jesus Christ? I think that I really have it over you as far as enjoyment is concerned. So that if you are right, I should lose nothing by having committed myself to faith in Christ. But if I am right, what will become of you? My fellowship with Christ assures me of joy in this life and eternal bliss in case there is life after death. I have nothing to lose. But you? If it turns out I'm right, you will be lost in the future. And on top of it all, you will find that you didn't enjoy the peace of heart and the joy of being on the side of right in this life, as I did."

198. Not Presumptions, but Certainties

The name of Michael Faraday is known to scientists and students everywhere. He was a British physical scientist whose discoveries contributed much to our knowledge of electricity. The modern world has deified science—physical science. But we must never forget that all scientific investigation is based upon the premise that for every effect there must be a cause, and that the universe is governed by laws. All experiments are based on the laws we are continually discovering, and only a pseudo-scientist would claim that we have reached the end of our discoveries. Where would we be if we had no faith in the trustworthiness of physical laws? We would never entrust ourselves to an airplane.

When Faraday was dying someone asked him, "Mr. Faraday, what are your presumptions, your hypotheses now?" "I do not entrust my head to presumptions at this moment, but to certainties," he replied. " 'For I know whom I have believed, and am persuaded that he is able to keep that which I committed unto him against that day' " (2 Tim. 1:12).

Doctrine

Sanctification

199. A Parable From Nature

A person who is "sanctified in Christ" is like the water spider which is a very peculiar insect. We are peculiar, also, to the environment in which we live. The water spider lives at the bottom of muddy pools and has the distinctive power of ascending to the surface of the pool and there surrounding itself with a tiny globule of air. Thus enveloped it descends to the sludge and ooze at the bottom of the pool and remains there unsullied by its environment until the air is exhausted. Then it rises again to the surface and the process is repeated. So those "sanctified in Christ" find spiritual rejuvenation in daily Bible reading and Christian fellowship, unsullied and undirtied by the hostile environment around them.

200. God's Model

A shipbuilder steps out into his yard and looks around him. There are the vast skeletons of ships just commenced; there are others advancing to completion. But there is nothing in the scene to satisfy. The big hulls are at present good for nothing. A thousand hammers are tapping in vexatious discord. The miry ground is strewn with wood and metal. Yet the owner stands content amid the imperfection. He never thinks of even doubting the process he beholds. In his mind he carries the ideal of a perfect ship, and he justifies the imperfect ships by imputing to them that ideal. God is like that great shipbuilder. The ideal man exists in His mind. He has the blueprint; man is like the ship being built. When God looks at it He does not despair, because He knows what He can do with the imperfect man.

The Trinity

201. Arithmetic of Heaven

A gentleman passing a church with Daniel Webster asked him, "How can you reconcile the doctrine of the Trinity with reason?" The statesman replied by asking, "Do you understand the arithmetic of heaven?"

202. The Godhead—a Family

There is ample evidence in the Scriptures that the Godhead is a unity made up of God the Father, God the Son, and God the Holy Spirit. We should not feel that it is an insult to our intelligence to expect us to accept this revealed truth of Scripture. Let us be as open to the truth as that converted Indian who gave the following illustration, imperfect though it is, for his belief in the Trinity: "We go down to the river in winter and we see it covered with snow; we chop through the ice and we come to the water. Snow is water, ice is water, water is water; therefore the three are one." In this way, God demonstrates his triune nature through the natural world.

Mysteries

203. Physical and Spiritual Mysteries

The farmer who turns up the ground and sows the seed seldom pauses to reflect on the mystery of its growth. Even the philosopher who understands the wonderful process of vegetation is conscious of difficulties he cannot solve in its several stages toward maturity. The farmer doesn't refuse to sow the seed because he can't see the actual plant in it. A sperm cell is almost invisible, yet it contains the full potential for a perfect human organism. Think of the mystery in such natural phenomena. We accept them because we can't live without them. God hasn't given us the freedom to reject natural laws and mysterious phenomena in connection with our physical lives. But He has chosen to give us the ability to reject His spiritual laws and not immediately feel the consequences. If we refuse to eat we'll die. There

are no two ways about it. But in the spiritual realm we feel no immediate physical impact of disobedience to God's laws. There is a spiritual consequence, but those who have no spiritual sensibility or life don't feel it. It would be just like inflicting punishment on a corpse; it couldn't feel it. Just so the spiritually dead can't feel the spiritual consequences of their disobedience.

204. The Great Touches the Mysterious

Parker says: "There is a mystery about religion, but there is ten thousand times more mystery without it. There is mystery with the Bible, but there is nothing but mystery without it. There is a mystery of grace; yes, and there is the mystery of sin. Life is a mystery. All that is great touches the mysterious. In proportion as a thing rises from vulgarity and the commonplace, it rises into wondrousness—and the wondrousness is but the first round in the ladder whose head rests upon the infinite mysteries."

205. No Explanation

Take a hyacinth bulb, for instance. Put it in a glass jar of water and watch it day by day. The leaves and the buds unfold above. The roots develop below. Then as the days get warmer it bursts into full and beautiful bloom. Why should the bulb break out this way into flower, leaf, and root before your eyes? "Why," you might say, "they always do." Yes, but why? You say it is the law of growth; but what do you mean by that? You don't explain anything by merely labeling it. You fail to explain either what it is in itself, or why it should be at work here under these conditions. You can't deny its existence, yet the moment you try to penetrate below the surface it eludes you altogether.

Judgment

206. The Immutable Law of Sowing and Reaping

The farmer who plants certain seeds knows what to expect. He knows he will reap what he sows. He may not know exactly how many bushels of corn he'll get to an acre, but he knows it will all be the result of the seeds he planted. That is an unbreakable law of nature: we reap what we sow, but we can never know exactly how much the harvest will be. This also holds true in the spiritual realm. We find immutable laws of sowing and reaping there also. I know some people try to deny the existence of such a realm as the Kingdom of God. They are like moles who are ignorant of the existence of the sunlit world because they are blind.

207. Future Punishment

The doctrine of future punishment is so clearly taught in God's Word that no one can escape it. It is not that God wants to threaten or frighten people into being good. As Dr. S. M. Merrill says, "It is the

last resort of God's wisdom and holiness. . . . In it God takes no delight. Yet the necessities of good government, the maintenance of order under rightful authority, and the highest regard for the welfare of the good, require this ultimate vindication of righteousness at the expense of the incorrigibly wicked."

Faith and Works

208. The Arms of Faith

On a wall in the Vatican, an artist sought to express the relationship between three spiritual gifts. He represented Love as standing up attending to the needs of those around her, and Hope as looking upward with prophetic expectation. Both of them, however, are standing on another form named Faith who has her arms around the cross to which she clings for support.

209. The Finished Work

A great many people find it extremely difficult to accept Christ's death on the cross as sufficient ransom for their sins. They want to do something themselves. "But I can't see it," said a certain cabinetmaker to a friend who was trying to show him how the death of Christ completed the work of atonement. At last an inspiration struck his friend, who, lifting the plane, moved as if to plane the top of a beautifully polished table that stood near. "Stop!" cried the cabinetmaker. "Don't you see that's finished? You'll simply ruin it if you use that plane on it," "Why," replied his friend, "that's just what I have been trying to show you about Christ's work of redemption. It was finished when He gave His life for you, and if you try to add to that finished work you can only spoil it. Just accept it as it stands—His life for yours—and you go free."

210. Faith Plus Works

When a soldier was leaving to fight for his country, a minister said to him, "I shall pray constantly that you may win." The soldier replied: "I don't see the necessity of your prayers. If God wants to give us victory, then He will do it without your prayers. And if it is our luck to lose, do you think your prayers could prevent this?" The minister thought for a moment and said, "All right. Take off your helmet. Take off your uniform. Put your rifle away. Go and rest. It's not necessary for you to fight. Nor is it necessary for the other soldiers to fight. If God intends to defeat the enemy, He is going to do it anyway without your arms." The soldier got the point. God helps those who fight, not those who do nothing. The sower plants the seed. That is our job, to sow the seed in human hearts. But we must also pray that God will give the increase which is salvation. Then what a joy to witness the result and to give all the glory to God!

Angels

211. Our Guardian Angels

If an angel from heaven suddenly became visible to you as you were sitting alone, what would your reaction be? An ancient saint admonished Christians in these words: "In every area . . . in every corner, pay a respect to your angel. Dare not do before him what you dare not do before others. Consider with how great respect, awe, and modesty we ought to behave in the sight of the angels lest we offend their holy eyes and render ourselves unfit for their company. Woe to us if they who could chase away our enemy would be offended by our negligence and deprive us of their visit."

212. Angels in Charge

The story is told of a little boy who asked his mother if he could take his baby sister out to play. She had just begun to walk alone and could not step over anything that lay in the way. His mother said "Yes, if you'll be careful not to let her fall." The man who tells the story says, "I found them at play, very happy, in the field. I said, 'You seem to be very happy, George. Is this your sister?' 'Yes sir,' he replied. 'Can she walk alone?' 'Yes sir, on smooth ground.' 'Then how did she walk over those big stones between here and the house?' 'Well, Mother told me to be careful she didn't fall, so I put my hands under her arms and lifted her up when she came to a stone so she wouldn't hit her foot against it.' " "He shall give his angels charge over thee. . . . They shall bear thee up in their hands, lest thou dash thy foot against a stone." God charges His angels to lead and lift His people over difficulties in the same way.

Eternal Security

213. God's Hold Is Sure

There were two brethren who differed on the question of the believer's safety in Christ. They were discussing the question, and one said to the other: "I'll tell you, a child of God is safe only so long as he stays in the lifeboat. He may jump out, and if he jumps out he is lost." To this the other replied, saying: "You remind me of an incident in my own life. I took my little son out with me in a boat. I realized, as he did not, the danger of his falling or even jumping into the water. So I sat with him all the time, and all the time I held him fast, so he could neither fall out nor jump out of the boat." "But," said the first speaker, "he could have wriggled out of his coat and got away in spite of you." "Oh," said the other, "you misunderstood me if you supposed I was holding his coat; I was holding him."

Hope

214. Kind Providence

If we think it all through, we shall agree that it is better that futurity be hidden from our view. What little child would have the heart to begin the alphabet if, before he did so, his teacher put clearly before him all the school and college work of which the alphabet is the beginning? The poor little thing would give up at once. And so it is that Providence, kindly and gradually bringing things into our lives day by day, wiles us onward, still keeping hope and heart through the trials and cares of life. Knowledge of the future would certainly be the deathknell of hope, for why hope if we could know? Hope is a wonderful element of human happiness which is based on our ignorance of the future here on earth.

Envy

215. The Crush of Envy

An incident is related in Greek history of a wrestler who was so envious of Theagenes, the prince of wrestlers, that he could not be consoled in any way. After Theagenes died, a statue of him was erected in a public place. His envious antagonist went out every night and wrestled with the statue, until one night he threw it over. The statue fell on him and crushed him to death.

216. No Time for Envy

Many Christians are like that person who, one day, looked extremely sad. One who knew him well said, "Either some great evil has happened to him, or some great good to another." It has been very aptly said, "The man who keeps busy helping the man below him will not have time to envy the man above him; and there may not be anyone above him."

217. Be Not High-Minded

A story is told of a watch which became dissatisfied with its little sphere in a lady's pocket. It envied Big Ben, the great tower clock in London. One day, as it passed over Westminster Bridge with its mistress, the little watch was heard to say, "I wish I could be up there. I could then serve the multitude."

"You shall have your opportunity, little watch," said a voice. Magically the watch was drawn up to the tower by a slender thread. When it reached the top, its mistress said to it, "Where are you, little watch? I cannot see you." Nor could anybody else. Its elevation became its annihilation.

218. A Wish Granted

A little snail that lived by the ocean noticed with envy the big, beautiful shell in which the lobster lived. "What a grand palace the lobster carries on his back! I wish I lived in his place," whined the little snail. "Oh, wouldn't my friends admire me in that shell!"

In time a wonderful thing occurred. The watching, envious snail beheld the lobster walk right out of his shell to grow up in another, larger one. When the empty lobster shell lay neglected on the beach the snail said, "Now I shall have my wish." And he boasted to all his friends that he was going to take up residence in a grand palace.

The birds and the animals then watched the snail pull himself loose from his own little shell and proudly crawl into the towering lobster shell. He huffed, puffed, blew, and gasped in an effort to make himself fit. But with all his efforts he felt very small inside the grand lobster shell. He grew tired, too. That night he died because the large, empty shell was so cold.

A wise old crow then said to the younger crows, "You see! That's what comes of envy. What you have is enough. Be yourself and save yourself from a lot of trouble. How much better to be a little snail in a comfortable shell than to be a little snail in a big shell and freeze to death!"

Faith

219. Operative Faith

A Christian farmer was constantly jeered at by a non-Christian because he would not work on Sunday, went to church, and gave his tithes to the Lord's work. At the end of a poor harvest season the non-Christian said to him, "Where is your God? He has certainly failed you, hasn't He?" "Oh, no," the Christian said, "my God does not close His books at the end of the harvest season."

220. The Rich Employer

Peter Eldersveld tells of a rich Christian who had a large company of employees, and many of them owed him money. He was constantly trying to teach them something about Christianity, and one day he hit upon a plan. He posted a notice for his employees to see that said, "All those who will come to my office between eleven and twelve o'clock on Thursday morning to present an honest statement of their debts will have them canceled at once." The debtors read the notice with a great deal of skepticism, and on Thursday morning, although they gathered in the street in front of his office, not one of them went to the door. Instead they gossiped and complained about their employer, and ridiculed the notice he had posted. They said it didn't make sense.

But finally, at 11:45, one man jumped forward, dashed up the steps into the office, and presented his statement. "Why are you here?" the rich man asked him. "Because you promised to cancel the debts of all those who would come as you instructed," the other replied. "And do you believe the promise?" "Yes, I do." "Why do you believe it?" persisted the employer. "Because, although it was too much for me to understand, I know that you are a good man who would not deceive anyone." The rich man took the bill and marked it "Paid in full," at which time the poor man, overcome, cried out, "I knew it! I told them so! They said it couldn't be true, and now I'm going out to show them." "Wait," said his benefactor, "it's not quite twelve o'clock. The others are not entitled to any special proof of my sincerity." When the clock struck twelve, the forgiven debtor ran out waving his receipt in the face of his fellows. With a mad rush they made for the door, but it was too late. The door was locked.

221. Cost of the Step of Faith

An old, low-caste woman in India was once asked the cost of a temple being built. She turned to the missionary in surprise and said, "Why, we do not know! It is for our god. We do not count the cost!" She could certainly have put many followers of Christ to shame. Before we take the step of faith we want to know the cost.

222. Look Over the Wall

Two men were discussing worry; one was blaming God because He didn't let us know what was going to happen. As they walked along, they came to a pasture where a cow was gazing dreamily over a stone wall. "Do you know why this cow has her head stretched over the wall?" asked one man. "No," said his friend. "I'll tell you. It's because she's not able to see through the stone wall. Imitate her. Quit banging the wall with your head. You won't break the wall down, but you will break your head. Stand tall, look over, and you'll be able to see farther on." It's the same lesson the Lord taught when He told people to look at the birds of the air and the lilies of the field, and consider who cares for them (Matt. 6:28). They have less cares than we who can think and reason, but God provides for them, and He will for us, too, if we trust Him.

223. God Governs the World

One night when an ambassador and his valet were obliged to sleep in the same room in a hotel, the valet noticed his master tossing and turning in bed. "Sir, what bothers you?" he asked. "Oh, I have so many things on my mind. The burden of my responsibility is hard to bear." "Forgive me, sir, but do you think God has been governing the world up till now?" "Of course." "And do you think He'll manage even after you've left this world?" "Undoubtedly." "Then don't you think it's possible for you to trust Him to do it even during your lifetime?" The ambassador got the point and was soon fast asleep.

224. Working Faith

Two gentlemen were crossing the river in a little boat. They began to argue about faith and works. The man who was rowing them across the river was a fine, enlightened Christian and on hearing their discussion he turned to them and said, "I believe I can solve your difficulty. I hold in my hands two oars. The one I call faith and the other works. Now watch it. I pull the oar of faith alone. You see, we can only go around and around; we cannot go forward. Now I pull the oar of works; again we move around and around. Now, see, I pull both of them together and on we go." Then the Christian ferryman added his conclusion, "In my opinion, a faith without works is dead, or works without faith will not suffice" (James 2:26).

225. Two Parts to the Gospel

An old country preacher used to say: "There are two parts to the Gospel. The first part is believing it, and the second part is behaving it." The hearer only is the one who is satisfied with just believing without behaving. That is what James describes as dead faith (James 2:17).

226. Saving Faith

Phillips Brooks defined faith by saying, "Faith means Forsaking All, I Take Him." Saving faith is leaving the spot where we are now standing and jumping into the arms of Jesus with full confidence that He is able to bear us up. It is like trying to swim. Swimming is work as we know. Before we can swim, we must believe that the water is able to bear us up; saving faith is believing on the Lord Jesus Christ first and then swimming in the great sea of His love and everlasting mercy. This is a faith that saves.

227. God Must Have You— You Must Have God!

A soldier being dealt with by a Christian worker put it very well when he said, "I see it now! God does not expect me to live His life without first giving me His nature." Faith which implants God's nature in the heart of man is a saving faith, and the faith which does not is not saving faith. Even if a man says he believes there is eternal salvation in Jesus Christ, this declaration will not save him, but going to Jesus Christ and losing himself in Him saves him. Faith which makes us run into the arms of Jesus saves; faith that makes us stand still does not save. Our works of faith emanate from a source of moral standards which we did not set up and which we cannot pull down, one

that is ever above the laws of human fabrication.

228. Practical Faith

A minister tells how in his first parish a banker occasionally came to his church, and every time he came the minister happened to be preaching on faith. The banker said to him, "Why don't you preach on something other than faith? Why don't you preach on something practical?" A few days later there was a run on his bank, and the minister went down to see what was going on. He found the people demanding their money; they were alarmed and suspicious, and the banker was going up and down the line saying to these people, "Everything is all right. There is nothing wrong with the bank." The minister touched him on the shoulder and said, "What is the matter?" "Why," he said, "there is nothing wrong, but these people have lost faith in the bank." The minister replied, "Do you remember when you told me to preach on something more practical than faith?" "Oh, yes," he said, "I remember it very well, and I take it all back. After all, there is nothing so fundamental to the business interests and commercial life as faith."

229. Faith and Reason

An old writer says, "Faith and reason may be compared to two travelers: Faith is like a man in full health who can walk twenty or thirty miles at a time without suffering. Reason is like a child, who can only with difficulty accomplish three or four miles. On a given day Reason says to Faith, 'O good Faith, let me walk with thee.' Faith replies, 'O Reason, thou canst never walk with me!' However, to try their paces, they set out together, but they soon find it hard to keep company. When they come to a deep river, Reason says, 'I can never ford this,' but Faith wades through it singing. When they reach a lofty mountain, there is the same exclamation of despair; and in such cases, Faith, in order not to leave Reason behind, is obliged to carry him on his back; and, oh, how dependent upon Faith is Reason!" Why has God made faith the indispensable ingredient in man's approach to Him? Is it not precisely because man's reason can go only so far? Where reason comes up against an insurmountable obstacle, faith soars above it and apprehends God and heavenly mysteries by this divinely given faculty.

230. Trust Him Fully

An old Methodist preacher once offered this prayer in a meeting: "Lord, help us to trust Thee with our souls." Many voices responded with a hearty, old-fashioned "Amen!" "Lord, help us to trust Thee with our bodies," he continued. Again the response was a vociferous "Amen!" Then with still more warmth he said, "And, Lord, help us to trust Thee with our money." Not an "amen" was heard in the house, except that of an impoverished old lady.

231. Lessons in Faith

There was a devout Christian mother who was always teaching her daughter lessons of faith and trust, especially telling her that she need never be afraid at any time because God was always near. One summer evening she tucked her little girl in bed after her prayers, put out the light, and went downstairs. Then an electrical storm came rolling out of the west with vivid flashes of lightning and a reverberating roar of thunder. Suddenly there was a simultaneous blinding flash and a deafening crash, and when the echoes died away, the mother heard the little girl calling desperately, "Mama! Mama! Come and get me." The mother found her trembling, little girl in tears. After she had soothed her somewhat, she thought it might be an opportune time to teach a spiritual lesson, and said, "My little girl, has Mother not taught you many times that you need never be afraid, that God is always near, and nothing can harm you?" The little one put her arms around her mother's neck and said, "Yes, Mama. I know that God is always near, but when the lightning and the thunder are so awful, I want someone near me that's got skin on him."

232. One Day at a Time

Did you ever try to lift all the burdens of life at once? It is hard to bear yesterday's, today's, and sometimes tomorrow's burdens and temptations in one day. A doctor was once asked by a patient who had met with a serious accident, "Doctor, how long shall I have to lie here?" The answer, "Only a day at a time," taught the patient a precious lesson. It is the same lesson that you and I need—the day's portion in its day. Let us be faithful for one short day, and the long years will take care of themselves.

233. That Is Faith

A skeptical physician said to his Christian patient, "I could never understand saving faith. I believe in God and I suppose I believe in Jesus Christ—I am not conscious of any doubts. I believe that Jesus Christ was the Son of God, and I believe in the Bible, yet I am not saved, I do not feel God near me. What is the matter with me?" "Well," said the patient, "a week ago I believed in you as a very skillful physician. I believed that if I put myself in your hands I would recover from my illness. In other words, I trusted you. For a week now I have been taking some mysterious stuff out of a bottle. I don't know what it is; I don't understand it, but I am trusting in you. Now, whenever a person turns to the Lord Jesus Christ and says, 'Lord Jesus, Christianity seems to me to be full of mysteries. I do not understand them, but I believe Thou art trustworthy and I trust Thee; I commit myself to Thee,' that is faith. A very simple thing, isn't it?" The faith of the patient did not heal him; it was the remedy that healed him; but in faith he took the remedy.

234. Faith Tested by Trials

Have you ever seen a blacksmith work with a piece of iron? He holds it in the fire to soften it and make it pliable. That is exactly why God permits the testing of your faith by temptations and trials. He wants you to acquire patience, to acquire pliability. If you and I are constantly out of the fire of affliction, we become stiff and useless. God wants to reshape us according to His image, for in the fall of Adam we lost our divine shape, our divine image.

235. A Test of Belief

Two boys stood at the edge of a frozen pond. One of them said to the other, "Billy, I believe it will bear our weight." "Do you?" asked the other. "Yes." "Then get on it." "No," said he, "I don't want to." "Then," said the other, "you don't believe it will bear you."

236. High in the King's Estimate

A poor but devout Frenchman came to his spiritual advisor and said with a sorrowing heart: "I profess faith in God, but at times, against my will, I'm overwhelmed with doubts as I try to live a Christian life in this world. Surely, God must be displeased with me as I struggle to overcome them." The clergyman answered with much kindness, "The King of France has two castles in different areas and sends a commander to each of them. The castle of Mantleberry stands in a place remote from danger, far inland; but the castle of La Rochelle is on the coast, where it is liable to continued sieges. Now which of the two commanders, do you think, stands highest in the estimate of the King—the commander of La Rochelle, or he of Mantleberry?" "Doubtless," said the poor man, "the King values him the most who has the hardest task, and braves the greatest dangers." "You are right," replied his advisor, "And now apply this matter to your case and mine."

237. Faith and Works

A bishop once told of two men, one of whom asked the other for a contribution for his church. The reply was that the church was always wanting money. The other friend said, "When my lad was a boy, he was costly; he always wanted boots and shoes, socks and clothes, and wore them out fast, and the older and stronger he grew the more money had to be spent on him. My son died and now does not cost me anything." A faith that descends from God is manifested toward men in acts of love and generous giving.

238. Proven Faith

A grocer was down in the cellar of his shop when he noticed his small son standing at the edge of the open trap door. He called up, "Here I am, Sonny, jump down." But the boy hesitated. "I can't, Daddy; I can't see you." Up came the answer, "No, but I can see you; trust me and jump, and I will catch you." At this point, the boy jumped

because he trusted his father.

239. Count The Promises

Two little girls were counting their pennies. One said, "I have five pennies." The other said, "I have ten." "No," said the first little girl, "You have just five cents, the same as I." "But," the second child quickly replied, "my father said when he comes home tonight he would give me five cents, and so I have ten cents." Trustfully, she counted what her father had promised. That's exactly how a Christian can be poor in the estimation of the world and at the same time be rich. He counts as his whatever his Heavenly Father has.

240. Faith and Obedience

Ralph Erskine, that eminent Scotch divine of the seventeenth century, put the relation of faith and works in a most revealing way when he wrote, "True faith is never alone, but still joined with Gospel-obedience: 'As ye have received, so walk.' He that would separate faith from obedience endeavors to walk with one foot, which is impossible. Faith and works, faith and holiness, are the two feet by which a man walks in Christ; when the Spirit of Christ promotes the one, He promotes the other also. If a man should try to go upon one foot, he could not walk but only hop, which would be impossible for him to continue long. Neither can obedience be consistent without faith, and such consistency will be the measure of the Gospel-walk."

241. Spiritual Enamel

A preacher once visited a coal-mining district and noticed how very dingy the town appeared. The coal dust seemed to blacken the buildings, trees, shrubs, everything. But, as he was walking with the foreman, he noticed a beautiful white flower. Its petals were as pure as if it were blooming in a daisy field. "What care the owner of this plant must give it," said the preacher, "to keep it so free from dust and dirt!" "See here," said the foreman, and taking up a handful of coal dust, he threw it over the flower. It immediately fell off and left the flower as stainless as before. "It has an enamel coating." This reminds me of being clothed in the righteousness of God by faith in Jesus Christ (Rom. 3:22).

242. The Last Request

A wounded soldier said to his comrades who were carrying him, "Put me down. Don't bother to carry me farther. I am dying." They did as he requested and returned to the scene of battle. A few minutes later, an officer saw the man weltering in his blood and said to him, "Can I do anything for you?" "Nothing, thank you." "Shall I get you a little water?" "No, thank you. I am dying." "Isn't there anything I can do for you?" persisted the kind-hearted officer. "Shall I write to your friends?"

"I have no friends that you can write to. But there is one thing for which I would be much obliged.

In my pack you will find a Testament. Will you open it at the 14th chapter of John, and near the end of the chapter, you will find a verse that begins with 'Peace'. Will you read it to me?" The officer did so and read the words, "Peace I leave with you, my peace I give unto you: not as the world giveth, give I unto you. Let not your heart be troubled, neither let it be afraid" (John 14:27).

"Thank you, sir," said the dying man. "I have that peace; I am going to that Savior—God is with me—I want no more," and he was gone.

243. Understand with Your Heart

W. J. Dawson gives his testimony as follows: "Well do I remember how like a flash of light that verse of Romans 10:10 illumined my soul one day, when all was at its darkest for me. And then I saw what it all meant: that God did not ask me to believe with my intellect at all, but to trust Him with my heart. From that hour the world has brightened in me, for I know now that I have found God. Often and often now I cannot believe with the intellect, but I can with the heart."

244. Does Your Faith Show?

Dr. J. M. Buckley, a Methodist preacher, was once asked to conduct what they used to call in those days an "experience meeting" at a church in the South. That was a meeting similar to a testimony meeting such as we sometimes have today. A woman arose and bore witness to the preciousness of her religion as light bringer and comfort giver. "That's good, sister!" commented Dr. Buckley. "But now about the practical side, the positive side. Does your religion make you strive to prepare your husband a good dinner? Does it make you look after him in every way?" Just then Dr. Buckley felt a yank at this coat tails by the host preacher, who whispered ardently, "Press those questions, doctor; press those questions. That's my wife!" Does our faith show by what we do for others?

245. Faith Healing by Works

When I become sick, I go to a certain doctor because I have faith in him and in his ability to make me well. What is the goal of placing my faith in the doctor?—my getting well. But is that faith enough?—no. I must also do all the things which the doctor asks me to do, take all the medicine, whether it is sweet or bitter. Just faith, abstract faith, will not reach its goal without my doing the things which the man in whom I place my faith asks me to do. As a result of that obedience I can reach the goal of my faith.

246. Two Kinds of People

Charles Haddon Spurgeon, that famous preacher of London, was a man with many responsibilities. He was going home after a difficult day, and his problems were so many that he was discouraged. While in this state of mind, however, he was reminded of a verse from the Word of God, "My grace is sufficient for thee." He looked up to God and said, "I believe it is sufficient for today, dear Lord." And then he burst into laughter. He understood how ridiculous it was to worry.

He began to think: "I'm like a fish that is very thirsty, who's beginning to worry lest it exhaust the water of the river. The big river answers, 'Drink, my little fish, all you want, there will be plenty for you.'" Again, Spurgeon said, "I thought that I was like a little mouse in the great big grain stores of Egypt after the seven year of abundance of harvest, and I was so fearful lest I would die of starvation. At that time Joseph appeared and said to me, 'Don't worry, little mouse, the wheat stores are sufficient for you.' And again I thought that I was someone on top of a mountain talking to himself and saying, 'I'm afraid I'm going to exhaust all the oxygen there is in the atmosphere.' But I heard the atmosphere saying to me, 'Do not be afraid, little man, you breathe all you want. Fill your lungs; there is enough oxygen for everybody.'" There are two kinds of people who are candidates for heaven. Those who have little faith and those who have much faith. Little faith will take our souls to heaven, but much faith will bring heaven to us. The important thing is for us to begin living in heaven now. In order for us to accomplish this we must stop the sighs produced by the various "ifs" of life and begin to face life as it is.

Fellowship with God

247. *I Want You*

If you really know God as your loving heavenly Father, you consider companionship with Him your greatest treasure. I've heard of a father who had to be away from home about seven months. On his return he took his family to a shopping center. Handing some money to his little girl, he said, "Lydia, take this money and buy anything you want." The child's eyes filled with tears as she clung more tightly to his hand. "What's the matter, Honey?" he asked. "I don't want money, Daddy," she said. "I want you!"

248. *Not Good if Detached*

Man often loses much of his worth when he is detached from the world of persons and things about him. There are some forms of life that can live in relative isolation. A sponge, for instance, fastens itself to the bottom of the sea and completes its life cycle there. A lichen grows on the side of a rock and, while it spreads around slightly, never moves from its original location. But man isn't made to be like that. His power and usefulness come, not in isolation, but through union and cooperation with others. No life can be truly valuable in God's sight that isn't attached to Jesus Christ. We need Him, just as every member of our body needs to be attached to it, if it's going to be of any value. We also need fellowship with other believers who are attached to Christ. A soldier fighting a battle alone, or a single man working with pick and shovel trying to dig a Panama Canal, would scarcely be more effectual than a Christian trying to establish God's Kingdom all by himself. There are people in every community who are essentially Christian in spirit who have nothing to do with the Church. "Not good if detached" is the label we might put upon their lives.

249. *Fellowship with the Father*

A happy Christian met an Irish peddler one day and said to him, "It's a grand thing to be saved." "Aye," said the peddler, "It is. But I think something is equally as good as that." "What can you possibly think is equal to salvation?" "The companionship of the Man who has saved me," was the reply. When we know that, we can rejoice with John and say "Truly our fellowship is with the Father, and with his Son Jesus Christ" (1 John 1:3).

Forgiveness

250. Practicing Forgiveness

It is said of Samuel Johnson, the great English writer and lexicographer, that "the way to get a favor from him was to do him an injury." Evidently it was characteristic of him to forgive his enemies and pray for them. Emerson said of Lincoln: "His heart was as great as the world, but there was no room in it to hold the memory of a wrong." Spurgeon advised, "Cultivate forbearance until your heart yields a fine crop of it. Pray for a short memory as to all unkindness." That is how the truly wise man acts.

251. Good Forgetters

Two little boys had quarreled. But the next morning Johnny took his cap and headed for Bobby's house again. Surprised, an older member of the family said teasingly, "What! Going to play with him again? I thought you quarreled only last evening and were never going to have anything more to do with each other. Funny memory you have." Johnny looked a little sheepish, dug his toe into the carpet for a moment, then flashed a satisfied smile as he hurried away. "Oh! Bobby and me's good forgetters!"

252. No Condemnation

A man was viciously attacked by another who sought to kill him. The face of the injured man was badly scarred for the rest of his life. He cherished no enmity, however, against the person who made the attack and later sought to have him pardoned. The announcement was made to the prisoner. As he read the pardon he said, "I want something more than pardon, sir; I want friendship." "What kind of friendship do you want?" asked the warden. "I can do without anyone else's friendship except that of the man I injured." The man with the scarred face came to see the prisoner, the tears in his eyes assuring the assailant of both his pardon and friendship.

253. Trampled Flowers

A girl was asked what forgiveness is. She gave the following beautiful answer: "It is the odor the flowers give off when they are trampled upon." For the merciful Christian, this odor reaches far, far away, even up to the judgment seat of Christ; the Christian need not be afraid when he gets there.

254. Willing to Forgive

This incident occurred between John Wesley and Joseph Bradford.

Bradford was for some years the traveling companion of Mr. Wesley for whom he would have sacrificed health and even life, but to whom his will would never bend. "Joseph," said Mr. Wesley one day, "take these letters to the post office." Bradford replied, "I will take them after your preaching, sir." Wesley again said, "Take them now, Joseph." Bradford turned to Mr. Wesley and said, "I wish to hear you preach, sir; and there will be sufficient time for the post office after the service." Wesley was not at all pleased and said, "I insist upon your going now, Joseph." Bradford rather angrily replied, "I will not go at present." "You will not!" "No, sir." "Then you and I must part," said Wesley. "Very well, sir," was Mr. Bradford's quick response. The good men slept over it. Both were early risers. At four o'clock the next morning, Wesley said to Bradford, "Joseph, have you considered what I said—that we must part?" "Yes, sir," was the reply. "And must we part?" "Please yourself, sir," Then Wesley said, "Will you ask my pardon, Joseph?" "No, sir," came the quick reply from Bradford. "You will not?" "No, sir," Bradford said again. "Then," answered Wesley, "I will ask yours, Joseph." That is what a Christian should do—be willing to ask forgiveness instead of expecting others to ask forgiveness of him.

Gifts

255. Give Your All

God's gift is always enough for any individual to accomplish something. If we compare it with what others have, we will find that there are two kinds of people—those who have never done anything with their gifts and those who have fully utilized theirs. You and I must say, "I may not accomplish as much as they have, but I'm going to give it all I've got!" We're never going to get anywhere unless we use the gifts God has given us.

256. The One Talent

Hide not thy talent in the earth,
However small it be;
Its faithful use, its utmost worth,
God will require of thee.
His own, which He hath lent on trust,
He asks of thee again;
Little or much, the claim is just,
And thine excuses vain.
Go, then, and strive to do thy part,
Though humble it may be;
The ready hand, the willing heart,
Are all heaven asks of thee.
— William Cutler

257. Use or Lose

The Lord has given to each one of us at least one gift, and probably many more than that. The most im-portant thing in life is to find what gifts we have; secondly, to recognize that they are from God; thirdly, to be faithful and dependable in using them. Anything that is not used doesn't develop. A pianist said, "You know, I must practice every day. If I don't practice one day I know the difference. If I don't practice two days, those who hear me know the difference."

258. Spiritual Gifts

Paul compares the possessors of spiritual gifts to members of the human body because as the members of our body are none of our doing or deserving, neither are the spiritual gifts we possess. They are God's gifts entrusted to us for a purpose. If that purpose isn't fulfilled, His gifts are wasted. What's the use of having an eye or a hand that doesn't serve the entire body? A test of the genuineness of any gift is whether it benefits the body of Christ as a whole, or only the possessor. Does it tend to unite the body or to divide it? Does it make members who are different from us feel estranged or fellow members with us of one and the same body?

259. A "Call" to Preach

An elder of the church was talking to a young mechanic who

thought he had a call to give up his shop and go into the ministry. "I feel," said the young enthusiast, "that I have had a call to preach." The elder, knowing his deficiencies as a speaker, shrewdly asked, "Have you noticed whether people seem to have a call to hear you?" Before you subject others to the sound of your voice, make sure that preaching comes naturally to you and that you have a call from God to exercise this ability. Paul knew he was "sent" to preach.

260. God Shall Supply

C. H. Spurgeon once said, "God is satisfied with Himself, and sufficient to His own happiness. Therefore, surely, there is enough in Him to fill the creature. That which fills an ocean will fill a bucket; that which will fill a gallon will fill a pint; those revenues which will defray an emperor's expenses are enough for a beggar or poor man." Didn't Paul say, "My God shall supply all your need according to his riches in glory by Christ Jesus" (Phil. 4:19)? And He sees fit to bestow these riches on us as an inherent gift. Thus all believers possess Christ, but not every one has all His gifts, for He gives them as it pleases Him. His pleasure is according to His knowledge.

Giving

261. The Uncommitted Christian

Two close friends, a Jew and a Christian, often discussed their religions. Finally they decided to visit each other's place of worship. They went to the synagogue first. The time for the offering came and the Jew took a check out of his pocket and placed it in the offering plate. The Christian was very inquisitive so he moved about until he could see the amount of the check. It was for $27.50. He immediately turned to his Jewish friend and said, "Abe, is this your weekly or your monthly offering?" Abe turned to his Christian friend and said, "Why, don't you know I am an orthodox Jew and the Old Testament tells me that I should give one tenth of all that I make to the Lord? I thought you Christians did exactly the same thing." "Oh, no," the Christian replied. "Don't you know that we have been emancipated from the law and we are now under grace. We are free people; we are not bound by this law or any other." "And what do you do when it comes to your offerings to the church?" "Oh, Abe, that is simple. At the end of the week, we just give what is left over." "Really?" Abraham answered with surprise,

"You almost persuade me to become a Christian."

262. Gain by Giving

On a farm in New York state is a pond and a little brook. When I last saw them, it was in the rainy season, and both were full to the brim with clean, pure water. It is in the dry season the difference in their natures shows up. The stream, constantly flowing to water the banks all along its course, still keeps pure and sparkling; it continues to draw from the underground springs at its source and to give freely as it goes along. The pond, neither receiving nor giving, hoards its precious moisture only to have its waters become foul and stagnant. It is the same lesson our Lord was trying to teach His disciples: We gain by giving and lose by keeping. After sharing the mercy of God and thus maintaining and increasing our own purity, we receive the peace of God in such abundance that it overflows to all around us.

263. Willing to Give All I Don't Have

A new convert declared his determination to give all that he had for the Master. He said, "Pastor, if I had fifty pigs, I'd give twenty-five of them to the Lord." "That's very nice," said the pastor. "If you had thirty would you give fifteen to the Lord?" "Of course I would," said the new Christian. "If you had ten would you give five of them?" asked the pastor again. "You know I would," he answered. Then the pastor said, "If you had two, would you give one to the Lord?" "Now Pastor, don't ask me that. You know I have only two pigs."

264. A "Nickel" Heart

"Ah!" said a woman who in her poverty had done much for Christ and who had a great sum willed to her, "I cannot do as much as I used to do." "But how is that?" someone asked. Said she, "When I had a nickel purse I had a silver heart, but now I have a silver purse and I have only a nickel heart."

265. A Drop in the Bucket

Let's not refuse to give the little we have; God will multiply it. I remember an elderly man who was giving very little, but it was truly sacrificial. He had a younger friend who was always making fun of him. "Such need in the world, and yet you think that with your few dollars you will make a difference! Old friend, what you give is only a drop in the bucket." But the old man with rejoicing in his face turned to his friend and said, "Yes, all that God expects of me is my drop and He will see to the filling of the bucket."

God

Creator

266. Seeing God in Nature

A Christian was invited to admire a great skyscraper. After looking at its majestic height, he called his host's attention to a little flower that he had on his lapel, saying, "True, this building speaks of man's achievement, but this flower with its life speaks of God's creation. I can see God more clearly in the flower than in the skyscraper."

267. A Doctor's Testimony

Here is the testimony of a medical doctor: "In an anatomy room, a dead body meant nothing to me. I could not visualize the man or woman it might have been. Life left few records on the immobile face. For weeks I worked, and each day the wonder grew. Then one day I was working on an arm and hand, studying the perfect mechanical arrangements of the muscles and tendons, how the sheaths of certain muscles are split to let tendons of other muscles through, so that the hand may be delicate, small and yet powerful. I was all alone in the laboratory when the overwhelming belief came: a thing like this is not just chance but a part of a plan, a plan so big that only God could have conceived it. Religion had been to me a matter of form, a thing without conviction, but now everything was an evidence of God—the tendons of the hand, the patterns of the little butterfly's wings—all are a part of God's wonderful design."

268. God Gives Life

A city missionary visited a poor old woman in an attic room who had scarcely enough money for her bare existence. He observed a strawberry plant growing in a broken teapot on the windowsill, and on a subsequent visit remarked how it continued to grow and with what care it was watched and tended. "Your plant flourishes nicely; you will soon have strawberries on it." "Oh, sir, it is not for the sake of the fruit that I prize it. It is a great comfort to have that plant living, for I know it can only live by the power of God. As I see it live and grow day by day, it tells me God is near." This lonely Christian wanted something to remind her constantly that life in its continuance and growth was a direct result of God's activity.

269. Consider the Heavens

One evening when Napoleon was returning to France from the expedition to Egypt, a group of French officers entered into a discussion concerning the existence of God. They were on the deck of the vessel that bore them over the Mediterranean Sea. Thoroughly imbued with the skeptical and atheistical spirit of the times, they were unanimous in their denial of God. It was decided to ask the opinion of Napoleon, who was standing alone wrapped in silent thought. On hearing the question, "Is there a God?" he raised his hand and pointing to the starry firmament simply responded, "Gentlemen, who made all that?"

270. The Wonderful Recreation

John Ruskin was walking along the streets of London one rainy day when he noticed the great quantities of mud at his feet. The thought occurred to him that it would be interesting to have the mud analyzed to find out exactly what inorganic elements were in it. This was accordingly done, and it was found that London mud consisted of sand, clay, soot, and water. He was struck by the fact that these are the very substances from which our precious jewels and gems are formed. From the sand come the onyx, agate, beryl, jasper, amethyst; from the clay come the sapphire, ruby, emerald, topaz; and from the soot, the diamond. London mud composed of precious jewels! Man cannot transform the mud into those glittering points of light, but God

transforms and recreates the mud—poor, sinful, wayward humanity—into redeemed souls who sing a new song and carry with them glad tidings of great joy!

271. Follow the Architect's Plan

Beecher, that great preacher, once said, "If the architect of a house had one plan and the contractor had another, what conflicts would there be! How many walls would have to come down, how many doors and windows would need to be altered before the two could harmonize! Of the building of life, God is the architect, and man is the contractor. God has one plan, and man has another. Is it strange that there are clashings and collisions?" How much better if the contractor follows the Architect's plan. How wonderful for man to accept God's will for his life without any questioning whatsoever.

272. Who Made You?

"Who made you?" someone once asked a little girl. She replied, "God made me that much," indicating with her two hands the ordinary size of a newborn infant, "and I growed the rest myself." The little girl said this in her simplicity. Profound thinking must surely lead us to the same conclusion—that God made us for He made all things. But we may be tempted to think that we have done a great deal ourselves, not acknowledging even God's providential care.

273. God, the Creator

A businessman once gave the reasons why he knew there was a God. He had been earnestly considering the wonders of the stars and planets, their system and order. Then he said, "It takes a girl in our factory about two days to learn to put the seventeen parts of a meat chopper together. Some may believe that these millions of worlds, each with its separate orbit, all balanced so wonderfully in space— that they just happened; that by a billion years of tumbling about they finally arranged themselves. I am merely a plain manufacturer of cutlery. But this I do know, that you can shake the seventeen parts of a meat chopper around in a washtub for the next seventeen billion years and you'll never make a meat chopper."

274. Not Mere Chance

To think is to grow in awareness. Think as you look at a flower, a sunset or gaze at the starry sky. Someone has said that the unbelieving astronomer is mad. "What do you see?" a friend asked a famous botanist who was scrutinizing a flower. "I see God," was the reverent answer. A Scottish doctor wrote with his finger in the garden soil the letters of his little son's name, sowed cress in the furrows, and smoothed the ground. Ten days later, his son ran to him in astonishment and said that his name was growing in the garden and insisted on his father seeing it. "Is it not a mere chance?" asked the father. "No, someone must have arranged it that way." "Look at yourself," said the doctor. "Consider your hands, finger, legs, feet; did you come here by chance?" "No, something must have made me." "And who is that something?" As he did not know, the father told him the name of the great God who had made him and all the world. He never forgot that lesson.

Faithfulness

275. Never Disappointed

A pastor who visited an old man suffering from painful rheumatism found him with his Bible open in front of him. The minister noticed that the word "proved" was written repeatedly in the margin. He turned over a few pages and found, "God is our refuge and strength, a very present help in trouble." "Proved." And so it went on through the Book. Next to John 1:12 he had written "Proved." He had received Christ by believing and had indeed become a child of God. He had proved that promise of God's Word. Millions of other born-again believers could write "proved" next to this verse. There isn't a single one who has put this promise of God to the test and been disappointed.

276. God's Noble Reserve

The fact remains that God does keep many secrets, and it seems to me that there are some secrets that every good government ought to keep to itself for the good of its citizens. Responsibility demands a certain amount of reserve. God is certainly responsible and He exercises authority. But He keeps secrets. These are both for His glory and the glory of those who have become His children through faith in Christ. This is not understood by unbelievers, even as some unrealistic citizens do not concede the necessity of a certain amount of secrecy on the part of their government. Sometimes men cultivate the habit of concealment so that they may circumvent opposition and accomplish their own crafty aims more adroitly. This reflects an attitude of contempt for others. But God's reserve is always noble. It is always in favor of man. And the mystery of mysteries is that it is both for His glory and the believer's glory.

277. Confidence in God

All curiosity implies more or less skepticism and mental uneasiness. If our faith were unlimited, we should not seek to have so many questions answered. Imagine a physician whose fidelity and skill have inspired such confidence that, when he is called in, no one ever dreams of asking what treatment he is adopting or of cautiously checking his diagnosis; or a commander to whom his chief gives a free hand, not being asked to divulge his plan of campaign. The man is not yet born who commands that kind of unlimited confidence. But God demands and

deserves this matchless honor. He ordains not a few of the mysteries that confront us so that we may have occasions for glorifying Him by our unquestioning trust in His wisdom and goodwill.

Father

278. Seeing and Believing

A blind girl, whose eyes had been opened by a surgical operation, delighted in the sight of her father who had a noble appearance and presence. His every look and motion were watched by his daughter with the keenest delight. For the first time his constant tenderness and care seemed real to her. If he caressed her or even looked upon her kindly, it brought tears of gladness to her eyes. "To think," she said, holding his hand closely in her own, "that I have had you for a father all these years, and never really knew you.

279. Father Revealed by His Son

Let's suppose an artist sent you a picture of himself that he had painted. The picture would tell you something about him, give you a glimpse of his knowledge and ability. However, if he sent you a long descriptive letter explaining his innermost thoughts and feelings, you would begin to feel you really knew him. And finally, if he decided to send to you his son who possessed the same features as he and was like him in ability and character, this would reveal the father to you much better. "The only begotten son, which is in the bosom of the Father, he hath declared him" (John 1:18).

Forgiving

280. Death and Taxes

It's a flip saying, but true: death and taxes are the two things we can count on. But there is a difference: we know on what day the taxes fall due; we can't predict the day of death. We can put money aside to take care of taxes; but what provision can we make in anticipation of death? If we die before our taxes are paid, they'll not be forgiven. The government will take them out of our estate. If we die as unrepentant sinners, our sins will not be forgiven after death. We'll have to pay the penalty for them hereafter. But there is a difference: God has made a way of escape for us. He has already paid the penalty for our sins—yours and mine. All He asks is that you accept what He has done for you in a true spirit of repentance and faith.

281. The Open Door

The story is told of a girl who turned her back on her widowed mother who had worked so hard to bring her up, and left home without telling her mother where she was going. Night after night the mother waited for the girl, but she did not come back. In her perplexity and sorrow the mother went to her pas-

tor to ask his help. He suggested that she have some pictures taken of herself and bring them to him, which she did. Then he asked her what message she wanted to send her lost girl. In tears the mother said, "All I want to tell her is 'Come back.' " "Write that on each picture," said the minister, and then he proceeded to send these pictures to places of amusement in other large towns which he felt the daughter was most likely to frequent. He requested that the picture be posted on the bulletin board where it could be easily seen. One night, the daughter came to one of these places and was attracted by something familiar about the picture on the bulletin board. Little did she imagine that it could be her mother's picture. She came closer to it, and there it was—her own mother, looking much older than when she had left. Then she saw what was written on it, "Come back," and knew it was addressed to her. She could not proceed with her plans for that night. With a heart burning with remorse, she went back to her room, packed her clothes, and took the first train home. Arriving in the early hours of the morning, she was surprised to find the door of the little apartment open; in she went. There was her mother in tears, not sleeping, but sitting up, praying for her prodigal daughter. She threw her arms around her, and the first thing she asked when she could speak was, "Mother, why did you leave the door open?" "Oh, Louise, the door has never been closed since the day you left. I left it open all the time expecting your return. I didn't want you to find it shut when you came back."

Graciousness

282. Beggar and Giver

Sir Walter Raleigh was continuously submitting requests to Queen Elizabeth on behalf of convicts. Once the Queen said to him: "Sir Walter, when will you stop being a beggar?" "When Your Majesty ceases to be a giver," was the wise answer. Oh, how wonderful to know that God is the inexhaustible source of blessing!

283. Give Thyself First

Socrates had a trusted servant who, seeing others giving presents to his master, came to him one day and said, "Because I have nothing else to give you, Master, I here give you myself." Socrates saw the earnestness of the servant and said, "Do so." After bestowing upon him gifts, and advancing him to the head of his servants, he called him one day and said, "I now give you back to yourself better than when I received you." God bestows rich spiritual gifts on the one who gives his life to Him.

284. The King with the Open Hand

There is a legend told of an ancient kingdom whose sovereign had just died, and whose ambassadors were sent to choose a successor from twin infants. They found the little fellows fast asleep, and looking at them carefully, agreed that it was difficult to decide, until they happened to notice one curious small difference between them. As they lay, one infant had his tiny fists closed tight; the other slept with his little hands wide open. Instantly they made their selection of the latter. The legend very properly concludes with the record that, as he grew up in his station, he came to be known as the King with the Open Hand. We could say the same thing of our God. His hand is always open to give.

285. God's Nature

A little girl and her mother were reading the New Testament one morning when they came to John 3:16, "For God so loved the world, that he gave his only begotten Son, that whosoever believeth in him should not perish, but have everlasting life." Stopping for a moment in the reading the mother asked, "Don't you think it is wonderful?" The child, looking surprised, replied in the negative. The mother, somewhat astonished, repeated the question, to which the little daughter replied, "Why, no, Mommy, it would be wonderful if it were anybody else, but it is just like God." The little girl was absolutely right. It is God's nature to give freely of His grace and of His mercy.

286. More to Follow

A rich man and a poor man were both members of a certain congregation. The rich man desired to do an act of benevolence, so he sent a sum of money to a friend, asking him to give it to the poor man as he thought best. The friend sent him only twenty-five dollars and said in the note: "This is yours. Use it wisely. There is more to follow." After a while he sent another twenty-five dollars and said, "More to follow." Again and again, he sent money to the poor man, always with the cheering words, "More to follow." So it is with the wonderful grace of God. There is always more to follow. We shall never be able to exhaust it.

287. Heaven Is a Part of My Garden

A philosopher was asked by a friend to show him the splendid garden of which he was always boasting. He led him to a bare rocky space behind his house. "Where is your garden?" the friend asked. "Look up," said the philosopher; "heaven is a part of my garden." Every good gift in the garden really comes from above; should God command the clouds to send no rain, the earth would soon be like iron. Heaven shields, broods over, and enriches every fruitful plot of ground. Turn, then, your whole being fully toward the sunshine of God's grace, and pray that the garden of your soul may always be as ready to receive heavenly blessing as is the garden around your dwelling. When, by God's enablement, you become a planter, remember that the seed is God-made, and when you become a waterer, remember that the water is also God-made.

288. God's Offer of Grace

Picture a table set with delicious food. Hungry people are gathered around it. God has prepared the food. It is free. If there are some who sit at this table and do not taste the food, it is their own fault. To be in the midst of plenty and to go hungry is certainly unreasonable behavior. Yet that is what is happening all the time. God's bounty is not taken advantage of. God provides spiritual food, but He will not force it on anyone. Man must reach out and partake of it.

289. Bursting Boilers

It was in a large prayer meeting that a rather pompous man arose and said, "Brethren, I am on board the old ship Zion, and I am sailing heavenward, and I am going at the rate of sixteen knots; I shall soon sail up the harbor of the blessed." Then another man with more arrogance rose and said, "I, too, am on board the old ship Zion, and I am sailing heavenward at the rate of thirty knots; I shall soon sail up the harbor of the blessed," and he sat down. Then another man with even more arrogance got up and said, "I, too, brethren, am on board the old ship Zion. It is a steamship with a terrific horsepower, and on this steamship I shall soon sail up the harbor of the blessed," and he sat down. Then a plain Christian woman rose and said, "Well, brethren, I have been going to heaven seventy years, and I have been going afoot; I suppose from the looks of things that I shall have to go afoot the rest of the way. If some of you people that are going by steam don't look out, you'll burst your boilers." As a dear saint of God said, let us make our boasting as follows: "I am not what I ought to be, I am not what I wish to be, I am not what I hope to be; but by the grace of God I am not what I was." Never leave the grace of God out.

290. God's Grace

A convict, who has just finished his term of penal servitude, wishes to lead an honest life. He comes to a man who has a large jewelry establishment and who requires a night watchman. He is engaged to watch this building through the quiet hours of the night when he has everything under his care and every opportunity to rob his employer. On the first evening, he meets one of his old companions, who questions him, "What are you doing here?"

"I'm the night watchman."

"Over this jeweler's shop?"

"Yes."

"Does he know what you are?"

"No, keep quiet; if he knew, I should be dismissed."

"Suppose I let it out that you are a returned convict!"

"Oh, please don't; it would be my last day here, and I wish to be honest."

"Well, you have to give me some money to keep quiet."

"Very well, but don't let anyone know."

Thus the poor man would live in fear, lest it should come to the ears of his employer what his previous character had been.

Let us suppose, however, that instead of the employer's engaging the man in ignorance of his character, he went to the convict's cell and said, "Now I know you—what you are, what you've done, every robbery you've committed, but I am about to give you a chance of becoming honest. I'll trust you as my night watchman over my valuable goods." The man is faithful at his post. He meets an old companion who threatens to inform his employer about his past. He asks, "What will you tell about me?"

"That you were the ringleader of thieves."

"Yes, but my master knows all that; he knows me better than I know myself."

Of course, this silences his companion forever. Jesus Christ is the only Master who is "full of grace and truth." Jesus Christ is gracious to you and me because He knows the truth about us, that we deserve nothing but hell. But through His grace heaven can be our share, if we personally and by faith appropriate His grace.

291. An Example of Plenty

A poor woman who had had a hard struggle to make ends meet, and knew what it meant to have very little food, was taken on an outing to the seaside. She was delighted with the scene. As she looked out over the vast expanse of waters, tears filled her eyes and she exclaimed, "Thank God for a sight of something there is enough of!" That is how it is with the soul when it gets its first vision of the infinite fullness of God's grace in Christ. His grace is quite enough for the soul's every need.

292. The First Step to Heaven

Sometimes I go to the store to buy cheese. Almost invariably I ask for a taste before I make my purchase, and the grocer very cheerfully gives it to me. Why is he willing to do this? Because he knows that his cheese is of superior quality. God does not hesitate to have us taste His grace. He is sure we shall want more once we have had a sampling of it. Now would it not be stupid of me to stand before the grocer's counter and, without sampling his cheese say to him, "No, I don't think I'll take any of your cheese. It is not good." I would have no right to pronounce an opinion about something of which I have no personal knowledge. The valid challenge of the grocer is "Taste and see." We have often done that. We did not want to eat, but we finally decided to take a taste, and then we wanted to keep on eating. Oh, that initial step, that initial experience is so important! The first step is most of the way to heaven.

293. Our Gracious Savior

God's attention is attracted by our weakness. A mother responds in exactly the same way. She loves all her children, but if she has one who is weak and sickly, while the others are healthy and strong, her care and attention are lavished upon the one who has most need of her protection, most claim upon her love. Her other children are able to take care of themselves, but the little delicate one, whose life hangs almost by a thread, appeals by his very weakness to her strongest instincts of maternal love. So it is with our gracious Savior. He loves us, oh, so tenderly because of our very weakness.

294. Not a Rascal by God's Grace

A good Scotsman called to see Rowland Hill, that eminent English clergyman who did so much for the betterment of his countrymen. Without saying a word, he sat still for some five minutes looking into Rowland Hill's face. At last Mr. Hill asked him what held his attention. Said the Scotsman, "I was looking at the lines of your face." "Well, what do you make out of them?" "Why," said he, "that if the grace of God hadn't been in you, you would have been the biggest rascal living!"

295. Do We Question the Blessings?

A young girl in an institution for the handicapped was approached by a well-meaning but tactless woman who wrote on her slate, "My dear, why are you deaf and dumb?" Tears came into the girl's eyes. Then, after a pause, taking the pencil and slate she wrote, "Even so, Father, for so it seemed good in thy sight." She could very well have asked in turn, "Why do you hear and speak?" Isn't it strange that we ask all our questions about life's sufferings and not about its blessings? Do we take it for granted we deserve them?

296. Sufficiency of God's Grace

A man stood up in a meeting and facing the preacher who had spoken about the sufficiency of God's grace, said: "You can talk like that about Christ—that He is dear to you, that He helps you—but if your wife were dead as my wife is, and you had some babies crying for their mother who would never come back, you could not say what you are saying." A little later the preacher lost his wife in an accident. After others had conducted the funeral service, he stood by the casket, looked down into the face of the silent wife and mother and said, "The other day when I was preaching, a man said I could not say Christ was sufficient if my wife were dead and my children were crying for their mother. If that man is here, I want to tell him that Christ is sufficient. My heart is broken, my heart is crushed, my heart is bleeding, but there is a song in my heart, and Christ put it there. And if that man is here, I tell him though my wife is gone and my children are motherless, Christ comforts me today." That man was there, and down the aisle he came and stood beside the casket and said, "Truly, if Christ can help in a time like this, I surrender to Him."

297. Not Rejected

Once a large and beautiful block of marble was brought from the Greek island of Paros. Out of this marble it was planned to chisel a statue of the great Napoleon. The famous sculptor, Canova, surveyed it with critical eyes before commencing work upon it and discovered a slight red mark traversing the block. To the unskilled it was an insignificant matter, but Canova said, "I cannot work upon this; it has a flaw. It is not perfectly pure and white. I will not lay my chisel upon it." Therefore he rejected it. Think what imperfections the omniscient eye of God detects in the purest of human characters. Yet, He does not reject us on this account. How humbling, indeed, is this thought!

298. I Am What I Am

Two or three years before the death of that eminent servant of Christ, the Rev. John Newton, an aged friend and brother in the ministry called on him at breakfast.

Family prayer followed, and the portion of Scripture for the day was read to him. In it occurred the verse, "By the grace of God, I am what I am" (1 Cor. 15:10). After the reading of this text, he uttered this affective soliloquy: "I am not what I ought to be—ah! how imperfect and deficient! I am not what I wish to be. I abhor what is evil, and I would cleave to what is good. I am not what I hope to be. Soon, soon, shall I put off mortality, and, with mortality, all sin and imperfection. Yet though I am not what I ought to be, nor what I wish to be, nor what I hope to be, I can truly say I am not what I once was—a slave to sin and Satan; I can heartily join with the apostle and acknowledge, 'By the grace of God, I am what I am.' "

Incomprehensible

299. Answer to a Hard Question

"Mother, who made God?" "That's a hard question, Jimmy. Why don't you go out and play for awhile?" answered the puzzled mother. When Jimmy insisted on an answer, the mother was inspired to take off her ring and hand it to her little boy, saying to him, "Here, Jimmy, show me the beginning and the end. God is the same way, Son. He has no beginning and no end."

300. Were You There?

An amusing radio comedian of many years ago, known as the Baron Munchausen, used to spin wild and improbable tales. When anyone challenged him he would ask, "Vas you dere, Sharlie?" God was there before there was any beginning; He was there when His only begotten Son came into the world, for He entered into human flesh through Him. He was there on the cross, for in Christ He suffered, bled and died for you and me. To anyone who questions this, you can retort, "Were you there? God was, and I prefer to take His Word for it."

301. The Great "I Am"

Bishop Beveridge gave a wonderful illustration of one of the names by which God has chosen to call Himself, "I AM": "He does not say, I am their light, their guide, their strength, or tower, but only 'I AM.' He sets, as it were, His hands to a blank, that His people may write under it what they pleased that is good for them. As if He should say: Are they weak? I am strength. Are they poor? I am riches. Are they in trouble? I am comfort. Are they sick? I am health. Are they dying? I am life. Have they nothing? I am all things. I am wisdom and power. I am justice and mercy. I am grace and goodness. I am glory, beauty, holiness, eminency, super-eminency, perfection, all-sufficiency, eternity. Jehovah, I am. Whatever is amiable in itself, or desirable unto them, that I am. Whatsoever is pure and holy, whatsoever is great or pleasant, whatsoever is good or needful to make men happy, that I am."

302. Don't Reject the Medicine

The mysteries of God are like a bottle that contains medicine. It is the medicine that cures you, not the bottle. Without even questioning it, you accept the fact that the medicine could not be presented to you without its container. You do not reject the medicine simply because you do not understand the composition of the bottle.

303. The Infinite God

The late Dr. Clarence Edward Macartney, while a theological student, visited the home of a skeptic. The skeptic's argument was as follows: "If a man tells me that he has a horse which can trot a mile in three minutes, I tell him to bring out the horse and prove it. If you tell me that there is a God, I ask you to produce God and prove His existence." Macartney replied, "No Christian claims to know God, nor would want to know Him in that way. By that kind of searching we cannot know the Almighty to perfection. The Christian believer does not say, 'I know God,' or 'I see God,' or 'I think there is a God,' but 'I believe in God.' "

304. One God

A little boy, on being asked "How many Gods are there?" replied, "One." "How do you know that?" "Because there is only room for one, for He fills heaven and earth." He was right. How, then, can puny little man expect to see Him in all His majesty and glory?

305. The Glory of the Creator

"You teach," said the Emperor Trajan to Rabbi Joshua, "that your God is everywhere, and boast that He resides among your nation; I should like to see Him." "God's presence is indeed everywhere," replied Joshua, "but He cannot be seen. No mortal eye can behold His glory." The Emperor insisted. "Well," said Joshua "suppose we try to look first at one of His ambassadors." The Emperor consented. The Rabbi took him into the open air at noonday and bade him look at the sun in its blazing splendor. "I cannot," said Trajan. "The light dazzles me." "You are unable," said Joshua, "to endure the light of one of His creatures, and can you expect to behold the resplendent glory of the Creator? Would not the brightness of His glory annihilate you?" This same thought is expressed in the Bible in 1 Timothy 6:16, "Who only hath immortality, dwelling in light unapproachable; whom no man hath seen, nor can see: to whom be honor and power eternal. Amen." (Author's translation.)

306. The Great God

We have discovered new worlds in the splitting of the atom. Democritus, the ancient Greek physical philosopher who coined the word "atom," would never have believed it. With our telescopes we find a system in every star, but with our microscopes we find a world in every atom. There surely must be more things that we don't know than those things we do. It is logical, then, to concede that we cannot know the God of the universe in His full essence.

307. The Great—a Mystery

Why does Paul call all that God bestows upon us "mysteries"? Not because they are myths, but because they are facts that we can neither understand nor explain. As Joseph Parker points out: "We know how easy it is to reduce everything to the mystery of darkness and to suppose that, because we can't see, therefore all things that are declared to be in existence cannot possibly be where they are said to be. When night comes down upon us, and the sea is covered, and the great rocks around our coast are all hidden, what would you think of a man who said, 'There is no sea; there are no rocks; there are no mountains. I deny it; I swear there is no sea! . . . Why, if there was an ocean, should I not see it? If there were rocks, would I not behold them?' He forgets that he is surrounded by conditions that have obscured from his vision the facts which he so emphatically denies. It should not surprise us that God's actions and providences are mysteries to us. It is natural; it could not be otherwise." "The great must always be a mystery to the little," continues Parker. "The arch must always be a mystery to the column; God must always be a mystery to His creatures. If I could understand all, I should be all. Only the whole can comprehend the whole. Only God can understand God."

308. Blind Men and the Elephant

Six blind men approached an elephant. Each man put out his hand to touch some part of the elephant's anatomy and thought he had grasped the whole. To one the elephant was like a tree, to another like a wall, to a third like a fan, to a fourth like a snake, to a fifth like a spear, and to a sixth like a rope—depending on whether they had touched his leg, his side, his ear, his trunk, his tusk, or his tail. The poem in which this fable is contained concludes that all of them were right, though each of them was wrong. It takes a synthesis of all aspects of God and His creation to get a complete picture of Him—and none of us is so gifted as to be able to comprehend this, though we make some progress as we open our hearts and minds to the various facets of truth we encounter on our heavenward journey.

309. Where Is God?

A youngster returning from Sunday school sat by a man in a bus. The man, apparently an unbeliever, seeing her Sunday school paper, decided to make fun of the child and said to her, "Tell me where God is and I'll give you an apple." The little girl thoughtfully turned to her fellow passenger and said in return, "Sir, if you tell me a place where God isn't, I'll give you a basket of apples."

310. *Manifestations of the Light*

"God is light, and in Him is no darkness at all" (1 John 1:5b). Light is a synonym of all that is beautiful and glorious in the universe of God, whether in the material or in the spiritual realm. Perhaps the most magnificent declaration ever uttered is that recorded in the book of Genesis by Moses: "God said, Let there be light: and there was light" (Gen. 1:3). Light is the most perfect emblem of purity we can imagine. We cannot conceive of the possibility of its defilement. Light is the source of beauty; we could have no concept of beauty without it. The colors of the rainbow, the endlessly varied and pleasing pictures portrayed before us in the flowers, the ever-changing shades in sky or forest, the delicate tints in the plumage of the bird, the flush of health on the human cheek, the glory of the sunrise, the splendor of the sunset—all these and ten thousand other manifestations of beauty are creatures of the light.

Judge

311. *Take God at His Word*

Getting children to eat what is good for them can be quite a problem. Convincing them that you mean business takes more strength of character than some parents possess. Yet the mother who lets her child indulge his preference for sweets, instead of such body-building foods as milk, meat, and veg-etables, does not really love him as much as the mother who does her best to see that he gets a balanced diet. The parents who give in to a child on matters that affect his future health and character are not loving. They are merely encouraging him to go on getting his way in all future contests of will. They are laying the foundation for trouble for the rest of his life. So it is with God. Unless people believe that He means what He says, they will run to all kinds of excesses, and ruin their lives for time and eternity. Although the Bible consistently proclaims that unbelief and sin, if unrepented of in this life, will result in eternal loss, too many people refuse to take God at His Word. They choose to believe He is too soft-hearted ever to condemn anyone to eternal punishment.

312. *God the Judge*

Returning home from school one day, my little boy came to me with the evidence of what he had had for lunch smeared all over his mouth. I told him to go wash his face and come back to show me the results. He returned in a hurry, saying, "I am all clean now, Daddy." "Are you?" I asked. "Sure. I washed just like you told me to." From his point of view he was clean, but from where I stood he still looked dirty. It is not what we think of ourselves that counts, but what God our Creator thinks of us.

Loving

313. The Mystery of God's Love

One day, as a minister sat in the office of his church to meet anyone who might have spiritual difficulties, only one person came. "What is your difficulty?" asked the minister. The man answered, "My difficulty is the ninth chapter of Romans, where it says, 'Jacob have I loved, but Esau have I hated.' " "Yes," said the minister, "there is great difficulty in that verse; but which part of the verse is difficult for you?" "The latter part, of course," said the man. "I cannot understand why God should hate Esau." The minister replied, "The verse has often been difficult, but my difficulty has always been with the first part of the verse. I never could understand how God could love that wily, deceitful, supplanting scoundrel Jacob."

314. God Is Love

A preacher tells us how one of his children said to the youngest, "You must be good or Father won't love you." He called the child to him and said, gravely and tenderly, "That is not true, my boy." "But you won't love us if we are not good, will you?" asked the child. "Yes, I shall love you always; when you are good, I shall love you with a love that makes me glad; when you are not good, I shall love you with a love that hurts me." That's exactly what the love of God is toward us.

He was not obliged to love us because we were either bad or good, but He did love us because of what He is—Love—and for that reason He came. His coming was neither forced nor deserved.

315. Loving Encouragement

"Your child will walk again," said a wise physician to a polio victim's parents, "if you keep up a regular course of exercise that I will prescribe for him, and if you do not wait on him more than necessary, but insist that he try to help himself." At first the exercises were painful, and the child cried out. But though the parents' hearts were full of pity, their concern for his future would not let them give in. They continued hour after hour, day after day, month after month, kindly but firmly encouraging their little boy to exercise his partly paralyzed legs, and to follow as nearly as possible the routine of a normal child. Now a young man, this once crippled youngster walks without the trace of a limp. Is this not an illustration of the way that God loves us, and the way we are to love and help others?

316. God So Loved!

Ancient Greek poetry tells of a warrior, the hero of Troy, dressed in all his military armor, stretching out his arms to embrace his little son before going into battle. His child was frightened as he looked at the helmet and full military dress, and instead of falling into his father's arms he screamed in terror. However, under all the battle array was hidden a heart of fatherly love. The warrior threw off his armor, gathered his little boy in his arms, and held him tightly against his chest where he could hear the beating of his father's heart, as if saying, "I love you, I love you."

That's how God revealed Himself at Bethlehem. There He does not instill fear but attracts with His love.

317. Loving Chastisement

The newspapers once carried the story of a father and mother who, finding that their little girl had taken and eaten something from the cupboard, began to shake and slap the child. When the child became drowsy, they did not let up, but continued their shaking and slapping for four hours. What cruel punishment for such a little offense! No, it was compelled by love. The child had swallowed ten sleeping tablets, and the doctor said the only hope of saving the child's life was in keeping her awake. We do not always understand the path through which God leads us, but we may be certain His chastisement is always born of love. God does not choose to stop the harshness of the winds, but He rather directs us through them.

318. Daddy, Are You There?

A little girl and her father were returning from the funeral of their dearly loved mother and wife. Some kind neighbors invited them to spend a few days with them so they wouldn't be alone in the house with all its sad memories. However, the father decided it would be better to go home. That night the father placed the little girl's bed next to his, but neither could fall asleep. Finally the child said, "Daddy, it's dark, I can't see you. But you're there, aren't you?" "Yes, dear, Daddy's here right next to you. Go to sleep." The little one finally dropped off to sleep. In the darkness and the depth of sorrow, the father in tears said aloud, "O Heavenly Father, it's so dark, and my heart is overflowing with sorrow. But You're there, aren't You?" And immediately there came to him a passage from the prophet Isaiah: "Fear thou not; for I am with thee: be not dismayed; for I am thy God: I will strengthen thee; yea, I will help thee; I will uphold thee with the right hand of my righteousness" (Isaiah 41:10).

319. Our Loving God

God reminds us of an ancient king sitting with his council, deliberating on high affairs of state involving the destiny of nations. Suddenly he hears the sorrowful cry of his little child who has fallen down and been frightened. He rises and runs to his relief, assuages his sorrows and relieves his fears. This was not an unkingly act. It was rather a natural one.

320. Our Loving Guide

Many things must be hidden from a child, and the more sensitive he is the stricter the concealment. We are so timid and unschooled that

God has to often place the shadow of His hand across our vision, just as the Alpine guide will blindfold a nervous traveler so that he may guide him unharmed across some terrifying chasm. Many of God's mysteries are things that He has hidden from us to the glory of His pity and gentleness. He has to guide us over a great many of the perilous places of life.

Merciful

321. The Just God

A certain man misappropriated a sum of money, never believing that his good Christian friend would take steps to have him punished for embezzlement. Now that he is in jail he knows he depended too much on the kindness and mercy of this Christian, instead of reckoning with his justice. There is great danger in misunderstanding God's essential character. He is a God of justice as well as of love. He will inflict punishment where punishment is due. There is mercy available through Jesus Christ, but that mercy becomes effective only to those who appropriate it, who accept it.

322. Be Merciful

J. H. Evans said, "I believe that God often permits me to be chastened by my sin, because I do not make use of my mercies." We often lose our mercies by loving them too well, as the ball of snow is melted by the heat of the hand that holds it, or a rose is spoiled by pressing it too tightly. Theophilus Gale very well said, "Whatsoever I thankfully receive, as a token of God's love to me, I part with contentedly as a token of my love to Him."

323. Peaches or Pumpkins

The members of the Ladies' Society had all been complaining that the dry season would ruin the crops. But there was one lady who was not complaining. They asked her if the drought had not hurt her fruit or garden. She said, "Yes, but I'll tell you what cured me of worrying. I used to fret over everything, and one spring when I sat down to have a good cry because an untimely frost during peach blossoming threatened to ruin our splendid prospect for fruit, my Aunt Martha came in and reminded me that she had lived eighty years, and the world's crop of provisions had never failed yet. 'If we don't have peaches, we'll have punkins,' said she. And I have noticed since then that, in spite of all the frosts and droughts, I've never suffered from lack of food, and I don't believe you have, either." They all smiled rather sheepishly, and the president said thoughtfully, "That's true. 'Peaches or punkins.' I'll try to remember that." We, too, should try to remember that everything continues to exist because of God's providential care in spite of us and our sinfulness.

Omniscient

324. *God Meets Each Individual Need*

God has His own way of speaking to every soul. He starts with something known. We have all heard about Helen Keller, who became blind, deaf, and mute as a child. What could be the use of such a life? She was a prisoner of darkness, deprived of the outside light. However, behind the darkness and silence there was a unique intelligence waiting to be kindled by a spark from without. Her dedicated teacher was the one who led her out into the larger world and enabled her to communicate by the sense of touch. But how could Helen Keller communicate with God, or God with her? Her teacher decided to try to tell her the story of God's revelation in Jesus Christ. Using the language of touch, she did her best. At the end the child responded, "Oh, I knew He must exist, but I didn't know His name!" God had revealed Himself to her in a very special way. He can do this for every human being who is willing to listen. He has some way in which He can reach us according to our individual need and ability to comprehend.

325. *Mature Understanding*

Bill comes to the alley where for years he has parked his car, only to find a ticket on it. He fumes and fusses because there was no sign prohibiting parking in that area. Nevertheless he pays his fine and resolves never to park his car there again. Still, he can't understand the why of it. Some days later, however, he has his answer. During a windstorm a mammoth oak had fallen right across the place where he had been parking his car. Had it been in its accustomed place, it would have been smashed. Thanks to the ticket that cost him three dollars it was not there. Of course, it pleases God sometimes never to explain to us the reasons for many of His actions in our lives. But Paul maintains that the more mature we become as Christians the more God will reveal to us.

326. *You Can't Distract God*

I remember that when I was in high school we had a mathematics teacher who loved to talk. If our lesson was difficult and we wanted to avoid tackling it, one of the students would adroitly put a question to the teacher to get him started. Good-bye to the lesson for that day! We often try to treat God in a similar manner, thinking to distract Him from His subject. When He tells us we must repent in order to be saved from sin, we resort to a philosophical argument as to what constitutes sin. Be careful. God is not an easily distracted professor of mathematics. He knows all our tricks.

327. *Under God's Watchful Eye*

Let us not be like the two little boys on the hilltop, one of whom was up a tree stealing apples and the other watching to make sure they were safe from observation. They were blissfully unaware that someone watched them through a telescope several miles away, noting each motion and even the guilty expression of their faces as plainly as if he had been in the tree with them. How absurd for the boys to conclude that observation ended with their own vision, and that safety was the result of what they could distinguish! In this universe, which is but the result of God's handiwork, we are no more intelligent than these two little boys, if we conclude that God cannot observe us, since we cannot see Him with our own two eyes.

328. God's Way

A little boy asked, "Why is it that when I open a marigold it dies, but if God does it, it's so beautiful?" Before anyone could answer him, he said, "I know! It's because God always works from the inside." That's God's wise way of working with men—from the inside.

329. The Exact Meaning

A Christian businessman who had suffered heavy losses was tempted to doubt the goodness of God. "Why did He allow these reverses to come to me?" he questioned. One night as he sat dejected and discouraged before the fireplace, his six-year-old son came and sat in his lap. Over the mantle hung a motto that read, "God's works are perfect." "Daddy, what does perfect mean?" asked the boy. Before the father could reply he continued, "Does it mean that God never makes a mistake?" The thought was just what the father needed. Hugging his son to him he said, "Yes, Johnny, that's just what it means!"

330. Our Omniscient God

Dr. Robert E. Speer tells the story of an old sculptor who was cutting a figure that was to stand in a niche in the wall so that its back would never be seen, yet he was working with the same painstaking care on the back as on the front. Someone asked, "Why are you working on the back of that figure? No one will see it." "Ah," replied the sculptor, "God will always be looking upon it." "I am not sure," continues Dr. Speer, "that it is not on the obscurities of our lives that God looks, far more than on what we regard as our real life, upon which men look. What He looks at, after all, is what is back of the life." That is the heart.

331. Intelligent Architect

Existing things are not the result of chance. No one ever saw a rude heap of bricks dumped from a cart onto the ground arrange themselves into the walls, rooms, and chimneys of a house. The dust filings on a brassfounder's table have never been known to form themselves into the wheels and mechanism of a watch. The types loosely flung from the founder's mold never yet fell into the form of a poem, such as Homer, or Dante, or Milton would have constructed. Only an illogical person could believe that nature's magnificent temple was built without an architect, her flowers of glorious beauty were colored without a painter, and her intricate, complicated, but perfect machinery constructed without an intelligent mind. That man gave the atheist a crushing answer, who told him that the very feather with which he penned the words, "There is no God," refuted the audacious lie. It takes logic to come to the conclusion that there must have been a *lógos,* an intelligence behind what we see.

332. God Knew What He Was Doing

For a number of years our family had supported an orphan girl in Greece. We finally brought her to the United States to live in our home. One day I took her with me to a church, and while there she gave her testimony. Among other things she said: "God permitted me to become an orphan. Evil men killed my father. My mother died of cancer. But God knew what He was doing. As a result of being left an orphan, I entered a Christian orphanage where I found Christ. If I had not become an orphan, I might never have come to know Jesus Christ."

Grace

333. A Very Beautiful Hand

John Wesley and a preacher of his acquaintance were once invited to lunch with a gentleman after the service. Wesley's preacher friend was a man of very blunt speech. This well-meaning man, while talking with their host's beautiful daughter, who had been profoundly impressed by Wesley's preaching, noticed that she wore a number of rings. During a pause in the meal he took hold of the young lady's hand and raising it, called Wesley's attention to the sparkling gems. "What do you think of this, sir," he asked, "for a Methodist hand?" The girl turned crimson. The question was extremely awkward for Wesley whose aversion to all display of jewelry was well known. With a quiet, benevolent smile he looked up and simply said, "The hand is very beautiful." He had not denied the implied rebuke but had taken the sting out of it. The young lady appeared at evening worship without her jewels and became a firm and dedicated Christian.

334. A Gracious Reproof

John Wesley once had for a fellow-passenger in a coach an officer who was intelligent and agreeable in conversation; but there was one serious drawback—his profanity. When they changed vehicles, Wesley took the officer aside, and after expressing the pleasure he had enjoyed in his company, said he had a great favor to ask him. The young officer replied, "I will take great pleasure in obliging you for I am sure you will not make an unreasonable request." "Then," said Wesley, "as we have to travel together some distance I beg that, if I should so forget myself and swear, you will kindly reprove me." The officer immediately saw the motive, felt the force of the request and smiling said, "None but Mr. Wesley could have conceived a reproof in such a manner." It worked like a charm.

335. Grace in Temptation

A Korean Christian showed that he had grasped the meaning of the injury caused by anger when he got up in prayer meeting and said, "I heard the missionary say that every burst of anger pierced the heart of Jesus. So I hung a picture of the Lord Jesus on my wall, and every time I lost my temper, I put a thorn on that picture. The picture was soon covered with thorns. A great love welled up in me that He should suffer because of my temper; now He gives me grace in temptation. I say, 'Not I, but Christ within me,' and His sweetness comes instead of my bad temper."

336. Honesty—Not Pride

A United States President asked a certain general a question about another officer. Overhearing his reply which praised the officer, a friend approached him afterwards and said, "General, do you know that the man of whom you spoke is one of your most bitter enemies and misses no opportunity to malign you?" "Yes," replied the officer, "but the President asked my opinion of him; he did not ask for his opinion of me."

337. The Imperfect Saints

We should be lenient in our judgment of those who accomplish so much in the vineyard of God. They are men of like infirmities and weaknesses as ourselves. Let us remember they are not perfect. Are we then to reject their message because of their imperfections? No. In a pipe which conveys water into a house, there may be a flaw that will sometimes permit rust or earth to mix with the water. Shall we, therefore, reject the water itself, and say, if we may not have it just as it comes out of the fountain or source, we will not have it at all? What if we live far from the fountain itself and can have no water but what is conveyed in pipes subject to such defects?

338. Love Catches a Thief

A Quaker had a bundle of hides stolen from his warehouse. He wondered what steps he should take to prevent a repetition of such an act. Instead of putting the machinery of the law in motion, he placed the following ad in the newspapers: "Whoever stole a quantity of hides on the 5th of this month is hereby informed that the owner has a sincere wish to be his friend. If poverty tempted him to take this step, the owner will keep the whole transaction secret and will gladly help him to obtain money by means more likely to bring him peace of mind."

A few nights later, when the family was about to retire to rest, a man knocked at the door of the Quaker's house, carrying with him a bundle of skins. "I have brought them back," he said. "It is the first time I ever stole anything, and I have felt very bad about it." "Let it be the last, friend." said the Quaker. "The secret still lies between ourselves." He spoke to the man faithfully and affectionately about the folly of dishonesty and of the claims of the gospel. He also took him into his employment, and the man became a changed character, living an exemplary life from then on.

339. Love Your Enemies

A story is told of Peter Miller, a plain Baptist preacher living in Ephrata, Pennsylvania in the days of the Revolutionary War. Near his church lived a man who maligned the pastor to the last degree. The man became involved in treason and was arrested and sentenced to be hanged. The preacher started out on foot and walked the all seventy miles to Philadelphia to plead for the man's life. Washington heard his plea, but he said, "No, your plea for your friend cannot be granted." "My friend!" said the preacher. "He is the worst enemy I have." "What!" said Washington, "you have walked nearly seventy miles to save the life of an enemy? That puts the matter in a different light. I will grant the pardon."

Greed

340. Common Characteristic

One day, in Springfield, a neighbor of Lincoln's was drawn to his door by the sound of crying children. He saw Lincoln passing by with his two sons both crying lustily. "What is the matter with the boys?" asked the man. "The same that is the matter with the whole world!" answered Lincoln. "I have three walnuts, and each boy wants two."

341. Six Feet of Earth

Leo Tolstoy, the famous Russian writer, had a deep insight into human nature. In one of his books he speaks of a Russian peasant who was told that he could have all the land he could measure by walking in one day, from sunrise to sunset. The agreement stipulated that by sundown he must be back at his starting point. The man envisioned great holdings. Early in the morning he began walking; but as he realized that every foot of land on which he stepped belonged to him, he began to run at a feverish pace. The agreement stipulated that by sundown he must have returned to his starting point. His greed was so great, however, that more than half his time had elapsed before he turned back. He had to run at top speed to beat the setting sun. It was a real struggle. If he were not at the appointed place, he would lose all. He finally made it. But even as his foot touched the starting point, he fell dead from exhaustion. All that he gained in the end was sufficient land for his dead body—six feet of earth. That was his final inheritance.

342. Never Enough

It's a strange thing that some people can never have enough of the world; but no matter how little of the Lord they have, they seem to feel it is enough. When I was a lad an old gentleman took some trouble to teach me a little knowledge of the world. With this in view, I remember, he once asked me when is a man rich enough? I replied, "When he has a million dollars." He said, "No." "Two million?" "No." "Ten million?" "No"; "A hundred million?" which I thought would settle the question. He still continued to say, "No." I gave up and confessed I could not tell and asked him to tell me. He gravely said, "When he has a little more than he already has, and that is never."

343. Overabundance Can Destroy

A philosopher said: "I was walking in a garden when I saw a tree whose branches were so loaded with fruit that they bowed down to the earth. Some of them broke under the heavy weight. 'Poor tree!' I thought. 'Here's one who was destroyed by the overabundance of his success.' " He continued his walk and saw a shepherd at whose feet lay a dead sheep. A wild dog had killed it. All the other sheep had run into the fold and were safe. They had managed to get through a hole in the fence. But the sheep that was killed couldn't get through because it was too fat, and the dog jumped on it. And the philosopher thought, "Another life destroyed by an overabundance of blessings." The philosopher went on until he met a man hobbling along on two wooden legs with the aid of two canes. "Tell me, sir, how did you lose your legs?" asked the philosopher. "I'll tell you. In my youth I served in the army. Some of my fellow soldiers and I attacked the enemy and put them to flight. Then we began helping ourselves to the loot. My comrades just grabbed a few things and left quickly. But I wanted to take as much as I could carry. Meanwhile the enemy overtook us. My friends escaped, but I was so heavily loaded down I couldn't run fast, and I was wounded. I escaped with my life, but I lost my legs." "Indeed," said the philosopher, "success, riches and greed can all equally destroy."

Growth

344. No Progress

If we plant a tree, it begins to grow; if we set a post, it begins to decay. There was an old farmer who, in the prayer meetings of his church in describing his Christian experience, always said: "Well, I'm not making much progress, but I'm established." One spring when the farmer was setting out some logs, his wagon sank in the mud in a soft place in the road, and he could not get out. As he sat on top of the logs viewing the situation, a neighbor who had never accepted the principle of the old farmer's religious experience came along and greeted him: "Well, Brother Jones, I see you are not making much progress, but you're established."

345. No Substitute

A devout Frenchman was right when he said, "Beware of a religion which substitutes itself for everything—that makes monks. Seek a religion which penetrates everything—that makes Christians." Chlorophyll is essential to green trees. As it is acted upon by the sun, it purifies the dirty air, absorbing the carbon dioxide that poisons us. Just so, the action of the Holy Spirit is essential to the believer, to purify his spiritual life.

346. Needy Children

Some people have the idea that once the relationship is established between God and man, nothing more is needed. This is a mistake. When a child is born it has the general nature and characteristics of its parents, but does it not continue to need their loving care? It could not live without it. So it is with us and God. He gives us of His nature, His fullness; we become His children, but we need Him constantly and uninterruptedly if we are to go on living spiritually. Our lives as Christians cannot be maintained at all unless it is He who maintains them. This is unlike our earthly parent-child relationship in one sense, however. In our relationship with God we never outgrow our need to be dependent on Him. And though, in the New Testament, Christian maturity is enjoined on all believers, this process of spiritual growth never brings us to a point where we may become independent of God. We are given to understand that our relationship to Him is always that of children. Woe unto anyone who ceases to be a child of God in his own estimation and thinks he has grown up sufficiently to be independent of God!

347. *The Young Christian*

"The young Christian is still carnal," says Andrew Murray. "Regeneration is a birth: the center and root of the personality, the spirit, has been renewed and taken possession of by the Spirit of God. But time is needed for its power from that center to extend through all the circumference of his being. The kingdom of God is like unto a seed; the life in Christ is a growth, and it would be against the laws of nature and grace alike if we expected from the babe in Christ the strength that can only be found in the young men, or the rich experience of the fathers."

348. *Strive for Spiritual Maturity*

Dr. Shelton, a former president of the National Bible Institute in New York City, used to recount with a twinkle in his eye the story of the first time he took his little daughter to a restaurant. She began prattling in her high, clear childish voice to the amusement of the other diners and the embarrassment of her father. "Hush, Marjorie," he said, "people are looking at you." "But Daddy," she protested, "Marjorie must speak!" May it not be that immature Christians by their foolish talk and thoughtless behavior cause those around them to laugh at Christians in general and bring embarrassment to their heavenly Father? Let us consciously strive for spiritual maturity so that with Paul we may say, "When I became a man, I put away childish things" (1 Cor. 13:11).

349. *Responsible for Growth*

God made you essentially what you are. Don't find fault with Him because you are different from others. Discover what you are and grow in the pattern He has designed for you. We are responsible for growing, but not for the essential element of our being. A little girl expressed it beautifully when she said, "Mother made me this much"— indicating the smallness of a baby—"and I growed that much" —showing how tall she had become. How tall have you grown in your Christian life?

350. *A Spiritual Photograph*

Spurgeon says: "We have the likenesses of our boys taken on every birthday . . . so that we see them at a glance from their babyhood to their youth. Suppose such photographic memorials of our own spiritual life had been taken and preserved; would there be a regular advance, as in these boys, or would we still have been exhibited in the perambulator? Have not some grown awhile, and then suddenly dwarfed? Have not others gone back to childhood? Here is a wide field for reflection."

Heaven

351. Prepare for Eternity

In the days the eastern emperors were crowned at Constantinople, it is said to have been a custom to set before his majesty a certain number of marble slabs, one of which he was to choose to be his tombstone. It was considered good for him to remember his funeral at his coronation. Life is time, and the purpose of time is to prepare for eternity. A Greek philosopher, Anaxagoras, was asked why he thought he was born. His answer was, "That I may meditate upon heaven."

352. The Afterlife

To the uninformed eye, a caterpillar turns into a completely different creature when it becomes a butterfly. If a child had never been instructed that one emerged from the other, he would not recognize them as being related. But the scientist knows that when a caterpillar changes into a chrysalis, the whole of its body material undergoes a complete transformation except for a central and essential nerve that controls its entire system. This is retained. Then why shouldn't our spirits have greater powers in the next life? Why should they not be able to repeat our likeness in a celestial and sanctified form, so that we shall be as easily recognized by other spirits in the next world as we are by other bodies in this world?

353. Occupants of Heaven

Someone has very well said: "At three things I shall wonder in heaven: first, that I shall not find many there of whom I was certain; second, that I shall find many there whom I was sure I wouldn't find; but lastly, and most wonderful of all, that I am actually there myself."

354. But I Am a Christian

A pious person who was perplexed by denominational differences had a dream. He thought that he had died and arrived at the gates of heaven. When he applied to the watchmen to admit him within the sacred walls, they inquired, "Whom do you want?" He replied that he belonged to the Independents and wished to join them in that place. "There are no such people here!" was the answer he received. "Well," said he, "I have had some connection with the Baptists; may I join them?" "We don't know any by that name," replied the heavenly watchmen. It was in vain that he asked for Episcopalians; they had never heard of them. There were not even any

Wesleyans, Catholics, Greek Orthodox, or Presbyterians there. He
was just going away in despair
when, as a last resort, he said, "But
I am a Christian." At this term the
gates of bliss flew open, and he
was received as a welcome guest.
Being a Christian is the only thing
that really matters in the sight of
God. We may call ourselves by any
other name, but, when we come to
God, what counts is whether or
not we are truly born-again Christians.

355. No Glass Between!

There was a little boy who came
from an extremely poor family. He
received no gifts at Christmas time,
but he often looked into the store
windows at the exciting things
other little boys could have but he
could not. One day he was run over
by a car and taken to a hospital.
One of the nurses brought him
some toys—a troop of soldiers. As
he touched them, he said, "There
isn't any glass between!" There is a
glass separating us now from the
things that many of our fellowmen
enjoy in this life, even great honor
and respect in the house of God,
but the day will come when there
will be no glass.

356. Eternal Joy

Charles H. Spurgeon once wisely
observed, "If a man might have a
cottage on a hundred years' lease,
he would prize it much more than
the possession of a palace for a
day." Of course he would, and this
is what adds so much preciousness

to the joys of heaven, for they are
eternal.

357. Seeing Heaven

One Sunday, a minister preached
a sermon about heaven. Next morning, as he was going to town, he
met one of his wealthy members.
This man stopped the preacher and
said, "Pastor, you preached a good
sermon on heaven, but you didn't
tell me where heaven is." "Ah," said
the preacher, "I am glad of the opportunity this morning. I have just
returned from the hilltop up there.
In that cottage there is a member of
our church. She is a widow with
two little children. She is sick in
one bed and her two children are
sick in the other bed. She doesn't
have anything in the house—no
coal, no bread, no meat, and no
milk. If you buy a few groceries
and go there yourself and say, 'My
sister, I have brought these provisions in the name of the Lord Jesus,'
ask for a Bible, read the Twenty-
third Psalm, and then go down on
your knees and pray—if you don't
see heaven before you get through,
I'll pay the bill." The next morning
the man said, "Pastor, I saw heaven
and spent fifteen minutes there.
There's no bill for you to pay."

358. The Christlike Heart

There is one additional factor that
will enable us to know Christ "as he
is," and that is "we shall be like him"
(1 John 3:2). Being like Him will
make us sensitive to all that we
have missed in our relationship
with Him on earth. You may have

had a close friend for years, yet never truly known him, just because you are radically different from him. But someone who has a real affinity of nature with him will be able to see in him what you have never seen; he is like him and sees him as he is. You must have the Christlike heart to see the Savior; and in heaven our hearts will be perfectly tuned to His.

359. *Land of the Living*

A man who was dying called upon his secretary to write a letter to a friend. "I continue to be in the land of the living," his secretary wrote in her desire to help him. But he corrected her. Instead, he instructed her to write, "I am still found in the land of the dying, but soon I shall be found in the land of the living."

Hell

360. A Place Too Much Like Hell

A young lawyer, an atheist, boasted that he was going west to locate some place where there were no churches, no Sunday schools, and no Bibles. Before the year was over, he wrote to a classmate, a young minister, begging him to come out and start a church. "Be sure to bring plenty of Bibles," he urged. "I have become convinced that a place without Christians, Sunday schools, churches, or Bibles is too much like hell for any living man to stay in."

361. Unpopular Subject

"Oh, you preachers make me sick!" a fellow said to a witnessing Christian on the train one day. The Christian assured him he was not a preacher. "I don't care what you are. You Christians are always talking about a man going to hell because Adam sinned." "No," the Christian said, "you need not go to hell because Adam sinned. You will go to hell because you refuse the remedy provided for Adam's sin. Don't keep complaining about something that has absolutely been taken care of. If you go to hell, you will go over the broken body of Jesus Christ, who died to keep you out."

362. Hell a Possibility

When a Brooklyn traffic officer handed a young woman a ticket, she told him, according to the press report, "You can go to hell." When she appeared in court, the magistrate dismissed the officer's complaint about her language, saying, "It wasn't a command or a wish, but a real statement of fact, for going to hell is a possibility." How terrible it is, however, that multitudes today have forgotten this possibility. A humorous magazine, poking fun at "advanced theology," remarked, "Nowadays most of the churches and preachers are so advanced that it takes considerable ingenuity to get into hell."

363. The Reality of Hell

A dying girl said to her father, "Father, why didn't you tell me there was such a place?" "What place?" "A hell!" "Jenny," he said, "there is no such place. God is merciful. There will be no future suffering." She said, "I know better! I'm slipping into eternity this moment. I am lost! Why did you not tell me there was such a place?" We do not want to be accused one day of not having told others, for that will be a witness against us.

364. Where Is Hell?

A companion of a newly converted Christian said to him one day, "Can you tell me where hell is?" After a moment's hesitation the young Christian said, "Yes, it's at the end of a Christless life."

Holy Spirit

365. Energized by the Holy Spirit

Seneca, the Roman historian and philosopher, said, "No one is free who is a slave to the body." In 1 Corinthians 6:19 Paul specifically refers to the body of the believer as the temple of the Holy Spirit. "What? know ye not that your body is the temple of the Holy Ghost which is in you, which ye have of God, and ye are not your own?" Yet in 1 Corinthians 3:16 he says, "Know ye not that ye are the temple of God, and that the Spirit of God dwelleth in you?" Is there a contradiction here between the body as the temple, and the whole person as the temple? No, both are correct. Our spirit pervades our body, and it is through the works of the body that the spirit, the real person, is shown. This is why the stress is on the body, because that is what people can readily discern, while the spirit is invisible. Paul knew that the body is the last area of man to be brought entirely under the Spirit's influence and power, just as the twigs and leaves are the last parts of a plant to be energized by the sap. Thus the bodily temple presents to us the complete picture of the fully consecrated man.

366. Enthusiasm—the Unquenchable Fire

John Henry Jowett has beautifully expressed what characterizes the life of power. "Another element in a forceful character is heat, the fire of an unquenchable enthusiasm. . . . The Acts of the Apostles is a burning book. There is no cold or lukewarm patch from end to end. The disciples had been baptized with fire, with the holy, glowing enthusiasm caught from the altar of God. They had this central fire from which every other purpose and faculty in the life gets its strength. This fire in the apostles' souls was like a furnace-fire in a great liner, which drives her through the tempests and through the envious and engulfing deep. Nothing could stop these men. Nothing could hinder their going. 'We cannot but speak the things that we have seen and heard. We must obey God rather than men.' This strong imperative rings throughout all their doings and all their speech. They have heat, and they have light, because they were baptized by the power of the Holy Ghost."

367. The Spirit as the Receiver

There must be a correspondence between the receiver and the transmitter. When we listen to a radio broadcast, there are many sound waves all around us, but the only way for us to become aware of them is to have an appropriate receiver able to catch them and make them audible. We would never know that anyone was talking to us from a distance if we expected our watch to pick up the sound waves. There is only one way in which man can know God, and that is through man's own spirit. God is a Spirit and can be known only by a spirit. We must not expect to feel Him with our fingers, or see Him with our physical eyes. It cannot be done. Yet that which can be perceived only by the spirit of man is just as real as that which can be perceived by his physical senses.

368. Christ in You

Benjamin West, the great painter, speaking of Gilbert Stuart, a brother artist famed for his beautiful coloring, used to say to his pupils, "It's no use to steal Stuart's colors; if you want to paint as he does, you must steal his eyes." When we are baffled in our efforts to live as Christ lived, the record of His life, however wonderful it is, will not enable us to be like Him. What we need is His heart, His nature. Only divinity within us can recognize divinity without. Without the Holy Spirit, we cannot know Him as God.

369. The Work of the Holy Spirit

Mr. Spurgeon once preached what in his judgment was one of his poorest sermons. He stammered and floundered and felt that his message was a complete failure. He was greatly humiliated and when he got home, he fell on his knees and said, "Lord God, Thou canst do something with nothing. Bless that poor sermon." All through the week he

uttered that prayer. He woke up in the night and prayed about it. He determined the next Sunday he would redeem himself by preaching a great sermon. Sure enough, his sermon the next Sunday went off beautifully. At the close, the people crowded him and covered him with praise. Spurgeon went home pleased with himself and that night he slept like a baby, but he said to himself, "I'll watch the results of those two sermons." What were they? From the one that had seemed a failure he was able to trace forty-one conversions. From the magnificent sermon he was unable to discover even a single soul that had been saved. Spurgeon's explanation was that the Spirit of God used the one and did not use the other.

370. Give the Lord Control

In his observations on 1 Corinthians 2:1, J. Stuart Holden gives a beautiful illustration. He says, "I have around my home a garden. In that garden and its possibilities I have the mind of nature. For instance, I know what soil and what seed should produce this, that, and all the other kinds of flowers and fruit; I see set forth in the seedsmen's catalogues the wonderful things that the garden should bring forth. . . . But mark you, the flowers and the fruit are only produced by labor, by obedience to the laws of nature. When the garden has been made beautiful and fruitful, it has been made so only by intelligent cooperation with nature. Similarly, we Christians have the mind of

Christ. We know full well what a Christian life should be." The fruits of the Spirit are only made evident in our lives as we wholeheartedly cooperate with the Lord in full submission and obedience to Him by letting His Spirit have full control of us—body, soul and spirit.

Humility

371. Giving God the Glory

A woman doctor on the mission field restored to health the greatly loved child of a native. In gratitude he knelt at her feet and not only thanked her but worshiped her as a god. She remonstrated, saying that she was a mortal like himself and worship belonged only to God. He replied that no one but a god could have saved the child's life. "Whom would you thank and praise," the missionary replied, "for a princely gift sent by the hand of a messenger—the servant or his generous master, the giver? I am but God's servant by whose hand he has been pleased to send you this great gift of healing." May a like humility and faithfulness possess us as we use our gifts, small or great, in the service of our Lord and among those in the sphere where He has placed us.

372. Mock Humility

If the Christian wants to receive any benefit as he looks in the mirror of the Word of God, he must approach it with humility. A man can counterfeit hope and all the other graces, but it is very difficult to counterfeit humility. One soon detects mock humility.

373. Plain Earthenware Bottles

Some years ago, a party of Americans were leaving Cairo, Egypt, on a journey across the desert and bought vessels in which to carry water. Each one chose the kind of vessel that pleased him. One found jars of brass whose fine designs attracted him. Another purchased porcelain vessels of rare beauty. A third, however, took some plain earthenware bottles. The way across the desert was long and wearisome. The heat was intense. Every drop of water was of value. The brass vessels heated; the water became impure, unfit to drink. The costly porcelain jars cracked in the heat and the water was lost. But the plain earthenware bottles kept the water pure and fresh to the journey's end.

374. The Blessing of Humility

When you are in the process of humbling yourself, the Lord will load you with blessings. God wants you to be like the stalk of wheat that is full of beautiful grains. The more it is loaded the lower it stoops down. Thus, my dear friend, your real riches will be manifested by your humility.

375. The Humble Monk

A subtle temptation that comes to the new believer in Christ is to become proud of his position. He finds it all too easy to take the lead and to assign to Christ a position of lesser importance. Thomas Aquinas was a true saint of God, whose crown of glory never faded because he never polished it himself. One day when he was walking in the cloisters of a monastery in Bologna where he was lecturing, a monk came hurrying up to him and told him to come with him on an errand to the city. The monk had been ordered by his superior to bring with him the first brother monk he saw; not knowing Thomas by sight, he told him to come.

The great teacher never said a word but followed the monk as well as he could, though a bit slowly, for he was rather lame. "Hurry up, can't you?" the monk said impatiently, and Thomas did his best. After a while, the monk noticed that all the people in the street were looking at his companion, and many of them were saluting him with great respect. Presently one of them asked, "Isn't that the great teacher, Thomas Aquinas, who is with you?" The monk was horror-stricken! He had disturbed one of the most important men in the city and then treated him with scant courtesy. With tears in his eyes he begged the master's pardon.

376. What Hath God Wrought

The inventor of the telegraph, Professor Samuel F. B. Morse, was asked by a friend, "Professor Morse, when you were making your experiments in your rooms at the university, did you ever come to a standstill, not knowing what to do next?"

"Oh, yes, more than once."

"At such times what did you do next?"

"Whenever I could not see my way clearly, I prayed for more light."

"And the light generally came?"

"Yes. And may I tell you that, when flattering honors came to me from the invention which bears my name, I never felt I deserved them. I had made a valuable application of electricity, not because I was superior to other men, but solely because God, who meant it for mankind, must reveal it to someone, and was pleased to reveal it to me."

The first message sent by the inventor of the Morse code was, "What hath God wrought!"

377. How to Be Fruitful

A government official in India who was engaged in irrigation work came to the owner of a field and offered to make it fruitful, to which the owner answered, "You needn't attempt to do anything with my field; it is barren and will produce nothing." The official replied, "I can make your field richly fruitful if only it lies low enough." He meant that a lowland would be much easier to irrigate than higher ground. If you and I are willing to accept God's estimate of us as revealed in Scripture—as fallible, weak, and unfruitful apart from His enabling grace in Christ—He can fill us with the living water that will bring forth fruit. One of the last messages of a great philanthropist was, "Tell my younger brethren that they may be too big for God to use them, but they cannot be too small."

378. An Outstanding Memory

I had the opportunity of conversing with Mrs. May Moody Whittle, D. L. Moody's daughter-in-law. I asked her what was her outstanding memory in the life of Dwight L. Moody. Do you know what she said? "He could tell his children that he was wrong and ask them to forgive him." She went on to tell me that one day the children let the horses out of the stable and it took him a long time to get them back. He really told them off. Finally, at night when the children were in bed, Mr. Moody went up and apologized to them for having spoken as he did. This trait is what his children esteemed more than anything else in their father.

379. The Holy Shadow

It is said that long ago there lived a saint so good that the angels came down to see how a mortal could be so godly. He went about his daily work diffusing virtue as a star diffuses light, as a flower emits perfume, without being aware of it. Two words told the story of his days—he gave; he forgave. Yet these words never fell from lips; they were only expressed by his smile, in his forbearance and charity. The angels asked God that the gift of miracles might be given to this good man. The answer was, "Yes; ask him what he wishes." So

the angels spoke to him about it. Would he choose that the touch of his hand should heal the sick? He said, no, that he would rather God should do that. Would he have power to convert souls? He answered, no, that it was the Holy Spirit's work. What, then, did he desire? He said, "That God may give me His grace." When pressed further to give the particular power he would have, he replied, "That I may do a great deal of good without ever knowing it." Then it was decided that every time the saint's shadow should fall behind or on either side, so that he could not see it, it should have the power to cure disease, soothe pain, and comfort sorrow. Thus it came to pass that, falling thus out of his sight, his shadow made withered plants grow again, and fading flowers sweet, gave health to pale children and joy to unhappy mothers. But the saint was never aware of the blessings that flowed from him. And the people, respecting his humility, even forgot his name and spoke of him as the Holy Shadow. How different this dear saint was from some of the present-day leaders in our religious circles whose names almost overshadow the name of Him whom they preach.

380. Praise Detested

One of the things St. Chrysostom detested was the applause and flattery of those to whom he preached. He said: "To me it is nothing when I am applauded and well spoken of. There is only one thing I ask of you—to prove your approval of me through your works. That is how you can speak well of me, and that is what is going to do you good. This, to me, is the greatest honor. I prefer it to a material crown. I do not desire applause and being well spoken of. I have one request to make—for you to listen to me in quiet attentiveness and to put my advice into practice. This is not a theater. You don't sit here in order to admire actors and to applaud them. This is a place where you must learn the things of God." God greatly honored Chrysostom in the sowing of the seed of His Word because he was a humble man.

381. Take No Credit

"Look, Daddy, I wrote my name all by myself!" cried a little boy proudly waving a paper. His mother had held his hand and helped him form the letters for several days, and now this wavering scrawl is suddenly his own accomplishment. We smile at this, but do we not often behave in similar fashion? When by God's grace we give our hearts to Jesus Christ, and His love comes to dwell within us, how can we take credit to self for His working in and through us? Paul's question, "What hast thou that thou didst not receive?" (1 Cor. 4:7) should restore us to a proper sense of humility before God and our fellowmen.

382. Ego Reduction!

The naturalist William Beebe told of an exercise in humility practiced during visits he made to Theodore Roosevelt at Sagamore Hill. Often, after an evening's talk, the two men would stroll over the wide-spreading lawn and look up into the night sky. They would see who could first find the pale bit of light near the upper lefthand corner of the Great Square of Pegasus. Then either Beebe or Roosevelt would exclaim, "That is the spiral galaxy of Andromeda! It is as large as our Milky Way. It is one of a hundred million galaxies. It is two and a half million light-years away. It consists of one hundred billion suns, many of them larger than our own sun!" After a moment of awesome silence, Roosevelt would grin and say, "Now I think we are small enough. Let's go to bed!"

383. Stoop Down to Reach God's Highest Gifts

F.B. Meyer once said: "I used to think that God's gifts were on shelves one above the other, and that the taller we grew in Christian character the easier we could reach them. I now find that God's gifts are on shelves one beneath the other. It is not a question of growing taller but of stooping lower; that we have to go down, always down, to get His best gifts."

384. Dying to Self

The great artist Michelangelo fastened a little lantern to his headpiece so that his shadow wouldn't fall on the marble on which he was working. When self becomes obtrusive, it casts a shadow on all we do. This is true even in prayer.

385. *I Don't Know the Way*

A mother once sent her son on an errand to a place he'd never been. He was a little fellow, but he didn't want to show he was afraid. That's human nature. The younger we are, the more we hate to lose face. Humility often comes with age. As this youngster got ready to leave the house, he stopped at the door, turned to his mother, and said, "It's so far, and I don't know the way. I'm not afraid, you know, but could you come along with me for a little bit of the way?" The mother understood how disturbed the little one was. "Of course," she said. "Mother will come with you all the way." The little fellow put his hand in hers and went out in full confidence that everything would be all right.

386. *Humble Enough to Be Used*

When someone asked St. Francis of Assisi why and how he could accomplish so much, he replied: "This may be why. The Lord looked down from heaven upon the earth and said, 'Where can I find the weakest, the littlest, the meanest man on the face of the earth?' Then He saw me and said, 'Now I've found him, and I will work through him. He won't be proud of it. He'll see that I'm only using him because of his littleness and insignificance.' "

387. *From Heaven Comes All*

On March 27, 1808, a grand performance of the *Creation* took place in Vienna, and the composer himself, Franz Joseph Haydn, who was seventy-six, was able to be in attendance. He was so old and feeble that he had to be wheeled into the theater in a chair. His presence aroused intense enthusiasm among the audience which could no longer be suppressed as the chorus and orchestra burst with full power into the passage, "And there was light." Amid the tumult of the enraptured audience the old composer was seen striving to raise himself. Once on his feet, he mustered up all his strength, and in reply to the applause of the audience, cried out as loudly as he was able, "No, no! Not from me, but," pointing to heaven, "from thence—from heaven above—comes all!" He then fell back on his chair, faint and exhausted, and had to be carried out of the room. What a humble acknowledgment for a great musician to make.

388. *Give Him the Reins*

In the horse and buggy days, a man was driving with his wife along a dangerous road. At a very narrow place the wife became frightened and seized the rein nearest to her. Her husband quietly passed her the other rein and let go. Then more frightened than ever she said, "Oh, don't you let go!" He answered, "Two people cannot drive one and the same horse; either I must drive or you must." Then she gave him the reins and he drove safely past the danger.

389. All Equal

It is related that once when the Duke of Wellington remained to take communion at his parish church, a very poor old man went up the opposite aisle, and reaching the communion table, knelt down close by the side of the Duke. Someone came and touched the poor man on the shoulder, and whispered to him to move farther away, or to rise and wait until the Duke had received the bread and wine. But the eagle eye and the quick ear of the great commander caught the meaning of that touch and that whisper. He clasped the old man's hand and held it to prevent his rising; and in a reverential undertone but most distinctly, said, "Do not move; we are all equal here."

390. The Converted Hindu

"I am by birth," said a converted Hindu, "of an insignificant and contemptible caste; so low, that if a Brahmin should chance to touch me, he must go and bathe in the Ganges to purify himself. Yet God has been pleased to call me, not merely to the knowledge of the gospel, but to the high office of teaching it to others." Then addressing a number of his countrymen, "My friends, do you know the reason of God's conduct? It is this: If God had selected one of you learned Brahmins and made you the preacher, when you were successful in making converts, people would say it was the amazing learning of the Brahmin, and his great weight of character, that were the cause. But now, when anyone is convinced by my instrumentality, no one thinks of ascribing any of the praise to me; God gets all the glory."

391. God's Theater

The open-air theater in ancient Corinth attracted great crowds of people. The people who played in the theater were often quite famous. In our day we call them stars. Popularity and theater performances are almost synonymous. Paul told the Corinthians that God's theater is larger than theirs—that it extends under the vault of heaven. But the apostles were not leading the lives of popular theatrical stars. Their lives were not rich or famous. They were last on the social and economic ladder. Yet they performed with an audience larger than those who were swimming in pleasure. They had an audience above as well as an audience before them. Angels from above watched them, and men from every walk of life.

392. Mary Magnified the Lord

On one occasion an orchestra presented Handel's "Messiah" so beautifully that the applause was thunderous, and everyone turned toward the composer. Handel stood up and with his finger pointing upward, silently indicated that the glory should be given to God rather than to himself. This is exactly what the Virgin Mary did as she talked to Elizabeth. It is as if she were saying, "Don't praise me, but magnify the Lord who is my Savior."

Hypocrisy

393. Know Your Destination

The town of Pisa, Italy, is famous, of course, for its leaning tower. Not so well known, but far more significant, is a painting on the wall of a cemetery there. The artist has depicted the last judgment, with Christ, the Virgin Mary, the Twelve Disciples, and a number of angels. In this painting, groups of people are coming out of their graves, some going to the right and others to the left of the scene. But there appears to be some confusion. Some who thought they belonged on the right and destined for heaven, are being shifted back to the left, destined for hell—and vice versa. What was the basis for their judgment? Christ said, "Not every one that saith unto me, Lord, Lord, shall enter into the kingdom of heaven; but he that doeth the will of my Father which is in heaven" (Matt. 7:21). The Italian artist was inspired by his vivid imagination and the prophetic words of the 5th chapter of Matthew.

394. Test of Salvation

One of the best ways to test the genuineness of our salvation is to find out whether the old nature within us responds when it is called by an outside voice. A French woman was being sought by the police. As soon as she descended from the train, a policeman approached her and asked her who she was and from where she was coming. She gave him false information and started walking away. Then the voice of the policeman was heard behind her: "Rosine." That was her real name. She immediately turned. Are you responding to the hypocritical name of a Christian in church and in the world by your real name?

395. The Bark on the Inside

A child was walking along a street when a large dog came out of a yard barking. She stood terrified. Soon a stranger came by and said to her, "Come on, little girl, the dog has stopped barking." "Yes," she said, "but the bark is still on the inside." She saw in the eyes of the dog an unfriendly spirit.

396. The False Christian

"Look, Mommy, this potato is so big and nice, isn't it?" Then the mother peeled it and cut it in half. How surprised was the little girl when she saw it all black and hollow in the middle. "Oh, Mommy," she said, "this potato is not a real Christian, is it?"

397. Deceit

A woman, enlarging on her husband's inconsistencies, said, "At a theologically liberal meeting he's a liberal and at a conservative meeting he's a conservative." Someone asked, "What is he at home?" She replied with emphasis, "He's a real demon!"

398. The Bat's Reward

Aesop, probably the most renowned writer of myths, speaks in one of his fables about a time when the beasts and the fowls were engaged in war. The bat tried to belong to both parties. When the birds were victorious, he would wing around telling everyone that he was a bird; when the beasts won a fight, he would walk around assuring everyone that he was a beast. Soon his hypocrisy was discovered, and he was rejected by both the beasts and the birds. He had to hide himself, and now he can appear openly, only by night. You cannot hold on to the world with one hand and to the Lord with the other. If you do, you will enjoy neither the world nor the Lord. A house divided against itself cannot stand, was the verdict of the Master (Mark 2:25).

399. The Condemning Evidence

There was a very well-thought-of deacon who was a zealous advocate of the cause of temperance. One day he employed a carpenter to make some alterations in his living room. As the worker was tearing things down, he came upon a very nicely concealed closet. He was shocked when he saw a jug and tumblers in the hidden closet. The carpenter, with wonder-stricken countenance, ran to the proprietor with the announcement of the discovery. As soon as the deacon heard of it, he said, "H'm! Well, I declare, that is curious. Sure enough, it must be that Captain Brown left those things here when he occupied the premises thirty years ago." "Ah, perhaps he did," answered the carpenter; "but say, deacon, that ice in the pitcher must have been well frozen to have remained solid all this time."

400. Sour and Sweet Apples

Spurgeon used to illustrate hypocrisy with the following story: An American gentleman said to a friend, "I wish you would come down to my garden and taste my apples." He asked him about a dozen times, but the friend did not come. At last the fruit grower said, "I suppose you think my apples are good for nothing, so you won't come and try them." "Well, to tell the truth," said his friend, "I have tasted them. As I went along the road I picked one up that fell over the wall, and I never tasted anything so sour in all my life. I do not particularly wish to have any more of your fruit." "Oh," said the owner of the garden, "I thought that would happen. Those apples around the outside are for the special benefit of the boys. I selected the sourest kinds to plant all around the orchard so the boys might give them up as not worth stealing. If you will come inside, you will find that we grow a different quality there, sweet as honey."

401. *Violating the Gospel*

We are so eager to defend the cause of Christ that sometimes in our defense of it we violate the very gospel we defend. We are like the man who wrote a famous tract entitled, *Come to Jesus*. Soon after the writing of that tract, which was mightily used of God, he engaged in a theological dispute in which he wrote to an opponent's publication an invective article bristling with sarcasm, and sharp and cutting as a razor. Reading it to a friend, he asked, "What do you think of it?" "It is a masterpiece of invectiveness," was the reply. "You fairly flay him alive. What have you decided to call it?" "I have not thought of a title. Can you suggest one?" "Well," said his friend, "how about calling it, *Go to the Devil*, by the author of *Come to Jesus?*"

Inconsistency

402. A Christian Off and On

Gypsy Smith once asked a man in an after-meeting, "Are you a Christian?" "Yes." "How long?" "Twenty-eight years, on and off." "More off than on, I guess," replied the evangelist.

403. Erring Christians

In the Greek, the verb to "err" is *planōmai*. This is the word from which we get the English word "planet." These heavenly bodies are called planets because they seem to wander ("err") in the sky. There are not only planets in the solar system, but also erring ones in the Christian church.

404. Authority Questioned

A medical doctor, sitting in the company of friends, quickly cut in on a lay person who was talking about a particular disease with an air of authority. "Only a specialist who has devoted his life to medical science is entitled to speak with authority," he declared. He was right. Before long, however, the conversation turned to a religious question. Without a moment's hesitation the doctor became equally dogmatic. When it was politely pointed out to him that he had not made a study of the Bible and was not religiously inclined, he confi-dently voiced the assumption that all people are equally entitled to an opinion on questions of religious truth and experience. According to him, the person who hardly gives five minutes' serious attention to the claims of the Spirit is entitled to rank equally with those to whom the reverential fear of God is a daily study and passion.

405. Hot And Cold

Aesop's fables contain many helpful moral lessons for us. One of them is about a man and a satyr who, having struck up an acquaintance, sat down together to eat. The day being wintry and cold, the man put his fingers to his mouth and blew upon them. "What's that for, my friend?" asked the satyr. "My hands are so cold," said the man, "I do it to warm them." In a little while some hot food was placed before them, and the man, raising the dish to his mouth, again blew upon it. "And what's the meaning of that, now?" asked the satyr. "Oh," replied the man, "my porridge is so hot, I do it to cool it." "Then," said the satyr, "from this moment I renounce your friendship, for I will have nothing to do with one who blows hot and cold with the same mouth."

406. Double-minded Christians

The worst pronouncements Christ ever made were not against the out-and-out sinner and unbeliever but against the hypocrite. We can see this for ourselves in the twenty-third chapter of Matthew. Both God and your fellowmen can tell the difference between the real and the counterfeit, the real and the imitation. These people are like an old apple tree which stood at the fence line by the roadside. Its branches spread both into the field and out over the highway. There was always a contention as to whether the fruit of this tree belonged to the farmer or to the public. An unwritten law said it belonged to the first one to club it down. Every boy, big and little, watched to see when the apples were beginning to turn red, and then the battle was on. The owner never got a ripe apple from that old tree. The tree on the side of the highway always had lodged in its branches a lot of broom handles, sticks, and old wagon spokes. That tree got more clubbing than a whole orchard. It presents a true picture of the professing "Christian" who hangs on both sides of the fence and thus receives clubs from every direction.

407. Christian Living

Henry Drummond, that great Scottish professor, told how the Infidel Club was started in Glasgow. Some men were standing at the corner of a street when a very prosperous looking man went past. One of the men said, "That is the founder of the Infidel Club in Glasgow." "What do you mean by that?" said another of the men. "Why, that man is an elder of the church." "Elder or no elder," replied the man, "he is the founder of Glasgow's Infidel Club." Then he told how the man's inconsistent life had been bearing for years a false witness to Christ. So false, in fact, that it had undermined the faith of several young men who joined together to form the Infidel Club.

Jealousy

408. Kill the Spirit of Jealousy

D. L. Moody told of two merchants between whom there was great rivalry and bitter feeling. One of them was converted. He went to his minister and said, "I'm still jealous of that man, and I don't know how to overcome it." "Well," said the minister, "if a man comes into your store to buy goods, and you cannot supply him, just send him over to your neighbor." He said he wouldn't like to do that. "Well," said the minister, "you do it and you will kill jealousy." Sure enough, when he began sending customers over to his rival for goods he himself could not supply, the rival began to send customers over to this man's store, and the breach was healed.

409. Earthly Wisdom

Those who study bees tell us when a honeybee drives its barbed stinger into flesh, it becomes so firmly imbedded that the only way the bee can escape is to leave the stinger behind. This, however, is sure to cause the death of the bee. It receives such a wound that it cannot possibly recover. So it is with us. Sometimes we sting others because they are a little better than we are. Being jealous of them, we not only leave the sting in those who happen to disagree with us, but the act brings about spiritual harm to ourselves. If our zeal embitters others, it will multiply bitterness within our own hearts. Thus, when others feel the bitterness of our zeal, they will surely come to the conclusion that we do not possess Jesus Christ who descended from heaven to give us new life.

410. Overcoming Jealousy

Dr. F. B. Meyer told the following experience to a few personal friends: "It was easy," he said, "to pray for the success of Campbell Morgan when he was in America, but when he came back to England and took a church near to mine, it was somewhat different. The old Adam in me was inclined to jealousy, but I got my heel upon his head, and whether I felt right toward my friend or not, I determined to act right. "My church gave a reception for him, and I acknowledged if it was not necessary for me to preach Sunday evenings, I would dearly love to go and hear him myself. Well, that made me feel right toward him. Just see how the dear Lord helped me out of my difficulty. There was Charles Spurgeon preaching wonderfully on the other side of me. He and Mr. Morgan were so popular and drew such crowds that our church caught the overflow, and we had all we could accommodate."

411. Beware of Jealousy

Mrs. Wesley was extremely jealous of her husband. His work set him in the position of friend and counselor to many women. Among his helpers and in the institutions that were springing up under his care, women were employed, and each one was for his insanely jealous wife an object of deadly suspicion. Wesley on his part was apt to be tolerant, in a masculine and broad-minded way, of the facts and relationships of some women, which other women, even the best, would hardly forgive. Sally Ryan, for example, the housekeeper at one of his orphanages, was a woman with a past. She was at this time only thirty-three, but she had three husbands living and was separated from them all. Wesley was in constant correspondence with her, a fact which kindled his wife to fury. She stole Wesley's correspondence to satisfy her doubts. She would travel one hundred miles to see who his companions were at a particular stage of his preaching tour. Her fury threw her sometimes into paroxysms of mad violence and sometimes into acts of almost incredible treachery. She not only stole her husband's letters to satisfy her doubts, but she tampered with them so as to give them an evil sense and put them into the hands of his enemies to be published. Beware of jealousy. It can make the light of God in your heart so dark you see only evil, never good, in everyone.

412. The Squawking Canary

In a home where a lady had two canary cages, one on either side of a window, a visitor made some comment about the birds. Whereupon the hostess remarked that one of the canaries was exceedingly jealous. She then proved her statement. Going to the cage of the bird that was not jealous, she began petting it, calling it pretty names and chatting with it. The reaction of the other canary was remarkable. Its feathers ruffled up, it fluttered all about the cage and made angry squawks of protest. There was no question about its jealous nature. Man, too, displays a jealous nature by his actions.

Judgment of Others

413. A Judgmental Character

A man said once to Mr. Dawson, "I like your sermons very much, but the aftermeetings I dislike. When the prayer meeting begins, I always go up into the gallery and look down, and I am disgusted." "Well," said Mr. Dawson, "the reason is, if you go on the top of your neighbor's house and look down his chimney to examine his fire, of course you get only smoke in your eyes."

414. One Talent—Bury It

Some people are like the man who said he was afraid he was going to be of no use in the world because he had only one talent. "Oh, that need not discourage you," said his pastor. "What is your talent?" "The talent of judging others, of criticism." "Well, I advise you," said his pastor, "to do with it what the man of one talent did with his, bury it. Criticism may be useful when mixed with other talents, but those whose only activity is to criticize the workers might as well be buried, talent and all."

415. Negative Judging

Let us not be like that man who is always quick to judge his fellowmen: If he is poor, he is a bad manager. If he is rich, he is dishonest. If he needs credit, he can't get it. If he is prosperous, everyone wants a favor from him. If he's in politics, it's for pie. If he is out of politics, you can't place him, and he's no good for his country. If he doesn't give to charity, he's stingy. If he does, it's for show. If he is actively religious, he is a hypocrite. If he takes no interest in religion, he's a hardened sinner. If he shows affection, he's a soft specimen. If he seems to care for no one, he's cold-blooded. If he dies young, there was a great future ahead of him. If he lives to an old age, he has missed his calling.

416. Judging Others

Many people sit in judgment on everybody. They seem to delight in imputing unworthy motives to others, and in this respect perhaps they are judging others by themselves. When they see someone working for the Lord, they'll say, "Oh, yes, George is a real saint, but he gets paid for what he does, you know." The inference is that if he weren't paid he'd not be so zealous for the Lord. It may be that the financial compensation for his work had something to do with his decision to engage in it; but it may not have been his main motive by any means. It's all too human to exaggerate the secondary motives of others. We seem to derive some sort of satisfaction in pointing out the flaws in their characters. It seems that the only way some people can build themselves up in their own eyes is by tearing others down.

417. Exercise Patience

The builders and decorators of a great cathedral made the mistake of admitting visitors while the work was in progress. They heard nothing but criticism. Finally they had to close the doors and admit no one but workmen. When it was all finished, the exquisiteness of the structure was universally acclaimed. The previous judgments had been premature. When we are tempted to judge people, let's recognize that just as in our own case success comes gradually as a rule, so it does to others. Let us not dishonor God by attributing ugliness to Him in any of His works in nature or humanity. He is not through yet. God is in the process of perfecting much that we see now as unfinished and imperfect. Don't judge Him prematurely for permitting the sickness, accident, deformity, and seeming injustice of this world. Wait. Exercise patience. He is still at work.

418. Overcoming Temptation

A man in a responsible position, entrusted with large sums of money, was tempted one day to put some of the cash into his own account. He knew that it would be a long time before his theft could be discovered. He resisted the temptation but felt that he must tell somebody the anguish of mind through which he had passed. He went, therefore, to the man who had occupied the position before him, told him all about the temptation, and how he had almost fallen. To his surprise, the man did not reprove him but put his hand on his shoulder in a fatherly sort of way. "I know exactly how you felt," he said quietly. "I went through it all myself when I occupied your position." It was, of course, humiliating for both of these men to admit the temptation of the heart, although it did not result in a crime. Realizing that whatever victories we score, we do so merely by the grace of God, how hesitant we should be to criticize others who may have allowed sins of the thought and will to materialize a little more than we have ourselves. Let us not, therefore, speak evil of our brethren, even in our minds, even to ourselves.

419. Judgment of Brethren

Many critical Christians are like that Persian youth who was very meticulous about his religious duties. He would rise up in the middle of the night to watch, pray, and read the Koran. One night as he was engaged in these exercises his father, a man of practical virtue, awoke while his son was reading. "Behold," the religious youth said to his father, "thy other children are lost in irreligious slumber, while I alone wake to praise God." "Son of my soul," the wise father answered, "it is better to sleep than to awake to notice the faults of thy brothers!" If the knowledge of the sins of others arouses in us the spirit of censoriousness and criticism, confession has not accomplished its intended and hoped-for purpose.

420. Prejudice Is Evil

Those who speak evil of others are usually too quick to draw conclusions. If they see a man coming out of a bar, they immediately decide he must have been drinking. They lack the charitable nature that would let them consider that he may very well have gone in to distribute Christian tracts in a place where they were desperately needed, or he may have gone in to try to persuade a weaker brother to leave the place and go home.

421. The Lord's Admonition

At the conclusion of the Civil War, when hatred and vindictiveness were rampant in the land, President Lincoln sought to stem the tide of judgment and reprisal. When Senator Sumner of Massachesetts pressed him to have Jefferson Davis summarily hanged, Lincoln twice repeated our Lord's admonition, "Judge not, that ye be not judged" (Matt. 7:1). Though he had vanquished Davis as an enemy, Lincoln refused to condemn him as a man. He chose to leave that final judgment to his Creator.

422. No Cross Examination Allowed

There was a juvenile court judge who had a very unusual experience during the course of one of his trials. An elderly man who owned a watermelon patch had caught a boy stealing his melons and had him arrested. When the time came for the trial, the man made his complaint to the court, after which the judge turned to the boy and said, "Son, what do you have to say for yourself?" The boy looked up at the judge with questioning eyes and answered, "Judge, did you ever steal a watermelon when you were a kid?" The judge was somewhat startled at the turn of events, dropped his head into his hand for a few moments of thought, and finally responded, "No cross-examination of the court allowed. The case is dismissed."

Kindness

423. Business as Usual

A young man left his employer, a lumber merchant, and began business in competition with him. For a while he prospered greatly and got many orders that would have gone to the firm he had left. But just when his business seemed to be most flourishing, and he had more orders than he could supply, a huge fire in his yard destroyed all his lumber. The day after the fire he saw his old employer coming toward his office. He said later, "I could have hated him, for I thought he was coming to gloat over my misfortune. But he came to me as a friend in need and said, 'I know you have agreed to supply lumber to your customers by certain dates, and this unfortunate fire makes it impossible for you to do it. My lumber yard is at your disposal. You can have what you need and pay me at your own convenience. Your business may go on as usual.' " The young man was overwhelmed by this embodiment of the Golden Rule; the rivalry and hatred that he had felt gave place to love.

424. Oil of Kindness

There was an old man who carried a little can of oil with him everywhere he went. If he passed through a door that squeaked, he poured a little oil on the hinges. If a gate was hard to open, he oiled the latch. So he went through life lubricating all the hard places and making it easier for those who came after him. People called him eccentric, queer, cranky, odd, and other degrading names. But the old man went steadily on, refilling his can of oil when it became empty and oiling the hard places he found. He did not wait until he found a creaky door or a rusty hinge and then go home to get his oil; he carried it with him. There are many lives that creak and grate harshly day by day. They need lubricating with the oil of kindness, gentleness, or thoughtfulness. That can of oil is predominantly one that characterizes the Christian religion. The task of using it belongs to those who claim to be Christians. As the old man kept his oil with him, so we need to keep our Christian kindness handy. It does no good if left at home or in the church.

425. Kindness

Alexander Maclaren says, "Kindness does not require us to be blind to facts or to live in fancies, but it does require us to cherish a habit of goodwill, ready to show pity if sorrow appears, and slow to turn away even if hostility appears."

426. A Grateful Friend

A gentleman had found a shelter for a ragged, homeless boy and was walking down the street with him. He was stopped by another gentleman who, after a short conversation, said, "You are surely not walking through the streets with that dirty boy?" "Why not?" said the gentleman. "He is my friend." Overhearing the first remark the lad was slinking away, but the answer made him the life-long, devoted follower of his new-found friend. God calls us His friends. Can we ever express enough gratitude and honor to Him?

427. One Hurts—All Hurt

A man passing a small group of children noticed they were all crying noisily. He stopped one lad and asked, "What's the trouble? Why are you all crying?" Between sobs the boy answered, "We all have a pain in Billy's stomach." That's real sympathy for the one who is suffering. Paul possessed such sympathy for the Christian brethren who should have been spiritual but were actually carnal. He still calls them brethren. His desire is not to condemn but to lift them up. This is the spirit of the third chapter of First Corinthians.

428. Spirit of Kindness

"I once lived in the country," said a preacher, "next to a very excellent man who, nevertheless, had his weaknesses. I recollect an occasion on which he became angry and manifested his displeasure in a striking manner. Wanting a place to hang up a trowel in my yard, I drove a nail into the fence between his yard and mine. It went through on the other side. One day I heard a racket in my yard and looking to see what was the reason, I found my trowel ringing over the pavement. My neighbor with his hammer had hit the nail and sent the trowel and everything else flying. My first feeling was to fire the trowel over at him and give him a piece of my mind, but my second thought was, 'Well, that's the way he is, but he is a very good fellow, a quiet neighbor so I won't say anything about it.' I was going to be satisfied; but then I decided I had better say something to him. I stepped in and said, 'I ask your pardon, sir. It was thoughtless my driving that nail through the fence, and I am glad you reminded me of it.' He shook hands with me and said, 'Well, well, let us not say anything more about that.' The result showed the wisdom of treating the matter in a spirit of simple kindness. It was evidently the course of conduct that was best for him."

429. Kindness Rewarded

Two boys who were working their way through Leland Stanford University found themselves almost without funds. One of them conceived the idea of engaging the great Polish pianist, Paderewski, for a piano recital, and devoting the profits to their board and tuition. The pianist's manager asked for a guarantee of $2,000. The boys proceeded to stage the concert, but the proceeds totaled only $1,600. The boys sought the great artist and told him of their efforts. They gave him the entire $1,600 and a promissory note for the $400, explaining that they would earn the balance and pay it off at the earliest possible moment.

"No, boys, that won't do," said Paderewski. Then, tearing up the note, he returned the money to them, saying, "Now take out of the $1,600 all of your expenses, and keep ten percent of the balance for each of you for your work, and let me have the rest."

The years rolled by. The war came, and Paderewski was striving with might and main to feed the starving thousands in his beloved Poland. There was only one man in the world who could help Paderewski. Thousands of tons of food began to come into Poland for distribution. After the starving people were fed, Paderewski journeyed to Paris to thank Herbert Hoover for the relief sent them.

"That's quite all right, Mr. Paderewski," was Mr. Hoover's reply. "Besides, you don't remember how you helped me once when I was a student working my way through Leland Stanford, and I was in a hole." Remember the words of the Master, "With what measure ye mete, it shall be measured to you again" (Matt. 7:2).

Knowledge

430. Can the Finite Understand the Infinite?

The story is told of a blind tortoise which lived in a well. Another tortoise, a native of the ocean, in its inland travels happened to tumble into this well. The blind one asked of his new comrade whence he came. "From the sea," was the response. Hearing of the sea, the tortoise swam round a little circle and asked, "Is the water of the ocean as large as this?" "Larger," replied he of the sea. The first tortoise then swam round two-thirds of the well and asked if the sea was as big as that. "Much larger than that," said the sea tortoise. "Well, then," asked the blind tortoise, "is the sea as large as this whole well?" "Larger," said the sea tortoise. "If that is so," said the other, "how big then is the sea?" The sea tortoise replied, "You only know about the water in your well. Your capability of understanding is small. As to the ocean, though you spent many years in it, you would never be able to explore the half of it, nor to reach the limit, and it is utterly impossible to compare it with this well of yours." The tortoise replied, "It is impossible there can be a larger body of water than this well; you are simply praising your native place in boastful words." This is only a Mongolian myth, but one that can teach man a great deal concerning his prejudiced view of his own knowledge. If man knows so little of the natural surroundings of his life, how much less must he know about the Infinite Creator of all things.

431. The Infinite God

The finite can neither see nor comprehend the Infinite. The Infinite has to reveal Himself. Henry Ward Beecher said: "When Columbus drew near to the eastern coast of this continent, he could see that there were mountains, but do you believe he knew what minerals were in them? Do you suppose he knew all the trees, all the shrubs, all the vines, all the herbs there? He knew something about the outlying islands of this great continent, but he did not understand the details that went to make it up. I can understand there is such a being as God, but when it is said that He is infinite, I am so finite that my comprehension ends right there. I cannot understand infiniteness. All things in the natural world symbolize God, yet none of them speak of Him but in broken and imperfect words. High above all He sits, sublimer than mountains, nobler than lords, truer than parents, more loving than lovers. His feet tread the lowest places of the earth, but His head is above all glory; everywhere He is supreme."

432. The Depths of God

At one time, that thoughtful man who became St. Augustine was greatly disturbed because he could not understand the essence of God. "I admit there is a God," he mused, "but how can I know of what He consists?" Christ had come down to earth with the claim that He was God. By His resurrection, which He Himself predicted, He proved that claim. He revealed that God is a Trinity: God the Father, God the Son, and God the Holy Spirit. But how could a mind as developed as that of Augustine accept this? One day as he was walking by the sea, he saw a small boy who, with the help of a shell, was emptying water from the ocean into a hole he had dug in the sand. "What are you doing, son?" asked Augustine. He was impressed by the naive answer, "I'm going to empty all the sea into this hole." Augustine smiled. An inner voice, however, was saying to him, "You are trying to do the same thing by thinking you can understand the depths of God with your limited mind."

433. Our Limited Knowledge

A woman who had recently returned from a trip to Europe was asked if she had seen the Rhine in Germany. "Oh, yes," she gushed, "and the view from the top was magnificent!" In the same manner,

some Christians claim to know more than they actually do or even more than it is possible for a believer to know, especially about heaven and the life to come. They fail to recognize how imperfect our knowledge is in this life, even of revealed truth. Then they wonder at the rejection of Christianity by so many thoughtful people who try to arrive at the truth of God by their unaided intellect and hence fail miserably to discover a Christ who is so far beyond their mind's grasp.

434. Just a Handful of Peanuts

George Washington Carver was not only one of America's greatest agriculturists and scientists, he was also the pioneer of the synthetics industry which has revolutionized life in this country and around the world. When he was old and bent with years, he shared with a group of students one day the story of his single most crucial undertaking— unlocking the mysteries of the simple peanut. He first cried out, "Oh, Mr. Creator, why did You make this universe?" "Then," he told the students who were listening intently, "the Creator answered me. 'You want to know too much for that little mind of yours,' He said, 'Ask me something more your size.' So I said, 'Dear Mr. Creator, tell me what man was made for.' Again He spoke to me, and He said, 'Little man, you are still asking for more than you can handle. Cut down the extent of your request and improve the intent.' And then I asked my last question. 'Mr. Creator, Why did You make the peanut?' 'That's better!' the Lord said, and He gave me a handful of peanuts and went with me back to the laboratory and together, we got down to work." The results of that conversation with God are history. God wanted Dr. Carver to realize that his knowledge was only partial, and that his mind was not great enough to unravel all the mysteries of the universe, or even of man. He showed him that such a simple thing as a lowly peanut had enough potential within it to keep his brilliant mind well-occupied for a lifetime.

435. The Prize of Folly

One of Aesop's fables tells of a lottery that Jupiter held for the gods. It happened that the best prize, "wisdom," fell to his daughter Minerva, upon which a general murmur arose that the wheel had been rigged. In order to punish and silence the protesters, Jupiter awarded them the prize of "folly" instead of "wisdom," and they went away perfectly contented. And from that time, it is said, the greatest fools have looked upon themselves as the wisest men.

436. Finite Mind

Can a man born blind conceive in his mind all of the varieties and properties of color merely by hearing of them? How foolish it would be for a blind man to conclude that because he cannot see colors they do not exist. He simply lacks the capacity for seeing them. It would be equally foolish for us to reject the existence, the reality, of that which is mysterious to us, but which has been revealed to us by God. As Paul says in 1 Corinthians 2:10, 11, "But God hath revealed them [the elements of mystery in the gospel] unto us by his Spirit: for the Spirit searcheth all things, yea, the deep things of God. For what man knoweth the things of man, save the spirit of man which is in him? Even so the things of God knoweth no man, but the Spirit of God."

437. Near-sighted

A forester near Hamburg, Germany, found an unusual bird's nest. It was a tiny tin can in which a full-grown cuckoo was imprisoned. Apparently the can had been used by some smaller bird for a nest, and the cuckoo egg had been left there in accordance with the custom of the cuckoo of leaving eggs in other birds' nests. When the eggs hatched, the foster parents discovered that they had a stranger in their home—a cuckoo. When flying-time came, all were able to leave the nest but the cuckoo who was too large to get through the opening in the can. So the foster parents continued to feed the imprisoned bird who, for lack of exercise, had become so fat that it filled the entire can. Its misery was ended only when the forester opened the can and let the bird out. Many men never fly, spiritually speaking, because they are never able to break the bonds that hold them to the narrow restrictions of the single viewpoint of truth they have chosen. God will break the bonds of the man of faith who deliberately opens his heart and mind to "the whole counsel of God" as found in His Word from Genesis to Revelation.

438. Limited Perception

When Paul says, "For now we see through a glass, darkly" in 1 Corinthians 13:12, he is not speaking of seeing through a dirty windowpane but of looking into a shadowy mirror such as those manufactured in Bible times in Corinth. All our attempts to look at truth as we see it reflected in creation, in history, in our own consciousness, and even in the Bible, can give us only a dim and imperfect idea of God and of heavenly realities because of human finiteness and sin. Our perception of realities may be more or less the truth as far as our perception goes, but this is always dim and imperfect.

439. Obedience—Gateway to Knowledge

It is difficult to tell which is more important, the proclamation of the grace of God or submission to the Lord Jesus Christ, since the two are so interrelated. Anne Sullivan, who tutored young Helen Keller who was deaf, dumb, and blind, said, "I saw clearly that it was useless to try to teach her language or anything else until she learned to obey me. I have thought about it a great deal, and the more I think, the more certain I am that obedience is the gateway through which knowledge, yes, and love, too, enter the mind of a child."

Love

440. A Kind Teacher

F. W. Farrar tells how, when Dwight L. Moody was an ignorant, ragged, shoeless boy in the streets of Chicago, he found his way to a Sunday school by one of those unseen providences that men call chance. He was shy and sensitive and very nervous lest the other boys would laugh at him because he could not find the places in the Bible. The teacher observed his embarrassment, and with gentle, silent tact saved him from his shame by finding the places for him. But for that little nameless act of love and sympathy, a career of memorable beneficence might have been lost to the world.

441. Warmth of Love

Have you ever seen a tailor place a piece of absorbent paper over a spot of grease and press down on it with a hot iron? Why does he do it? The heat melts the grease, and the paper absorbs it. Real love absorbs the spots in the lives of others, making them feel the warmth of our own hearts for them.

442. The Christian Grocer

A Christian grocer was in financial difficulties because his customers thought they could run up their bills indefinitely. They felt that such a saintly man would never press them for payment or take them to court. Their ready excuse was, "We don't have money to pay our bills." "How can I pay my creditors, if the people I have trusted do not pay me?" puzzled the grocer. What should a Christian do in such a case—believe all things and all men and go bankrupt? A novel idea came to him. He posted the following notice on the bulletin board in front of his store: "On this bulletin board, thirty days from now, will appear the names of all persons who have been indebted to me for one year or more and who, after repeated requests, have refused to pay! Some have told me that they are unable to pay, but they are able to build homes, drive cars, and have other things that I could have if I had the money due me. I hope I don't have to put any names on the board, but I won't be put off any longer!" Results followed immediately. Many paid their old accounts, while others promised to do so on the next payday. This grocer's action was wholly consistent with Christian love. He refused to believe the falsehoods of others and by so doing didn't allow them to continue in deceit and dishonesty. Love believes all things that encourages honesty and virtue in others. Love does not believe lies but endeavors to correct them.

443. Parental Love

A young man who had committed a crime was sent to prison without his parents knowing about it. When he finally wrote and told them where he was, they hastened to the distant city to see him. Sullen and stony-faced, he greeted them in the visiting room. Braced for their recriminations and anger, he was completely unprepared for their loving concern. "I thought you would never forgive me—that you would disown me!" he cried. "Why should we do that?" asked his father. "You're our son, and we only want to help you." The fact that their love toward him had not changed was the beginning of that young man's redemption.

444. Blind to the Truth

A wife whose husband had embezzled thousands of dollars simply would not believe it of him. She loved her husband. So did a close friend, but this friend had to appear in court for the truth's sake and witness against him. The man was pronounced guilty by two courts and sentenced to a jail term, but his wife still refused to believe the truth. Was her kind of love of any help to his sinful and eternal condition? No, it only encouraged him to persist in perpetuating a lie. Real love is not blind to the truth. It does not reject truth for fear that it will not survive the blow. It ac-

cepts truth as the basis of the redemptive work of love.

445. No Burden

An American missionary who was walking down the streets of a Chinese city was greatly interested in the children, many of whom were carrying smaller children upon their backs and managing at the same time to play their games. "It is too bad," the American sympathetically said to one little fellow, "that you have to carry such a heavy burden!" "He is no burden," came the quick reply; "He is my brother." "Well, you are chivalrous to say so!" said the man, and he gave the boy some money. When the missionary returned home he said to his family, "A little Chinese boy has taught me the fullest meaning of the words, 'Bear ye one another's burdens, and so fulfill the law of Christ.' " He recounted his interview and added, "If a little Chinese boy can carry and care for his brother and refuse to consider him a burden, surely we ought not to think it a burden to carry our brother, the weak and the needy ones, who look to us for help. Let us rejoice as we carry one, and say, by our actions, 'He is no burden; he is my brother.' "

446. An Act of Love

Let us imitate the barber who one week noticed that there was a good increase in his business. When he tried to find out why, he discovered that his competitor, another barber in the village, was ill. When the week ended, he took all that he had made above his average earnings and carried it to his competitor with his Christian love and sympathy.

447. *They Killed My Brother*

I vividly remember an incident that took place at our Greek Keswick in Macedonia one year. The Lord had just opened the door for a special ministry among the Turks. After I announced it, a devout Christian woman came up to me, placed some Greek currency in my hand, and said, "I want this used to win Turks to Christ. They killed my brother, but I want to be the first to contribute to their cause." There will be a special reward for that woman at the day of judgment for believers.

448. *Encouraging Friends*

One winter in Chicago, a young man of dissipated habits was happily converted to God. His life was so radically changed that not a soul who knew him doubted the depth and genuineness of God's work of grace in his heart. He lived like a Christian for many months. One stormy evening in November, after business hours, he was on his way home when he was delayed by an open drawbridge. A large, brilliantly lighted bar stood right at hand. He had often frequented such places before his conversion, but never since that time. This evening, however, as he waited for the bridge to turn and let him through, he stepped into the bar for no other reason than to get out of the pelting

sleet. Suddenly, all the familiar temptations closed around him, and almost before he was aware of his danger, he had ordered a drink. One drink led to another, and before he left the place he was partially intoxicated. Before he reached home he despaired of his salvation. "My family, my friends, the church, will all know about it," he groaned within himself. "No one will have any confidence in me. I am disgraced, lost."

But two young men from his church who had seen him leave the bar came up to him and said, "Charlie, don't go home tonight. Come with us and we'll take care of you. We promise that no one in the world shall ever hear from us a word of what happened tonight." They encouraged him, saying that God would forgive and restore him. Next morning he was himself again. They knelt together in earnest prayer, and when he rose from his knees it was with the glad assurance of pardon and God's favor restored. This young man never again yielded to such a temptation and went on to become a successful minister of the gospel.

449. *The Valuable Picture*

When a certain wealthy man died, his will could not be found. Since his wife and only son had preceded him in death, his possessions were sold at auction. Everything was disposed of except a picture of the son. Nobody seemed to want it until an elderly woman approached and pleaded with the auctioneer to let her have it for the few dollars in her possession. When he gave her the picture, she hugged it to her heart, for she had been the son's nurse in his infancy and boyhood days. Attached to the back of the painting she discovered an envelope addressed to an attorney. Taking it to him, she was astonished to hear him exclaim, "Woman, you have a fortune! This is the man's will, and in it he has left a large sum of money to anyone who loved his son enough to buy the picture."

450. Christian Love

That great blind preacher, George Matheson, adequately grasped the idea of Paul when he wrote: "Christian love is the only kind of love in which there is no rivalry, no jealousy. There is jealousy among the lovers of art; there is jealousy among the lovers of song; there is jealousy among the lovers of beauty. The glory of natural love is its monopoly, its power to say, 'It is mine.' But the glory of Christian love is its refusal of monopoly. The spiritual artist— the man who paints Christ in his soul—wants no solitary niche in the temple of fame. He would not like to hear anyone say, 'He is the first of his profession; there is not one that can hold a candle to him.' He would be very sad to be thus distinguished in his profession of Christ, marked out as a solitary figure. The gladdest moment to him will always be the moment when the cry is heard, 'Thy brother is coming up the ladder also; thy brother will share the inheritance with thee.' "

451. Love Demonstrated

A class of little girls was learning to spell. They spelled a number of small words, such as "pig," "cat," "dog," "cow," and amused themselves by imitating the sounds that these animals make. Then little Mary was asked to spell "love." She didn't stop to give the letters, but ran and threw her arms around the teacher's neck and kissed her on the cheek. "We spell 'love' that way at our house," she said. The girls laughed, but the teacher said, "That is a beautiful way; but do you know another way to spell 'love'?" "Oh, yes," cried Mary, "I spell love this way," and she began to put the books in order on her teacher's desk. "I spell love by helping everybody when they need me."

452. Punishment Necessary

A young man speeding along a highway crashed into an oncoming car, and the resultant chain reaction caused the death and crippling of several innocent victims. Yet the judge, after only five minutes deliberation, let him go free. The ensuing public uproar caused a re-opening of the case and a conviction—although ultimately the sentence was suspended. The public outrage in this case, and in similar instances where justice is flouted, shows that men have a built-in recognition of the fact that, where wrongdoing goes unpunished, the law-abiding are threatened and the innocent victimized. Parental love cannot allow disobedience to go unchecked or let continued rejection of authority go unpunished. To do so would be to encourage anarchy and to discourage those who are trying to do what is right. The doctrine of love that the Lord Jesus Christ preached was no wishy-washy affair of permissiveness, of "anything goes," but was balanced by stern warnings about sinning against God and man.

453. Love in Deed and Truth

A young man spent an entire evening telling a girl how much he loved her. He said that he could not live without her; that he would go to the ends of the earth for her; yes, go through fire for her, or die for her. However, on leaving, he said, "I'll see you tomorrow night if it doesn't rain." How often we say we love God yet deny it by our actions. Christ will give His crown of life only to those who love Him in deed and in truth.

454. Be Merciful

J. H. Evans said, "I believe that God often permits me to be chastened by my sin, because I do not make use of my mercies." We often lose our mercies by loving them too well, as the ball of snow is melted by the heat of the hand that holds it, or a rose is spoiled by pressing it too tightly. Theophilus Gale very well said, "Whatsoever I thankfully receive, as a token of God's love to me, I part with contentedly as a token of my love to Him."

Meekness

455. Soft Answers to Rough Questions

A missionary in Jamaica was once questioning some little boys on the meaning of Matthew 5:5 and asked, "Who are the meek?" A boy answered, "Those who give soft answers to rough questions." We shall do well to remember this child's definition. The one who has wisdom in his head and heart does not need to shout at others. Wisdom speaks softly and persuasively, instead of impelling and forcing. Through the use of our tongues people will know whether we are wise or not. As that great theologian, Charles Hodge, said, "The doctrines of grace humble a man without degrading him and exalt him without inflating him."

456. The Meek Shall Inherit the Earth

Men cannot understand how meekness is going to inherit the earth. Men believe in physical strength. They believe in arms and armies. They believe in craft and cunning. They believe in energy, will, and perseverance. They believe in things. They believe in matter. They believe in influencing their fellowmen, working upon them by threats, by pain, by fear. There are few men who believe that a humble man is being used in the strongest possible manner. They cannot credit that his humility shows that he is governed by his highest nature. They cannot conceive that an attitude of meekness is in perfect accord with the divine nature, which is dwelling in that meek one as a result of his new birth in Christ. In saying that the meek shall inherit the earth, our Lord declares this is the potential accomplishment of the man who is indwelt by Christ, by the Spirit of God within man.

457. The Fruit of Meekness

A Brahmin compared the Christian missionary to the mango tree. All its branches hang with fruit. It is then assailed with stones and clubs by passersby. How does it respond—by dropping fruit at every blow at the feet of those who assail it. At the close of the season, it stands scarred and battered, its leaves torn off, its branches broken. But the next year it bears more fruit than the previous year. That is what our meekness should do in the world—not try to conserve its self-esteem but bear fruit, fruit that descends low at the attack of cruel words and actions. Christian meekness cannot be exercised in isolation. It must be manifested within the framework of society, a society that hates the Lord Jesus Christ, openly or subtly, and all who stand for Him.

458. A Sense of God's Goodness

One night during an evangelistic meeting, a paralytic was wheeled down the aisle and placed near the platform. In the preliminary part of the service, the song leader caught sight of him and asked, "What is your favorite hymn?" He immediately answered, "Count Your Blessings!" There was no wail of complaint from the handicapped man, just a vivid sense of the goodness of God. Our submissiveness to God spells satisfaction for our lot on earth. This is the lesson of this Beatitude, "Blessed are the meek: for they shall inherit the earth." This paralytic is surely heir to a greater part of earth than many a millionaire. Meekness, in this sense, is a power—the power to feel satisfaction with what God gives, the power not to merely endure it but to enjoy it to the fullest and to use it for His purpose.

459. A Room Nobody Wants

When Sammy Morris, a Kru boy from Africa, came to America to be trained for Christian service, he presented himself for matriculation at Taylor University. He revealed a spirit all too rare among Christians. When the President of the Univer-

sity asked him what room he wanted, Sammy replied, "If there is a room nobody wants, give that to me." Of this incident the President later wrote: "I turned away, for my eyes were full of tears. I was asking myself whether I was willing to take what nobody else wanted. In my experience as a teacher, I have had occasion to assign rooms to more than a thousand students. Most of them were noble, Christian young ladies and gentlemen; but Sammy Morris was the only one of them who ever said, 'If there is a room that nobody wants, give that to me.' "

460. Meekness of Wisdom

A preacher once received a letter with a pathetic story of a muddled and disordered life which ended: "It just beats me. A doctor of philosophy and unable to solve my own troubles!" It takes more than a friend of wisdom to help us in our troubles; it takes Wisdom personified, the Lord Jesus Himself. When everything goes wrong and troubles abound and the Christian can still go about his duties in life without revolting against God, against Wisdom, then he is possessed with this wonderful meekness of wisdom. Meekness of wisdom is accepting Wisdom's dealings with us without a murmur and without a sigh. It is that temper of spirit which at all times says, "Yes, Lord, Thou knowest best."

Money

461. Blessings of Poverty

It was Andrew Carnegie who said, "Comrades, I was born in poverty and would not exchange its sacred memories with the richest millionaire's son who ever breathed. What does he know about mother or father? These are mere names to him. Give me the life of the boy whose mother is nurse, seamstress, washerwoman, cook, teacher, angel, and saint, all in one, and whose father is guide, exemplar, and friend—no servants to come between. These are the boys who are born to the best fortune. Some men think that poverty is a dreadful burden and that wealth leads to happiness. What do they know about it? They know only one side; they imagine the other. I have lived both, and I know there is very little in wealth that can add to human happiness beyond the small comforts of life. Millionaires who laugh are rare. My experience is that wealth is apt to take the smiles away."

462. Silver Makes the Difference

One day a wealthy old miser visited a rabbi who took him by the hand and led him to a window. "Look out there," he said, pointing to the street. "What do you see?" "I see men and women and little children," answered the rich man. Again the rabbi took him by the hand and led him to the mirror and said, "What do you see now?" "Now I see myself," the rich man replied. Then the rabbi said, "Behold, in the window there is glass, but the glass of the mirror is covered with silver, and no sooner is the silver added then you fail to see others but see only yourself." If you see self and all the respect and honor others ought to give you, you are on dangerous ground. You won't be able to see others if self is in the image you hold in front of you.

463. Wealth without Happiness

The historian, Gibbon, tells us that Abdulrahman, of the Muslim Caliphs of Spain, built for his pleasure the city, palace, and gardens of Zehra, beautifying them with the costliest marbles, sculptures, gold, and pearls. He had sixty-three hundred persons—wives, concubines, and eunuchs—at his service. His guard had belts and scimitars studded with gold. At his death, the following authentic memorial was found: "I have now reigned above

fifty years in victory and peace. . . .
Riches, honors, power, pleasure—
the days of pure and genuine happiness which have fallen to my lot:
they amount to fourteen."

464. Rich Yet Poor

An Arab, losing his way in the desert, was in danger of dying from hunger. At last he found one of the cisterns out of which the camels drink and a little leather bag near it. "God be thanked!" exclaimed he. "Ah, here are some dates or nuts; let me refresh myself." He opened the bag, but only to turn away in disappointment. Alas, they were only pearls, and what good were they to a man who was dying of hunger? Was this man rich or poor? He was rich yet poor.

465. Money Defined

A London newspaper offered a prize for the best definition of money. It was awarded to a young man whose definition was, "Money is an article which may be used as a universal passport to everywhere except heaven and as a universal provider of everything except happiness."

466. Riches Like Nuts

In our constant struggle to acquire things for the preservation of life we wear out life itself. Wise is he who said: "Worldly riches are like nuts: many clothes are torn in getting them, many a tooth broken in cracking them, and never a belly filled with eating them." Jesus gives us very excellent advice which we

shall do well to heed, "Don't wear yourselves out for things which perish so easily."

467. Burden of Riches

A businessman once overtook a black man trudging through the snow, humming to himself. He talked with him and found that he was very poor. Finally he asked him if he didn't think he'd be happier if he were rich. "No, Boss, all the rich men I work for never laugh."

468. That Which Makes a Deathbed Terrible

A minister once visited a notable rich man. He was shown all the gardens, the beautiful estate, the statutes, pictures, etc. The rich man was very anxious to see what ideas all these things would arouse in the mind of the minister. He confidently expected a faltering compliment. Instead the preacher said, "Ah, David, David, these are the things which make a deathbed terrible."

469. Poverty of Riches

Once there were rich parents who left their children constantly in the care of servants. But, like the flower of the grass, riches passed by. The parents could not afford servants which necessitated their taking care of the children. One evening when the father had returned home after a busy and frustrating day at work, his little girl climbed upon his knee and twining her arms around his neck said: "Daddy, don't get rich again. You did not come into the nursery when you were rich, but now we can be with you and get on your knee and kiss you. Don't get rich again, Daddy."

470. The Pride of Riches

The moth looks like such a harmless creature. In its pearly white color it hovers about without sound at twilight, or in our dark rooms and especially in our closets where our woolen clothes are kept. It is not impertinent like the robust flies of the summer. It does not have the sting of a mosquito. It does not sound in our ears the shrill notes of the cricket. It does not nibble and gnaw like the mouse and rat, nor, as roaches do, indecently overrun our food. It is most fair, silent, and apparently harmless. Yet every housewife springs after it with electric haste. It is a dreaded pest, not for what it is but for what it does. Once a garment is moth-eaten, it is almost impossible to repair it. How true this is in the case of the proud rich. Once one begins to suffer the sickness of pride of riches, the cure is very difficult. Let us beware, for, once the moths have done their work upon us, there is hardly any hope. Let us remember, also, that the moth does its work secretly, without our realizing it; so does the pride of riches. We may be proud of the things we wear and possess without ever realizing it. How stealthily the moths work; pride of the soul even more so.

471. Quest for Happiness

The Persians tell a story about an unhappy king. In an attempt to find the answer to his dissatisfaction, he consulted his astrologers who told him he could find happiness by wearing the coat of a perfectly happy man. Immediately the king set out on his quest. He knocked at the doors of the very rich, for it seemed logical to find happiness there, but in vain. He visited the institutions of higher learning, thinking the erudite must be happy in their wisdom. That, too, proved a dead end. Finally he stumbled across a common laborer singing at his work who confessed he was perfectly happy. "Sell me your coat," cried the king. "I'll give you a bag of gold for it." But the laborer only laughed and said, "I'd gladly give it to you, Sir, but I have no coat." This is only a legend of course, but it illustrates a profound truth. Achieving riches is not synonymous with achieving happiness. That doesn't mean the rich have to become poor in order to be happy. The ranks of the happy include both poor and rich as well as those in between. King Solomon had the right idea when he prayed, "Give me neither poverty nor riches; feed me with food convenient for me: lest I be full, and deny thee, and say, Who is the Lord? or lest I be poor, and steal, and take the name of my God in vain" (Prov. 30:8, 9). Paul said it even more succinctly when he wrote to Timothy, "Godliness with contentment is great gain" (1 Tim. 6:6).

472. Futility of Riches

"You are to be more envied than anyone I know," said a young man to a millionaire. "Why so?" responded the millionaire. "I am not aware of any cause for which I should be envied." "What, sir!" exclaimed the young man in surprise. "Why, you are a millionaire! Think of the thousands your income brings every month!" "Well, what of that?" replied the millionaire. "All I get out of it is my food and clothes, and I can't eat more than one man's allowance and wear more than one suit of clothes at a time. Even you can do as much as I can, can't you?" "Yes, but think of the hundreds of fine houses you own, and the rentals they bring you." "What good does that do me?" replied the rich man. "I can only live in one house at a time. As for the money I receive for rents, why, I can't eat or wear it; I can only use it to buy other houses for other people to live in; they are the beneficiaries, not I." Then, finally, after a little more discussion, the millionaire turned to the young man and said: "I can tell you that the less you desire in this life, the happier you will be. All my wealth can't buy a single day more of life, cannot buy back my youth, cannot procure power to keep off the hour of death. Then what will happen? In a few short years at most I must lie down in the grave and leave it all forever. Young man, you have no cause to envy me."

Mother

473. Mother's Share

Professor William James, Harvard's famous psychologist and the author of that well-known book, *The Varieties of Religious Experience*, said: "A teacher asked a boy this question on fractions: 'Suppose that your mother baked an apple pie, and there were seven of you— your parents and five children. What part of the pie would you get?' 'A sixth, ma'am,' the boy answered. 'But there are seven of you,' said the teacher. 'Don't you know anything about fractions?' 'Yes, teacher,' replied the boy, 'I know all about fractions, but I know all about Mother, too. Mother would say she did not want any pie!' "

474. The Obedient Son

A distinguished French officer asked Washington's mother how she managed to rear such a splendid son. She replied, "I taught him to obey."

475. A Mansion Near the Throne!

Ian MacLaren, that great preacher of the Word of God, once visited a home and found an old Scotch woman standing in her kitchen, weeping. She wiped her eyes with the corner of her apron, and when the minister asked her what was the matter, she confessed, "I have done so little. I am so miserable and unhappy." "Why?" asked MacLaren. "Because I have done so little for Jesus. When I was just a wee girl, the Lord spoke to my heart, and I did want so much to live for Him." "Well, haven't you?" asked the minister. "Yes, I have lived for Him, but I have done so little. I want to be of some use in His service." "What have you done?" "Nothing. I have washed dishes, cooked three meals a day, taken care of the children, mopped the floor, and mended the clothes. That is all I have done all my life, and I wanted to do somthing for Jesus." The preacher, sitting back in the armchair, looked at her and smiled. "Where are your boys?" he inquired. She had four sons and had named them after Bible personalities. "Oh, my boys? You know where Mark is. You ordained him yourself before he went to China. Why are you asking? He is there preaching for the Lord." "Where is Luke?" questioned the minister. "Luke? He went out from your own church. Didn't you send him out? I had a letter from him the other day." Then she became happy and excited as she continued. "A revival has broken out on the mission station, and he said they were having a wonderful time in the service of the Lord!" "Where is Matthew?" "He is with his brother in China. Isn't it fine that the two boys can be working together? I am so happy about that. John came to me the other night—he is my baby and is only nineteen, but he is a great boy. He said, 'Mother, I have been praying and, tonight in my room, the Lord spoke to my heart about going to help my brother in Africa! But don't you cry, Mother. The Lord told me I was to stay here and look after you until you go home to glory.' " The minister looked at her: "And you say your life has been wasted in mopping floors, darning socks, washing dishes, and doing the trivial tasks. I'd like to have your mansion when we are called home! It will be very near the throne."

476. A Mother Rebuked

Are all your thoughts for this life and none for eternity? A young lady of twenty, a child of rich parents, was trained by her mother in all the arts of fashionable life. The daughter was happy amid the flatteries of her admirers, and the mother's pride was satisfied. Soon sickness came, and the minister was called in. He talked of death, judgment, and eternity, and the young lady trembled. In her dying hour, she called for her fine clothes. They were brought; looking up to her mother, she said, "These have ruined me. You never told me I must die. You taught me that my life in this world was to be happy and to enjoy the vanities of life. What could you mean? You knew I must die and go to judgment. You never told me to read the Bible or go to church unless to make a display of some new clothing. Mother, you have ruined me." A few moments later, she died.

477. The Disappointed Mother

A widow whose children had left her one by one to go to the "new country" (as she called it) heard each of them promise to save money and to send for her "very soon." Time passed; the children married and had children, but no mention came of sending for the old mother. She longed to see them, but thinking they lacked the means, she saved up enough money herself to pay them a surprise visit. But, her reception was the reverse of what she had fondly anticipated. Her children, who had prospered, seemed annoyed at their mother's coming, criticized her old-fashioned dress and speech, and had no room for her. The disappointed woman came back and entered a home for the aged, where she proved a blessing to all about her, shedding on those around her the love that her own children had rejected. No bitterness remained in the heart of the aged saint. "It seems to me that I knew what our Lord suffered," she told a friend, "when He came to His own dear people and they gave Him the cold shoulder. Just think! He came unto His own and His own received Him not! I can understand how that wounded His loving heart." Yet she could praise God for the experience since it drew her closer to her Savior and made her more compassionate toward others.

478. Christ in a College Dorm

A university student who had filled his wall with indecent pictures received an unexpected visit from his mother. She never said a word about them or gave any indication she had noticed them. But before she left she hung a picture of Christ in the middle of the other pictures. When she visited him again, the only picture hanging on the wall was Christ's. God had radically changed her son's heart.

479. Mystery of Love

A young man who was tired of the monotony and the restrictions of home decided to leave, to go to a place where he could wander and be free. He got fed up with that, however, as he realized it was not what he had dreamed it would be. He decided to write to his mother and tell her that he was going to take the train back home. He told her that if she still wanted him, she should hang a white handkerchief on top of the tree in their yard which could easily be seen before the train stopped at the little home-town station. How amazed the wandering young man was when he found that his mother had used every available handkerchief to hang on the various branches of the tree. He could not understand how his mother could continue to love him. It was a mystery to him that his mother's love had increased instead of diminished. It is so with the love of God for the wandering child.

Peace

480. Peace in the Storm

A story is told by William Gilbert of how Dante, wandering one day over the mountains of Lunigiana, eventually drew near to a lone, secluded monastery. It was at a time when his mind was wracked with internal conflict and was seeking refuge from the strife. So he loudly knocked at the monastery gate. It was opened by a monk, who in a single glance at the sad, pale face, read its pathetic message of misery and sorrow. "What do you seek here?" said he. With a gesture of despair, the poet replied, "Peace." It was the same old craving followed by the same old search. But neither the solitary places, nor the anchorite's cell ever brought true peace to the afflicted heart. Peace comes not from without but from within. We can have it in the winter of age or the spring of youth; in the lowly cottage or the stately mansion; in distressing pain or in buoyant health. The secret of it is in comradeship with Christ. You can have peace in the midst of the storm, if you have Christ. He is the shelter from the tempest, the soul's haven of rest. If we have learned to value His friendship, we have mastered the secret of the "peace which passeth all understanding."

481. Patience Pays

"My dear boy," said a father, "take a word of advice from an old man who loves peace. An insult is like mud; it will brush off much better when it is dry. Wait a little till you both are cool; then the broken relationship will be easily mended. If you go now, it will be only to quarrel." That is good advice for you and for me—patience will induce peace.

482. It Takes Two to Quarrel

I don't know if you are old enough to remember the organ grinder who used to go around in the streets with a little monkey to collect pennies. One such entertainer had an especially clever monkey. On one occasion, when a big dog broke away from some children with whom it had been playing and made a dash for the monkey, the bystanders were surprised to see that the monkey did not seem in the least afraid. He stood perfectly still in evident curiosity, waiting for the dog to come up to him. This disconcerted the dog, for it would have much preferred to chase something that would run and not stand its ground. As soon as the dog reached the monkey, the funny little scarlet-coated creature courteously doffed its cap. Instantly there was a laugh from the audience. The dog was nonplused. Its head drooped and its tail dropped between its legs. It looked like a whipped cur and not at all like the fine dog it really was. It turned and ran back home, and the laughing children could not persuade it to return. As for the monkey, he wanted no disagreement, and he knew instinctively that it took two to make a quarrel. You can often avoid strife by being the one who refuses to fight with a brother in Christ, even if he is somewhat different from you or belongs to another group.

483. Divine Peace

Oilcloth and linoleum may both look bright and shiny, but under the stress of daily wear the cheap oilcloth soon wears out, while the inlaid linoleum gives good service for many years. The stresses of life soon show up the shoddy material of which human peace is made, but stress only brings out more brilliantly the divine peace that Christ brings to the heart.

484. How to Live in Harmony

Christ's basic law for harmonious co-existence with others is found in Luke 6:31: "As ye would that men should do to you, do ye also to them likewise." Matthew states it this way: "All things whatsoever ye would that men should do to you, do ye even to them: for this is the law and the prophets" (Matt. 7:12). It is said that the Roman Emperor Severus was so enchanted by this law when he heard it for the first time that he appointed a reader to repeat it aloud every time someone came before him for judgment. He also ordered it to be written in large letters in the most frequented rooms of the palace and in many public buildings. Though an idolater, the Emperor honored Christ as the One who had told them how to live justly, and he was even disposed to include Christ among the gods.

485. True Peace

Two painters were asked to paint a picture illustrating peace. The first painted a beautiful evening scene in the foreground of which was a lake, its surface absolutely calm and unruffled. Trees surrounded it, meadows stretched away to the distant cattle gently browsing; a little cottage, the setting sun—all spoke of perfect rest. The second painter drew a wild, stormy scene. Heavy black clouds hung overhead; in the center of the picture an immense waterfall poured forth huge volumes of water covered with foam. One could almost hear its unceasing roar, yet perhaps the first thing to strike the eye was a small bird, perched in a cleft of a huge rock, absolutely sheltered from all danger, pouring forth its sweet notes of joy. It is the second painter who could describe the peace that passeth all understanding which is the Lord Jesus Christ, the wisdom of God in the heart of the redeemed. One can only have peace with himself if he has peace with God.

486. Shut the Door and Pray

A missionary in West Africa visited a sick church member. Since the sick man's wife was also present, he asked them several questions, one being, if they lived in peace together. The man answered, "Sometimes I say a word my wife doesn't like, or my wife talks or does what I don't like; but when we start to quarrel, we shake hands, shut the door, and go to prayer. So peace is restored again." This is a very good formula for us to follow, since we are surely apt to do or say something that others in our Christian community don't like, or others are apt to say or do something that we do not like.

Prayer

487. Answer to Prayer Requires Preparation!

A rather lazy student noticed that a fellow student always recited her lessons well, so he said to her, "How is it that you always say your lesson so perfectly?" She replied, "I always pray that I may say my lessons well." "Do you?" said the boy somewhat surprised. "Well, then, I will pray, too." However, the next morning he could not even repeat a word of his assigned lesson. Perplexed, he ran to his friend and reproached her as deceitful. "I prayed," said he, "but I could not say a single word of my lesson." "Perhaps," rejoined the other, "you didn't study hard enough!" "I didn't study at all," answered the boy. "I thought I didn't have to study after praying about it."

488. Good Retreat

In the Korean conflict, which was never officially termed a "war," the Eighth United States Army and the North Korean Communists ravaged the city of Seoul three times. It was a battle of wits as well as of arms because the American soldiers were thousands of miles from the source of their ammunition supply. At the outset of the conflict, they had to be ready to fight, to dig in and hide, or to retreat, if ordered. The very word "retreat" has always had a shameful connotation on the battlefield, so the generals and colonels chose to call it "a strategic withdrawal." Sometimes, when the battle against sin and Satan becomes hot in the Christian's life, discretion is the better part of valor, and a hasty retreat to the place of prayer is not only indicated but wise.

489. Prayer Limited

There was a sexton in a church who was very devoted to the pastor. A new pastor came, and someone asked the sexton what he thought of the new preacher. "Well," said the sexton, "I like him pretty well, but when it comes to praying, the former preacher asked the Lord for things the new preacher doesn't even know the Lord's got." Our immaturity and finite nature many times do not permit us to see what God has for us, blessings which are far better than those we want for ourselves.

490. Kill the Spider

A Christian who attended prayer meeting faithfully always confessed the same things during testimony time. His prayer was seldom varied: "O Lord, since we last gathered together, the cobwebs have come between us and Thee. Clear away the cobwebs, that we may again see Thy face." One day a brother called out, "O Lord God, kill the spider!"

491. Action Needed

We are reminded of the little girl who told a friend who was visiting her father that her brothers set traps to catch birds. He asked her what she did. She replied, "I prayed that the traps might not catch the birds." "Anything else?" "Yes," she said, "I prayed that God would keep the birds out of the traps." "Anything else?" "Yes, then I went and kicked the traps all to pieces." That little girl was bright enough to understand that life needed action as well as prayers.

492. They Stayed On

A small party of missionaries were invited to go to Tibet at a time when missionary activity was forbidden there. They were told their task was to help stem the tide of a plague that was raging out of control. When the plague was over, the government asked the missionaries to leave. But these servants of Christ felt a responsibility to minister to the souls of the Tibetans as well as to their bodies. The authorities threatened to kill them, but the fear of death did not deter them from their purpose. They stayed on.

One night the Tibetans encircled their house with flaming torches. They began dancing around in a wide circle, ever diminishing in size

seeking to achieve their aim of setting the place ablaze. The missionaries fell to their knees in prayer, and became so intent as the wild chanting came closer that they never realized it had ceased. When they arose, the mob had dispersed, and they were allowed to remain. Years later, one of their converts told them that he had been in the circle, and they had every intention of burning the missionaries to death in their house. However, as they approached the dwelling, there stood before the door a figure in white apparel holding a flaming sword. They fled in fright. And thus the door was opened for the gospel in Tibet, because God honored the faith of those who were willing to die at any time for their Lord.

493. Answer to Prayer

A man prayed fervently every morning at family worship for the poor in the community, but he was never known to give anything to the poor. One morning at the conclusion of family worship, after the usual prayer had been offered for the poor and destitute, his little son said, "Father, I wish I had your corncrib." "Why, my son?" asked the father. "Why, because then I would answer your prayer myself."

494. Use the Battering Rams

When St. Paul's Cathedral in England was being demolished to make room for a new edifice, thirty men operated a battering ram for one whole day on a certain part of the wall. Not seeing any immediate effect, they thought this a colossal waste of time, but they were told nonetheless to continue. On the second day, the wall began to tremble at the top and fell in a few hours. If our prayers and repentances do not appear to overcome our inner corruption, we must still continue to use these battering rams, for through faith in Christ the power of evil shall be overthrown.

495. God Our King

It is related of Alexander the Great that on one occasion a courtier asked him for some financial aid. The great leader told him to go to his treasurer and ask for whatever he wanted. A little later, the treasurer appeared and told Alexander the man had asked for a large sum and that he hesitated to pay out so much. "Give him what he asks for," replied the great conqueror. "He has treated me like a king in his asking, and I shall be like a king in my giving." Oh, for the realization of the greatness of the God to whom we come in prayer! From such a God we can only beg humbly; we cannot demand anything.

496. Prayer Answered

One day a lady was giving her little nephew some lessons. He was generally a good, attentive child, but on this occasion he could not fix his mind on his work. Suddenly he said, "Auntie, may I kneel down and ask God to help me find my marble?" His aunt gave her consent, and the little boy knelt by his chair,

closed his eyes, and prayed silently. Next day, almost afraid of asking the question lest the child had not found his toy and so might lose his simple faith, the lady said to him, "Well, dear, have you found your marble?" "No, Auntie," was the reply, "but God made me not want to." That is the way God many times answers our prayers and thus rids us of division within ourselves.

497. Ask for Rain, Carry Umbrella

Dr. Guthrie, that great Scotch preacher, prayed in the morning service for rain. As he went to church in the afternoon, little Mary, his daughter, said, "Here is the umbrella, Papa." "What do we need it for?" he asked. "You prayed for rain this morning, and don't you expect God will send it?" They carried the umbrella, and when they came home they were glad to take shelter under it from the drenching storm.

498. Belief in Prayer

A little boy came to the preacher and asked him to have the folks in prayer meeting pray that the Lord might cause his sister to read the Bible. The preacher made the request known, but as soon as someone began to pray about it, little Johnny got up and left. Everyone thought him very rude, and the next day the preacher scolded him for it. But Johnny said, "Sir, I wanted to go and see my sister read the Bible for the first time."

499. Needs or Wants

A parent does not give a child everything that he asks for. If my little boy came to me and told me just before supper that he wanted a lollipop, should I give it to him? Of course not. Then, if he turns to me and says, "But Daddy, I need it," he can say it as many times as he wishes. He is not going to get a lollipop just before supper. The expression of a need does not always represent a true need. Many times we act more inconsiderately before our Heavenly Father than our children act before us. We give utterance to our wants as if they were real needs. Let us watch this tendency. God is never fooled. He knows a real need from a want.

500. Praying in His Name

A little child who had just learned the alphabet kept repeating time after time the letters of the alphabet in an attitude of prayer. A missionary approached her and asked what she was saying. The little girl's answer was, "I am praying." "But why do you repeat the alphabet?" "I felt that I should pray, and because I did not know how to pray, I repeated the letters of the alphabet, knowing that the great Lord would fit the letters together to make words out of them." The little girl was only expressing something that we do unconsciously every time we close our prayer "In the name of the Lord." We invoke the totality of His revelation to us, all His attributes and all His omnipotence. We call upon Him as our Priest, our Mediator, our Prophet, our Redeemer, our Savior, our All in all.

501. Pray for Each Other

A minister was praying at the bedside of a dying woman. "Wait a moment," she said, as he started to rise from his knees. "I want to pray for you." Very tenderly she prayed with her hands upon his head. "For ten years, ever since you became my pastor, I have offered that prayer for you every morning and night," she told him. The minister went away with tears in his eyes and a strange warmth in his heart. He had known that this woman was sweet-spirited and true, but he had never guessed that he had a place in her prayers day and night. "I wonder how many of my six hundred members pray for me," he asked himself. Let us remember others in our prayers even as we want others to remember us.

502. Effectual Prayer

A lady lay in bed suffering violent head pains. While thus suffering she said to a friend who was watching by her side, "If only I could get ten minutes' sleep, I should feel better." The friend said nothing but offered up a silent prayer to God to grant the ten minutes' sleep. True, the petition was feeble, and the faith feeble, but the Lord, who is very tender, did not despise either the feebleness of the faith or the smallness of the subject of the request. The patient presently slept and described her sleep as most delicious. Specific prayer availeth much. We must narrow down our prayers if we want God to give us that which we need. Our children feel free to come to us and ask us for even the most insignificant things. The only hope of their getting that which they want is by asking, and asking specifically.

503. Jesus, Have Mercy

One time the plane in which I was traveling was caught in a violent storm. All the passengers, including myself, were getting sick. To take my mind off what was happening, I opened my New Testament to Luke 17:12-19, which deals with Christ's encounter with the ten lepers. When I couldn't finish reading the passage because the plane was being blown about like a bird in the wind, I had reached verse thirteen. The lepers standing afar off had cried out, "Jesus, Master, have mercy on us."

504. Happy Prayer Time

During the Welsh revival a minister was approached by a humble saint in his church and was asked this question. "Can you guess what is the happiest time I have in religion?" The minister thought he could easily answer and so he said, "Why, we are all as happy as we can be during these revival days, and at our prayer meetings night after night." The old man seemed somewhat surprised. "Well," he said, "That is true, but I was not thinking about that. Try again."

"Then," said the minister, "it must be when you are at prayer." "You are getting near it now," said the old man, "but it is not exactly when I pray. It is when I am done praying, and God and I are just chatting." If we knew that a great dignitary would accept us if we went to him, would we not go? If he invited us to stay with him and be on intimate terms with him, would we not stay? How much more wonderful it is when we think that the dignitary is God Himself. He will be our eternal Companion, if we go to Him through Jesus Christ.

505. Forty Martyrs of Sebaste

St. Basil was a great man of God, one of the greatest of the Church Fathers. One of his noble orations is dedicated to the memory of forty martyrs of Sebaste who were ordered by the officers of Licinius, in the year A.D. 320, to offer sacrifices to heathen idols. These were soldiers who had proven to be excellent in every respect. But Licinius the emperor issued a decree that they must renounce Christ or else their lives would be in danger. Those who refused to give up Christ were submitted to indescribable brutalities and tortures.

"The torturers were called forth. The first was ready and the sword was sharpened. . . . Then some of the persecuted Christians fled, others succumbed, others wavered, and some before even being submitted to the tortures, were afraid because of their threatenings. Some, when facing the tortures, became faint.

Others entered the battle, but were not able to persevere to the end in suffering the pains, and in the middle of the martyrdom they renounced Christ.

"However, the invincible and gallant soldiers of Christ proceeded visibly to the middle, at the time when the judge was showing the decree of the king and was asking them to submit to it. Without being afraid of anything which they saw, nor losing their heads as a result of the threatenings, they confessed that they were Christians.

"These Christians soldiers were offered money and honors in order to induce them to join the ranks of the heathen. To earthly honors they would not yield. Then came threats of indescribable tortures. What an answer these Christian soldiers gave: 'Do you have blessings of equal value to those you endeavor to deprive us of, to give us? We hate your gift because it will mean our loss. We do not accept honor which is the mother of dishonesty. You offer us money which remains here, glory which fades away. . . . We have despised the whole world. Those things which we see in the world do not have for us the value of the heavenly things which we hope and long for. . . . We are afraid of only one punishment, the punishment of hell. We are here ready to be tortured . . . for you to twist our bodies and to burn them.'

"The judge was infuriated by the courage of these brave Christians, and so he devised a slow and most painful way of putting them to death. It was very cold. He waited for the night when the wind was violent and the air freezing. He ordered these soldiers to be thrown naked on a frozen lake in the center of the town to die from freezing. There is no more atrocious and painful death than that. These Christian soldiers did not have to be forced to take off their clothes. They took them off themselves and marched on to the frozen lake. As each went, he said, 'We are not merely putting off our clothes, but we are putting off "the old man, which is corrupt according to the deceitful lusts" ' (Eph. 4:22). All together they shouted, 'The winter is bitter, but heaven is sweet; the freezing painful, but sweet the rest. Let us persevere a little longer and we shall be warmed in the bosom of the Patriarch [meaning Christ]. Let us exchange all of eternity for the pains of one night. Let the leg be burned so that it may ever dance with the angels. . . . How many soldiers have died in battle remaining faithful to a mortal king, and we, for the sake of remaining faithful to the true king, shall we not sacrifice this life? . . . We are going to die anyway; let us die so that we may live.' Their prayer was unanimous and ascended with one voice, 'Forty have we entered this ordeal, may all forty of us receive the crown of martyrdom. Oh, Despot, grant that not one of our number may yield. . . . You honored this number because you fasted forty days.'

"In spite of this earnest prayer, one of their number did not persevere and gave in to the offers of the heathen persecutors. Great sorrow came upon the others because only thirty-nine remained in the arena of death. Their plea became even more vigorous to their Heavenly Father. Forty entered the ordeal and forty wanted to see the face of the Lord. The deserter came to the warm place prepared by the emperor's executioners. But going from the extreme cold to the warm place, and plunging himself into warm water, he died instantly. The guard, a heathen who was watching all the developments and saw angels ministering to these saints of God, on hearing their prayers, decided to answer them. He took off his clothes and declared with a loud voice, 'I am a Christian, too,' and jumped naked on the frozen lake joining the thirty-nine to complete their number to forty. Thus their prayer was answered, forty entered the ordeal of martyrdom and forty saw the face of Jesus Christ. Now, whose memory was cursed and whose was blessed? We call the saints who persevered unto death blessed, indeed."

506. Praying for Others

Unfortunately, countless Christians become selfish in their prayers. They pray for themselves and their families and care little about others. The moon is a lavish giver that owes all her beauty to her habit of giving. Suppose the moon should swallow up and keep to herself all the years of light which the sun gives her and should refuse to share them with us; what would the effect be? She would stop shining. The moment she stopped shining, she would lose all her beauty. All the beauty and the brilliancy of a diamond are caused by its reflecting, or giving away, the light which it receives. It is the same way with the moon. If it should stop shining, or giving away the light it gets from the sun it would hang up in the sky like a great, black, ugly-looking ball. All its brightness and beauty would be gone. Which would we rather be, as we pray: a black ugly ball in God's sky, or a shining light, constantly giving of the light we so abundantly receive?

507. Power of Prayer

A man dreamed, while traveling, that he came to a little church. On the roof was a devil fast asleep. He went along farther and came to a log cabin which was surrounded by devils all wide awake. He asked one of them what it meant. Said the devil, "I will tell you. The fact is that the whole church is asleep, and one devil can take care of all the people; but here are a man and a woman who commune with God in prayer, and they have more power than the whole church."

508. Don't Play God

If the President of the United States invited us to visit him, and we tried to assume the prerogatives of the Presidency ourselves, he'd soon put us out. Yet, this is how some of us act toward God. He has told us to ask, but our asking often demonstrates an attitude of irresponsibility on our part. We ask Him to overrule His natural laws, to act as our servant who must accede to our command. We must never play God when we pray.

509. Seek and Find

Carey, the great missionary to India, found his Savior in a cobbler's workshop at Kackleton. Mary Slessor discovered the riches of Christ in a factory in Dundee; Livingstone found them at his loom in Blantire; and John Bunyan in the streets of Bedford, while he carried on his work as an itinerant mender of household utensils, a tinker. Yes, and God's richest treasure, His only begotten Son, was found by simple shepherds, not in a gilded cradle in a palace of splendor and wealth, but in the manger of a Bethlehem stable. You and I might find that same Savior while carrying on our daily duties in the workshop, office or home. "Seek," said Jesus, "and ye shall find."

510. Selfish Prayer

"I have prayed long for the conversion of my husband," said a woman, "but he's as far off from conversion as ever." "Why do you want your husband converted?" she was asked. "Oh," she replied, "it would be so nice. How different the house would be." "You are forgetting," was the rebuke, "the good of your husband and the glory of God. You appear to be thinking mainly of yourself. Pray for his conversion simply for the glory of God and your husband's need of a Savior."

Preacher

511. A Question for the Preacher

When the Rev. George Pentecost had finished a discourse in the city of Edinburgh, Horatius Bonar put his hand upon his shoulder and said, "You love to preach to men, don't you?" and Dr. Pentecost answered, "Yes." Then Mr. Bonar said, "Do you love the men you preach to?"

512. The Lord's Servant

One day as G. Campbell Morgan prayed, the Lord seemed to say to him, "Which do you want to be—a servant of mine or a great preacher?" Morgan replied, "May I not be both, Lord?" A spiritual struggle ensued as he thought, God may want me to be an unknown minister in an obscure place. Then Morgan submissively prayed, "O Lord, my greatest wish is to be a servant of Thine!" The Lord responded by making him one of the greatest preachers of his time.

513. Near the Gates of Heaven

A certain person listening to Bramwell speak asked another in the audience how it was that Bramwell had something that was new to tell every time he preached.

"Why," said he, "you see, Brother Bramwell lives so near the gates of heaven that he hears a great many things that we don't get near enough to hear anything about." Is this true of you and me or are we near enough to hear God when He speaks?

514. Blot Him Out!

Dr. J.H. Jowett, speaking of the time when he was in Northfield, says, "I went out early one morning to conduct a camp meeting away off in the woods. The camp dwellers were two or three hundred men from the Water Street Mission in New York. At the beginning of the service, prayer was offered for me, and the supplication opened with these inspired words: 'O Lord, we thank Thee for our brother. Now blot him out.' Then the prayer continued: 'Reveal Thy glory to us in such blazing splendor that he shall be forgotten.' "

515. Skeptic Converted

A minister preached a sermon one evening and went home utterly discouraged. He felt that he was a failure in the ministry, though at the same time he was greatly burdened for the lost. Some time past midnight his doorbell rang, and the leader of the choir, who was known as a bit of a skeptic, came to him saying, "Doctor, I am in agony concerning my soul. Your sermon tonight has convicted me of my sin, and I must have help or I shall die." In a very short time he was rejoicing in Christ. When asked what it was in the sermon that had impressed him, he said, "It was not so much what you said as the way you said it. I could see by the look in your eye and by the very pathos in your voice that you were longing for men to be saved, and I could not resist your message."

516. Failing at His Job

A young preacher fresh from seminary went to the front as a chaplain. He announced to the soldiers that he would let them choose whether they wanted him to preach a sermon or tell them funny stories. A tall, blunt-speaking fellow arose and said, "If you have come three thousand miles to talk to a bunch of soldiers, some of whom are going into eternity within three days, and you don't know whether to preach to them or tell them funny stories, I suspect you had just better go ahead and tell something funny."

517. Sleepy Preachers

"How can I get crowds to attend my services?" asked a young preacher of John Wesley. Replied Wesley, "Get on fire and people will come out to see you burn." It is pathetic that we have so many sleepy preachers and noiseless sermons. Henry Ward Beecher used to say,

"If a man sleeps under my preaching, I do not send a boy to wake him up, but I feel that a boy had better come and wake me up." We need resounding preaching and testifying so everybody can hear and some by the grace of God may heed.

518. The Humble Preacher

Dr. Westfield, the Bishop of Bristol in the reign of Charles I, was so excellent a preacher that he was called "a born orator." Yet he was so conscious of his own insufficiency that he never ascended the pulpit without trembling, even when he had been fifty years a preacher. Preaching once before the King at Oxford, he fainted away. His Majesty awaited his recovery, and then heard a sermon that powerfully moved him. The more conscious a preacher is of his own weakness, the more powerful and effective may be the message that he preaches.

519. Serve and Please Only One

A young man had just become pastor of a large church. At a reception given him by his people, one of the gossips, a woman with a dangerous tongue, came up and said, "I do not understand how you dared attempt the task of pleasing seven hundred people." Quick as a flash the Lord gave him the answer. He replied, "I did not come to this city to please seven hundred people. I have to please only One; and if I please Him, all will be well."

520. Importance of Messenger

A tight-fisted Christian, annoyed by the appeals of his preacher for funds, burst out one day, "Pastor, doesn't the Bible declare that the water of life is free, that grace is without money?" "Yes," replied the preacher, "but it takes pipes to channel the water to the people, and pipes cost money."

521. Each His Own Way

Two ministers, given to arguing about their respective faiths, were in a very heated discussion. "That's all right," said one calmly. "We'll just agree to disagree. After all, we're both doing the Lord's work— you in your way and I in His." Too many of us are tempted to feel and act that way. This type of behavior often is a manifestation of the attitude that we know in full, that we prophesy in full—that we are superior even to the Apostle Paul, although we may not say that in so many words.

522. Increasing by Decreasing

A minister who had to move to an obscure country parish in England because of ill health never gained acceptance among the villagers whom he sought to serve. Being unable to do much work, he procured a preacher from Wales who attracted large congregations. His family was a little jealous of this unexpected preference, but he rebuked them. "Take me to hear him," he said. "God honors him, and I will honor him. Have you ever studied that text, 'He must increase, but I must decrease'? 'A man can receive nothing except it be given him from heaven.' " How many preachers would be able to accept a more popular man in their pulpit in that spirit?

523. Delivered from Fear of Man

Bishop Latimer once preached a sermon before King Henry VIII that greatly offended his royal auditor by its plainness. The King ordered him to preach again the next Sunday and to make public apology for his offense. The Bishop ascended the pulpit and read his text, and thus began his sermon: "Hugh Latimer, dost thou know before whom thou art this day to speak? To the high and mighty Monarch, the King's most excellent Majesty, who can take away thy life if thou offendest. Therefore take heed that thou speakest not a word that may displease. But then, consider well, Hugh! Dost thou not know from whom thou comest—upon whose message thou art sent? Even by the great and mighty God, who is all-present and beholdeth all thy ways, and who is able to cast thy soul into hell! Therefore take care that thou deliverest thy message faithfully." And so beginning, he preached over again, but with increased energy, the self-same sermon he had preached the week before. The fear of God delivered him from the fear of man.

524. One of the Rarities

One day a very learned preacher was met by an illiterate preacher who despised education. "Sir, you have been to college, I suppose?" "Yes, sir," was the reply. "I am thankful," replied the illiterate preacher, "that the Lord opened my mouth without any learning." "A similar event," answered the learned clergyman, "took place in Balaam's time, when his ass spoke; but such things are of rare occurrence in the present day. Maybe you are one of the rarities."

525. Preachers Consider!

What Woodrow Wilson said about preachers is worthy of the careful consideration of every one of us: "When I hear some of the things which young men say to men by way of putting the arguments to themselves for going into the ministry, I think they are talking of another profession. Their motive is to do something. I know you do not have to be anything in particular to be a lawyer. You do not have to be anything in particular, except a kind-hearted man, perhaps, to be a physician, nor undergo any strong spiritual change in order to be a merchant. The only profession which consists in being something is the ministry of our Lord and Savior— and it does not consist of anything else. That conception of the ministry which rubs all the marks off and mixes him in the crowd so that you cannot pick him out, is a process of eliminating the ministry itself."

526. The Proper Attitude

A church was in need of a pastor. A candidate came who preached on hell. The next Sunday another candidate came whose sermon was also on hell, and his fundamental teaching was the same as that of the first one. When the members of the church were called upon to vote, they voted for the second candidate. When they were asked why, the answer was, "The first one spoke as if he were glad that people were going to hell, while the second seemed sorry for it."

527. The Divine Commission

An examining committee of ministers once met to determine the qualifications of Billy Sunday for ordination as a gospel minister. Among other questions fired at the world-famous baseball player was a request that he identify a well-known church father and name some of his writings. Billy was stumped. After fumbling around for a moment, he looked up with a twinkle in his eye and said, "I never heard of him. He was never on my team." The learned theologians deliberated together, but found it hard to make a decision. Finally, one of them moved that Billy Sunday be recommended for ordination, adding, "He has already won more souls for Christ than the whole shebang of us put together." The secret—he was sent by God.

528. A Spiritual Lesson

A preacher was watching an old man trout-fishing, briskly pulling them in one after the other. "You manage it cleverly, old friend," said the preacher. "I passed a good many fishermen below who don't seem to be catching anything." The old man lifted himself up and stuck his rod in the ground. "Well, you see, sir," he said, "there are three rules for trout fishing: first, keep yourself out of sight; the second is, keep yourself farther out of sight; and the third is, keep yourself still farther out of sight. Then you'll do it."

529. *Feed, Don't Beat the Sheep*

We preachers desperately need the advice which an aged minister gave a young man who was just entering upon his life work as a shepherd of God's flock. "My son," he said, "feed the sheep; do not beat them. If a sheep is well fed, he can endure and will submit to some harsh treatment, but to starve and beat him at the same time is likely to prove fatal."

Preaching

530. The Archbishop and the Actor

Said an archbishop to the manager of the acting group, "Tell me, how is it that you actors hold the attention of your audience so vividly that you cause them to think of things imaginary as if they were real, while we of the church speak of things that are real but our congregations take them as imaginary?" The reason is plain," answered the actor. "We actors speak of things imaginary as if they were real; while too many in the pulpit speak of things real as if they were imaginary." It was said of one famous old preacher, "He showed us the fires of hell, and then he swept our souls up to the gates of heaven." When you talk about Christ, you have to believe in the transforming power of the gospel if you expect to convince anyone of its power to save.

531. Practice What You Preach

A fountain pen salesman persuaded a merchant to order five hundred pens. He was writing the order in his notebook when suddenly the merchant exclaimed, "Hold on! I'm cancelling that order!" and turned to wait on a customer. The salesman left the store in angry perplexity. Later, the merchant's bookkeeper asked, "Why did you cancel that pen order?" "Why?" responded the man. "Because he talked pens to me for a half-hour, using a number of forcible arguments, and then booked my order with a lead pencil."

532. Applied Religion

On a certain occasion Gladstone said: "One thing I have against the clergy . . . I think they are not severe enough on congregations. They do not sufficiently lay upon the souls and consciences of their hearts and bring up their whole lives and actions to the bar of conscience. The class of sermons which I think are most needed are of the class which once offended Lord Melbourne. He was seen coming from church in the country in great anger. Finding a friend, he exclaimed, 'It is too bad; I have always been a supporter of the church, and I have always upheld the clergy, but it is really too bad to have to listen to a sermon like that we have heard this morning. Why, the preacher actually insisted upon applying religion to a man's private life!' But that is the kind of preaching which I like best, the kind of preaching which men need most, but it is also the kind of which they get the least."

533. Preach the Gospel

A young minister in a college town was embarrassed by the thought of criticism from his cultured congregation. He sought counsel from his father, a wise old minister, saying, "Dad, I am handicapped in my ministry in the pulpit I am now serving. If I cite anything from geology, there is Prof. A, teacher of this science, right before me. If I use an illustration from Roman mythology, there is Prof. B ready to trip me up for any little inaccuracy. If I mention something in English literature that pleases me, I am cowered by the presence of the learned man that teaches that branch. What shall I do?" The sagacious old man replied, "Do not be discouraged; preach the gospel. They probably know very little of that."

534. Dignity in Simplicity

John Wesley's preaching was marked by his constant use of the plainest, simplest words our language affords. Writing to one whose style was very high-sounding he said, "When I had been a member of the university about ten years I wrote and talked much as you do now, but when I talked to plain people, I observed that they gaped and stared. This quickly obliged me to alter my style and adopt the language of those I spoke to; and yet there is a dignity in this simplicity which is not disagreeable to those of the highest rank." Another preacher said, "If you preach so that the simplest person in the audience can understand you, the most educated is also sure to get the message."

535. The Simple Message

A minister felt that the words he spoke from Sunday to Sunday were not bearing the fruit they should. One Saturday morning after he had finished writing his sermon, the thought occurred to him, "Perhaps I shoot too high. I will go down and see if Betty can understand it." Betty was a trusted kitchen helper. He went to the kitchen and called her to come and hear his sermon. She hesitated but came when he insisted. After he had read a few sentences he asked, "Do you understand that?" "No," she replied. He repeated the idea in simpler language and then asked her if she saw it. "I see it a little," she said. Again he simplified it. She saw it more clearly and showed deep interest but said to him, "Plane it down a little more." And once again he simplified it. Then she exclaimed with ecstasy, "Now I see it! Now I understand it!" He returned to his study and rewrote his sermon in the simple style that Betty could understand. On Sunday morning he went to church in fear and trembling lest his people should be contemptuous of his sermon but he fully resolved to try the experiment. To his surprise, he found he received better attention than ever before, and there were tears in the eyes of many of his congregation. From that time on, he changed his style of language and had no further cause to feel that his work was unsuccessful. Clarity of thought and expression do not rob our testimony of its depth and significance. A witness for Christ need never fear oversimplification.

536. The Old Time Gospel

A critic told a renowned evangelist, "Your preaching has put Christianity back one hundred years." The evangelist replied, "That's not back far enough. We must go back to the cross of Christ and to the 'faith which was once delivered to the saints.' "

537. Preach to Broken Hearts

That forthright English clergyman, Dr. R. W. Dale, made this response to a young preacher who insisted that ministers must preach relevantly, to the times. "Young man, don't preach to the times. Go and preach to broken hearts and you will preach relevantly."

538. Lesson in Homiletics

At the close of a service, a preacher was stopped by a gentleman who, after conceding that the sermon possessed certain commendable features, added, "But it had one noticeable defect!" The startled minister, on inquiring what this defect was, received the following reply: "I am a Jew. I have only recently been born again. Up to that time I attended the synagogue. But there was really nothing in your sermon that I could not have heard in the synagogue, nothing that a Jewish rabbi might not have preached." "That," said the preacher in later years, "was the greatest lesson in homiletics I was ever taught."

539. Watch Your Choice of Words

Once that great Puritan preacher, Thomas Manton, had to speak before the Lord Mayor and Aldermen of London. He chose a subject in which he had an opportunity of displaying his learning and judgment. He was heard with admiration by the intelligent part of his audience, but as he was returning from dinner with the Lord Mayor, a poor man pulled him by the sleeve and asked if he were the gentleman that preached the sermon. He replied that he was. "Sir," said the man, "I came with the hopes of getting some good to my soul, but I was greatly disappointed, for I could not get a great deal of what you said; you were quite above my understanding." "Friend," said Dr. Manton, "if I have not given you a sermon, you have given me one. By the grace of God, I will not play the fool in such a manner again."

540. Correcting Not Conforming

Someone told G. Campbell Morgan that the preacher must catch the spirit of the age. Immediately this great preacher answered, "God forgive the preacher who does that. The preacher's business is to correct the spirit of the age." May we add that a witness for Christ must endeavor thoroughly to understand the spirit of the age—without conforming to it—in order to know what to correct.

541. Lifting Christ before Men

James Inglis was a graduate of Edinburgh University, learned and eloquent. He became the most popular preacher in Detroit, Michigan. Eager listeners filled his church to overflowing. One day, when he was preparing sermons for the following Sunday, it seemed as though a voice said to him, "James Inglis, whom are you preaching?" Startled, he answered, "I am preaching good theology." "I did not ask what you are preaching, but whom you are preaching." Inglis answered, "I am preaching the gospel." Again the voice said, "I did not ask you what you are preaching; I asked whom you are preaching." Silent, with bowed head, the preacher sat for a long time. Then rousing himself he cried, "O my God, I am preaching James Inglis, but henceforth I will preach Christ and Him crucified." Inglis went to a chest of drawers in his study, took his eloquent sermons from the files and burned them one by one. From that day he turned his back upon popularity and gave himself wholly to God's service by lifting Christ before men. God honored his consecration by giving him ever-widening influence.

542. A Sermon Lived

A minister preached a powerful sermon on the surrendered life. As he made an appeal to his hearers to make the surrender, a woman sitting near another woman said, "That is excellent preaching, but I wonder if such a life is possible?" The other woman smiled back at her and said, "Well, I know the preacher lives such a life because I happen to be his wife."

543. A Preacher's First Concern

Two young men broke into a photo studio one Sunday night. They murdered the aged owner and robbed the cash drawer. Headlines of the crime appeared on the front page of Monday morning's papers. The two youths had been apprehended and charged with murder. Because their names seemed familiar to the secretary of a local church, she looked them up in the visitor's book. Sure enough, they had attended the church on Sunday morning and that night they committed murder! The pastor's subject that morning had been "An Educated Ministry." Only God knows what the end result might have been if the minister had preached on Christ's power to save and to change sinful hearts.

544. Getting along Famously

Many people today treat religion as a matter of convenience. They have to belong somewhere to be considered respectable. A clergyman once met an old schoolmate of whose activities he had long been ignorant, and finding him a judge of good standing congratulated him upon his success in life. As they were parting, the clergyman said to him, "And best of all, Judge, I find you are a member of our church." "Well," said the judge, "that's more a matter of chance than anything else. You see, when I was getting established in my profession, my wife and I thought we ought to join a church—it was the respectable thing to do. So, after mature deliberation, we settled down with a certain denomination and got on very well for a time; but they kept harping on *faith,* till we pretty soon discovered that they required more *faith* than we had; so it became necessary to make a change. We turned the matter over considerably and at last, for various reasons, made up our minds to join another denomination. Here we found the demand was *work, work* incessantly; and it was presently apparent that they demanded more *work* than we were able to perform. It was with great reluctance that we concluded that we must change again, and we cast about with much caution, that this move might be final. At last we decided to connect ourselves with your church, sir, and have gotten along famously ever since *without* either *faith* or *works.*"

545. A Sermon without the Gospel

The story is told of three people who went into a church. The first was a business man who had failed and was contemplating suicide. The second was a prodigal youth, deep in sin, who was planning a robbery. The third was a young woman who was tempted to depart from the path of virtue. The service started. The choir arose and sang an anthem about building the walls of Zion. The minister addressed an eloquent prayer to the Lord and then preached on the theme, "Is Mars Inhabited?" Afterward, the businessman committed suicide, the boy stole and landed in jail, and the young woman began a life of moral shame. What might have happened if only the gospel of personal salvation in Christ had been preached!

546. The Sermon's Omission

Years ago it was the custom in a certain theological college for the student who had preached a sermon in class to go into the principal's office next morning for a quiet talk about his work. On one such occasion, the revered and saintly old principal said to the young man before him, "It was a good sermon you gave yesterday; the truth you dealt with was well-arranged and well presented. But your sermon had one omission, a grave one. There was no word in it for a poor sinner like me."

547. Preach It Again

A minister, on taking a new church, was highly complimented on his first sermon. A number of people told him it was just what the congregation needed. The next Sunday he preached well again, but the congregation was greatly puzzled because he preached the same sermon as before. The third Sunday, when the same sermon was preached again, the session waited on the preacher for an explanation. He said, "Why, yes it is the same sermon. You told me the first Sunday how much you needed just that, and I watched all week for some change in your lives, but there was none, so I preached it again. I watched all next week; still no change; and I don't see any yet. Don't you think I'd better prepare to preach it again next Sunday?"

548. Not Deep—But Muddy

"Isn't Rev. So-and-so a deep preacher?" asked a friend. "Well," replied the other smiling. "I'll tell you a story. When I was a boy I was amusing myself with some other boys in a pool. Some of them were going farther out than I was disposed to go, and I was frightened. To a man who was passing by I called out, 'Is the pool deep?' 'No, son,' he replied, 'it's only muddy.' "

549. Invitation—Important

A layman visited a great city church in Ohio during a business trip. After the service he congratulated the minister on his service and sermon. "But," said the manufacturer, "if you were my salesman, I'd discharge you. You got my attention by your appearance, voice, and manner; your prayer, reading, and logical discourse aroused my interest; you warmed my heart with a desire for what you preached; then you stopped without asking me to do something about it. In business, the important thing is to get people to sign on the dotted line."

550. Should Sermons Offend?

"I always write my sermons," said one preacher to another, "and then carefully revise them, so that if anything is written that might offend any of my hearers, I may at once erase it." The older preacher friend replied, "Do you mean that forcible statements, either of your own or from Scripture, concerning sin, the cross, and the judgment to come, are either toned down or avoided?" "Yes," replied the young novice clergyman. "If I think they will offend anyone, I do so."

551. Dictionary Sermon

A woman who went to hear a visiting preacher took along her Bible so that she might refer to any Scripture passages he happened to mention. On coming away from the service she said to a friend, "I should have left my Bible home today and brought my dictionary. The doctor does not deal in Scripture but in such learned words and phrases that you need the help of an interpreter to render them intelligible."

552. Flying on One Wing

Dr. Andrew Bonar told a story of a plain man in one of the Scottish Presbyterian country churches who had learned the precious doctrine of Christ's promised return for His own. He had spent a Sunday in Edinburgh to play the part of a sermon taster. When he returned to his village, the people asked him how he liked the Edinburgh preachers. His reply was, "They all fly on one wing. They all preach the first coming of Christ, but they do not preach His second coming."

553. Man Can't Live on Flowers

It's fruit that you want when you present the gospel. Someone who had heard a moving sermon was asked by a friend what he remembered of it. "Truly," he said, "I remember nothing at all, but I am a different man as a result of it." Contrast that with what another man answered when he was asked what he thought of a sermon that had produced a great sensation among the congregation. His reply may hold an important lesson for some of us. "Very fine, sir; but a man cannot live upon flowers."

554. Unfinished Sermon

"Is the sermon done?" asked one member of the congregation of another. "No, the preacher is done, but the sermon has to be worked out in our lives," replied the practical listener.

555. No Rain!

An Indian had attended services one Sunday morning. The sermon which contained very little in the way of spiritual food had been rather loud in spots. The Indian, a good Christian, was not impressed. When asked how he liked the sermon, he said, "High wind, big thunder, no rain."

556. Love Them All?

A brilliant, liberal preacher pleasing his congregation with flowery phrases as he talked on the importance of breadth of view and the danger of bigoted opinions, was bidding farewell to them as he was about to leave for a new parish. A young man approached him and said, "Pastor, I am sorry we are losing you. Before you came, I did not care for God, man, or the devil, but through your delightful sermons I have learned to love them all!" Unfortunately, that is the kind of messengers many churches have.

557. Keep It Simple

Vincent Ferrier, an eloquent preacher of the fifteenth century, was called to preach before a high dignitary of state. He took care to prepare his sermon according to the rules of oratory, but it was a notable failure. Next day he preached in his usual style, without pretentiousness, and electrified his hearers. The dignitary, who had heard him on both occasions, asked him how he could account for so great a difference in his sermons. He answered, "Yesterday Vincent Ferrier preached; today Jesus Christ."

Pride

558. Self-Proclaimed Expert

It is said that Billie Burke, the Hollywood actress, was enjoying a transatlantic ocean voyage when she noticed a man at the next table was suffering from a bad cold. "Uncomfortable?" she asked sympathetically. The man nodded. "I'll tell you what to do for it," she offered. "Go back to your stateroom and drink a lot of orange juice. Take five aspirin tablets. Cover yourself with all the blankets you can find. Sweat the cold out. I know what I'm talking about. I'm Billie Burke of Hollywood." The man smiled warmly and said, "Thanks. I'm Dr. Mayo of the Mayo Clinic!"

559. Pride Goeth before a Fall

The Emperor Justinian built the Church of St. Sophia, that gem of human architecture. He collected marble and treasures from all over the world to make it beautiful. At last the moment for dedication arrived. The words uttered by Justinian seemed full of humility as he said that all had been done for the glory of God. But as he allowed his eyes to drink in the beauty of the building, he could hardly contain himself. Someone heard him whisper, "Solomon, I have surpassed thee."

560. That Isn't Sin

Paul is telling the Corinthians that he who adds to the Scriptures is likely to be a proud and arrogant person, one who looks down upon others because they lack his abilities. He is in the same class as the young girl who went to her priest and confessed her sin of vanity. "What makes you think that?" asked the priest. "Because every morning, when I look into the mirror," she replied, "I think how beautiful I am." "Don't worry" said the priest, "that isn't sin; that's just a mistake." How true it is that those who are the proudest in their assumption of the right to think and act above what is written are the most mistaken. They need to humbly accept what God says of them in His Word.

561. I Did It All Myself

A young woman who won a coveted award smiled when her mother said, "I was praying you would get it." "Well, thank you," she replied, "but I earned this by my own hard work." Some people feel so sure of their self-sufficiency that they resent any implication that they owe God a word of thanks for the good things that come their way. Such an attitude could be justified only if a person were able to say, "I brought myself into the world, I endowed myself with all my talents and abilities, I raised myself, taught myself all I know, and control my present and future."

562. A Bag Tied in the Middle

A New Zealand preacher described a Pharisee as being like a bag tied in the middle. Anything put into the top will not reach the bottom. The Pharisee opens his mouth wide when he prays, but his heart is tightly shut. With his lips he asks for things that his heart does not really desire. If God were to give him the spiritual blessings he asks for, it would only be a waste of good gifts, for they could not get to the bottom of the bag. His pride would choke them off, and they would never touch his heart.

563. Need of Squeaky Shoes

Whether we want to recognize it or not, many of us are like the Christian who went to the village merchant to purchase a pair of shoes. He was outfitted with a suitable pair and went away happy. Some weeks later he brought the shoes back. "Didn't they fit? Weren't they good?" asked the merchant. "Yes." "Then why are you returning them?" "Because they don't have a squeak." It appeared the man wanted a pair of shoes that would squeak as he walked up the aisle of the church. He wanted something that would draw attention to himself.

564. The Wise Philosopher

It only takes a fifty-cent piece held close to your eye to blind you to the sight of the sun. Alexander the Great, full of pride over his recent triumphs, once came upon that wise philosopher Diogenes who was basking in the glory of the noonday sun. The powerful Alexander condescended to speak to the philosopher, asking if there was anything he could do for Diogenes. "Yes," was the reply. "Alexander can step aside from between me and the sunshine." Diogenes was wise in this respect. Alexander was great in conquest, but he was a fool to think he was more important to Diogenes than the sun.

565. Spiritual Pride

Too many of us are like the gourd that wound itself around a lofty palm tree, and in a few weeks climbed to the very top. "How old are you?" asked the gourd. "About one hundred years," said the palm. "About one hundred years, and no taller! Look, I have grown as tall as you in fewer days than you count years." "I know that well," replied the palm. "Every summer of my life a gourd has climbed up around me as proud as you are, and as short-lived as you will be."

566. The Proud Banker

A very richly dressed man stepped into a streetcar and with a haughty air sat down beside an old man who was poorly clad. When the conductor collected the fares he said to him in a loud voice, "Let me off at my bank." Evidently knowing him, the conductor assured him he would do so. Then he reached for the fare of the poorly clothed man next to him. He evidently was just as well known to the conductor as the banker, and so he said, "Please let me off at my peanut-stand, will you, Mister?" "Yes, George," was the distinct but kindly reply. The proud man didn't smile, but all the other passengers seemed suddenly possessed with unusual cheerfulness. This rich man had a right and a duty to dress in keeping with his station; he was not sinful because he owned a bank; but it was definitely wrong for him to seek to impress others with his importance. Instead he earned their ridicule.

567. Man Is Full of Himself

A householder left a patch of land completely unattended. On returning from a journey he found it full of stones, old bottles, and other rubbish. Though he had never attempted to garden before, he took a spade and began to dig up the ground and clear away the debris. Then he sowed a few seeds. With tremendous excitement he watched his garden patch. When at last he saw little shoots pushing up through the ground he was almost in ecstasy. Gradually the plants grew and at last the flowers appeared. To him it looked beautiful. One day his pastor stopped by. He couldn't get the pastor excited about his garden. Finally the pastor said, "Yes, it is wonderful what Almighty God does with a patch of ground like that." "Oh, it is,"

said the man, "but I wish you had seen this place when the Almighty had it all to Himself!" Unfortunately, the man failed to acknowledge that it was man's fault the patch of ground was such an eyesore in the first place. But it's true that God does not choose to make a garden without a gardener. The beauties of nature may occasionally surpass man's best efforts. A field of wild flowers in bloom shows the quality God has put into nature. But in most instances God commits the raw elements to man and lets him bring beauty, order, and usefulness out of them.

568. The Showpiece

A woman came into a milliner's store and wanted to have the trimming on her new hat changed, saying it had been placed on the wrong side. "But," said the saleslady, "the trimming is on the left side. That is where it ought to be." "It doesn't make any difference where it ought to be; it's got to be on the church side." "Church side!" gasped the astonished girl. "Yes, I sit next to the wall. I want it on the other side so the whole congregation can see it."

569. Praise of Self

If we stopped to listen to God's and others' opinions of us, it would have a sobering effect, and we would surely be less critical of others. We would not be like Rabbi Simeon who said, "The world is not worth thirty righteous persons such as our father Abraham. If there were only twenty righteous persons in the world, I and my son should be of the number. If there were only ten, I and my son should be of them, if there were only five, I and my son should be of the five. If there were but two, I and my son would be those two, and if there were but one, myself should be that one." Praise of self results in criticism of others.

570. The Superior Dress

All of us readily admit that Christianity advocates justice, equality, and opportunity for all. When it comes to practicing it, do we really mean what we preach, or are we like the little Sunday school girl who was observed by her teacher trying to move as far away as possible from the little girl next to her? They were both poor children, neatly but plainly dressed. The teacher said, "What is the matter? Why don't you sit still?" "Oh," she replied, "I have a silk dress, and she has a cotton one, and I don't want her to sit by me."

Priorities

571. Choice Made the Difference

Dr. Pierce Harris, a former pastor of the First Methodist Church of Atlanta, Georgia, preached to some prisoners. One of the prisoners got up and introduced him to the others with these words: "Several years ago, two boys lived in a town in north Georgia. They went to the same school, played together and attended the same Sunday school. One dropped out of Sunday school and said that it was 'sissy stuff.' The other boy kept on going. One rejected Christ; the other accepted Him. The boy who rejected Christ is making this introduction today. The boy who accepted Christ is the honored preacher who will speak to us today!" Choice made the difference.

572. Christian Grammar

The Bishop of Cambridge once taught a class. He said, "We have all learned to say in school: 'First Person—I; Second Person—You; Third Person—He.' But that is wrong in Christian grammar, so wrong that, to put it right, one has to turn it upside down. The Christian grammar is: 'First Person—He; Second Person—You; Third Person—I,' and 'He' means God, the First Person in the first place. Then 'You' means one's fellowman, and 'I' myself comes last."

573. Remove the Cup

Leonardo da Vinci once took a friend of his to see his masterpiece of the "Last Supper." The friend's first comment was, "The most striking thing in the picture is the cup." The artist immediately took his brush and wiped out the cup, saying, "Nothing in my painting shall attract more attention than the face of my Master."

574. Love of Money

A father was in the basement of his daughter's house trying to fix something for her when the blow torch exploded and he was badly burned. As if that was not enough, the daughter is suing her father for damages to get all the money that she can out of him. This is a perfect illustration of what happens when you put money, material things, first in your life.

575. Seeking God

A prominent American who was visiting Argentina was asked by the president of the republic, "Why has South America gotten on so poorly and North America so well? What do you think is the reason?" The visitor replied, "I think the reason is the fact that the Spaniards came to South America seeking gold, while the Pilgrim Fathers came to North America seeking God."

576. Tigers or Souls

Two men returning from India got into conversation. One was a sportsman and the other a missionary. "I've been in India for twenty-five years, and I never saw one of the natives converted as you Christians claim," said the sportsman. "That's queer," said the missionary. "Did you ever see a tiger?" "Hundreds of them," was the reply, "and I've shot dozens of them." "Well, I've been in India for many years," said the missionary, "but I've never seen a tiger. But under the power of the gospel of Christ I've seen hundreds of the natives of India turn to the Savior." You see, one was looking for tigers, the other was looking for souls.

577. Worldly Standard

The story is told of a Persian prince who, dressed as a poor man, went to a feast. He was pushed about, could not get to the table, and soon had to withdraw. He went home, dressed himself in his best cloth-of-gold robe and jewelled slippers, and returned to the feast. The guests made room for him, and the host rushing up cried, "Welcome, my lord! What will your lordship please to eat?" The prince stuck out his jewelled foot and said in a mocking tone, "Welcome, my lord slipper!" Then fingering his golden robe, "Welcome, my lord robe! What will your lordship please to eat?" Turning to his surprised host he said, "You ought to ask my lordly clothes what they would like to eat since the welcome was solely to them."

578. Man, You're a Fool

A student of ancient Greek in an English university surprised his teacher by his rapid grasp of the subject. When asked if someone were helping him, he mentioned his uncle. The professor said he'd like to meet him, and a date was set. The teacher was astounded with the uncle's knowledge of Greek. "What work do you do?" he asked. "I'm an itinerant preacher. I preach God's Word." Dismayed that such a gifted man should waste his time preaching, the professor blurted out, "Man, you're a fool!" The wise preacher retorted, "In which world, Professor?"

579. Man's Greatest Possession

Man's greatest possession is an unhindered relationship with God. I think of two friends who were passing a large tract of land that belonged to one of them. "What do you think this land and the buildings cost me?" asked the landowner. "I don't know what they cost you in money," replied his friend, "but I think I know what they cost you otherwise." "What?" "They cost you your soul," was the sorrowful reply.

580. Ready to Endure

Misjudged by a fellow missionary, David Livingstone gave up his house and garden at Mabotsa, with all the toil and money they had cost him, rather than have any scandal before the heathen. He began in a new place the laborious building of a house and school, and gathered the people around him. His colleague was so struck with his generosity that he said if he had known his intention, he never would have spoken a word against him. Parting with his garden cost Livingstone a great pang. "I like a garden," he wrote, "but Paradise will make amends for all our privations here." Paul says, "I endure all things for the elect's sakes, that they may also obtain the salvation which is in Christ Jesus" (2 Tim. 2:10).

581. Right Priorities

The time to begin to do the things that are important in your life is the very moment you become a believer in Jesus Christ. Your first thought should be, "This life on earth is not forever; therefore the things that count for eternity will have priority in my life." Don't be like someone who greatly distinguished himself in worldly achievements. In his last moments, he exclaimed, "I have provided in the course of my life for everything except death; and now, alas! I am to die, although entirely unprepared." How or when one dies is not important. The important thing is to prepare for the unavoidable happening while you are alive.

582. Safe on the Lord's Side

President Lincoln was once told by an associate, "I am very anxious that the Lord should be on our side." "Oh," said Mr. Lincoln, "that does not give me the least trouble in the world, sir. The only question is whether we are on the Lord's side. If we are on the Lord's side, we are perfectly safe."

583. Look for Lasting Qualities

A husband volunteered to accompany his wife on a shopping expedition to purchase dress goods for herself and the children. "This is pretty material," said the husband, indicating a colorful print. The wife fingered it briefly and said, "Too flimsy. It won't wear well." "Then how about this?" persisted the man, pointing to another bolt of cloth. "Strong enough," said the wife, "but will it wash?" The husband in his inexperience was allowing himself to be influenced by eye appeal. The wife was looking for more lasting qualities.

584. Satisfied with Second Best

Robert Browning tells of a famous musician who, under financial pressure and the influence of popular demand, lowered his standards and produced some inferior works that brought in ready cash and a measure of success. One evening as he stood on the platform enjoying the applause of the audience, he happened to glance at a private box and see the master, Rossini. His eyes fell and his color rose. The mob applauded, but he knew that the master condemned the cheap and unworthy work.

585. Wrong Choices Are Destructive

You may have read about the war of Troy, but do you know how it was supposed to have started? It was the judgment and choice of Paris that were responsible for it. Beautiful Thetis was getting married to Pileas, the King of the Myrmidons. During their wedding ceremony, says the legend, the golden apple of dispute was given to the most beautiful woman. There were three that sought the prize: Hera, Athena, and Aphrodite. According to the command of Zeus, Paris, the shepherd of Troy, had to choose which of these three was the most beautiful. Hera represented power, Athena wisdom, and Aphrodite pleasure. Paris chose Aphrodite, the goddess of pleasure, and because of this the war of Troy was declared with all its resultant suffering and unhappiness. Because Paris chose pleasure, he brought destruction upon himself and others. This is what many of us choose also, and we suffer alienation from God.

586. Lunch or Appetite?

A poor man had his meager lunch stolen by one of his fellow workers. Hungry after the lunch hour, he sang and praised the Lord, and the workers made fun of him. They said, "My goodness, your very lunch has been stolen from you and you're praising God. What for? You're stupid!" "Oh, no," he said, "I'm not stupid. They may have stolen my lunch, but they couldn't steal my appetite from me."

587. The Christian's Choice

There's much truth in saying that every man is the architect of his own fate. Your choices affect your destiny. Out of a rough block of stone one man may make a beautiful statue, another, gravel. Both products are good and useful under certain conditions. But a statue can be immoral in conception, and gravel can be the grudging and punitive work of a criminal condemned to a rockpile. The point is, whether you are a gifted artist or a competent gravel maker, you can choose whether to use your abilities worthily or unworthily. In building a Christian life you have the same choice.

588. Just an Expensive Casket

A young man asked his minister to officiate at his brother's funeral. "Let me see," said the minister. "Your brother was thirty-two years old?" "Yes." "He worked hard for twenty years, didn't he?" "Yes." "Well, what did he get out of it?" "He left eighty acres of fine land, money in the bank, and thousands of dollars in insurance." "Yes, that's what you get out of it; but what did he get out of it?" "Oh, we are going to buy him an expensive oak casket!"

589. Take Alarm

Thomas Guthrie used to say: "If you find yourself loving any pleasure better than your prayers, any book better than the Bible, any house better than the house of God, any table better than the Lord's table, any person better than Christ, any indulgence better than the hope of heaven—take alarm."

590. Feed the Hungry

"Why do you insist upon having the largest piece of pie, Harry?" asked a mother reprovingly. "Isn't your big brother entitled to it?" "No, Mama, not the way it looks to me," replied Harry. "He was eating pie three years before I was born." Preacher, feed the new Christians who are hungry for the Word, a double portion of it.

Purity

591. Kept Pure

A woman from Berne, Switzerland, tells us this story of her country's flower, the edelweiss. The very name of this plant is a story in itself. Edelweiss is a compound word which in the German means "noble and white." It is a small perennial herb of the aster family whose pure white blossom must be sought after, since it nestles in the highest snowy crags of the Alps. It is so absolutely white that it blends perfectly with its environment, losing its identifying characteristics completely in its surroundings. Even when picked and pressed in paper for preservation, it remains free from discoloration for many years. If we would be like the edelweiss, we must keep ourselves pure and noble, striving to attain the heights with God. Then, as He keeps us pure in heart and motive, He will enable us to accept with humility the loss of our own status in the scope of His larger landscape.

592. A Pure Heart

A girl in Sunday school had read the Beatitudes in Matthew. She was asked which of the things mentioned she would most like to have. She said, "A pure heart." When asked why she preferred that, she said, "If my heart were pure, I believe I would have all the other virtues mentioned in this chapter."

593. The Healthy Eye

What our Savior wanted to teach by the analogy of the eye and the lamp is that everything we see depends on the condition of the lamp. If the lamp is dim, we won't see very clearly. If our eye is dim, diseased, the whole body will be darkened. Similarly, if the lamp is burning brightly, we see things as they are. We recognize the books upon the table and the photographs upon the wall. But if the lamp is flickering or smoky, everything is distorted or obscured; so it is with the eye. If we are color-blind, we cannot see the glorious redness of the rose. If we are near-sighted, we cannot see the friend who is signaling to us from a little distance. If we suffer from impending cataracts, we cannot clearly distinguish a friend sitting next to us. Still, the rose is red, though we cannot see it in our color blindness. Still, the friend is waving to us or seated by our side. There is nothing the matter with reality. The trouble is that we are seeing badly. Now the Lord tells us that the eye can be either single (healthy), or it can be evil. As the eye brings good or evil impressions to the body so the heart of man is that organ by which the spiritual self is enlightened. The heart can be single or evil.

191

Quotes

594. Reason for a Mirror

Socrates, that great father of philosophy, advised young men to carry a mirror. If they were good looking, they should remind themselves that an ugly life was out of keeping with good looks. If their appearance was not attractive, they were told to remember that handsome actions offset ugly looks.

595. Humble before God

Moody used to say, "You can always tell when a man is a great way from God—he is always talking about himself, how good he is. But the moment he sees God by the eye of faith, he is down on his knees, and like Job, he cries, 'Behold, I am vile.' " This is not an easy realization to come to—to see that while you may be morally clean you are vile in your own self-righteousness.

596. A Great Man

One of the finest descriptions of a magnanimous man is Emerson's brief characterization of Abraham Lincoln: "His heart was as great as the world, but there was no room in it to hold the memory of a wrong."

597. Secret of Peace

Helen Keller wrote, "If we trust, if we relinquish our will and yield to the Divine will, then we find that we are afloat on a buoyant sea of peace and under us are the everlasting arms."

598. John's Message

Jerome, the Church historian, relates of the Apostle John that when he became old he used to go among the churches and assemblies everywhere repeating the words, "Little children, love one another." His disciples, wearied by the constant repetition, asked him why he always said this. "Because," he replied, "it is the Lord's commandment; and if it only be fulfilled, it is enough."

599. Rich or Poor?

As Beecher said, "No man can tell whether he is rich or poor by turning to his ledger. It is the heart that makes a man rich. He is rich or poor according to what he is, not according to what he has."

600. Not One Grain Too Many

The words of Henry Ward Beecher come to mind in times of trial: "No physician ever weighed out medicine to his patients with half so much care and exactness as God weighs out to us every trial. Not one grain too much does He ever permit to be put on the scale."

601. *Never Choose Sin*

These are the words of Anselm, Archbishop of Canterbury, who died at the beginning of the twelfth century: "If I should see the shame of sin on the one hand, and the pain of hell on the other, and must of necessity choose one, I would rather be thrust into hell without sin than go into heaven with sin."

602. *Two Good Answers*

Someone asked Augustine where God was before the heavens were created. Augustine replied, "He was in Himself." He is indeed that only self-contained Being; for He is the only Infinite One. And when Luther was asked the same question, he answered, "He was creating hell for idle, proud, and inquisitive spirits like you."

603. *Indwelt by Christ*

Martin Luther said, "If anyone knocks at the door of my breast and says, 'Who lives there?' my answer is, 'Jesus Christ lives here, not Martin Luther.' "

Repentance

604. Real Sorrow

Two little boys were playing together one afternoon. They had not been playing long when the larger boy took advantage of his weaker playmate. Georgie, the smaller one, too proud to complain, withdrew some distance and sat by himself, manfully winking back the ready tears. After a short time, the larger boy grew tired of his solitary play and called, "Say, Georgie, come back. I'm sorry." Georgie, warned by previous experience, did not respond to the invitation at once. "Yes," he replied cautiously, "but what kind of sorry? The kind so you won't do it again?"

605. No Retribution

When Robert Southey was a small boy, he tells of another boy in his neighborhood by the name of Jim Dick. A number of children began tormenting Jim one evening, calling him names because of his racial origin. The poor little fellow was reduced to tears and slunk away. One day Southey wanted to go skating, but his skates were broken, and the only boy from whom he could borrow a pair was Jim Dick. "I went and asked him for them," said Southey. " 'Oh, yes, Robert, you may have them,' was his answer.

When I went to return them, I found Jim sitting by the fire in the kitchen reading the Bible. I told him I had returned the skates and thanked him for letting me use them. He looked at me as he took his skates and with tears in his eyes, said, 'Robert, don't ever call me names again,' and immediately left the room. The words pierced my heart; I burst into tears, and from that time resolved never again to abuse a member of a minority group."

606. A Christian's New Nature

A Hindu said to a native missionary, "I am sure if I lead a good life and do what is right, giving up my bad habits, God will be pleased with me and receive me into heaven." "That is the way most people reason today," replied the missionary. "You know the babul tree (a tree with long, sharp thorns). Now, suppose you break off from its branches a hundred or more of the nasty thorns, then will the tree cease to be a babool tree?" "Certainly not." "Suppose you should apparently stop one or another or even many of your evil ways and habits, you would still remain the same like the babool tree. You must have an entirely new nature, must become a new man, in order to please God. Only Christ can give you a new heart." The missionary's reply was sound and scriptural. The message of Christ, His first and only message to sinful man, is his need of repentance.

607. To Repent

Francis Fuller very wisely said, "To repent is to accuse and condemn ourselves; to charge upon ourselves the desert of hell; to take part with God against ourselves, and to justify Him in all that He does against us; to be ashamed and confounded for our sins; to have them ever in our eyes and at all times upon our hearts that we may be in daily sorrow for them; to part with our right hands and eyes, that is, with those pleasurable sins which have been as dear to us as our lives, so as never to have more to do with them, and to hate them, so as to destroy them as things which by nature we are wholly disinclined to. For we naturally love and think well of ourselves, hide our deformities, lessen and excuse our faults, indulge ourselves in the things that please us, are mad upon our lusts, and follow them, though to our own destruction."

608. The Pharisaical Sinner

An evangelist, wanting to comfort someone who had just accepted the Lord, said to him, "You see how even a publican was accepted when he cried for mercy." "Ah," said the man, "but I have been a greater sinner than a publican: I have been a Pharisee!"

609. Too Much or Too Little

A very practical man was known to confess: "I have too much religion or too little; I must either give up what I have or get more. I have too much religion to let me enjoy a worldly life, and too much worldliness to let me enjoy religion." He solved the dilemma triumphantly by a wholehearted acceptance of Christ as his living Lord. He put an end to divided loyalty and doubtful obedience.

610. A Changed Disposition

An excellent story of a good man's deliverance from the tyranny of bad temper is told by Dr. Alexander Whyte in his *James Fraser, Laird of Brea*. It seems that Fraser, a minister, was at times, by his own admission, of a sullen and peevish disposition. One day when he was visiting his people, he called on one of his elders to have a conference with him. All the time Dr. Fraser was talking, the elder sat patting a pet dog to whom he paid more attention than to his minister. When his wife came into the room to give them tea and ventured a word or two in the conversation, he turned on her with an angry look and curt remark that sent her out of the room with reddened cheeks. Fraser rode slowly back home that night giving himself time to think. "After all my evangelical preaching," he said to himself, "to see an elder of mine such a brute at home!" But gradually Fraser began to see that it was a case of like minister like elder; at any rate, in the matter of mulishness and glumness at home. The minister was much later than usual in arriving home that night. But from that time, his whole household connected that night with a great change in the head of the house. A sermon he preached on the following Sunday was so conspicuously blessed to the bad-tempered elder that his household also took immediate note of a miracle. James Fraser and his elder had entered into newness of life.

611. Repent—Not Penance

A minister found some young people reading the Douay Version of the New Testament. On noticing a passage in the chapter which was translated "do penance," where the English Version rendered the same word as "repent," he asked them if they knew the difference between penance and repentance. A short silence followed; then a girl asked, "Is this right? Judas did penance, and went and hanged himself; Peter repented and wept bitterly." The girl had it right. "Repent, therefore, and be converted, that your sins may be blotted out" (Acts 3:19).

612. Wandering Boy

There was a young civil engineer of western Kentucky who assisted his father in his business of railroad prospecting and surveying. As he traveled from place to place, he fell into the society of loose men and acquired intemperate habits, more than his father seemed to be aware of. He shrewdly managed to conceal his evil habits from his parents who were wonderful Christians, the father being the choir leader and the mother a soprano soloist. Once, while the young man was employed on a section of road forty miles from home, it became necessary to lay over from Thursday noon till Monday. His father would be detained till Saturday, reaching home in time for the choir rehearsal. The son, instead of going to his home, went to a bar to begin a spree. The bartender understood his case too well and kept him hidden in his own apartment. When his father came home, he expected to find the boy there. Trouble began when the question, "Where is Harry?" informed the startled mother that he should have come earlier. During the Sunday evening service she was to sing a solo, and by special request—because she sang it so well—her selection was to be, "Where Is My Wandering Boy?" It seemed impossible to her to sing that song under the circumstances. When on Sunday morning, a policeman found Harry, the certainty was no more comforting than the suspense had been. She was advised that he would be "all right tomorrow morning," and that she had better not see him until he sobered up. Toward Sunday night Harry began to come to himself.

His father had hired a man to stay with him and see to his recovery. When Harry learned that his mother had been told of his plight, the information cut him to the heart and helped to sober him. When the bells rang, he decided to go to church. He knew nothing of the evening program. He was still in his working clothes, but no reasoning could dissuade him. His attendant, after making him as presentable as possible, went with him to the service. Entering early by a side door, they found seats in a secluded corner, but not far from the pulpit and the organ. After the usual succession of prayer, anthem, and sermon, the time for the solo came. It was probably the first time in that church that a mother had ever sung out of her own soul's distress:

Oh, where is my wandering boy tonight,

The child of my love and care?

Every word was to her own heart a cruel stab. The congregation caught the feeling of the song, but there was one heart as near to breaking as her own. She sang the last stanza,

Go for my wandering boy tonight,

Go search for him where you will,

But bring him to me with all his blight,

And tell him I love him still.

Oh, where is my wandering boy?

Just then a young man in a woolen shirt, corduroy trousers and jacket made his way down the aisle to the choir stairs with outstretched arms, and sobbing like a child, cried, "Here I am, Mother!" The mother ran down the steps and folded him in her arms. The astonished organist, quick to take in the meaning of the scene, pulled out all his stops and played, "Praise God From Whom All Blessings Flow." The congregation joined in the great doxology, while the father, the pastor, and the friends of the returned prodigal stood by him with moist eyes and welcoming hands.

613. Under Christ's Supervision

A poor German girl announced that she was going to give a piano concert. In order to attract people to come, she mentioned in the advertisements that she was the student of the famous Hungarian professor, Franz Liszt. But it was a falsehood. To her dismay, she learned the professor was going to visit her town on the day before the concert. What should she do now? She went to meet him, confessed her guilt, and asked him to forgive her. The professor answered, "You made a mistake. All of us make mistakes. The only thing that you can do now is to repent; and I believe that you have already repented. Sit down and play." At the beginning, she played with much fear. The professor corrected a few of her mistakes and said, "Now truly you can say that I taught you. Go ahead and play at your concert tomorrow evening, and the last piece will not be played by you, but by your teacher." You are like this girl. You have sinned. There is nothing else you can do but repent. Then you will play the role of your life under the supervision of Christ Himself. The last and the best piece will be played by Him.

Resurrection

614. A Glorious Body

In the days when any country boy could stand in front of a blacksmith's shop and watch with fascinated eyes what happened there, something analogous to the resurrection of the body occurred. The smith would put a rusty, cold, dull piece of iron into the fire, and, after awhile, take that identical piece of iron out of the fire, but now bright and glowing. Thus it will be with our bodies: they are laid down in the grave, dead, heavy, earthly; but at the general resurrection this dead, heavy, earthly body shall arise living and glorious.

615. The Corruptible Made Incorruptible

A professor of biology made it his custom to stand before his students holding up a little seed between his thumb and forefinger. When he bowed before the seed, his students were mystified. This university professor had spent his whole life studying the beginning of life, and he acknowledged to his students that it was still a mystery to him. He said: "I know exactly what this seed consists of in the exact proportions of water, carbon, and other elements. I can mix these individual elements and make a seed that will look exactly like this one. If I plant the seed that I have compounded, it will rot. The various elements I have put together will be absorbed by the ground. However, if I sow the seed that God made, it will spring up into a plant, because it contains that mysterious element we call life." The physical resurrection of Christ is just as much a mystery. In fact, the life you now possess which causes your body to function and renew itself continually, and not collapse into a putrefying mass, is also a mystery. He, therefore, who in the beginning created our present corruptible bodies, will also create a new body without having to collect the various elements of our old ones from the earth.

616. My Resurrection Has Come

Suppose a visitor to our earth from another planet were to see a caterpillar on a rosebush, and a conversation could take place between them. It might go something like this: "How ugly you are and how gross, doing nothing but eat, eat, eat, all day long," says the visitor. "True," replies the caterpillar, "but I won't always be like this. Some day I'll have beautiful wings, and fly from flower to flower." "A likely story," says the visitor with a laugh. A few days later, this stranger finds a hard brown chrysalis on the rosebush and is surprised to hear the caterpillar's voice saying, "Now I'm worse off than before. You think I'm dead because I can neither move nor eat, but soon I shall have a resurrection and fly in the sun." "Poor deluded worm," says the visitor, "you'd better accept the fact that your life is over." But about three weeks later, the stranger, strolling in the rose garden, is surprised to hear the caterpillar's voice again. Looking for the chrysalis, he sees one beautiful wing and then another unfolding from its cracked shell. "You see," says the voice, "my resurrection has come," and spreading its wings the butterfly flits away to enjoy its wonderful new existence.

617. *The Living One*

A Mohammedan and a Christian were discussing their religions and had agreed that both Mohammed and Christ were prophets. Where, then, lay the difference? The Christian illustrated it this way: "I came to a crossroads and I saw a dead man and a living man. Which one did I ask for directions?" The response came quickly, "The living one, of course." "Why, then," asked his friend, "do you send me to Mohammed who is dead, instead of Christ who is alive?" This is the basic difference between Christ and every other religious leader. All the others came into the world, lived, and died—but none of them lived again. The resurrection of Christ was the one event that persuaded His disciples once for all that He was the Christ, God's Son.

Salvation

The Cost

618. Counting the Cost

Let's ask ourselves this question: "Am I concerned about the sacrifices I may be called upon to make in serving Christ?" Two young men were talking about this very thing. One of them said, "I cannot tell you all that the Lord Jesus is to me, or what He has done for me. I do wish you would enlist in His army." "I'm thinking about it," answered the other young man, "but it means giving up several things—in fact, I am counting the cost." A Christian officer, just passing, heard the last remark, and laying his hand on the shoulder of the young soldier said, "Young man, you talk of counting the cost of following Christ, but have you ever counted the cost of not following Him?"

619. Sovereign Grace

A father sees his child drowning. If he remains indifferent and does not come to the rescue of his child while he can, I am sure the law will condemn him. He will be punished because he did not save his child while he could. That is a case where power carries with it the responsibility of saving action. The father has to save his child whether he wants to or not. It was not so, however, with God. God could save you and me, but He did not have to, since He knew the tremendous cost of saving man. Remember, He did not do what He did under the compulsion of some law, but out of His pure free will and sovereign grace. When we think of that, how much more we appreciate what He has done for us.

620. Salvation Too Cheap?

A miner once said to a preacher, "I'd like to be a Christian, but I can't receive what you said tonight." "Why not?" asked the preacher. "Well, I'd give anything to believe that God would forgive my sins, but I can't believe He'll forgive me if I just turn to Him. It's too cheap." The preacher looked at him and said, "Have you been working today?" Surprised, the man replied, "Yes, I was down in the pit as usual. Why?" "How did you get out of the pit?" "The way I usually do. I got into the cage and was pulled to the top." "How much did you pay to come out of the pit?" The miner looked at the preacher in astonishment. "Pay? Of course, I didn't pay anything." "Well," said the preacher, "weren't you afraid to trust yourself to that cage? Wasn't it too cheap?" "Oh, no," he said; "it was cheap for me, but it cost the company a lot of money to sink that shaft." Then the implication of what he had said struck him, and he saw that though he could have salvation without money and without price, it had cost the infinite God a great price to rescue lost men.

Explanation

621. Salvation Assurance

Nothing disqualifies us for doing God's work more than a doubt as to our salvation. Mr. Moody used to illustrate this by saying: "If I were in the river, and I didn't have a firm grip on something, I couldn't help anybody. I've got to get a good hold for myself before I can help someone else." There is no liberty, peace, rest, joy, or power until we have assurance.

622. Not a Dying Thief but a Living Thief

A minister was talking to a man who professed conversion. "Have you united with a church?" he asked him. "No, the dying thief never united with a church and he went to heaven," was the answer. "Have you ever sat at the Lord's table?" "No, the dying thief never did and he was accepted." "Have you been baptized?" "No, the dying thief was never baptized and he went to heaven." "Have you given to missions?" "No, the dying thief did not, and he was not judged for it." "Well, my friend, the difference between you two seems to be that

he was a dying thief and you are a living thief."

623. The Cross of Christ— Key to Salvation

A little girl once begged a famous preacher to visit her dying mother. "Come and get my mother in," she pleaded. He followed the girl to a slum tenement, and sitting by the mother's bed began to speak of the beautiful example of Christ. But the woman interrupted him saying, "That's no good, mister, no good for the likes of me. I'm a poor sinner and I'm dying!" He was one of those preachers who did not think it proper to speak of the cross and the blood of Christ. But he remembered the simple story of Jesus dying on the cross, which he had heard from his mother, and he explained it all to the woman. "Now," she cried, "you're getting at it! That's the story for me!" The minister said afterward, "The gospel message got her in, and got me in, too!" That's the message that can bring salvation—the cross of Christ.

624. The Bridge of Repentance and Pardon

Across the River Zambesi, below the Victoria Falls, is a bridge which spans the widest chasm and overlooks the most terrific turmoil of waters to be seen on any river in the world. That bridge was made by building out an arm from either shore and uniting the two outstretched arms in the center above the roaring stream. Neither arm could have reached the opposite bank by itself; the two were needed to meet each other. Such are repentance and pardon which form the bridge across that tumultuous stream and those stupendous falls which separate the soul from God. At first one is inclined to say, "Why cannot the bridge of pardon be thrown over exclusively from God's side?" Perhaps others are tempted to say, "Surely the bridge of repentance will span the chasm and bring the soul to the unregarding God." But no, the truth lies here: pardon without repentance is impossible, and repentance without pardon is useless. When repentance and pardon meet, the soul is joined with God.

625. Illuminated by the Light

After a mission service, the preacher of the evening was hurrying away to a late train. He had just three minutes to catch it when he saw a man running after him. "Oh, sir," he said breathlessly as he came up, "can you help me? I am very anxious about my salvation." "Well," replied the preacher, "my train is just here, and it is the last one; but look up Isaiah 53:6. Go in at the first 'all' and go out at the last 'all.' Good night." The man stood staring after him until he had disappeared into the station and then he muttered, "Go in at the first 'all' and go out at the last 'all.' What does he mean?" When he arrived home he took down his Bible and turning to Isaiah 53:6 read these words, "All we like sheep

have gone astray; we have turned every one to his own way; and the Lord hath laid on him the iniquity of us all." "Go in at the first 'all,' " he repeated. " 'All we like sheep have gone astray.' I am to go in with that 'all.' Yes, I see. It just means that I am one of those who have gone astray. And go out with the last 'all.' 'The Lord hath laid on him the iniquity of us all.' I see. Yes, I am to go out free with those whose iniquity has been laid on Christ." At last he realized his individual lost condition and his individual redemption. This is actually the message of John 1:9. The eternal Light of Christ illumines the individual who responds affirmatively. "Go in at the first 'all' and go out at the last 'all.' "

626. The Needy Community

On a cold winter day Thomas Carlyle was sitting near his fireplace when the door opened and the new pastor of a nearby church came in. After they had exchanged a few words, the young preacher asked the philosopher, "What do you think our community needs more than anything else?" Without hesitation Carlyle answered, "What our community needs more than anything else is a man who knows God experientially, not simply from what he has learned from others."

627. Put Yourself among Sinners

Dwight L. Moody once said, "The great trouble is that people take everything in general, and do not take it to themselves. Suppose a man should say to me, 'Moody, there was a man in Europe who died last week, and left five million dollars to a certain individual.' 'Well,' I say, 'I don't doubt that; it's rather a common thing to happen,' and I don't think anything more about it. But suppose he says, 'But he left the money to you.' Then I pay attention; I say, 'To me?' 'Yes, he left it to you.' I become suddenly interested. I want to know all about it. So we are apt to think Christ died for sinners; He died for everybody, and for nobody in particular. But when the truth comes to me that eternal life is mine, and all the glories of heaven are mine, I begin to be interested. I say, 'Where is the chapter and verse where it says I can be saved?' If I put myself among sinners, I take the place of the sinner, then that salvation is mine and I am sure of it for time and eternity."

628. Available to All

An unbeliever once ridiculed the power of the gospel of Jesus Christ by saying, "If Jesus Christ is able to save to the uttermost, why is it that there are so many unbelievers?" The Christian to whom he was speaking stopped a very dirty little boy who was passing by and turning to the unbeliever said, "Can you blame soap and water for the filth of this boy?" It was available to all, but only those who accept it experience its regenerating power.

629. Simple Faith

An evangelist was holding spe-cial meetings for boys and girls. One day after the children's meeting, little Helen came home, rushed into her father's study, threw her arms around him, and said, "Daddy, I am a Christian!" "Well, Helen, I am glad to hear that," said her father. "When did you become a Christian?" "This afternoon, Daddy," she replied. He asked her to tell him what had occurred. "Oh," she said, "the evangelist told us that Jesus Christ was there in the room and that, if we would receive Him, He would come in and live in our hearts and make us His own; that He would receive us." "Well," he said, "go on; tell me what else happened." "Why," she said, "I received Him and Jesus took me in." "But how do you know that when you received Jesus He took you in?" the father persisted. She gave him a look which he would never forget as she answered, "Why, Daddy, because He said He would!" That's exactly what it means to believe in the name of Christ—to believe what He is and what He said He would do for us when we receive Him. It is so simple that explanations only serve to complicate it.

630. Saved by Faith

The recognition of your sinful and lost estate does not necessarily mean that you have to understand fully how and why it all happened before you can cry out for help and salvation. A man once came to a preacher and asked, "How is it that I was born with an evil heart? Is that fair, that I should inherit the sin of Adam?" The preacher replied, "The question that should concern you more is how to get rid of your evil heart. You have an evil heart which renders you completely unfit for the Kingdom of God; you must have a new heart or you cannot be saved. The question which now most deeply concerns you is, how shall you obtain it?" But the man insisted, "I wish you would tell me how I came by my wicked heart." "I shall not do that at present," replied the preacher, "for if I could do it to your entire satisfaction, it would not in the least help you toward obtaining a new heart. The great thing for which I am desirous is that you should become a new creature and be prepared for heaven." Then he continued, "You are like a man who is drowning. Along come his friends to save him, but he insists on being told exactly how he came to be drowning before he will consent to be rescued." The man started to think. The preacher was right. The most urgent thing for him and for you is not the full understanding of why and how you came to be what you are, but to come to the Savior, to become what you can be—a child of God by receiving Jesus Christ.

631. Heavenly Light Brings Change

The light is willing enough to enter the window of the soul when it is allowed admission. No man passes from his natural darkness into heavenly light without being aware that a great change has taken place. When the light first comes in, it reveals much that before was unperceived. If a room has been shut for a long time and kept in darkness, the light has a startling effect. With the light of a candle we cannot detect the dust, but if we open the shutters and draw the curtains, the light makes the mold and the dust very apparent. The first effect of the light of God in the soul is painfully unpleasant. It makes us loathe ourselves and wish we had never been born. Things grow worse and worse to our consciences as the light shines more and more. We would have every idol discovered and broken, and every dark chamber exposed to the sun. We must not keep the light out of any part of our nature. The light should be permitted to continue to enter our souls, and as it does, it gradually illuminates. Our will by nature prefers the darkness. We claim the right to act as we please. The light must continue to enter if our will is going to consent to change.

632. Salvation in Three Tenses

Somebody asked a Christian, "Are you saved?" "In what tense?" was the queer retort of the Christian. "What do you mean?" "Well," said the Christian, "salvation is in three tenses: it is in the past: 'Not by works of righteousness which we have done, but according to his mercy he saved us, by the washing of regeneration, and renewing of the Holy Ghost' (Titus 3:5). Here is salvation in the present: 'Moreover, brethren, I declare unto you the gospel which I preached unto you, which also ye have received, and . . . by which also ye are saved.' The Greek word *sōzesthe* is inadequately translated in the King James Version. It should be 'ye are being saved' (1 Cor. 15:2). Not only were we saved in the past, but we need salvation continuously. Finally there is salvation in the future: 'Much more then, being now justified by his blood, we shall be saved from wrath through him' (Rom. 5:9)." Is your salvation in all three tenses?

633. Man's Way of Salvation

Billy Sunday told of a man who came to him and said, "I will cut out the booze and get on the water wagon." "Good; what else?" "Of course, I am a gambler; I will quit gambling and I will never touch a pack of cards." "All right; what else?" "I am a bad man, and I will live a clean life." "Good; what else?" He said, "If I quit these things, I think they cover about all. I will quit drinking, swearing, stop gambling, and I will quit being impure." Billy said, "Good. Give me your hand and say you will accept Jesus Christ as your Savior," He said, "No, I will not. If I stop those things, I won't need to do that."

God's Part

634. Found by the Savior

A young man who presented himself as a candidate for baptism was asked by one of the deacons when he had found Christ as his Savior. "I didn't find Him; He found me," was the reply. That's absolutely correct. God is constantly seeking the wandering sinner, confronting him with the cross of Christ at every turn.

635. Predestination—Settled

A woman hearing a preacher speak on predestination said, "Ah, I have long settled that point; for if God had not chosen me before I was born, I am sure He would have seen nothing to have chosen me for afterwards!"

636. The Concealed Angel

It is related that Michelangelo, the famous Italian sculptor, painter, and poet, once stood before a great block of marble that had been rejected by builders and cast aside. As he stood there with eyes staring straight at the marble, a friend approached and asked what he was looking at. "An angel," came the reply. He saw what the mallet, the chisel, and patient skill could do with that rejected stone. He set to work and produced one of his masterpieces. Likewise, God sees possibilities in us.

637. The World's Ignorance

The richest man in the world, Croesus, once asked the wisest man in the world, Thales, "What is God?" The philosopher requested a day in which to deliberate, and then for another, and then for another, and another—and at length confessed that he was not able to answer. The longer he deliberated, the more difficult it was for him to frame an answer. The fiery Tertullian, the early Church Father, eagerly seized upon this incident and said it was an example of the world's ignorance of God outside of Christ. "There," he exclaimed, "is the wisest man in the world, and he cannot tell you who God is. But the most ignorant mechanic among the Christians knows God and is able to make Him known unto others." If God is to be revealed at all, He has to reveal Himself, and He has done so through Jesus Christ.

638. Jesus, a Seeker

The kingdom of heaven is like treasure hidden in a field. The Lord finds faith in a Roman soldier. He finds faith in heathen women. He finds lost womanhood in the Samaritan woman at the well. He seeks and finds generosity in that tight person called Zacchaeus. He seeks and finds courage in Peter, that coward who wouldn't reveal even to a little maid who he was while Jesus was being tried. The Lord seeks and finds an apostle in a persecutor like Saul of Tarsus and makes him Paul.

639. God's Part

A man once rose up in a meeting to give his testimony to the saving grace of God. He told how the Lord had won his heart and given deliverance from the guilt and power of sin. He spoke of Christ and His work but said nothing of any efforts of his own. The leader of the meeting was of a legalistic mind, and when this man's testimony was ended he said, "Our brother has only told us of the Lord's part in his salvation. When I was converted, there was a whole lot I had to do myself before I could expect the Lord to do anything for me. Brother, didn't you do your part first before God did His?" The other was on his feet in an instant and replied, "Yes, sir, I clean forgot. I didn't tell you about my part, did I? Well, I did my part for over 30 years, running away from God as fast as ever my sins could carry me. That was my part. And God took after me till He ran me down. That was His part."

640. God Sets the Condition

A young man attended an informal gathering in a Christian home where those who attended were encouraged freely to express any perplexities that stood in the way of belief. "I went into the woods one day," this young man said to the group, "and sat down on a sandy patch of ground and said to God, 'God if you will destroy that little pine tree I am looking at, I will believe in you.' I sat there a long while, but nothing happened. Now, if there was a God, why didn't He reveal Himself to me when I asked Him to?" He was honestly troubled and obviously in earnest, yet, not knowing the Scriptures, he erred. Man does not set the conditions by which he will condescend to believe in God, but God sets forth the conditions under which He will reveal Himself to man. Man must come to Him through the provision He has made in Christ, repent of his sin, and yield his heart to the purifying action of the Holy Spirit. Then and only then will he "see God."

641. We Have Received!

In John 1:16, the verb *elabomen*, "we received," has an active sense. It means "to take, to take hold of, to seize." This always indicates man's part in the process of his salvation by the Lord Jesus Christ. It should never be thought that man either merits this salvation or takes the initiative in its process. It is as if I had a piece of candy to offer to my child. It is my offering that prompts his receiving. My little boy would not say, "Daddy, give me that," if "that" were not there. Or here is a spring of water; I am thirsty. I can take a cup and fill it with water to satisfy my thirst. My cup would be absolutely useless if there were no possibility of getting it filled. Or I am sick; medicine is available which the doctor prescribes for me. It is up to me to take it or leave it, and my choice would determine the consequences. But I, the patient, could never boast that it was my receiving the medicine that cured me. My receiving was actually nothing more than an active passivity—obedience and submission to the doctor's advice. No man, therefore, who is given the privilege of receiving of the fullness of God in Christ can boast of it, for without the offering and the giv-

ing there would have been no receiving. But, on the other hand, the offering and the giving would do a man no good if he did not receive it.

Invitation

642. Let Him In

One day the great artist, Michelangelo, stood outside a window. Inside he saw a canvas with a few brushes and paints next to it. All that was missing was the hand of the artist. "Oh," cried Michelangelo, "if I could only be inside, what a picture I could paint!" That's exactly what Christ wishes when He stands outside your life. "Oh, what I could accomplish, if only I could get in!" Allow Him to get in. Open the door of your heart. Believe on Him. Then He will bring peace to your troubled soul.

643. Get on Board

Suppose an artist sees a piece of canvas on which he desires to paint a beautiful picture. However, if that piece of canvas does not belong to him, do you think the painter would work diligently on that canvas? No! Yet people want Jesus Christ to bestow His grace upon them in taking away a bad temper or some other sin, though in their hearts they have not yielded themselves to His command and His keeping. It can not be. But if you will come and give your life into His charge, Christ Jesus waits to be gracious; Christ Jesus waits to fill you with His Spirit. It is the Holy Spirit alone who by His indwelling can make a spiritual man.

644. Taste and See

There was a little fellow who was returning home from a store with a pail of honey in his hand. A gentleman who walked beside him saw him slip one finger down into the pail. Then, because his mother had told him never to wipe his sticky fingers on his blouse or trousers, it found its only logical destination, his mouth. It really tasted good. After he had done this several times, the gentleman approached him and said, "See here, Sonny, what have you in that pail?" "Some honey, sir." "Honey—is it sweet?" "Yes, sir." "How sweet is your honey?" "It is very sweet, sir." "Well, I do not understand you. I asked you how sweet your honey was, and you have not yet told me. How sweet is it?" "Why, it is very, very sweet, sir." "Well, you are a funny little fellow; I asked you how sweet your honey is, and you just tell me it is very, very sweet. Now, can't you tell me really how sweet your honey is?" The little fellow was impatient by this time, so he stuck his finger down into the honey, and holding it up said, "Taste and see for yourself."

645. Seize the Opportunity

Long ago, in one of the old Greek cities, stood a remarkable statue. Every trace of it has vanished now. However, we still have an epigram which gives us an excellent de-

scription of it and the lesson which those wise old Greeks meant it to convey. The epigram is in the form of a conversation between a traveler and the statue:
"What is they name, O statue?"
"I am called Opportunity."
"Who made thee?"
"Lysippus."
"Why are thou on thy toes?"
"To show how quickly I pass by."
"But why is thy hair so long on thy forehead?"
"That men may seize me when they meet me."
"Why, then, is thy head so bald behind?"
"To show that, when I have once passed, I cannot be caught."
Remember, Christ says, that the present opportunity may never be yours again, seize it while it is near you.

646. Putting Salvation Off

An old man said to his pastor, "When I was seventeen, I began, at times, to feel deeply about settling my soul's estate, and this continued for two or three years. But I determined to put it off until I was settled in life. After I was married, I reflected that the time had come when I had promised to attend to religion. But I had bought a farm, and I thought it would not be convenient for me to become religious until it was paid for, since attending church would take time and money. I then resolved to put it off ten years; but when the ten years came round I thought no more about it. I sometimes try to think about it, but I cannot keep my mind on the subject one moment." The pastor urged him not to face death as an enemy of God, to repent, but he said, "It is too late; I believe my doom is sealed; and that is just as it should be, son, for the Spirit strove with me, but I refused."

647. *Jump, I Am Here*

When a fire broke out in a tenement house, everybody managed to escape except one child. Through the smoke-filled room he made his way to the window, where he started to cry, "Daddy, Daddy, how can I escape? I can't jump; it's too high. I can't get out through the door because it's full of flames." Because of the dense smoke, the child couldn't see the crowd in the street, but he heard their cries and especially the voice of his father. "Son, I'm here with my arms open to catch you. Jump and I'll save you. Never mind if you can't see me. I'm here."

648. *Whosoever Will, Come—the Final Invitation*

It was Dwight L. Moody who said, "Many men fold their arms and say, 'If I am one of the elect—in other words, one of those God willed to be saved—I shall be saved; and if I am not, I shall not. No use bothering about it.' I have an idea," he said, "that the Lord Jesus saw how men were going to stumble over this doctrine of election, so after He had been thirty or forty years in heaven, He came down and spoke to John. On the Lord's

Day in Patmos He said to him: 'Write these things to the churches.' John kept on writing. His pen flew very fast. Then the Lord, when it was nearly finished, said: 'John, before you close the book, put in one more invitation: "The Spirit and the bride say, Come. And let him that heareth say, Come. And let him that is athirst come. And whosoever will, let him take the water of life freely." ' "

The Requirements

649. *You Must Believe*

A young nurse was helping to care for a sick, Christian gentleman whom she loved very much. He said to her, "Ellen, it is time I should take my medicine. Measure just a tablespoon and put it in a glass." She quickly did so and brought it to his bedside. He made no attempt to take it from her but said, "Now, dear, will you drink it for me?" "Me drink it? What do you mean? I am sure I would in a minute if it would make you well, but you know it won't do you any good unless you take it yourself." "Won't it really?" "No, I am sure it will not." "If you cannot take my medicine for me, neither can I take your salvation for you. You must go to Jesus and believe in Him for yourself." The dear old saint of God had been trying to explain to his young nurse that she could not be saved on his account and by serving him, but rather through her own acceptance of Jesus Christ as her Savior.

650. Self-Made Spiritually

A little girl baked a cake without benefit of a cookbook or her mother's advice. She knew nothing about proportions of flour, baking powder, sugar, salt, and milk, and never thought of eggs or shortening. When the cake came out of the oven, it was well rounded and nicely browned. She exhibited it to her family with pride as "a cake I made my very own self," but when she took her first bite of it she found it bitter with too much baking powder, and hard as a rock. That's how our own concoctions turn out in the spiritual realm, when we blithely assume we "know that recipe" without reference to the cook or the cookbook. You must first know God in Christ through receiving Him as Savior and Lord, before you can have the spiritual discernment that will enable you to understand the doctrine revealed in His Word.

651. No Other Way

Once we have discovered any of the laws that govern the universe, we proclaim them with absolute certainty, and admit to no rival laws and theories. In school we don't find one teacher saying that two and two are four, and another that two and two are five. Once a physical law has been defined and established, we don't hold that any man's contrary claim is equally valid. The truth of physical phenomena render its laws exclusive. Yet the human mind often refuses to grant that this holds true regarding the laws of the spiritual realm. They prefer to accept the glib assumption that all roads in the religious world lead to God and heaven. The argument goes something like this: "There's only one God, and every religion is based on serving and following and worshiping that one God, by whatever name they call Him. After all, we're all children of one Heavenly Father." Strangely enough, even some who profess to follow the teachings of Jesus blandly ignore His unequivocal statement, "I am the way, the truth, and the life: no man cometh unto the Father, but by me" (John 14:6). Such words are totally unacceptable to non-Christians, and even some nominal Christians unthinkingly say that all religions are equally good and lead to God.

652. Only One Way

Jane, a deeply religious woman, presumed that the Virgin Mary, the mother of the Lord Jesus, could do the work of her Son just as effectively as He. And of course, being a woman, she identified more with a female. She was discussing her religious beliefs with a friend who, on the other hand, believed that no one could be what Jesus Christ was and is, and that no one else could effect the work of salvation in the human heart. But nothing could persuade Jane. The friend who believed in the exclusiveness of Jesus Christ to save was employed as a maid in a doctor's home. One day Jane became seriously ill and called for the doctor, her friend's employer. The friend answered the phone and said, "I am sorry, but the doctor is not in." Then this Christian woman, who had put all her trust in Jesus Christ, thought of all the theological discussions that she had had with her friend and added, "But, Jane, you know the doctor's mother is in. Maybe she can help you." "Is she a doctor?" "No, but she is the doctor's mother. She will do, won't she?" Immediately Jane could see what her friend was driving at. She wanted to show her in this vivid way that Mary, although highly respected and honored, cannot do the work of her Son.

653. Reward for Acknowledging Sins

In the early part of the reign of Louis XVI, a German prince traveling through France visited the arsenal at Toulon where the galleys were kept. The commandant, as a compliment to the prince's rank, said that he was welcome to set free any one galley slave whom he should choose to select. The prince, willing to make the best use of the privilege, spoke to many of them in succession, inquiring why they were condemned to the galleys. Injustice, oppression, false accusations were assigned by one after another as the causes of their being there. In fact, they were all injured and ill-treated persons. At last he came to one who, when asked the same question, answered to this

effect: "Your Highness, I have no reason to complain. I have been a very wicked, desperate wretch. I have deserved to be broken alive on the wheel. I account it a great mercy that I am here." The prince fixed his eyes upon him and said: "You wicked wretch! It is a pity you should be placed among so many honest men. By your own confession, you are bad enough to corrupt them all; but you shall not stay with them another day." Then, turning to the officer he said, "This is the man, sir, whom I wish to be released."

654. Baptism of Repentance

A certain man thought that by being immersed he could find salvation. A friend of his had quite a time explaining to him that it was not so. But this man insisted that, as water would purify the body, so water consecrated by a minister or priest would purify the soul. Finally, to demonstrate that baptism did not mean regeneration, the friend decided upon an object lesson. "Here," he said. "I take an ink bottle, cork it tight, put a string round the neck, and drag it through the river. How long will it take to clean out the inside?" The answer was obvious, "You will never in the world clean it out that way." We must understand once and for all that no outward act will ever cleanse us within. Repentance is an act that takes place within us, while baptism is an outward act that demonstrates to the world what has already happened in our hearts. Thus, neither John the Baptist nor anyone else in the New Testament speaks of "repentance of baptism" but of "baptism of repentance." Baptism depends upon and is caused by repentance and not vice versa. It does not make sense for the unrepentant to be baptized.

655. The "Yes" of Faith

A woman came up to an evangelist after hearing him preach and said that she could not understand salvation. The evangelist asked, "Mrs. Franklin, how long have you been Mrs. Franklin?" "Why, ever since I was married," she replied. "And how did you become Mrs. Franklin?" he asked. "When the minister said, 'Wilt thou have this man to be thy wedded husband?' I just said, 'Yes.'" "Didn't you say, 'I hope so,' or 'I'll try to?'" asked the evangelist. "No," she replied, "I said, 'I will.'" Then pointing her to God's word, he said, "God is asking you if you will receive His Son. What will you say to that?" Her face lighted up and she said, "Why, how simple that is! Isn't it queer that I didn't say 'Yes' long ago?" That is the simple belief the Bible calls for—for you to say "Yes" and God will receive you as long as you come in the name of Christ.

656. Only One Savior

It is said when one of the most noted English physicians was succumbing to a fatal disease, he went from one authority to another until he had reached the highest on the continent. Telling this man his trouble, he received the reply, "The only man who can save you is an English physician, Dr. Darwin of Derby." Sad was the reply, "I am Dr. Darwin of Derby." He was the best, but he could not save himself. Even the best of us cannot save ourselves.

657. The Father's Child

Dwight L. Moody gives us a fine illustration of the fact that the commandment of Christ to follow Him is given to His children and not to strangers "I was standing with a friend at his garden gate one evening when two little children came by. As they approached us, he said to me, 'Watch the difference in these two boys.' Taking one of them in his arms he stood him on the gatepost and, stepping back a few feet, he folded his arms and called to the little fellow to jump. In an instant the boy sprang toward him and was caught in his arms. Then turning to the second boy he tried the same experiment. But in the second case it was different. The child trembled and refused to move. My friend held out his arms and tried to induce the child to trust to his strength but nothing could move him. At last my friend had to lift him down from the post and let him go. 'What makes the difference in the two?' I asked. My friend smiled and said, 'The first is my own boy and knows me; but the other is a stranger's child whom I have never seen before.' And there was all the difference. My friend was equally able to prevent both from falling. The difference was in the boys themselves. The first had assurance in his father's ability and acted upon it, while the second boy, although he might have believed in the ability to save him from harm, would not put his belief into action." So it is with many today who give credit to the gospel story but are unwilling to cast themselves into the arms of the Savior.

658. Believe and Receive

There are radio waves all around us sent out by transmitters. Only a receiving set can catch them. If you don't tune your radio to the waves of the transmitter you'll never understand what the speaker is saying. If you're not tuned in to God, you'll never understand Him either. Don't try in your unbelief to understand and know God. It's impossible. You must believe before you can receive His regenerating nature. St. Paul knew this when he said, "I live; yet not I, but Christ liveth in me" (Gal. 2:20). Then your battles, the temptations that beset you, will be fought by Christ Himself. He can more easily bear the burdens of your life than you can by yourself.

659. Real Joy

A gentleman residing in the fashionable part of London, and thoroughly carried away with the follies of society life, was walking down the street one day with a Christian woman of his acquaintance. He turned to her and asked, "How is it that you religious people are always trying to rob us of our pleasure? I enjoy life, and I can't see why you should be forever trying to rob me of what pleasure this short life affords." "You are greatly mistaken if that is what you think," replied the woman. "We do not want you to give up anything, but to receive." The gentleman kept thinking of the word "receive." It refused to leave him. Not long after, he called on the woman, told her his life was miserable, and asked what he must do to receive peace of soul and joy of heart. She led him to the Savior, where he found pardon and joy he had never known before.

The Result

660. Light Reveals

A young woman asked me to tell her in a few words how she could know if she was really a Christian. I said: "If you are a Christian you are not afraid of the light because you live in it. You no longer run after sin, though it may run after you. When you belong to Christ, you will find it difficult to sin; but when you belong to Satan you will find it easy. You belong to the one whom you truly long to please."

661. The Truth Is Dynamite

A. W. Tozer says: "The truth received in power shifts the basis of life from Adam to Christ, and a new set of motives goes to work within the soul. A new and different Spirit enters the personality and makes the believing man new in every department of his being. His interests shift from things external to things eternal, from things on earth to things in heaven. He loses faith in the soundness of external values; he sees clearly the deceptiveness of outward appearances; his love for and confidence in the unseen and eternal world become stronger as his experience widens. . . . The gulf between theory and practice is so great as to be terrifying. . . . Wherever the Word comes without power, its essential content is missed."

662. A New Stomach

One time a former drunkard was praising God for taking away all his appetite for liquor. A physician argued with him, saying that he would have to have a new stomach in order to have the appetite for liquor removed. "Praise God!" said the former drunkard. "I knew I had a new heart, but this is the first time I knew I had a new stomach!" "Therefore, if any man be in Christ, he is a new creature: old things are passed away; behold, all things are become new" (2 Cor. 5:17).

663. New Creatures in Christ

Queen Victoria once paid a visit to a paper mill. The foreman showed her and her attendant over the works without knowing who his distinguished visitor was. She finally went into the rag-sorting shop where men were employed in picking out the rags from the refuse of the city. Upon inquiring what was done with this dirty mass

of rags, she was told that, sorted out, it would make the finest white paper. After her departure, the foreman found out who it was that had paid the visit. Some time later, Her Majesty received a package of the most delicate white stationery having the Queen's likeness for a watermark, with the intimation that it was made from the dirty rags she had inspected. That illustrates Christ's work in us. He takes us, filthy as we are, and makes us into new creatures. Receiving Christ is becoming Christ's. After receiving Him, we are as different from what we were before as pure white paper is from the filthy rags from which it was made.

664. Made Spotless

Dr. Guthrie, attending a school gathering in a slum area, followed a speaker who had referred to poor neglected children as "the scum of society." This roused the indignation of Dr. Guthrie. Taking a clean sheet of paper and holding it up, he said, "Yes, this was the scum of society once, only filthy rags, but they can be cleansed and made into spotless white paper on which you may write the name of God." So it is with a believer in Christ.

665. A Heartfelt Experience

Somebody was asked how he knew that he was converted. "Why, bless your heart," was the answer, "I was there when it happened!" When Jesus Christ comes into our hearts, we know it, and others will, too.

666. *His Perfect Salvation*

Someone has said, "The Redeemer who loved us from eternity and formed us for Himself will not leave the pining soul to the secondhand tinkering of others. He will closet us in with Himself." I believe God longs to give to each of us a perfect personal assurance of His perfect salvation. Yet how few seem to realize this as David Brainerd did. In his diary he wrote: "My discourse was suited to my own case, for of late I have found a great want of apprehension of divine grace and have often been greatly distressed in my soul because I did not suitably apprehend this fountain open to purge away sin, and so I've had to be laboring for spiritual life and peace of conscience in my own strength; but now God showed me in some measure the arm of strength and fountain of all grace. But do I hear someone say, can He meet me at the point of my need? Let me tell you that He absolutely can."

667. *The Heart a Better Interpreter*

That great English preacher, Joseph Parker, once said, "The divinity of the Son of God is not proved merely in proportions. I think that he who believes in the divinity of Christ has all history, etymology, and philosophy on his side. My dependence is not founded upon the construction of a phrase or the mood and tense of a verb, and yet we have nothing to fear from that side. I rely upon His moral reach and spiritual compass. When He touched my soul into life, I did not call for a Greek grammar, Hebrew lexicon, or volumes of encyclopedias, to find how the thing stood. I believe because 'once I was blind, and now I see.' The heart is sometimes a better interpreter than the understanding. What better proof do I want? 'He has redeemed my life from destruction.' "

668. *Second Birth*

A preacher was asked, "Where were you born?" "I was born in Dublin and Liverpool," he replied. The man with whom he was conversing thought there was some misunderstanding. "How can a man be born in two places at once?" he asked. But the preacher meant that he had been born in the flesh in Dublin and born again in the spirit in Liverpool. The second birth is just as definite an experience as the first. With the first birth man becomes a creature of God; with the second he becomes a child of God.

669. *Seeing the Gospel*

A missionary approached a native whom he had not seen before and asked, "Have you ever heard the gospel?" "No," he replied, "but I have seen it. I know a man who used to be the terror of the neighborhood. He was a bad opium smoker and as dangerous as a wild beast. But he became completely changed. He is now gentle and good and has left off opium."

670. *Mystery of Salvation*

A psychiatrist who visited a rescue mission listened intently to the testimonies of many converts. The superintendent asked him if he would like to say a word. This is what he said: "Tonight I have been given an opportunity to observe something I did not know existed anywhere. It has been my privilege to listen to the testimony of men who were glad to witness to what Christ had done for them. I know nothing about that, but I confess I cannot otherwise explain what has taken place in their lives. A few of these men I recognize. As drunkards, even as dope addicts, some of them have come under my observation at the hospital. But here they are, alive, well-dressed, delivered, and in their right minds. I do not know how the miracle has been wrought, but of one thing I am confident—nothing in science can account for this change in them. That kind of gospel is worth preaching to anyone, anywhere."

671. *The End of a Quest*

Justin Martyr, one of the early Church Fathers, started out in his youth on a search for the highest wisdom. He tried a stoic, who told him that his search was vain. He turned to a second philosopher, whose greed for money quenched any hope of assistance from him. He appealed to a third, who required a preliminary knowledge of music, astronomy, and geometry. Just think of a soul thirsting after God and pardon and peace, being told, "You can't have any of this until you've got a college degree." How many would be shut out from God's presence! In his helplessness, Justin Martyr applied to a follower of Plato, under whose guidance he began to have some hope that he was on the right track. But one day, when earnestly groping after the truth, he was met by a nameless old man who talked to him about Jesus Christ. Immediately he felt he was at the end of his quest. "Straightway," says Justin, "a flame was kindled in my soul," and if not in the actual words, yet in the spirit he sang,

"Thou, O Christ, art all I want;
More than all in Thee I find."

672. *Standing in the Lord's Shoes*

A poor, uneducated old woman was once met by a skeptic. "Well, Betty, you are one of the saints, are you? Pray what sort of folks are they? What do you know about religion?" "Well, well," replied the old woman, "you know, sir, I'm no scholar, so can't say much for the meaning of it; I only know I am 'saved by grace' and that's enough to make me happy here, and I expect to go to heaven by and by." "Oh, that's all, is it? But surely you can tell us something more than that. What does being saved feel like?" "Why, it feels to me," said that Spirit-taught one, "just as if the Lord stood in my shoes, and I stood in His."

673. The Light Within

An old sculptor had among other pieces of work in his shop the model of a beautiful cathedral. It was covered with the dust of years, and nobody admired it, although it was an exact model of a fine cathedral, inside and out. One day the attendant placed a light inside the model, and its gleam shone through the beautiful stained-glass windows. Then all stopped to admire its beauty. The change that was brought by the light within was marvelous.

674. Victory over All Sins

To a pastor's study one day came a young man from a good family. He was in the depths of despair and confessed that he had practiced the most loathsome sins. He hated his own body, the instrument of his shame. He wanted to die, and would have put an end to his life if he could have been sure that death ended all. The pastor, in recounting this incident, said that he shuddered to think of what would have been the result of that interview if he had not been able, on the authority of God's Word, to call him to repentance and conversion in Christ, and to assure him of a gift of power that can give victory over all sins. One genuine experience of Christ is worth more than all the arguments of a pagan philosophy.

675. The Willing Slave

During the time when slave trade was still practiced in some parts of the South, a handsome young man was up for sale. The bids kept rising. Finally, an Englishman gained possession. The young slave began to chide him, "Ha, you buy a slave when slavery has already been abolished in England." The purchaser, however, said, "I have bought you to set you free." The young slave, overcome with emotion, replied, "I will be your willing slave forever."

676. Fruit of the Spirit

A missionary teacher tells of a Japanese woman who asked her if only beautiful girls were accepted by her school. "Why no," she replied, "We take all the girls who come to us." "But," continued the woman, "all your girls seem to be very beautiful." "That's because we teach them the value of their souls in God's sight," explained the teacher, "and this makes their faces lovely." "Well," said the woman, "I don't want my daughter to become a Christian, but I would like to send her to your school to get that look on her face."

677. Spiritual Resurrection

"Oh, how many things I would have to give up!" said a sinner who was wondering whether to receive Christ or not. "So many things I do now I would no longer be able to do." "Don't be afraid," an experienced Christian told him. "Even now aren't there things you can't do? For instance, can you eat dirt?" "No, of course not," was the reply. "I don't even want to eat dirt."

"This is exactly what will happen when Christ begins His life in you," said his friend. "The sin that you now desire you will not want at all."

678. Proof—A Changed Life!

A changed life is an indisputable argument. Zeno, the subtle Greek philosopher was once trying to show that there is no such thing as motion; upon which Diogenes simply got up and walked about! So when cynics sneer at Christianity and say it is all a lot of nonsense, the best way to refute them is to produce the evidence of a changed life.

679. The Christian's Riches

John Bunyan wrote: The happy man was born in the city of Regeneration, in the parish of Repentance unto Life. He was educated in the School of Obedience; he works at the trade of Diligence and does many jobs of self-denial. He owns a large estate in the country of Christian Contentment and wears the plain garments of humility. He breakfasts every morning on spiritual prayer and sups every evening on the same. He also has "meat to eat that the world knows not of." He has gospel submission in his conduct, due order in his affection, sound peace in his conscience, sanctifying love in his soul, real divinity in his breast, true humility in his heart, the Redeemer's yoke on his neck, the world under his feet, and a crown of glory over his head. In order to obtain this, he prays fervently, works abundantly, redeems his time, guards his sense, loves Christ, and longs for glory.

Satan

680. The "Orphan"

A young man, under the influence of drink, stood on the outside of a crowd and boasted that he would make the open-air preacher stop preaching. He shouted: "Hi, Mister, you can go home; you don't need to preach any more—the devil's dead!" The preacher looked at the young man sternly and replied, "The devil's dead? Then you are an orphan!"

681. Satan Defeated

Dwight L. Moody said that one of the happiest men he ever knew was a man in Dundee, Scotland, who had fallen and broken his back when a boy of fifteen. He had lain on his bed for forty years and could not be moved without a good deal of pain. Probably not a day had passed in all those years without acute suffering. But day after day the grace of God had been granted him, and when Mr. Moody was in his room it seemed as if he was as near heaven as he could get on earth. When Mr. Moody saw him, he thought he must be beyond the reach of the tempter, and he asked him, "Doesn't Satan ever tempt you to doubt God and to think that He is a hard master?" "Oh, yes," he said, "he does try to tempt me. I lie here and see my old schoolmates driving along, and Satan says, 'If God is so good, why has He kept you here all these years? You might have been a rich man, riding in your carriage.' Then I see a man, who was young when I was, walk by in perfect health, and Satan whispers, 'If God loved you, couldn't He have kept you from breaking your back?' " "And what do you do when Satan tempts you?" "Ah, I just take him to Calvary, and I show him Christ, and I point out those wounds in His hands and feet and side, and say, 'Doesn't He love me?' The fact is Satan got such a scare there nineteen hundred years ago that he cannot stand it; he leaves me every time." That bedridden saint of God did not have much trouble with doubts; he was too full of the grace of God.

682. Proof of Conversion

Dwight Moody used to speak of a miserly farmer recently converted, to whom a neighbor in distress appealed for help. The miser decided to prove the genuineness of his conversion by giving him a ham. On his way to get it the tempter whispered, "Give him the smallest one you have." A struggle ensued and finally the miser took down the largest ham he had. "You are a fool," the devil said. And the farmer replied, "If you don't keep still, I'll give him every ham in the smokehouse!"

683. Later, but Lost

There is a story that Satan once had a conference in order to devise some effective method to harm the Lord's work on earth. One demon suggested, "Let us go down and persuade men that there is no God." This, however, was rejected by the majority of the demons and by the archdemon, Satan, who stated that it was impossible for any intelligent man not to believe in the existence of God. How could they persuade men of the non-existence of God when they themselves believed that there is a God? Another demon proposed that they should tell the people that Jesus Christ never really existed. This also was rejected since historical facts are historical facts, and Jesus Christ as a historical figure could not be denied. Then another demon suggested that they persuade everyone that death ended it all and that they should not worry about life after death. But this also was rejected because man would conclude that God must be a fool to have created man for this earth only. Finally the most intelligent of the demons got up and said, "I'll tell you what we'll do. We'll go down and tell everybody to believe that there is a God, that belief in Jesus Christ saves, but you can get by just by professing faith and go on

living in sin as you used to." Immediately this proposal was unanimously acclaimed, and ever since, the demons, Satan's agents, have been telling people to believe, but to live the way they want.

684. God Has the Keys

When the devil came to Martin Luther and asked him to open the door of his heart so that he could come in and discuss some very important matters with him, he said, "I don't have the keys to the door; God has them. Ask Him if you wish." Needless to say, Satan took to his heels.

685. Resist Satan

Billy Bray, the Cornish miner, whose rugged piety has been a blessing to many, says that one year his crop of potatoes turned out so poorly that, when he was digging them, Satan, at his elbow, said, "There, Billy, isn't that poor pay for serving your Father the way you have all the year? Just see those small potatoes!" He stopped digging and replied, "Ah, Satan, at it again; talking against my Father, bless His name! Why, when I served you I did not get any potatoes at all. What are you talking about?" And on he went digging and praising the Lord for small potatoes.

686. Satan Is Real

A man came to Charles Finney, the well-known evangelist, and said, "I don't believe in the existence of a devil." "Don't you?" asked Finney. "Well, you resist him for a while, and you will believe in it." That's what the second commandment of James is: "Resist the devil, and he will flee from you" (James 4:7b). A godly life is characterized by its conflicts with sin. The place most frequented by Satan is where holiness dwells.

687. Empty Houses

Suppose you had been house hunting in a development of new homes, and when you found an empty one you tried to get into it. If the house was full, occupied by people, you wouldn't dare try to get in. That's exactly what Satan does. He looks for vacuums. He looks for empty houses. They may be clean, but if God is not within you, having made you His temple, you can be sure the devil is going to occupy you. Be filled with the Spirit of God. That's the admonition and meaning of this parable of our Lord in Luke 11:24–26.

688. Satan's Big Trick

Luther says in one of his sermons: "The devil held a great anniversary at which his emissaries were convened to report the results of their several missions. 'I let loose the wild beasts of the desert,' said one, 'on a caravan of Christians, and their bones are now bleaching on the sands.' 'What of that?' said the devil. 'Their souls were all saved.' 'I drove the east wind,' said another, 'against a ship freighted with Christians, and they were all drowned.' 'What of that?' said the devil. 'Their souls were all saved.' 'For ten years

I tried to get a single Christian asleep,' said a third, 'and I succeeded, and left him so.' "Then the devil shouted," continues Luther, "and the night stars of hell sang for joy." One of the tricks of Satan is to make us believe that submission to God means a spiritual stupor. Far from it. It is a battle; it is resistance and first of all to Satan himself.

689. Satan's Tools

An old fable says that the devil once offered his tools for sale, intending to give up his business. He displayed these tools—malice, hatred, jealousy, deceit, and several others, with the prices marked on them. One of them was set apart, marked with a higher price than the others. When the devil was asked why this was, he said, "Because that is my most useful tool; it is called depression; with that I can do anything with people." How true! Let us watch, therefore, when it makes its appearance and take our stand against depression; it is often from the devil.

690. Fighting the Forces of Evil

Animal trainers say that the secret of handling lions, tigers, and leopards is to keep them constantly afraid of you. The instant they get over their fear, they will attack. They are treacherous beasts and often gather courage for an attack when the trainer's eyes are turned away from them. One never knows when they will spring at their keeper if they have a chance to do it from behind. Our fight with the forces of evil is like that. Satan is always seeking to attack us from the rear or in ambush. He goes about like a roaring lion, seeking whom he may devour, but he is a great coward when faced with courage. "Resist the devil and he will flee from you" is as true today as it was when the Apostle James first made the declaration (James 4:7).

691. The Cleansing Blood

It is related that once the devil came to Luther and tried to use the biblical truth of the fallibility of the Christian to create in him a defeatist attitude. He presented Luther with a long list of sins which Luther was guilty of; sins of commission and sins of omission. Then Luther with his characteristic wit turned to the devil and said, "No, you must have forgotten some, for sure. Think a little harder." Sure enough, the devil thought of some more, and he put them down. "That's very fine," said Luther. "Now write with red ink across them all, 'The blood of Jesus Christ his Son cleanseth us from all sin' (1 John 1:7)." There was nothing the devil could answer to that.

692. Self-reformation

A bent bow springs back, not merely to the perpendicular line, but bends to the opposite direction. A pendulum that is set swinging not only returns to the place from which it started but also swings as far in the other direction, and this is true of every great effort in life, whether intellectual or moral. After great intellectual strain, the mind returns, not to the condition of repose in which it was before, but to a condition of weariness. After great moral effort, there is danger of reaction, and this is especially true of penitence. After a great act of penitence there is a sense of joyous freedom from sin. The soul has been swept and garnished, swept by confession, garnished by the relief of knowing that it is not burdened any more. Yet this is only the negative side of spiritual life and is in itself a condition of peculiar danger. The old tenant has been driven out of the house. The house has been cleansed and prepared for a new tenant. But, alas, it is still empty. A great victory has been won, but there is often a tendency to exaggerate the results of the victory, let down the defenses and think the war is ended when only one battle has been fought. The enemy may have been routed, but if we give ourselves up to mere rejoicing, the enemy may return with recruited forces and fall upon us while we are feasting upon the memories of our first victory, and so we may become an easy prey.

693. Spiritually Dead

A young Christian who worked for a rich man was always telling his employer that Satan was constantly battling with him, but he always won over Satan. The master made fun of him, telling him that Satan never bothered him. How was that? The young Christian could not answer him. One day, however, they went hunting together. The employer shot at some wild ducks. Some he killed, and some he just wounded. "Run," the employer said, "and catch the wounded ones first before they run away." The young Christian came back laughing. He had the answer to the big question. "You know, sir," he said, "why Satan does not tempt you? Because you are spiritually dead, just like those ducks. He goes after the live ones, ones like me."

Second Coming

694. Longing for His Appearance

At one time the recording engineer of the author's radio broadcasts, a very dear saint of God, was almost completely blind. Whenever I visited him and prayed with him, he always wanted to hold my hand as I prayed. He told me that did something to him. Physical contact meant special inspiration and comfort to him. I thought he would not hold my hand when I prayed with him after the restoration of his eyesight, but he still continued to do so. I think this is a perfect illustration of the earnest desire of Christians for the physical appearance of the Lord Jesus.

695. Be Prepared

A servant whose master and mistress were away was uncertain when they would return. A friend visited her and feeling rather tired went in to rest. When she got up she saw that the servant had gone to all kinds of trouble to lay the table for tea as if her master and mistress were coming home that hour. She questioned the servant whether the master and mistress were coming home that day, but her friend answered, "I have not heard, but as the time is uncertain, I always have everything ready each day." What a lesson this is for the Christian—to have everything ready every day and every hour of the day.

696. The Patient Farmer

What good will it do the farmer to be angry at the plants because they are later in yielding fruit than he thinks they should be? It won't affect the plants. It is not in his power to ripen fruits at his pleasure. Therefore, as the farmer exercises patience and long-suffering waiting for the earth to yield her fruit, so should we in waiting for the presence of the Lord.

697. Be Ready

The Lord wants us to live all the time as if today would be our last. I believe it was John Wesley who was asked at one time, "What would you do if you knew that tonight you would die?" That great preacher of years gone by said, "I would do exactly what I have scheduled to do." Could you say that?

698. Looking for Jesus

A little girl had been listening while her mother's friends were speaking about the imminent return of the Lord. After some time she was missed, so her mother went in search of her. She found her looking out a window at the top of the house. Asked what she was doing she said, "Oh, Mother, I heard you say Jesus might come today, and I wanted to be the first to see Him. See, I washed myself and put on a clean dress."

699. Await His Coming

As that great preacher of the Word, Dr. G. Campbell Morgan, said, "To me the second coming is the perpetual light on the path which makes the present bearable. I never lay my head on my pillow without thinking that maybe before morning breaks, the final morning may have dawned! I never begin my work without thinking that perhaps He may interrupt my work and begin His own. This is now His word to all believing souls, till He comes."

Self

Self-centered

700. Simpson's Folly

Many years ago a man named Simpson built a house on the Canford Cliffs, near Bournemouth, England. Friends and neighbors tried to warn him he had chosen a site too near the edge of the cliff, that landslides frequently occurred along the coast, and the very weight of the house would precipitate such a catastrophe. But Mr. Simpson wouldn't listen. He built a very beautiful house there and for a time all went well. Then the inevitable happened, and the ominous warnings all came true. All that remains of his house is a heap of ruins on the beach known as "Simpson's Folly."

701. Rights—Ours and Others

A young lawyer negotiated a contract of which he was rather proud and took it to an old and wise counselor for his examination. To his surprise the old man, as he read it slowly, shook his head. "That is a great contract, John. It is most skillfully drawn," he remarked as he handed it back. "But, John, you have forgotten the other fellow. No contract is sound which neglects the rights or the equities of any party to it." We are not righteous if we think only of our own rights and neglect the rights of others.

702. No Responsibility

A young man applying for a job as usher in a theater was asked by the owner, "In case of fire, what would you do?" "Oh, don't be concerned about me," was the reply. "I'd be able to escape immediately." He did not even think of his responsibility toward others. Of course, he didn't get the job.

703. Preoccupation with Self

Someone remarked to the director of a mental institution, "I imagine all the people in here are 'beside' themselves." "No, you're wrong," the doctor replied. "They're shut in here, not because they're 'beside' themselves, but because they're 'inside' themselves. They think of nothing else but self." When preoccupation with self becomes your problem, you become a problem for the world and to God Himself.

704. The Peacock Syndrome

A rich man decided to take up fishing. He bought the most expensive equipment and bait, but he caught nothing. He passed by a farmboy who had an old stick and a rusty hook but had caught a big string of fish. "How did you manage to catch so many, when I couldn't catch a single one?" he asked. "Oh," said the boy, "I try to keep out of sight so the fish won't see me. Perhaps you show yourself too much."

705. *The Way of the World*

The fable of the fox and the wolf aptly illustrates the way of the world that the Christian is to avoid. It seems a fox was peering into a well from which people drew water by lowering an empty bucket, and pulling up the full one that was at the bottom. By accident the fox fell into the empty bucket and found itself at the bottom of the well. It made a lot of noise trying to get out. A wolf, hearing the noise, looked down and said to the fox, "What are you doing, my friend?" "I'm catching fish," was the sly answer; "Come down to help me." "How can I?" asked the wolf. "Jump into that bucket up there and you'll be down here in a moment." The foolish wolf obeyed, and because it was heavier than the fox it went down and the fox came up and started to run away. "Are you leaving me down here?" cried the wolf. But the fox answered slyly, "That's the way of the world, my friend; when one goes up, the other goes down."

706. *Share Your Blessings*

In her travels, a lady experienced some cold weather. As she was shivering she turned to her servant to remind her to send some warm blankets to the poor people when they got home. She arrived at her luxurious warm home, took off her furs, and over a cup of tea made herself comfortable. Later, when her servant reminded her of the promised blankets, her reply was, "Ah, yes, I remember; but it's nice and warm now."

Selfish

707. *Ruined by Selfishness*

A farmer inherited a rice field. The first year, the water covered his land so well that he had an abundant harvest. In fact, it even overflowed into his neighbor's field, making it fertile also. But he began to fret because his neighbor's field became as productive as his own. He decided that the water was part of his inheritance and belonged exclusively to him, so he cut it off from his neighbor's field the next year. The result? His own field was flooded and his crop ruined.

708. *Refusal to Face Reality*

When Marie Antoinette came to Paris as a bride, not a single ragged or starving person appeared on the streets along which the splendid procession passed. France was seething with discontent at the time, born of dire poverty—a discontent that was later to break out in the horrors of the Revolution—but Marie Antoinette was not to know anything about that. So the poor starving populace were swept into the side streets where they could not be seen and kept penned up there so that Marie Antoinette might think all was happy and prosperous in Paris. But an optimism based on ignorance is not optimism at all. An optimism gained by a refusal to face the facts is deliberate self-deception. Fear to face reality stems from fear of the sacrifice and labor of love that may be involved. Selfishness turns away its face from the sorrows, shames, and failures of others. But love dares to look at the head bowed with grief and the face paled with suffering.

Self-controlled

709. In His Presence

La Fontaine, chaplain of a Prussian regiment, preached a plain sermon on the sin of a hasty temper. The next day the major, a very passionate man, told him he had used his official liberty rather too freely. La Fontaine admitted that he had thought of him, but had no intention of being personal. "Well, it is of no use," said the major. "I have a hasty temper, I cannot help it, and I cannot control it. It is impossible." The next Sunday La Fontaine preached upon self-deception, and the excuses which men are apt to make, "Why," said he, "a man will declare that it is impossible for him to control his temper, when he very well knows that, were the same provocation to happen in the presence of his sovereign, he not only could, but would, control himself.

And yet he dares to say that the continual presence of the King of Kings imposes upon him neither restraint nor fear!" The next day the major again accosted him. "You were right yesterday, chaplain," he said humbly. "Hereafter, when you see me in danger of falling, remind me of the King." Let us always remember we are in the presence of Christ. Surely we would not wish to let our passions loose in the presence of the King.

710. The Invitation

There is a story of a young minister who was going home late one evening from church. He entered a crowded streetcar with his Bible under his arm and at once became the target for sneering remarks from some rough fellows. These remarks kept up, and as the young minister was leaving the car, to the amusement of his companions one youth said, "Say, Mister, how far is it to heaven?" What would be the actions of a consecrated Christian under such circumstances? Is it permissible to lose one's temper and blow one's top? Of course, one way to answer is to keep silent, but then one feels he is failing the Master. This young minister, with a quiet dignity and with all gentleness, replied, "It is only a step away; will you take it now?"

711. Not a Coward

A young soldier who was showing signs of panic on the eve of his first battle was chaffed by a veteran. "Why, sonny," he said, "you're shaking with fear. Don't be such a coward." "I'm not a coward," hotly retorted the youth. "If you felt half as scared as I do, you'd run away!" He was right. That young man was not a coward because he felt fear, but he would have been a coward if he had allowed it to master him and drive him from his post of duty.

Self-righteous

712. See the Wonders of God

A preacher wrote: "Last summer I stood looking over a Highland river valley lit with a beautiful sunset, and I marveled at the work of God in nature. I turned to a farmer friend and said, 'What a privilege it is for you to live amid such beauty!' He thought for a moment and said, 'Aye, man, it's grand sheep country.' I have many farmer friends who would have bared their heads at the very thought of the wonders of God in nature, but this man's sense of the beautiful was clouded by the pursuit of the material. Oh, how often we lift our eyes from the face of the vision God gives us and turn them on our mirrors and see only self; self counting the sheep and the cattle; self getting rich, climbing the ladder of earthly success; self winning favor in the eyes of men. Not that these things are not worthwhile in their place on earth—they are! But when we make them our only end in life, we miss all that is best and most beautiful."

713. Too Close to the Mirror

A stern old saint used to bemoan the wickedness of the world which to her was going from bad to worse. She seemed to be obsessed with the idea that, except for herself and her own circle of friends, no one else was saved. She stood so close to the mirror of life that she and her immediate surroundings dominated the view. Had she only stepped back or to one side, she would have had a much better perspective of life as a whole. Another Christian saw in the mirror all the wonderful manifestations of the working of God, news of which seemed to be reaching her from every quarter— from the slums, from the mission field, from all the darkened corners of the earth where light was dawning. How poor life seems to be when it is only a shadowy background to the all-absorbing form of self. How glorious when we step out of the picture and let the larger landscape sweep into view.

714. None Righteous

An Indian and a white man were brought under deep conviction of sin by the same sermon. The Indian was immediately led to rejoice in pardoning mercy. The white man was in distress for a long time, almost to despair. But at last he was brought to a joyous sense of sins forgiven. Sometime after, while meeting his Indian brother, he said to him, "How is it that I should be so long under conviction, when you found peace at once?" "Oh, brother," replied the Indian, "I will tell you. There comes along a rich prince. He proposes to give you a new coat; you look at your coat and say, 'I don't know; my coat looks pretty good; it will do a little longer.' He then offered me a new coat. I look at my old blanket; I say, 'This is good for nothing,' and accept the beautiful new garment. Just so, brother, you try to keep your own righteousness. You won't give it up; but I, poor Indian, could see that I had none, so I was glad at once to receive the righteousness of God—the Lord Jesus Christ."

715. Two Sides to Every Question

Someone once remarked, "There are two sides to every question—my side and the wrong side." An illustration of this concerns an argument that arose between two young chaplains of different denominations. The senior chaplain said, "Let's bury the hatchet, my brother. After all, we are both doing the Lord's work, aren't we?" "We certainly are," said the junior chaplain, quite disarmed. "Let us do it, then, to the best of our ability, you in your way, and I in His." I'm afraid too many of us are inclined to think our ways are the Lord's ways, and the ways of other fellow Christians fall short of that standard.

716. Average Morality Is No Morality

Many of us are like that man who prided himself on his morality and some specific virtues and said, "I am pretty good on the whole. I sometimes get mad and speak a couple of unnecessary words, but then I am pretty honest. I work on my farm on Sundays when there's work to be done, but I give a good deal to the poor and have never gotten drunk in my life." This man one day hired a Christian to build a fence around his pasture. He gave him very specific instructions. In the evening when the Scotsman came in from work, the man said, "Well, Jack, is the fence built, and is it good and strong?" "I cannot say it is all tight and strong," Jack replied, "but it's a good average fence, anyhow. If some parts are a little weak, others are extra strong. I have left a little gap here and there, a yard or so wide, but I made up for it by doubling the rails on each side of the gap. I dare say the cattle will find it a good fence on the whole and will like it, though I cannot say it is perfect in every part." "What!" cried the man, not seeing the point, "Do you mean to tell me that you built a fence around my lot with weak places and gaps in it? Why, you might as well have built no fence at all. If there is one gap or a place where an opening can be made, the cattle will be sure to find it and will be sure to go through. Don't you know, man, that a fence must be perfect or it is worthless?" "I used to think so," said the man, "but I hear you talking so much about averaging matters with the Lord, it seems to me we might try it with the cattle."

717. Respectable Sinner

A gentleman once took exception to a message based upon the Word of God concerning Jew and Gentile, that both are guilty before God. The preacher remarked, "But the Word of God distinctly says, 'There is no difference: for all have sinned, and come short of the glory of God' " (Rom. 3:22, 23). The preacher's friend then replied, "Do you mean to say that there is no difference between an honest man and a dishonest one, between an intemperate man and a sober man?" "No," the preacher remarked, "I did not affirm that there was no room for comparison between such cases; but my position is, if two men were standing here together, one an intemperate man and the other a sober man, I should say of the one, 'This man is an intemperate sinner; the other is a sober sinner.' " Our friend did not know how to meet the difficulty, but answered, "Well, I don't like such teaching." Very quietly the preacher replied, "Then I will make some concession and meet your difficulty. I will admit that many are 'superior sinners,' and that you are a superior sinner." What consternation was pictured on the face of the respectable sinner. Sometimes it is harder for respectable sinners to be justified because of their self-righteousness than it is for out-and-out sinners.

718. Hindrance to Spiritual Growth

A young preacher frequently talked with a wise old farmer. One day the question under discussion was, "What is the greatest hindrance to spiritual growth and happiness?" The preacher said, "Surely it is failure to renounce our sinful self." "No," said the farmer, "the greatest hindrance is failure to renounce our righteous self."

719. First, Look in the Mirror

A man prayed complainingly to Almighty God about a neighbor, saying, "O Lord, take away this wicked person." And God said, "Which?"

720. Layers of Self

"Man is like an onion," said A. T. Pierson, "layer after layer, and each a layer of self in some form. Strip off self-righteousness and you will come to self-trust. Get beneath this and you will come to self-seeking and self-pleasing. Even when we think these are abandoned, self-will betrays its presence. When this is stripped off, we come to self-defense, just as the Corinthians did—the word of the puffed up—and last of all, self-glory. When this seems to be abandoned, the heart of the human onion discloses pride that boasts of being truly humble."

Sin

721. *The Well of Kindness*

In ancient times in the East, a common practice among tribes at war was to fill each other's wells. Every well thus rendered useless was a public blessing destroyed. It is like a crime against humanity when a well of kindness in a heart is stopped. The world's need and sorrow are the losers. The thirsty come to drink where before their want had been satisfied, and are disappointed. But the most serious consequence is the harm that is done to the persons themselves whose love and compassion are thus restrained. One of the great problems of Christian living is to keep the heart gentle and sweet amid all the world's trying experiences. Nothing worse could happen to a person than to become cold toward human suffering, or bitter toward human infirmity and failure.

722. *The Unbreakable Chain*

It is told of a famous smith of medieval times that, having been taken prisoner and immured in a dungeon, he began to examine the chain that bound him with a view to discovering some flaw that might make it easier to break it. His hope was in vain, for he found from some marks upon it that it was his own workmanship. It had been his boast that none could break a chain that he had forged. Thus it is with the sinner. His own hands have forged the chain that binds him, a chain that no human hand can break.

723. *Don't Play with Sin*

Sin is nothing to play with. It has the strength to defeat you if you get too close to it with excessive confidence in your own strength. A well-to-do man advertised for a chauffeur. Three applicants came. His first question was, "How close to the edge of a cliff can you drive without going over?" One man said, "A yard." Another said, "A foot." The third said, "I always try to keep as far away as possible." The third man got the job. He who underestimates the strength of an enemy is in danger of defeat.

724. *Criticism Dangerous*

A student may turn his enlightened heart into darkness by starting to be critical, first with the things that may be criticized, and then proceeding to belittle those things that are beyond criticism. He is like a little boy with a new knife; he must cut something or other. He cuts up the Scriptures and decimates them; he has such a sharp knife that he must use it or otherwise he is not happy. From a critic, he advances to an irreverent faultfinder, and from that to an utter unbeliever. His light has blinded him.

725. Prepared to Sin

A little boy was once forbidden by his mother to go swimming, but she permitted him to go out for a walk. When he came back, it was quite evident that he had disobeyed her and had gone in the water. When asked why, the little fellow answered, "Well, Mother, I happened to have my swimming trunks with me, so I decided to go in." When the child saw the beautiful sea, it presented a real temptation to him. In his mind was born the desire to disobey his mother—to sin. After all, sin is nothing but disobedience. The desire, however, could not have been translated into sin if he had not had his swimming trunks with him.

726. Slay the Monster

A man with an axe was attacked by a vicious dog, and in defending himself had to kill the animal. The owner was furious and asked the man how he dared kill his dog. The man replied that if he had not killed it, the dog would have torn him to pieces. "Well," said the owner, "why did you hit with the blade? Why didn't you just hit it with the handle?" "I would have," replied the man, "if it had tried to bite me with its tail." So, when I have to deal with sin, some people say, "Why don't you go about it more diplo-

matically? Why don't you choose less offensive words to describe it?" I answer, "I would, if it would bite me with its tail, but as long as it deals roughly with me, I will deal roughly with it; any kind of weapon that will help to slay the monster, I'm going to feel free to use."

727. A Believer Like Zacharias

A gentleman who believed himself perfect called to see an old Christian neighbor. They began talking about the interesting subject of the believer's perfection. "Can you point to a single perfect man or woman in the Bible?" inquired the aged saint. "Yes," readily answered the other, "turn to Luke 1:6 and you will read there of two—Elizabeth and Zacharias—who walked in all the commandments and ordinances of the Lord blameless." "Then you consider yourself a believer like Zacharias?" "Certainly I do," said the visitor. "Ah," replied the old man, "I thought you might be; and we read a few verses further on that he was struck dumb for his unbelief."

728. Are You Sinless?

A lady came to her pastor after he had preached one day and said, "But does not John say, 'Whosoever abideth in him sinneth not' (1 John 3:6)?" Of course he consented to the fact, telling her that the Christian does not voluntarily wallow in sin, but that we should also remember that the same apostle says, "If we say that we have no sin, we deceive ourselves, and the truth is not in us. If we confess our sins, he is faithful and just to forgive us our sins, and to cleanse us from all unrighteousness. If we say that we have not sinned, we make him a liar, and his word is not in us" (1 John 1:8-10). Then he turned to this Christian lady and asked her, "Can you say you are sinless?" There was no answer.

729. No Rights

We claim things as our right, sometimes, to which we have no right at all. In fact, we have no right to anything, and sometimes God impresses this upon us by taking things from us. Let us not be like the sick man to whom a benevolent gentleman had been giving a quart of milk a day. At last, the time came for this poor man to die, and of course the gift of milk was expected to come to an end. When he was gone, the gentleman called upon the widow. "I must tell you, sir," said she, "that my husband has made a will and has left the quart of milk to his brother!"

730. Temptation Attracts or Repels

Thomas à Kempis has said, "First there comes to the mind a bare thought of evil, then a strong imagination thereof, afterward delight and evil motion, and then consent." His advice was, "Withstand the beginnings." If you apply a magnet to the end of a needle that moves freely on its pivot, the needle affected by a strong attraction approaches as if it loved it. Reverse the order, applying the magnet to the other pole, and the needle shrinks away trembling as if it hated it. One man rushes into the arms of vice; another recoils from it in horror. According as the nature it addresses is holy or unholy, temptation attracts or repels, is loved or hated. Our Lord Jesus said, "Watch and pray, that ye enter not into temptation: the spirit indeed is willing, but the flesh is weak" (Matt. 26:41).

731. Sins Buried

An earnest servant of Christ preached on the text, "Thou wilt cast all their sins into the depths of the sea" (Micah 7:19). His little boy, ten years old, afterwards said to him, "Daddy, when you were talking about the Lord casting sin into the sea, you ought to have said that sin was heavy like stones, and would drop out of sight, or they might think it would float like corks on the top." Praise God, our sins are covered by the blood of Jesus as stones thrown into the ocean.

732. Don't Neglect the Son

Emperor Theodosius, in the 4th century, denied the deity of Christ as do many in this 20th century. When his son Arcadius was about sixteen, he decided to make him his partner in the government of the empire. Among the great men who assembled to congratulate the new wearer of the imperial purple was Bishop Amphilocus. He made a handsome address to the Emperor and was about to leave when Theodosius exclaimed, "What! Do you take no notice of my son?" Then the bishop went up to Arcadius and putting his hands upon his head said, "The Lord bless thee, my son." The Emperor, roused to fury by this slight, exclaimed, "What! Is this all the respect you pay to a prince that I have made of equal dignity with myself?" Amphilocus replied, "Sir, you do so highly resent my apparent neglect of your son, because I do not give him equal honors with yourself. Then what must the Eternal God think of you when you degrade His coequal and coeternal Son to the level of one of His creatures?"

733. The Unseen Sin

A half-witted man wore a most curious coat. All down the front it was covered with patches of various sizes, mostly large. When asked why the coat was patched in such a remarkable way, he answered that the patches represented the sins of his neighbors. He pointed to each patch and gave the story of the sin of someone in the village. On the back of his coat there was a small patch. On being asked what it represented, he said, "That is my own sin, and I cannot see it."

734. Don't Let Your Light Grow Dim

There is a danger that there may be a dimming of the light within us. It is worth our while to note some of the things that bring this sad eclipse of the soul. Anything that corrupts, degrades, or debauches the soul; anything that mars its innocence, or robs it of its purity, will at the same time dull the keenness of its perception as to what is right and what is wrong. Innocence is often compared to cleanness or whiteness, while guilt is described by the words dark, black, mire, and dirt. Conscience is like a glass through which the light streams. But if we rub coal dust or smut of any sort over the glass, the light will shine through it but dimly. And if we cover the glass with a sufficient coat of filth, it will not shine through at all. So sin makes foul the glass of the soul. Where the light shines clearly and the man has no doubt at all about what is right, if he yields to temptation and sinful thoughts make conquest of him, it will be as though tar stained the glass in his window. If he continues to sin and impure thoughts come to get possession of his soul, the light from heaven will finally be shut out entirely.

735. Call It by Its Real Name

Dr. J. Wilbur Chapman told of a distinguished Methodist minister of Australia who preached on sin. One of his church officers came afterward to talk with him in his study. He said to the minister: "Dr. Howard, we don't want you to talk so plainly about sin, because if our boys and girls hear you talking so much about sin, they will more easily become sinners. Call it a mistake if you will, but do not speak so plainly about sin." The minister took down a small bottle of strychnine that was marked "Poison." He said, "I see what you want me to do. You want me to change the label, such as 'Essence of Peppermint.' Don't you see what would happen? The milder you make the label, the more dangerous you make the poison."

736. What Makes Sin Sinful?

What makes sin sinful? I remember when I was in the army I was brought before my commanding officer because while I was on night duty I had opened a telegram I wasn't supposed to. Nobody had told me this. I thought it was part of my duty to open it and to communicate its contents to the officer on duty. I ended my defense with the words of Paul, "Sin is not imputed when there is no law" (Rom. 5:13). I was not punished. They saw the reasonableness of my contention that one cannot break a law that does not exist.

737. Lure of Sin

Spurgeon was right when he said, "Where the most beautiful cacti grow, there the venomous serpents are to be found at the root of every plant." And it is so with sin. Your fairest pleasures will harbor your grossest sins.

738. Not Welcomed

It is only natural when you are eagerly expecting someone to welcome him with open arms. Just imagine the disappointment of a father returning to his family from the war to find that he is not recognized. All along the family has been praying and waiting for his return, yet when he arrives he is not welcomed. There could be no greater shock to a father than that. A welcome by one's own family is the instinctive hope of all. "He came unto His own and his own received Him not."

739. Wrong Standard

Pride comes from the fact that we measure ourselves by earthly standards, instead of by God's standard for us. We are like the little boy who came to his mother and said, "Mamma, I am as tall as Goliath; I am nine feet high." "What makes you say that?" asked the surprised mother. "Well, I made a little ruler of my own and measured myself with it, and I am just nine feet high!"

740. Don't Gold Plate Your Life

Ruskin told of visiting a famous cathedral in which there are a number of colossal figures high up among the heavy timbers that support the roof. From the pavement these statues have the appearance of great beauty. Curious to exam them, Ruskin climbed to the roof and stood close beside them. He was disappointed to find that only the parts of the figures that could be seen from the pavement were finished. The backs were rough and unsightly.

741. Sin Is Sin

Spurgeon writes: "The shops in the square of San Marco were all religiously closed, for the day was a high festival. We were much disappointed, for it was our last day, and we desired to take away with us some souvenirs of lovely Venice. Our regret soon vanished, for on looking at the shop we meant to patronize, we readily discovered signs of traffic within. We stepped to the side door and found, when one or two other customers had been served, that we might purchase to our heart's content, saint's day or no saint's day. After this fashion, too many keep the laws of God to the eye, but violate them in the heart."

742. Indulgence

Thomas Manton says on indulging: "There were but two common parents of all mankind, Adam the Protoplast (the first created), and Noah the Restorer, and both failed due to appetite, the one fell by eating, and the other by drinking."

743. A Lost Inheritance

The son of a rich father forsook his fine home for a life of crime and immorality, bringing disgrace to his family and causing his father many years of deep sorrow. One day he learned of his father's death and decided to return home at once. He wanted to be present at the reading of the will to see if he had been left anything. He thought possibly his father out of kindness had bequeathed him something. Together, with other members of the family, he assembled at the lawyer's office to listen to the reading of the will. The first part of it was a long recital of his son's sins. Father had set them down carefully, one by one, expressing the grief of heart which he had borne for so many years. The son became more and more restless as he heard that sad story of his evil doings. He began to fidget and fuss in his seat, obviously disgusted with the whole proceedings. Finally, he could stand it no longer and grabbed his hat, rose to his feet, stomped out of the room, and slammed the door behind him. But he left too soon. For the second part of the will said that his father had left him $25,000. He could not subsequently be located and thus never got the money for the simple reason that he declined to hear about the sins which he refused to confess. He lost his inheritance.

744. Us Only

There was a small Christian sect of an exclusive nature which was holding a convention. Outside the auditorium there was displayed the motto, "Jesus Only." A strong wind blew the first three letters away, so that the sign read, "Us Only." Isn't that too often the sign that our prayers, attitudes, and behavior present to the world? And then we expect God to bless us.

745. No Repentance, No Pardon

Caleb Young, in Kentucky, thought that a man in the state's prison who was serving a life term had been too heavily sentenced. Bringing influence to bear upon the governor, he obtained a pardon for the man. He went to the prison and had a talk with the man. He said to him, "If you were to be released from this place, what would you do?" The man vindictively replied, "I would go and shoot the judge that sentenced me, the lawyer that prosecuted me, and the witnesses that testified against me." Mr. Young said nothing to the man about the pardon. He went out of the prison and tore the pardon to pieces.

746. *Vanity*

Two geese about to start southward on their annual autumn migration were entreated by a frog to take him with them. When the geese expressed their willingness to do so, if a means of conveyance could be devised, the frog produced a long stick and got the two geese to take it at each end while he clung to it by his mouth in the middle. In this manner the three were making their journey successfully when they were noticed from below by some men who loudly expressed their admiration of the device and wondered who had been clever enough to discover it. The vainglorious frog, opening his mouth to say, "It was I," lost his hold, fell to the earth, and was dashed to pieces. Beware, Christians, lest you meet with the same calamity as that of the frog through your vain-glorying in self.

747. *Sinner Like You and Me*

There was a criminal who was awaiting execution. A minister went to visit him, but there was not much response to his exhortation. On his way back home, the minister met one of his elders and told him about his experience. He asked the elder to go and see the criminal. The elder came back with great joy in his heart for what had been accomplished with him. The minister was very anxious to know why he had failed and the elder succeeded. This is what happened. As soon as the elder saw the criminal, he sat beside him, took his hand in his and said with much fervor and simplicity, "Wasn't it only the great love of God to send His Son into the world to die for sinners like you and me?" In a moment the fountain of the man's heart was broken up and he wept bitter tears. Afterward the criminal said, "When the minister spoke to me, it seemed like one standing far above me, but when that good man came in and sat down by my side and classed himself with me, I could not stand it any longer."

748. *Sin's Chain*

An overladen coal barge stood in the river. A sailor reported to the captain that the water was gaining upon the vessel, but the captain drove him away with scoffing. Twice, thrice the warning was repeated, but each time it went unheeded. At last the barge began to give evidence of sinking. The captain ordered the men to the boats. As they took their places, he said, "See, I told you there was plenty of time." Then he took out his knife to cut the cable to the barge. He fell back with a cry of horror; the cable was an iron chain.

749. A Sinner Who Didn't Think

A young man once said to a preacher, "I do not think I am a sinner." Then the preacher asked him if he would be willing for his mother or sister to know all he had done, said or thought, all his motives and all his desires. After a moment the young man said, "No, indeed, I certainly would not like to have them known—not for all the world.

750. Forgiveness Necessary

When Mr. Wesley was on a voyage with General Oglethorpe to Georgia, the General threatened revenge upon an offending servant, saying, "I never forgive." "Then I hope, sir," said Mr. Wesley, "that you never sin." The General saw the force of this remark and modified his action toward the servant.

751. Avoid Strife

A man let an offender go instead of avenging himself for an insult. He was criticized in consequence, and he said to the friend who chided him, "Tell me, my friend, if you were climbing a hill, and a great stone or block rolled down toward you, would you consider it disgraceful to step aside and allow it to roll past? If not, what disgrace can

there be in avoiding and giving way to a man aroused by anger until he has had time for reflection, and his agitated mind finds rest in repentance?" There is an old legend that tells of Hercules encountering a strange animal on a narrow road. He struck it with his club and passed. Soon the animal overtook him, now three times as large as before. Hercules struck it fast and furiously, but the more he clubbed the beast, the larger it grew. Then Pallas appeared to Hercules and warned him to stop. "The monster's name is Strife," he said. "Let it alone and it will soon become as little as at first." This is valuable advice for those of us Christians who engage in counterblows, thinking that only thus can we stop the blows.

752. Strong but Weak

Edinburgh Castle was captured only once in the whole history of Scotland. Its defenders thought that the steepness of the rock on one side made it inaccessible and impregnable, so they put no sentries there. In the grey mist of the early morning a little part of the enemy crept up the precipitous slopes and surprised the garrison into surrender. It was captured at its strongest point. Paul said, "When I am weak, then am I strong" (2 Cor. 12:10). Yet the reverse is often true also. "When I am strong, then am I weak."

753. Treasure in Heaven

When a friend once wrote to Dr. Livingston about the sacrifices he was making in spending his days among the savages of Central Africa, he made the spirited reply: "Is that a sacrifice which brings its own best reward in healthful activity, in the consciousness of doing good, in peace of mind, and in the hope of a glorious destiny hereafter? Away with such a thought! I never made a sacrifice." May we, too, seek "first the kingdom of God, and his righteousness," rather than our own selfish satisfaction.

754. Christian Forewarned

A man once remarked that he could not swallow what the preachers called "original sin and Adamic nature." "My good fellow," said a Christian to him, "there is no occasion for you to swallow it—it's inside you already." The sooner we realize that grim fact in our Christian lives, the better. "Forewarned is forearmed" is especially good advice for the Christian. Dangers inducing us to sin are not all found outside ourselves; they are also inside; and sometimes the enemies within are stronger and more furious than those without.

755. The Regenerated Sinner

An old Scotch minister was really disturbed when a fellow minister came to preach in his church, because to his surprise he gave a sermon to sinners. The Scotch minister could not keep the disappointment within him, so he turned to the visiting preacher and said, "Well, Rev. McDonald, that was a very good sermon which you preached, but it is very much out of place. I do not know one single unregenerate person in my congregation."

756. Sick Sheep

A visitor saw the shepherds in Nazareth bringing their flocks to water them at the well. When the sheep had drunk their fill, the shepherds called and their sheep followed them. The visitor asked the shepherds if the sheep always followed their own shepherds when they called them. "Yes," said a shepherd, "except under one condition." "What is that?" "The sheep that do not follow the voice of the shepherd are the sick sheep. If a sheep is healthy, it will always follow the shepherd, but if there is something wrong with the sheep, it will follow anybody."

757. Feel in Your Pockets

A neighbor heard that a poor woman was reduced to extreme poverty by the loss of her cow, which was her only means of support. He was personally unable to replace the cow for the poor woman, so he went around soliciting funds. Each neighbor offered sorrow and regret, but none practical assistance. He became impatient, and after being answered as usual by a plentiful shower of feeling, exclaimed. "Oh, yes! I don't doubt your feeling; but you don't feel in the right place." "Oh," said one, "I feel with all my heart and soul." "Yes, yes," replied the solicitor, "I don't doubt that either; but I want you to feel in your pocket." If we can feel in our pockets but don't, we commit sin.

758. The Constant Dissenter

We read about a church which was calling a new pastor. There were only a few negative votes, the great majority being in favor of the nominee. A gracious member of the minority moved to make the choice unanimous. But one man in that minority, a stern old Scotchman, was by no means disposed to make any such soft surrender of opinion, and he wasted no words. His ultimatum was quick and straight: "There is one thing ye might as well understand right here and now. I'll let you know there'll never be anything unanimous in this church as long as I am in it."

759. No Trespassing

In olden times gardens used to be enclosed. In Palestine every garden was enclosed by a wall—as was Gethsemane—or by a prickly hedge. "A garden inclosed is my sister, my spouse" (Song 4:12). To separate one's garden plot from the open field and shield it from harm was always the gardener's first care. Man in his sinful condition also shuts himself in. He discourages others from entering his property. He is afraid they will harm him. But Christ has commissioned His followers to plant the seed of the gospel and to water it in the hearts of men.

760. This Wonderfully Made Body

Of course, the body compels a great deal of admiration as the farmer cannot help admiring the smooth shiny seeds from which a beautiful field of wheat will one day emerge. If you fully understand what is in your body, how intricate, how methodical all its functions are, you cannot help but admire and honor it. You could not possibly create such a masterpiece. Scientists may make a living virus, but that's far from constructing a whole living body. But this wonderfully made body has been corrupted by your sin and mine. We have caused corruptibility to enter the cosmos, which includes our bodies.

761. Avoid Boasting

We should not let the sickness of other Christians lead us to brag that we are well because we are sinless while other Christians are sick because they are sinners. The proud heart is detestable to God. Perhaps we need to pray the well-known prayer of an early Wesleyan preacher: "Lord, save me from that good man—myself." It must be awful in the sight of God to see His children boasting of their health while condemning others because they are sick.

Spiritual Blindness

762. Prisoner Recognizes Sin

One day, after a gospel meeting in a prison in Greece, the chief of chaplains of the prisons was discussing with the preacher the wonderful response by the prisoners of Greece to the message of the Gospel: "When you deal with a prisoner, you do not need to persuade him that he is a sinner. His imprisonment is a proof of it. But there are many out of jail who should be in, and because they are out they argue all is well with them and they need no Savior."

763. Eye Trouble

A friend of mine went into a drugstore the other day and pointed to some toothbrushes on a rack. "Let me have a pink one," she requested. To her surprise, the clerk took down an orange one. "No, pink," she reminded him. This time he selected a lavender one. My friend began to sense the difficulty. "No, I said pink," she repeated pleasantly; the clerk's finger hovered uncertainly over the rack and neared the desired color, "That one," she declared emphatically. "I see you're color-blind," she remarked as he wrapped her purchase. With a sheepish smile he confessed, "I always call blue 'green.' " But this same friend had a color-blind relative who doggedly insisted that certain colors were a figment of other people's imaginations because he could not distinguish them. Do not be surprised when those who do not know God cannot accept as real the spiritual truths He has revealed through His Word. The "eyes of their understanding" have never been opened.

764. To Each His Own

Public opinion has its own valid functions, but it is inappropriate and insufficient in guiding a Christian worker. A broom, for instance, is not adapted to clean an oil painting. It has its own function, that of cleaning a floor, and it discharges this much more efficiently than if it were a paintbrush. How disastrous it would be if a body of well-meaning and earnest persons, armed with brooms, were to burst into an art gallery with a view to improving the paintings. The best intentions won't enable a rough instrument to accomplish work for which it is unfit. Similarly, public opinion, by reason of its conglomerate nature and massive force, is unfit to deal with the secrets of the kingdom of heaven.

765. No God/No Morals

Two friends, meeting after a long time, were discussing the current breakdown in morals, especially among the younger generation. "What do you suppose really causes it?" asked one who in the past had openly declared she felt no need of God in her life. Her Christian friend hesitated, feeling it would be useless to give her own opinion as a believer since the other had so often rejected her attempts in the past to speak of religious matters. Before she could formulate a reply, however, her friend advanced her own theory. "Don't you think the breakdown in religious values has something to do with it?" "Yes, I do," agreed the other quickly. "If young people have turned their backs on religion and feel that God doesn't exist, they no longer have any absolute standards of right and wrong, no authority to turn to for direction, and the result is confusion. Everyone does that which is right in his own eyes." Surprisingly, her friend agreed with her. Even unbelievers are beginning to realize that if God doesn't exist, society has nothing on which to base its ethics.

766. New Birth, Not New Surroundings

The Roman philosopher, Seneca, wrote to his friend Lucullus: "My wife has a moronic child, Harpasti, who suddenly became blind. What I am about to tell you will be difficult to believe, but it is true. We cannot make her understand that she has become blind and that no change in her environment will help her. She insists that her nurse take her to a house where it is not dark. It seems to me," continued the philosopher, "that what has happened to her is happening to all of us. Not one of us realizes that he is both miserable and vengeful."

767. Mad Over Religion?

Two friends, one an army officer, met after an interval of ten years. They had been attached to each other and shook hands cordially. After a little chat, the civilian, looking at the other man with a curious air, said, "By the way, General, they tell me you have gone mad over religion." "Well," responded the general, "I'm not aware of being crazy; as far as I know I'm enjoying all my senses. But you know, if I am, there is one comfort; I've got Jesus Christ for my keeper and heaven for my lunatic asylum, so I think I shall not do badly after all." The world may consider the faithful, practicing Christian crazy, but what counts is that God declares him righteous over and over again.

768. A Rewarding Life

The closer to God we are, the more peace and happiness we shall experience. A baker never expects to get a better cake than the ingredients he puts into it. Yet many people who complain that life is not as rewarding as they expected it to be, forget that in leaving out God they have left out that which alone can give life its glory, hope, love, and joy.

769. *Ignorance on a Grand Scale*

A man left $200,000 in his will for anyone who, through research, could prove before a court of justice that there is a soul and of what it consists. No one has been able to claim the legacy. Only in the Bible will you find the divine revelation concerning the soul of man.

770. *Ask the One Who Knows*

Suppose a robbery had been committed in a store in your neighborhood; you join the crowd standing outside and ask, "What happened?" Someone starts to fill you in on what's going on, though he hasn't been inside the building himself. Then the storekeeper comes out, and you ask the same question. His account differs in many details from that of the bystander. Whom would you believe? The answer is obvious. You realize that the man who stands outside a building is a very poor judge of what is taking place within. Yet, frequently the man who stands outside the circle of born-again Christians refuses to enter or even listen to what is going on inside the circle of those who are in Christ. Unfortunately, when he desires to get information on spiritual things, he doesn't go to those who have experienced the indwelling of the Spirit of God, but turns to worldly philosophers and rationalists, those outside of the circle of believers. Therefore the information he gets of what is going on inside is totally perverted.

771. *No Man Is an Island*

One day a man was hiking in the mountains when he came upon the hut of a hermit who had isolated himself from other human beings. He struck up a conversation with the hermit who told the visitor that he was completely self-sufficient to meet his own needs. He said, "I cut the trees and hewed the logs for my cabin, and I put it together with wooden pegs. I grow or hunt all my own food, and I get along just fine. I don't need anybody else."

The man looked at him for a moment, then said, "Tell me, how did you cut the trees you used for your cabin?"

The hermit replied, "With my axe."

Then the visitor said, "But wasn't someone else responsible for making that axe and your other tools, and for mining the iron that was used to make them? What about your clothes, do you make all of them?"

"No," replied the hermit, "I have to make a trip outside about once a year to get new clothes."

"Then," said the man again, "what about the shells that you use in your gun when you hunt your food, and what about the gun itself? Weren't you dependent on someone else for both?"

"Well," said the hermit reluctantly, "I guess so."

"The truth is," said the visitor, "that you are not as independent of others as you like to think. Even if you could sustain yourself completely without any of the things we've mentioned, you're still forgetting one vital thing which you could never supply or maintain by yourself."

"What's that?" asked the hermit.

Looking him full in the face, the man said, "Your own life." Whereupon the hermit fell silent and had little else to say.

772. *Only as You See Him*

At the Grand Canyon, a guide took a group of tourists to the southern rim. Among the sightseers were an artist, a minister, and a cowboy. After they had beheld the spectacle for a few minutes, the guide asked the artist, "Could you paint a picture like that?" "Never!" the artist replied. "Only God could make that scene." The guide then turned to the minister. "Could you describe such grandeur in a sermon, Pastor?" The minister shook his head. "No, sir. Such majesty defies mortal description." Finally he turned to the cowboy. "And what do you think about this Grand Canyon, partner?" The cowboy answered in wonderment, "I was just thinking—what an awful place to lose a cow!" The unsaved look at Christ and see a good teacher, a moral man but not the Son of God.

Stewardship

773. *Wise Investment*

Baylor University is a thriving institution in Beaumont, Texas. The Christian who gave the money for building that school later lost all his property. Men of the world asked him, "Don't you wish you had the money back that you put into that school?" He replied, "Not at all. It is all that I have saved. If I had kept that money, I would have lost it too. I am thankful that I gave that building when I did." The world may judge us by what we do with the property God has placed in our keeping. Nevertheless, we should only be concerned with God's estimation of our stewardship of His gifts.

774. *Christians as Stewards*

What the Treasury Department requires in financial matters, the Word of God requires in spiritual matters. The apostle Paul tells us that Christians must regard themselves as "stewards of the mysteries of God" (Rom. 14:10c). We are not originators of these mysteries, we are simply the recipients of them, holding them in trust under God. Paul wants to remind us by this expression that we are accountable. He has just finished speaking of that day when the work of each one will be made manifest. Just imagine how careless a treasurer might be if he knew that he would never have to give an accounting of the funds entrusted to him. As Christians we are to live constantly in view of the day of accounting that is coming. We will have to give an accounting for everything God has given us.

775. *Only Today Is Ours*

John Bate said, "Today is given us by Him to whom belong days. We have the power to use it as we please; we compass our salvation or our damnation within it; we can travel twenty-four hours of time nearer to heaven or to hell. We are responsible for its proper use. How important that we do the proper work of today in the sphere of today. That man is blessed who, at the close of his day, can look upon his finished work and anticipate tomorrow as bringing nothing but the things which legitimately belong to it. Today God speaks to us in His Word that we harden not our hearts. Today is the day of salvation. All duties, all privileges, all trials, all joys, all sorrows; in one word, everything we have, we have today. Yesterday is gone, tomorrow is not, only today is ours, and only in today do we hold all our possessions."

776. *Purpose of Stewardship*

Would you call the farmer faithful who didn't care enough to cultivate, weed, and spray his fields after the seed was planted? He should change his methods if he's not getting an adequate yield of produce. The purpose of farming is to raise a good crop, and the purpose of stewardship is to multiply the investment entrusted to a manager by his employer. Christian stewardship entails the responsibility of investing whatever time, talents, and possessions God has given us to yield the best returns to Him.

777. *Spiritual Gems Must Be Sought*

On a visit to Sri Lanka I saw divers go down to the ocean floor and scoop up mud to find the precious stones hidden there. These gems can not be found on the beach but down in the ocean bed. All the secrets of God in nature have been wrested from Him by patient, painstaking investigation on the part of men.

778. *Stewardship Training*

When I was living in Khartoum, Sudan, a kind man named Stelios Costantinidies used to test me in a very interesting way. I will never forget it for it made a man of me. He would give me sufficient money and a little over to buy a small treat, and then wait to see whether I would return the change. He never asked how much the soda or ice cream cone cost—just how much I had spent. I had to be truthful, so I took the money out and gave him the right change. If you don't think this is a good test of character, try it on your own children.

Tests and Trials

779. *Win Where You Are*

"Did you ever notice," asked an old lady, as she smiled into the troubled face before her, "that when the Lord told the discouraged fishermen to cast their nets again, it was right in that same old place where they had been working all night and had caught nothing? If we could only go off to some new place every time we get discouraged, trying again would be an easier thing. If we could be somebody else, or go somewhere else, or do something else, it might not be hard to have fresh faith and courage. But it is the same old net in the same old pond for most of us. The old temptations are to be overcome, the old faults to be conquered, and the old trials and discouragements which we failed yesterday must be faced again today. We must win success where we are if we are to win it at all. It is the Master Himself who, after all these toilsome, disheartening efforts that we call failures, bids us, 'Try again.'"

780. *Trials Help Development*

One day a small boy saw a butterfly struggling to emerge from its cocoon. It was straining with all its might to get out of the opening which was too small. Thinking he was helping the butterfly, the boy took his knife and slit the cocoon. But to his dismay the butterfly emerged with small and shriveled wings and was unable to fly. Within a short time it was dead. When the boy asked his father about it, his father explained that the butterfly needed the struggle to get out of the cocoon, for this was the process that developed its wings and made them strong enough for flight. In trying to help by relieving the butterfly of its painful struggle, he had actually deprived it of that which was necessary for its development and its very life. This same principle carries over into all of human life— the struggles and the trials we face actually serve for our development, not only in the physical realm but also in the moral and spiritual.

781. *Patience by Tribulation*

A certain lady prayed a great deal for patience. She complained to another Christian that while she prayed for patience, all she seemed to get was trouble. "The Lord is sending you trouble in order to produce patience in you," was the reply. How many times have you prayed for patience, and the Lord sent along your way a child that was naughty, a boss who was demanding, a husband or wife who was exasperating to live with? It was all an answer to your prayer for patience so that you may have the opportunity to exercise and practice it. Accept it from the hand of God, for that is part of your training.

782. Music in the Storm

Legend has it that a German baron made a great Aeolian harp by stretching wires from tower to tower of his castle. When the harp was ready, he eagerly listened for the music. But it was the calm of summer, and in the still air the wires hung silent. Autumn came with its gentle breezes, and there were faint whispers of song. At length the winter winds swept over the castle, and now the harp answered in majestic music. This is a very good illustration of what our Lord meant when He said, "Blessed are the mourners." Their blessedness is more apparent at times when adversity and sorrow strike. If as a Christian you can laugh and be jovial when everything goes well, the world will think nothing of it. But they will be deeply impressed if you can sing in the time of storm. This is why the Lord associates blessedness with mourning and sorrow in this life.

783. How to Use Suffering

An unbeliever once read the story of the crucifixion of the Lord Jesus Christ. As he pondered it, he gave vent to the following expression: "There is a Man who not only suffered, but who knew how to use His suffering." This is the aim of pa-

tience. Let her have a perfect work, James 1:4 says. What does he really mean by that? The word translated "work" here is the Greek *ergon* which indicates that endurance should be active, not passive. James wants to correct a great misapprehension about the word *hupōmonē*, "patience." We have seen that this word "patience" actually means "to bear under." It gives the picture of someone who is under a terrific load. James is saying that as you are bearing that terrific load, don't remain stationary; move about, exercise your energy. There should be no passive endurance in the Christian life. The Christian should be aggressive, and in spite of the burdens of life he is carrying, he should move forward to the goal that is set before him.

784. Afflicted Hearts

Some of the greatest benefits to mankind have had their source in men who have experienced great affliction. The German poet Goethe said, "I never experienced affliction that did not turn into a poem." The music that gives man a taste of heaven has often come from afflicted hearts.

785. Jesus—The Refiner

Some years ago in Dublin, a company of women met to study the Bible. One of them was puzzled by the words of Malachi 3:3, "And he shall sit as a refiner and purifier of silver." After some discussion, a committee was appointed to call on a silversmith and learn what they could on the subject. The silversmith readily showed them the process. "But, sir," said one, "do you sit while the refining is going on?" "Oh, yes, indeed" he said. "I must sit with my eyes steadily fixed on the surface, for if the time necessary for refining is exceeded in the slightest degree, the silver is sure to be damaged." At once they saw the beauty and comfort of the Scripture passage. As they were leaving, the silversmith called after them, "Oh, one thing more! I only know when the process is complete by seeing my own image reflected on the silver." That is what the Lord Jesus wants to see in you and me as He refines us by fire—His blessed image. And it will be reflected to others, too.

786. Burdens Bring Blessings

An ant was seen carrying a long piece of straw. Finally it came to a crack in the rock which was like a precipice to the tiny creature. After attempting to take its burden across in several ways, the ant went to one end of the straw and pushed it in front of him over the crack till it reached to the other side, crossed over on the straw, and then pulled it after him. There is no burden which you and I carry faithfully and patiently, but will some day become a bridge to carry us. The God of circumstances will not place a burden upon us that is heavier than we can bear. Our burdens are only heavy enough to serve as a bridge to carry us over in such a manner that others may say after we have

gone, "Blessed is he who has endured."

787. Making You a Blessing

A fable tells of a little piece of wood that once complained bitterly because its owner kept whittling away at it, cutting it and filling it full of holes. But the one who was cutting it so remorselessly paid no attention to its complaining. He was making a flute out of that piece of ebony, and he was too wise to give up because the wood moaned so piteously. His actions seemed to say, "Little piece of wood, without these holes and all this cutting, you would be an ugly stick forever— just a useless piece of ebony. What I am doing now may make you think that I am destroying you when actually I am changing you into a flute whose sweet music will comfort sorrowing hearts. My cutting you is the making of you, for only thus can you be a blessing to the world."

788. Taste the Sweetness and Escape the Sting

It is said that the way the natives in the East collect honey without being stung by the bees is quite remarkable. They are not protected by their clothing for they hardly wear any. And yet, although surrounded by clouds of angry bees, they rarely suffer. The explanation given is that these natives are quite passive, deliberate in their movements, making no effort to protect themselves, not attempting to drive the swarm away. If a bee settles upon them, it does not sting them any more than it would attempt to sting a piece of wood. The Westerner, on the other hand, is nervous, restless, combative; he attempts to frighten the bees, is manifestly scared himself, makes a noise, gesticulates, runs away, and ends by being badly stung. Our troubles in life compass us about like bees. If we fret and fume, we shall feel the sting and miss the honey. But if we live in quietness and confidence, we shall taste the sweetness and escape the sting.

789. Not a Curse but a Blessing

Dr. Thomas Lambie, for many years a medical missionary in Abyssinia, said that while he was in Africa he learned something very significant from the natives. They often had to cross bridgeless streams, a difficult procedure because of the danger of being swept off their feet and carried downstream to great depths or hurled to death against the hidden rocks. Dr. Lambie learned from the natives the best way to make such a hazardous crossing. The man about to cross found a large stone, the heavier the better, lifted it to his shoulder, and carried it across the stream as ballast. The extra weight of the stone kept his feet solidly on the bed of the stream so that he could cross safely without being swept away. Thus, the spiritual man regards the heavy stones, the burdens he has to carry in life, not as

curses as the natural man would tend to interpret them, but as steadying influences, as God's provisions enabling him to cross safely to the realm beyond.

790. Real or Artificial?

It is related of the Queen of Sheba that she sent two wreaths of roses to Solomon, one real and the other artificial. To test his reputed wisdom she defied him to detect the genuine from the artificial. Solomon at once directed that some bees be brought into the room. Immediately they flew to the real flowers and ignored the counterfeit. The real disciples of Christ are known by the bees that cluster around to sting them. Artificial flowers don't attract stinging bees. Rejoice, therefore, when you are excommunicated from the organized world of artificial religion.

791. Learn from the Birds

Let us learn from the birds. What is it that enables them to fly? Wings? Of course, but not wings alone. It is the resistance of the air that makes flight possible. A bird flies much as an oarsman rows his boat. As oars are used to push against the resistance of water, thus sending the craft ahead, the scooped-out shape of the underside of the bird's wings helps it get a "grip" on the air. The air resists and the bird pushes against the resistance with the downward stroke of its wings. By such pushing movements, it succeeds in flying. Throughout life, progress is made only in the face of opposition. The bird flies through the resisting medium of air. The brook trout needs the resisting water if he is to swim. A democracy thrives through a system of opposing political parties and checks and balances in government. The spirit of a person grows stronger, not as life becomes easier, but as testings and temptations are met, struggled with, and beaten into submission.

792. Move a Great Load Smoothly

There is an analogy between our lives and the different kinds of boats we have today. There is the rowboat, the sailboat, and the steamboat. All three of them are able to carry loads. The rowboat carries the least because its motion depends on the strength of those who row. The sailboat carries a little more for its motion depends on the wind. However, there is a chance that the wind will toss the boat around quite a bit, and it will be difficult to reach the goal. The steamboat, however, depends neither on human strength nor on the winds, but on the power within which will move it to its destination in spite of the weakness of human strength and the fury of outside circumstances. This is what Christ desires of us. He desires His followers to develop the capacity to carry a heavy load in life without permitting that load to depress them, but rather allowing it to help them to move smoothly. I do not know if you have ever traveled on a boat which is empty, which has no cargo. The motion is terribly rough and the seamen dread it. But when the boat is loaded, it goes along smoothly. That is the goal of trials in the Christian journey. They help us to get settled on the sea, furious though it may be, and move smoothly on to our destination.

793. Joy in Affliction

One day I visited the little room where one of the missionaries of AMG lives in Athens, Greece. This man is an invalid who was condemned to execution by the Nazis during the occupation of Greece in World War II. Seven bullets went through his body and he was left for dead, but he escaped the ordeal alive. Through this experience, and the personal witness of a servant of Christ, he found Christ as his Savior. After becoming blessed in the Lord through the new birth, he did not want to keep the good news to himself but was anxious to share it with others. Although he suffered eighty percent incapacitation and constant excruciating pain so that he had to remain in bed most of the time, his great rejoicing in the midst of affliction attracted attention. A radio announcer came to visit him and told his story over the air in Athens, inviting suffering people to write to this invalid who knew the secret of being joyful in the midst of affliction. The same thing happened with respect to one of the leading newspapers in Athens. As a result, this consecrated missionary now has a congregation of about nine thousand people all over the world who write to him asking the secret of his joy. He has written about thirty-eight thousand letters to individuals thus far as he glories in his tribulation (Rom. 5:3).

794. *Double the Burden*

Once a porter in Asia, taking his carrying pole, went to meet a missionary at the train depot. At the station he found that the luggage consisted of one large, heavy bag instead of several smaller ones which the missionary usually carried. He couldn't divide that bag into two portions, and plainly he couldn't carry that heavy bag hanging from one end of his pole. He looked about until he found a stone about the same weight as the bag, hung that from one end of the pole, the bag from the other, and walked proudly home with his double burden! The easier way for him was to carry twice as much. By carrying the two when he needed only to have carried one, he balanced his burden. It's easier to carry two bags than one, for they balance. A one-sided load is a greater strain than a balanced burden that is twice as heavy. A milkmaid with the old-fashioned yoke always walked more easily and straightly carrying two full milk pails than under the awkward burden of one. By doubling a burden you actually make it easier to bear because you have balanced it. We all have our own burdens, and it often seems as if they are enough to carry. But the Bible says,

"Bear ye one another's burdens." Take on another's as well, and balance your own. That is the yoke of Christ. The way to carry our own burdens more easily is to help carry somebody else's burden. Perhaps that's one reason God gave us two hands—one for our own burdens and one for our neighbor's. "Look not every man on his own things, but every man also on the things of others" (Phil. 2:4).

795. *One Problem at a Time*

Try this simple experiment. Collect 365 little sticks, toothpicks, if you wish. Tie them together. Now try to break the bundle with your hands. No matter how strong you are, it will be a tough job. Make a smaller bundle, say 30, and it is still too difficult to break. But take just one at a time and, no matter how weak you are, you'll be able to break each one. You're exactly the same person who tried to handle all the sticks together, but this time you changed your way of solving the problem, and it became much easier. "Sufficient unto the day is the evil thereof" (Matt. 6:34).

796. *A Lesson From Suffering*

A bird had no interest in learning the song its master wanted to teach it while its cage was full of light. Its master covered the cage to darken it. He then whistled the same song over and over until the bird learned it by heart. When it could repeat it note for note, the owner uncovered the cage and the bird sang it beautifully. This is an illustration of the way God sometimes deals with us. He darkens the cage of our lives in order to teach us some divine song.

797. Tested for Strength

If steel is to be used in a reliable manner, it must be tested and proven. So must the servant of Christ. Someone describes his visit to a steel mill as follows: "All around me were little partitions and compartments. Steel had been tested to the limit, and marked with figures that showed its breaking point. Some pieces had been twisted until they broke, and the strength of torsion was marked on them. Some had been stretched to the breaking point, and their tensile strength indicated. Some had been compressed to the crushing point and also marked. The supervisor of the steel mill knew just what these pieces of steel would stand under the strain. He knew just what they would bear if placed in a ship, building, or bridge. He knew because the testing room revealed it." It is often so with us as God's children. God doesn't want us to be like vases of glass or porcelain. He doesn't want us to be hothouse plants, but stormbeaten oaks; not sand dunes, driven with every gust of wind, but granite rocks withstanding the fiercest storms. To make us strong He must bring us into His testing room of suffering. Better the storm waters with Christ than the smooth waters without Him.

798. Those Pesky Insects

Henry Ward Beecher wrote: "In the sultry insect-breeding days of summer, how insects abound! Every tree is a harbor for stinging pests. Wherever you sit they swarm around and annoy you and destroy your peace and comfort. By and by there come those vast floods of clouds that bring tornadoes and are thunder-voiced; up through the valleys and over the hills and mountains sweep drenching and cleansing rains. When the storm has ceased, the clouds are gone, and you sit under the dripping tree, not a fly, not a gnat, not a pestilent insect is to be seen. The winds and rains have driven them all away. Has it never been so with those ten thousand little pests of pride, vanity, envying, jealousy, and unlawful desire. For days they have teased and fretted you and kept you in conflict with conscience, affection, and all the higher motivations, until God sent you some great searching sorrow, some overwhelming trouble? In those hours He graciously sustained you and lifted you up towards Himself, so that, although you suffered unutterable affliction, you felt that it had cleansed you from jealousies, pride, envies, vanity, the whole swarm of venomous and stinging insects that beset you."

799. The Fruit of Affliction

A man completely dejected by life's afflictions was walking one day in the botanical gardens of Oxford when his attention was arrested by a fine pomegranate tree with a stem which was cut almost through. On asking the gardener the reason, he received an answer which explained the wounds of his troubled spirit. "Sir," said he, "this tree used to shoot so strongly that it bore nothing but leaves. I was therefore obliged to cut it in this manner, and when it was almost cut through then it began to bear plenty of fruit."

800. He Hasn't Made You Yet

A happily married woman with two children lost both of them. They were buried in the same grave, and she went into a deep emotional collapse. For some years she became as weak and helpless as a little child. She had to be fed by members of her family who ministered to her. One day as her aunt, who was a joyful Christian, took her turn at feeding her, this woman who was unusually despondent that morning said, "Oh, Auntie, you say that God loves us. You say it, and you keep on saying it. I used to think that way, too, but if He loves us, why did He make me as I am?" The aunt, after kissing her gently, said with the wisdom of years, "He hasn't made you yet, child. He's making you now!"

When through fiery trials thy pathway shall lie,
My grace, all-sufficient, shall be thy supply;
The flame shall not hurt thee; I only design
Thy dross to consume and thy gold to refine.

801. Overcoming Difficulties

Those who heard Jenny Lind, the sweet singer of Stockholm, have written of the wonderful quality of her voice and the charm of the songs she sang. Yet few realize that she owed as much to the school of suffering and sorrow as to the academy where her powers were developed. Her childhood was full of sadness. The woman with whom she lived locked her in her room each day when she went to work; the only means the child found of spending the long hours was to sit by the window and sing to herself. One day a music teacher in the city passing by heard the voice of the unseen singer and detected its possibilities. He called a friend to his side, and together they listened to the wonderful voice within. They got in touch with the child's guardian and made arrangements for the almost friendless girl to be given her chance. There were many difficulties to be overcome, but step by step she mounted the ladder of fame. She astounded London, Paris, Vienna, Berlin, and New York. Some say there never was such a voice, trilling like the thrush, pure as the note of the lark. But those who knew her best realized how the sorrows of her childhood gave a richness and depth to her song that otherwise would have been unattainable. She herself once wrote:

In vain I seek for rest
In all created good:
It leaves me still unblest,

And makes me cry for God.
And safe at rest I cannot be
 Until my heart finds rest in
Thee.

802. Affliction Unavoidable

The lawns which we wish to keep in the best condition we mow very frequently. But out in the fields there is no such repeated cutting. The tall unkept grass of the field may be proud that it has never experienced the power of the mower blades, but the cut grass is more beautiful and more serviceable. Do we as human beings before God have any more voice in the matter than the grass in our lawns? There is nothing that the grass can do to hinder the frequent cutting by the owner. Aren't we as impotent in the hands of God as the grass is under the mower? Affliction is a fact in life. Let us accept it and endeavor to find out, not so much why God permits it, as how God wants us to use it.

803. The Well of Love

In Northern Greece we have a beautiful summer camp at the foot of Mount Olympus. It is right on the shores of the blue Aegean Sea whose water is very salty. But stand where the water has just receded and dig a few inches, and the hole will fill up with the most refreshing, sweet water you have ever tasted. It has come from the mountains and hidden out of sight to be discovered only by digging. When the sea rolls in and pours its bitter flood over the little hole, though it covers it with a shroud of brackish waters, the stream of sweet water still flows. Such should be the stream of love in our hearts. When the flood of unkindness and wrong pours over us, we may be treated cruelly by the world. But whatever injustice we may have to endure from others, the well of love within us should never retain a trace of bitterness but remain pure and sweet.

804. Wrought by Fire

The Cathedral of Nuremburg contains some rare and exquisite workings in iron. But was the iron just pinched into shape? How many strokes did it receive? How many blows did it undergo on the anvil? How was it beaten here and there? How was it bent forward, and backward, and forward, and backward again? How was it distorted and contorted? How was it hammered and hammered till by and by it was covered with little speckles as multitudinous as those in frost-pictures, and far more permanent? Those speckles were wrought out by incessant workings in the fire and on the anvil under the hammer. Think also of the many pieces of iron that failed this trial. Their inner flaws could not endure, and they were cast aside. Similarly, suffering makes a man or spoils him. Our Christlikeness is measured by our willingness to suffer with Christ and for Christ. Since the Body of Christ is the Church, we must be willing to suffer for the other members of His Body. In this suffering there is an inbuilt joy.

805. The Hidden Opening

There is a place along the Hudson River where, as you sail, you seem to be entirely hemmed in by hills. The boat drives on toward a rocky wall, and it seems as if it must either stop or be dashed to pieces. Just as you come within the shadow of the mountain, an opening is suddenly discovered, and the boat passes out into one of the grandest bays on the river. So it is with temptation. You are not to seek it, not to enter into it; God promises no way out in such a case. But if it meets you on your heavenward journey, you are to go straight on, though you see no way out. The way will reveal itself in due time if you only keep on your way, being the way of duty—the way of the Lord. As in the river, the beautiful bay lies just around the menacing rock. So it will often be found that your sweetest and best experience in life lies just beyond your most threatening temptation.

806. Triumph over Adversity

Naturalists are amazed at the resistance of weak things in nature. There is security and triumph of frail things that baffles man's understanding and imagination. "It is a curious thing," wrote Kay Robinson, "that the extremes of heat and cold seem to be most easily endured by the flimsiest creatures. What is it that, when the frost is splitting our strongest metal water-pipes, protects the tiny tubes of life-giving moisture in the almost spectral organism of a gnat? Larger things get frostbitten and perish. In tropical countries the tiniest insects brave the blistering midday heat which shrivels the largest herbage, and drives men, birds and animals gasping under shelter. In India a small, blue butterfly flits all day about the parched grass or sits in full blaze of the sun where metal or stone becomes so hot that it burns the hand. What heat-resisting secret resides in the minute body of that little butterfly, scarcely thicker than notepaper? Nature's power of preserving life touches the miraculous." The same God who made the natural world made the spiritual also. Similarly, then, the saints have the least reason to be afraid when they most feelingly recognize their utter weakness and dependence. We prevail by yielding; we succumb to conquer like those sea-flowers that continue to bloom amid the surf when the rocks are pounded. In acquiescence and diffidence, in yielding and clinging, we triumph over adversity as the fern survives geological cataclysms and the butterfly the scorching sun. In our weakness we experience God's strength (2 Cor. 12:9).

807. New Power, New Joy

The treasures of His grace are never exhausted. In the realm of the spirit there is something that stirs within man, a deep-rooted instinct for seeking. God has hidden His treasures in the difficult and arduous ways of experience. Experience contains precious treasures that men find only as they journey faithfully along life's hazardous road. When we conquer and overcome, we find a treasure of God in the conquest of a certain sin, in the overcoming of a great temptation; we find the hidden manna which may be fresh courage, new strength to overcome another temptation that has harassed us for a long time. New strength and new joy are ours through conquest. In the midst of this difficult way of discovering new things about life, men learn to tackle it with new equipment and new determination. The story told by a certain man can be echoed by most of us: "I wrestled," he said, "all night, in the grip of a fearful sin that was slowly dragging my soul to hell. All through the night the fearful battle raged, and I felt that my soul was lost; but with the coming of the dawn there shone a light brighter than the dawn. The Son of Man was at my side and the temptation was thrust from me in His strength. I arose from my knees, strengthened in body and soul, and prepared to meet anything that might come my way." You and I have wrestled like that man and have found new power and new joy when we have conquered a temptation in the power of God. The man of faith can find, if only he will seek, the promise of a glorious dawn even in the darkest night.

808. Rescued from Difficulties

To quote G. Campbell Morgan: "I remember hearing a very dear friend of mine in a conference say that if the Lord leads us into difficulties, He leads us out; but that, if we get into difficulties of our own making, we have to get out ourselves. I thank God that is not true of my life. That is not what I have found out. Yes, it is true, if He leads me into difficulty, He will lead me out; but if I wander off in my own foolishness, He will still follow me, and lead me out."

Thankfulness

809. We've Won

Napoleon said, "Battles are won, not by men, but by a man." He was right in more ways than one. Victories are won, not by Christians but by Christ. It is our privilege and joy to share in His victory. Like the small boy who jumped up and down shouting "We've won, we've won!" at a football game—though he was not a member of the team or of the school represented by the team, we too can rejoice in a victory with which we associate ourselves. We can live in joy and triumph. We can shout, "We've won!" over the victory that was accomplished by our Lord Jesus Christ on Calvary nearly 2,000 years ago.

810. Count Your Blessings

A poverty-stricken woman was found on Christmas Day eating a dinner that consisted of a piece of bread and a small fish. A minister who visited her spoke commiseratingly of the poverty of her fare, to which the old woman with face aglow, replied, "Poor fare? Dear heart, don't you see that the Lord has laid tribute on land and sea to feed me this blessed Christmas Day?" This woman owned the earth, though she ate only bread and herring for Christmas dinner.

811. Victory through Christ

An American admiral had a small card printed and circulated among his subordinates and workers. On it in gray type was this background: "It Can't Be Done," and then, in bold black type across this was printed, "But Here It Is." As we look at sin and realize its strength, defeat would seem to be inevitable were it not for Christ. "But thanks be to God, which giveth us the victory through our Lord Jesus Christ." The phrase "which giveth us" is a present participle *(didonti)* in Greek. A better translation would be "who keeps on giving us." This is not just one victory that God gives us but a constant experience of victory through Christ.

812. Dumber Than the Animals

One year when Christmas Day came on a Sunday, a farmer decided to go to church. (Like some people, he thought he was fulfilling his religious obligation by going to church twice a year—at Christmas and Easter!) The sermon that day was preached from the text, "The ox knoweth his owner, and the ass his master's crib: but Israel doth not know, my people doth not consider" (Is. 1:3). Isaiah is saying that man is dumber than the animals. After church the farmer returned home and stood among his cows. One of them began to lick his hand—a practical demonstration of the sermon he had just heard. Strong man though he was, the farmer began to weep as he thought, "God did much more for me, and yet I never thanked Him. My cow is far more grateful than I am. What do I ever give her other than grass and water?"

813. Gratitude to God

Men will endure almost anything as long as they have hope. Cyrus Field said he was nearly in despair on many occasions as he sought to make his vision of the transatlantic cable a reality. Some called it a "mad feat of stubborn ignorance," that a man should endure all that he and his co-workers went through to make this feat possible. "Many times," he confessed, "when wandering in the forests of Newfoundland in the pelting rains, on the decks of ships on dark, stormy nights, alone, far from home, I have almost accused myself of madness and folly to sacrifice the peace of family, and all the hope of life, for what might prove, after all, but a dream. . . . And yet one hope has led me on; and I have prayed that I might not taste death til this work was accomplished. That prayer is answered. And now, beyond all acknowledgments to men, is the feeling of gratitude to God."

814. God's Gift of Laughter

It is said that Dr. Theodore Cuyler and Mr. Spurgeon were once out in the fields enjoying God's sunshine and the beauties of nature. Dr. Cuyler told a story at which Mr. Spurgeon laughed until his sides shook. Suddenly Mr. Spurgeon said, "Theodore, let's get down on our knees and thank God for laughter." And these two happy Christian preachers knelt in the field and thanked God for His great gift of laughter.

815. Recognize God's Blessings

A gentleman of wealth, but a stranger to a personal knowledge of God, was walking alone through his grounds one evening. Coming to the small hut of a poor man who earned his family's bread by his daily labor, he heard the continuous sound of loud speaking. Curiosity prompted him to stop and listen. The man of the house happened to be at prayer with his family. As soon as the gentleman could distinguish the words, he heard him give thanks to God for the goodness of His providence in giving them food to eat and clothes to put on, and in supplying them with what was necessary and comfortable in the present life. He was immediately struck with astonishment and confusion, and said to himself, "Does this poor man who has nothing but the meanest fare, and that purchased by hard work, give thanks to God for His goodness to himself and family, while I, who enjoy ease and honor, and everything that is pleasant and desirable, have hardly ever bent my knee or made any acknowledgement to my Maker and Preserver?" This incident was the means used by God to bring this rich man to a realization of his lack of what makes a person really blessed. It was not long before he accepted the Lord Jesus Christ, whose blessing is evidence in both poverty and riches.

The Tongue

816. Slander Hurts

There's no doubt that slander hurts. There's only a single letter's difference between "words" and "swords." Slanders are like flies; they light upon our sores where they know they will hurt the most. Sir Francis Bacon expressed a profound truth when he said, "The worthiest persons are frequently attacked by slanders, as we generally find it to be the best fruit which the birds will peck at."

817. The Lesson of the Tongue

Socrates of Constantinople, an early church historian, tells of an ignorant man who came to him asking him to teach him a Psalm or some part of Scripture. Socrates began to read to him the 39th Psalm, "I said, I will take heed to my ways, that I sin not with my tongue." As soon as he had read the first verse, Pambo, for that was his name, shut the book and took his leave saying that he would go learn that point first. His instructor waited and waited for him, but he did not come back. Finally, one day Socrates met Pambo accidentally and asked where he had been. Pambo said he was still learning that first lesson about the tongue. Forty-nine years later when someone else asked him why he did not learn anything else from the Scriptures, his reply was the same. Is it then any wonder that James takes almost the whole third chapter to discuss this all-important part of the body?

818. Little Things

We should mind little things in life—little courtesies, little matters of personal appearance, little extravagances, little minutes of wasted time, little details in our work. It seems that a thing cannot be too small to command our attention. The first hint Newton had, leading to his very important optical discoveries, was derived from a child's soap bubble. The art of printing was suggested by a man cutting letters in the bark of a tree. The telescope was the outcome of a boy's amusement with two glasses in his father's shop. Goodyear neglected his skillet until it was red hot, and the accident guided him to the manufacture of vulcanized rubber—little things, every one a little thing. Yet how important they proved to be to the man who had the wit to correlate these things with the idea in his head. So the tongue is like the helm of a ship. The helm is small, but it can direct a big vessel.

819. The Tongue—The Best and Worst

Xanthus, the philosopher, once told his servant that the next day he was going to have some friends for dinner and that he should get the best thing he could find in the market. The philosopher and his guests sat down the next day at the table. They had nothing but tongue—four or five courses of tongue—tongue cooked in this way, and tongue cooked in that way. The philosopher finally lost his patience and said to his servant, "Didn't I tell you to get the best thing in the market?" The servant said, "I did get the best thing in the market. Isn't the tongue the organ of sociability, the organ of eloquence, the organ of kindness, the organ of worship?" Then Xanthus the philosopher said, "Tomorrow I want you to get the worst thing in the market." And on the morrow the philosopher sat at the table, and there was nothing there but tongue—four or five courses of tongue—tongue in this shape and tongue in that shape. The philosopher again lost his patience and said, "Didn't I tell you to get the worst thing in the market?" The servant replied, "I did; for isn't the tongue the organ of blasphemy, the organ of defamation, the organ of lying?" Well done, servant; you certainly taught the philosopher a lesson, the same lesson the Apostle James wants to teach us in the third chapter. The tongue can do great good, and it can do great evil.

820. Undoing Gossip's Harm

There was a peasant with a troubled conscience who went to a monk for advice. He said that he had circulated a vile story about a friend, only to find out the story was not true. "If you want to make peace with your conscience," said the monk, "you must fill a bag with chicken feathers, go to every dooryard in the village, and drop at each of them one fluffy feather." The peasant did as he was told. Then he returned to the monk and announced he had done penance for his folly. "Not yet," replied the monk, "Take your bag, make the rounds again and gather up every feather that you have dropped." "But the wind must have blown them all away," said the peasant. Words are easily dropped, but no matter how hard you try, you can never get them back again.

821. Tongue Control

Once a young man came to that great philosopher Socrates to be instructed in oratory. The moment the young man was introduced he began to talk, and there was an incessant stream for some time. When Socrates could get in a word, he said, "Young man, I will have to charge you a double fee." "A double fee, why is that?" The old sage replied, "I will have to teach you two lessons. First, how to hold your tongue, and then how to use it." What an art for all of us to learn, especially for Christians.

822. A Forked Tongue

This is told of a Christian man whose most intimate friends could not find out anything about his religious affiliations. One day a friend of his, on being told that he belonged to the church, exclaimed, "Why, I have known him intimately for some years, but I never dreamed he was a Christian!" He could not possibly conceive how the mouth that spoke so violently and indecently of his fellow men could be opened in church to praise and bless God.

823. A Lie Is Forever

A little girl come to her mother, saying, "Which is worse, Mama, to tell a lie or to steal?" The mother replied that both were so sinful she could not tell which was worse. "Well, Mama," replied the little one, "I've been thinking a good deal about it, and I think it's so much worse to lie than steal." "Why, my child?" asked the mother. "Well, you see, Mama, it's like this," said the little girl, "If you steal a thing, you can take it back, unless you've eaten it, and if you've eaten it, you can pay for it; but a lie is forever."

824. Evil Use of the Tongue

I shall never forget going on a picnic with my schoolmates and my uncle who was the teacher. We were playing with a little ball, and it got caught in the top of a tree. The teacher was angry about it and wanted to know who threw it there. Because my uncle was the teacher, they all ganged up on me as the culprit. The result was that my uncle broke quite a good-sized stick on my back punishing me. That was punishment unrighteously administered because of a lie. Thus, this expression, "a world of iniquity" in James 3:6, actually means that both a great amount and a great variety of unrighteousness is caused by the evil use of the tongue.

825. The Steps and Stops

Once, when Dr. Pierson was in George Mueller's study, he took a glance into his Bible. As he was leafing through it he came to Psalm 37:23, "The steps of a good man are ordered by Jehovah." He noticed that George Mueller had written by the side of it in the margin, "and the stops!" If our tongues know when to go and when to stop, then our whole bodies, our whole personalities, will know when to move and when to stop. If we don't have God's bridle, these tongues of ours will keep going incessantly. Now we need the steps and the stops, too! If it were not for the bridle, the rider would find it very difficult, if not impossible, to stop the horse. Why does the horse stop? Because the bits in the bridle hurt his tongue. It is so with God in His dealings with us. We are moving so fast in the wrong direction, toward our own goal and destruction, that God has to pull hard on the bridle to cause us to stop.

Trust

826. Trusting Step by Step

A father asked his son to carry a letter from their camp to the village. He pointed out a trail over which the lad had never gone before. "All right, Dad, but I don't see how that path will ever reach the town," said the boy. "Do you see the trail as far as the big tree down there?" asked the father. "Oh, yes, I see that far." "Well, when you get there by the tree, you'll see the trail a little farther ahead, and so on until you get within sight of the houses of the village." Even so should we trust God, being willing to follow His directions one step at a time.

827. The Greatest Compliment

One wet, foggy day a little girl was standing on a street corner in a large city waiting for an opportunity to cross the street. She walked up and down and looked into the faces of those who passed by. Some looked careless, some harsh, some in a hurry; she did not see anyone who made her feel confident. At length an elderly man, tall and erect, yet with a kindly expression, came walking down the street. Looking up into his face she seemed to see the one for whom she had been waiting. She went up to him and asked timidly, "Please,

sir, will you help me over?" The old man saw the little girl safely across the street, and when he afterward told the story he said, "That little child's trust was the greatest compliment I ever had in my life."

828. Trust in God

As D. L. Moody said, "Trust in yourself, and you are doomed to disappointment; trust in your friends, and they will die and leave you; trust in reputation, and some slanderous tongue may blast it; but trust in God, and you are never to be confounded in time or eternity." Luther gave a similar testimony when he said, "I have held many things in my hands, and I have lost them all; but whatever I have placed in God's hands, that I still possess."

829. Childlike Trust

A frantic mother called her pastor one day. She was experiencing a bad case of "nerves" as so many of us do. He thought he heard a child's voice while she was speaking, so he asked, "Is your child as upset and worried as you are?" "No, of course not," she replied. "But why not?" persisted the pastor. "I suppose she puts her trust in me and lets me do the worrying," she answered. "Then make a transference. Try to think of yourself as a child of God and, just as your child puts her trust in you, put your trust in God."

830. The Miserable Supposer

There was a poor woman who earned her living by hard labor but who was a joyous, triumphant Christian. "Ah, Nancy," said a gloomy Christian lady to her one day, "it is well to be happy now, but I should think the thoughts of the future would sober you. Suppose, for instance, you should have a spell of sickness and be unable to work, or suppose your present employer should move away and no one would give you a job. Suppose. . . ." "Stop!" cried Nancy. "I never suppose. The Lord is my Shepherd, and I know I shall not want. You know, dear, it is all those supposes that are making you so miserable. You had better give them all up and just trust the Lord."

831. Fanatical Security

In the second century, a Christian was brought before a pagan ruler and told to renounce his faith. "If you don't do it, I will banish you," threatened the king. The man smiled and answered, "You can't banish me from Christ, for He says, 'I will never leave you nor forsake you.' " To this the king angrily retorted, "Then I will confiscate your property and take all your posses-sions." Again the man smiled and said, "My treasures are all laid up on high; you cannot get them." The king became furious and shouted, "I will kill you!" "Why," the man answered, "I have been dead forty years; I have been dead with Christ, dead to the world, and my life is hid with Christ in God, and you cannot touch it." In desperation the king turned to his advisers and asked, "What can you do with a fanatic like that?"

832. The Pilot's Smile

In Robert Louis Stevenson's story of a storm, he describes a ship caught off a rocky coast, threatening death to all on board. When terror among the passengers was at its worst, one man more daring than the rest, making the perilous passage to the pilot-house, saw the pilot lashed to his post with his hands on the wheel, turning the ship little by little into the open sea. When the pilot beheld the ghastly white, terror-stricken face of the man, he smiled, and the man rushed to the deck below shouting, "I have seen the face of the pilot and he smiled. All is well." The sight of that smiling face averted panic and converted despair into hope.

Unbelief

833. *Accounts Will Be Settled!*

An unsaved farmer, who gloried in his unbelief, wrote a letter to a local newspaper saying, "Sir, I have been trying an experiment with a field of mine. I plowed it on Sunday. I planted it on Sunday. I cultivated it on Sunday. I reaped it on Sunday. I hauled it into my barn on Sunday. Now, Mr. Editor, what is the result? I have more bushels to the acre in that field than any of my neighbors have had this October." He expected some applause from the editor who did not profess to be an especially religious man. But underneath the letter the editor published the simple comment: "God does not always settle his accounts in October"—the day of reckoning will come in His appointed time.

834. *The Dirt Floor*

Spurgeon, that great prince of preachers, was once staying at an inn in one of the valleys of northern Italy where the floor was dreadfully dirty. "I had it in my mind to advise the lady to scrub it," said Spurgeon, "but when I perceived it was made of dirt, I reflected that the more she scrubbed the worse it would be." Just so, God knew that there could be no improvement of the corrupt nature of man except through faith in His Son.

835. *Don't Speak of the Resurrection*

A missionary was preaching on the resurrection when the native chief cried out, "What are these words about the dead? The dead arise? Will my father arise?" "Yes," answered the missionary. "Will all that have been killed and eaten by lions, tigers, and crocodiles arise?" "Yes, and come to judgment." "Hark!" shouted the chief, turning to his warriors. "You wise men, did you ever hear such strange talk?" The chief then turned to the missionary and said, "Sir, I love you much; but the words of resurrection are too great for me. I do not wish to hear about the dead rising again. The dead cannot rise; the dead shall not rise!" "Tell me, my friend, why not?" asked the missionary. "Because I have slain my thousands. Do you think I want *them* to rise again?" The gospel was all right as long as he did not have to face his sins.

836. *An Ill-spent Life*

A millionaire in New York came to the end of his journey and died. On his deathbed he gave continual expression to remorse for what his conscience told him had been an ill-spent life. "Oh," he exclaimed, "if I could only be spared for a few years I would give all the wealth I have amassed in my lifetime! It is a life devoted to money-getting that I regret. It is this which weighs me down and makes me despair of the life hereafter!"

837. Success without God

"Father, are you going away?" asked a little girl of her dying rich father. "Yes, dear, and I am afraid you won't see me again." Then the little one asked, "Have you got a nice house and lots of friends there?" The successful man of the world lay silent for a while and then said, "What a fool I have been! I have built a great business here, but I shall be a pauper there."

838. The Unacceptable Excuse

During a revival a young man said that he did not wish to become a Christian. When asked for his reason, he replied, "Several years ago I was in a man's kitchen. Finding me there, he swore at me and kicked me out. He was a professing Christian, and from that time on I decided never to have anything to do with religion. And I never have to this day." The young man was asked to write down his reason in full and sign it. Then it was handed back to him with the words, "Take this, and when you are asked for your excuse on the day of judgment, hand this up."

839. No Comfort

Voltaire, that strange combination of freethinker, deist, and rabid denouncer of Christianity, gives scant comfort to atheists and agnostics in some of his pronouncements. "The world embarrasses me," he said, "and I cannot think that this watch exists and has no watchmaker." And in the same vein he confesses, "To whatever side you turn, you are forced to acknowledge your own ignorance and the boundless power of the Creator."

840. Little Lost Mary

A mother attended a service in a large and crowded auditorium with her little daughter, Mary. In some manner the two became separated. The mother sent a note to the platform which was read aloud: "If there is a little girl named Mary Moore in the audience, who is lost, will she please raise her hand so her mother can find her." No little girl raised her hand so the mother had the police searching the city for the child. Still not finding her, the mother came back and stood at the door of the auditorium as the people filed out. Among the last of them was Mary. Her mother snatched her up, crying, "Where were you, Mary?" "On the front row," replied the little one. "Didn't you hear the man read the notice, 'If there is a little girl named Mary Moore in the audience, who is lost, will she please raise her hand so her mother can find her?' " "Yes," said Mary, "I heard it." "Then why didn't you raise your hand?" "Why, Mother, it couldn't have meant me," said Mary, "for I wasn't lost. I knew where I was."

841. Fear of Death

Alfred Krupp of Prussia, the great cannon king, was literally a manufacturer of death. However, he had such a fear of death that he never forgave anyone who spoke to him of it. Every employee throughout his vast works was strictly forbidden to refer to the subject of death in conversation. He fled from his own home when a relative of his wife suddenly died there, and when Mrs. Krupp remonstrated, he became so enraged that lifelong separation ensued. During his last illness he offered his physician a million dollars if he would prolong his life ten years. But no amount of money could buy an extension of his life. How different it was with Jesus Christ, because He was not only God but man at the same time. When He became man, He came down for a definite time, that by His death and resurrection death might be conquered.

842. The Perplexed Skeptic

A young skeptic said to an elderly lady, "I once believed there was a God, but now, since studying philosophy and mathematics, I am convinced that God is but an empty word." "Well," said the lady, "I have not studied such things, but since you have, can you tell me where this egg comes from?" "Why, of course, from a hen," was the reply. "And where does the hen come from?" "Why, from an egg." Then the lady inquired, "Which existed first, the hen or the egg?" "The hen, of course," rejoined the young man. "Oh, then a hen must have existed without having come from an egg?" "Oh, no, I mean that one egg existed without having come from a hen." The young man hesitated: "Well, you see—that is—of course, well, the hen was first!" "Very well," said she, "who made that first hen from which all succeeding eggs and hens have come?" "What do you mean by all this?" he asked. "Simply this: I say that He who created the first hen or egg is He who created the world. You can't explain the existence even of a hen or an egg without God, and yet you wish me to believe that you can explain the existence of the whole world without Him!" Thus the old lady's common sense sent the young man's philosophy packing. Everything finite must have had a beginning. But the important issue is, what is behind every finite beginning? Is it self-begun, or is there an infinite and eternal mind, a personality, behind it, the same personality which is behind every finite beginning? This personality John chooses to call *ho Logos*, "the Word."

843. Admit Error

How do you go about curing a drunk? The answer to that is, you can't. Before a man can lead a consistently sober life, he has to be motivated from within. He has to admit to himself he has a real problem, and he has to want to lick it. Only then can anyone help him. It is the same way when a man is obsessed with a false idea. You can't change his opinions simply by telling him he is wrong. He will only become more firmly set against you, and more determined than ever to defend his idea. No, a man must first admit to himself that following his idea to its logical conclusion in his life has led to utter spiritual poverty; he must want to know the truth. He must be willing to follow it once he is convinced.

844. Decorations of an Empty Heart

There are many people today who are religiously decorated. These decorations deceive the owners into believing they are Christians, that they are born-again believers. They have bought some religious pictures or other items. They hang up pictures of saints or one of Jesus Christ knocking at the closed door, but they have never opened their own door to Christ. They have no love for the cross of Christ, but they may have a very handsome crucifix hanging on the wall, or even a cross on a chain hanging around their necks. They may be garnished with generosity, giving their tithes to the church but withholding their hearts from Jesus Christ. The Bible is on the table or in the bookcase, but it is never read. These are the decorations of religion that the Lord is speaking about. People may pray long-winded prayers, show zeal, go to church, volunteer to cut the church lawn, yet these may only be the decorations of an empty heart.

845. The Purpose of the Storms

Early one morning the doorbell rang at a pastor's home. There stood a young man, half drunk, in despair, at the end of his own rope. If ever there was a life on the way to shipwreck in a storm of his own creating, it was this young man's. His wife, too, had come through a similar experience. Only 20 years old, she had been married twice, and with children by both husbands had suffered indescribable beatings—a storm of her own making. But in the midst of it all she had seen the face of Christ through the ministry of this faithful pastor. She had been saved by the grace of the Lord Jesus, and her life had been radically changed. Now her husband had come before dawn to wake up the preacher and ask for spiritual help. He could no longer live in the storm he had created. What had made him come to himself?—the recent death of a young soldier killed in the line of duty. The whole town was speaking of this fine Christian lad, now dead. The prodigal husband questioned why God would take such a good man who was a blessing to the world, and leave him, a miserable sinner, behind. The answer, of course, is that the young soldier was ready to meet his God, while the prodigal was not. This may be the reason He is keeping you alive. The storms God permits are temporary, but the purpose for which He permits them is eternal.

846. Everybody but God

One day Mark Twain took his little daughter on his knee and told her all about the rulers and other prominent men whom he had met in his travels. She listened attentively. When he had finished, she said, "Daddy, you know everybody but God, don't you?" Mark Twain was certainly an intelligent person. Yet he rejected God.

847. A Pig in a Parlor

A Christian military officer, who visited the bedside of a dying soldier under his command, said to him, "I am going to ask you a strange question. Suppose you could carry your sins with you to heaven—would that satisfy you?" "The poor dying lad replied, "Why, sir, what kind of heaven would that be to me? I would be just like a pig in a parlor!" He was awakened to a sense of his lost state. The officer concluded, "The soldier was panting after a heaven of holiness, and was convinced if he died in his sin he would be quite out of his element in such a place of purity."

848. Modern Pharisee

If a person is a seeker after signs from heaven in order that he or others may believe, do you realize that he falls into the same category as those who tempted Jesus and is classified by the Lord Jesus as belonging to a wicked generation? The word of God should be the basis of our proclamation that Jesus Christ has done enough for Him to be declared the Son of God.

849. Stranger in Heaven

Robert Laidlaw, in his little gem of a tract, *The Reason Why*, asks: "Would it be kindness to transfer a poor ragged beggar into the glare of a beautiful ballroom? Would he not be more conscious of his rags and dirt? Would he not do his best to escape again to the darkness of the street? He would be infinitely happier there. Would it be kindness and mercy on God's part to bring a man with his sins into the holy light of Heaven if that man had rejected God's offer of the only cleansing power there is? If you and I would not wish our friends to see inside our minds now and read all the thoughts that have ever been there (and our friends' standards are perhaps not any higher than our own), what would it be like to stand before God, whose absolute holiness would reveal our sin in all its awfulness?" The Bible says you cannot sow thistles and reap figs. You cannot live for the lusts of the flesh here and expect to enjoy the things of the Spirit hereafter. "For he that soweth to his flesh shall of the flesh reap corruption; but he that soweth to the Spirit shall of the Spirit reap life everlasting" (Gal. 6:8).

850. A Child Shall Lead

A skeptical physician declared he could see no reason why he should have to come to the cross of Christ to be saved. A friend gave him a famous book on apologetics with a powerful defense of the reasonableness of the gospel. It satisfied the doctor's reason, but it did not move his will. A short time later he was called to the bedside of a little girl who was dying. She whispered that she had something to say to him, that she hardly had the courage to, as it was about his peace with God. But she added, "Tomorrow morning, when I am stronger, I will tell you." But in the morning she was dead. This led to the physician's conversion and a subsequent life of dedicated Christian service. God used a child rather than an apologist of the faith to lead a learned man to Christ. Very interestingly the word *mōron* in Modern Greek has come to mean "child, baby."

Thus we could paraphrase 1 Corinthians 1:27 as "But God has chosen the *mōra*—the foolish things or those who are like little children—and the weak ones of the world, to confound the wise and mighty ones."

851. Pride of Reason

A Christian once served on a parliamentary commission with Professor Thomas H. Huxley. One Sunday they stayed together in a little country inn. "I suppose you are going to church this morning," said Huxley. "I am. I always go to church on the Lord's Day," replied the Christian. Huxley said, "Suppose you sit down and talk with me about religion—simple, experimental religion." Sensing something of heart hunger in the great scientist, the associate replied, "If you mean it, I will." Then he spoke out of a rich, experimental knowledge of the saving and satisfying power of Christ. Huxley listened intently. Grasping the hand of the Christian, he said with deep feeling, "If I could believe what you have said about the cross of Christ and His pardoning love, I would be willing to give my right hand." He really didn't have to make that sacrifice. All he had to give up was the belief that the eye, the ear, the mind, could know all that there is to know and experience. Had he only been willing to swallow the pride of reason and to accept God's free gift, he too could have experienced the power of God unto salvation.

852. Everything but the Bible

Marshall Duroc, an avowed atheist, was once telling Napoleon a very improbable story, at the same time giving his opinion that it was true. The Emperor remarked, "There are some men who are capable of believing everything but the Bible." There are some people who say they cannot believe the Bible, yet their capacities for believing anything that opposes the Bible are enormous.

853. Spiritually Blind

A minister who faithfully proclaimed the Gospel in an open-air meeting was challenged at the close by an unbeliever who stepped from the crowd and said, "I don't believe in heaven or hell. I don't believe in God or Christ. I haven't seen them." Then a man wearing dark glasses came forward and said, "You say there is a river near this place? There is no such thing. You say there are people standing here, but it cannot be true. I haven't seen them. I was born blind. Only a blind man could say what I have said. And only a spiritually blind man could say what you have said. The Bible says of you, 'The natural man receiveth not the things of the Spirit of God: for they are foolishness unto him: neither can he know them, because they are spiritually discerned' (1 Cor. 2:14). Doesn't the Word of God say, 'The fool hath said in his heart, There is not God'?" (Ps. 14:1).

854. No Fear nor Hope in Death

When Robert Owen, the notorious freethinker, visited Alexander Campbell to arrange the preliminaries for the great debate that was to follow, they walked about the farm till they came to the family burying ground. "There is one advantage I have over the Christian," boasted Mr. Owen. "I am not afraid to die. Most Christians have fear in death, but, if some few items of my business were settled, I should be perfectly willing to die at any moment." "Well," replied Mr. Campbell, "you say you have no fear in death; have you any hope in death?" "No," said Mr. Owen after a thoughtful pause. "Then," said Mr. Campbell, pointing to an ox standing nearby, "you are on a level with that animal. He has eaten till he is satisfied, stands in the shade whisking off the flies, and has neither hope nor fear in death." How true is the saying, "They that die without dying thoughts shall die without living comforts."

855. The Blind Atheist

Shelley could write of the exquisite beauty of nature and yet was blind to its Source. He had often visited the Alps and exulted in their breath-taking majesty. Yet when he signed the guest book at the inn he added "atheist" after his name. The next visitor looked at it and added, "If an atheist then a fool; if not a fool then a liar."

856. Atheist Faces Death

For the person who is out of Christ, death is generally viewed with terror. It is said that the French nurse who was present at the death of Voltaire, being urged to attend an Englishman whose case was critical, said, "Is he a Christian?" "Yes," was the reply, "he is a Christian in the highest and best sense of the term—a man who lives in the fear of God. But why do you ask?" "Because," she answered, "I was the nurse who attended Voltaire in his last illness, and for all the wealth of Europe I would never watch another atheist die."

857. The One Supreme Mystery

A young man who was studying medicine could not accept the doctrine of the supernatural birth of Jesus Christ. He went to a preacher who reasoned with him but left him in greater perplexity than ever. When he had finished his medical studies, he went to practice medicine in a rural community. One Sunday he decided to go and hear a backwoods preacher, not thinking for a moment that such a man could change his viewpoint on the virgin birth of Jesus Christ. But this humble preacher knocked more skepticism out of the doctor in half an hour than he had accumulated in all his years of medical school. He said, "If anybody here is troubled about the mystery of God becoming man, I want to take you back to the first chapter of Genesis and the first verse. 'In the beginning God. . . .'" He looked down into the audience very searchingly. The doctor was so self-conscious that he felt the speaker was looking directly at him. Then the preacher continued, "My brother, let me ask you this: Do you believe God was in the beginning? That is to say, that before the beginning began, God was? Somebody had to be, to start things off. Science tells us how things evolve and grow, but not how they first started." The doctor whispered to himself, "Yes, I believe that." "Now," the preacher said, "if you believe that God was before the beginning, you believe the only mysterious thing of this universe." "If I believe that, God knows I could believe anything else in the world," thought the doctor to himself. His conclusion that memorable morning was, "I went to college and traveled through the mysteries of the theory of reproduction and cell formation, and now I realize that I was just a common fool; that if God was in the beginning, that was the one supreme mystery of all mysteries of this mysterious universe of God."

858. A Firm Stand for Christ

A wealthy unbeliever who had spent much money on the education of his daughter, returned home from a business trip to be informed by his wife that the girl had gone forward and accepted Christ at an evangelistic meeting. When she ran to greet him, he struck her several times and told her to get out and never come back. She took shelter in a friend's home and spent the night in prayer. Early next morning the repentant father sent for her to come back. He met her at the gate, saying, "I give you my heart and hand to go with you to heaven." The mother followed, and all rejoiced in the saving power of Christ. A firm stand for Christ did it all.

859. Power of God unto Salvation

A Bible-believing Christian was assailed by an atheist who said, "I don't understand how the blood of Jesus Christ can wash away my sin, nor do I believe it." "You and Saint Paul agree on that," answered the Bible student. "How so?" "Turn to the first chapter of 1 Corinthians and read verse 18: 'For the preaching of the cross is to them that perish foolishness; but unto us which are saved it is the power of God.'" The atheist looked startled and began to study the Bible, where he soon found the cross to be the power of God unto salvation.

860. Napolean's Question

As Napolean was blazing his trail to the throne, he sought to conquer Egypt. Along with him as assistants he had some of the best engineers and scientists of France. It was natural they should talk about the land of the Nile and the part religion had played in its history. They agreed that religion had colored and carved the history of Egypt, but that all religion was only legend and humbug. It couldn't be otherwise, seeing that even God was a myth. So they talked beneath the starry heavens, these thinkers of France. They were atheists, as indeed so many of their fellow countrymen were at that time. Napolean listened and contributed nothing to the conversation, but as he rose to leave he lifted his hand and pointed to the silent stars that shone so brilliantly through the deep black sky. "Very ingenious, Messieurs," he said, "but who made all that?"

861. The Challenged Atheist

An atheist who had just finished lecturing to a great audience invited any who had questions to come to the platform. After a short interval, a man who had been well-known in the town as a hopeless drunkard but who had lately been converted, stepped forward. Taking an orange, he turned to the lecturer and asked him if it was a sweet one. Very angrily the man said, "Idiot, how can I know whether it is sweet or sour, when I haven't tasted it?" To this the converted drunkard retorted, "And how can you know anything about Christ if you have not tried Him?"

862. The Atheist Persuaded

A young preacher once called upon an old atheist who was constantly arguing against the existence of God. He found him sitting in his sawmill just over the lever that lifts as the saw leaves the log. As the old man began to denounce the Deity, that lever sprang, catching him under the heels and flinging him backward and down into the stream. As he plunged, however, he shrieked as loudly as he could, "God have mercy!" The preacher ran around, waded into the water, and drew the struggling man ashore. Said the pastor, "I thought that you did not believe in a God." As soon as the atheist stopped struggling he said in a subdued voice, "Well, if there is not a God, there ought to be one, to help a man when he can't help himself!"

863. Who Made It?

One of the greatest atheists of the past was Robert G. Ingersoll. In spite of his atheism, he had for a friend the famous preacher, Henry Ward Beecher. In the preacher's study was an elaborate celestial globe which had been sent him with the compliments of some manufacturer. On the surface in delicate workmanship were raised figures of the constellations and stars which composed them. The globe struck Ingersoll's fancy one day when he was visiting the preacher. He turned it around and around with admiration. "That is just what I want," he said, "Who made it?" "Who made it, do you say, Colonel?" repeated Beecher. "Who made this globe? Why nobody, of course. It just happened." Well, we all know better than that. We know that things don't just happen but they have a cause, and there must be a First Cause of all things. That is as far as the mind of man will take him. The logical conclusion—there must be God, the Creator.

864. Fools for Christ's Sake

Henry M. Stanley found Livingstone in Africa and lived with him for some time. Here is his testimony: "I went to Africa as prejudiced as the biggest atheist in London, but there came for me a long time for reflection. I saw this solitary old man there and asked myself, 'Why on earth does he stop here—is he cracked, or what? What is it that inspires him?' For months after we met, I found myself wondering at the old man carrying out all that was said in the Bible— 'Leave all things and follow Me.' But little by little his sympathy for others became contagious. My sympathy was aroused, seeing his piety, his gentleness, his zeal, his earnestness, and how he went about his business. I was converted by him, although he had not tried to do it."

865. The Philosopher's Answer

A heathen philosopher, on being asked the question, "What and where is God?" desired two days in which to prepare an answer. Partly pressed with the difficulties of the subject itself, and partly encumbered and confounded by polytheistic prejudices, he doubled and redoubled the time. When required to state the reason for his delay, he acknowledged, "It is a question in which my insufficient reason is lost. The oftener I ask myself, 'What is God?' the less able I am to answer." How much more are you unable to reason why the omnipotent God, in order to save your soul, had to become man in the person of Jesus Christ and die on a cross. That is beyond reasoning, but it is within grasp of one's experience.

866. Wisdom Has to Go

The crust is bread itself; the ice is the very water of the river; and the hard ground is the very soil of the earth. It is the very substance of the thing that it imprisons. Each forms a barrier which resists outside influences. That's exactly what happens to man. His wisdom and self-assurance are the barriers that keeps God's wisdom from reaching him. A child is fit for the Kingdom of God because, as yet, he has not formed a crust-like barrier.

867. Man—Spiritually Blind

A minister was asked by a Quakeress, "Does not thee think that we can walk so carefully, live so correctly, and avoid every fanaticism so perfectly, that every sensible person will say, 'That is the kind of religion I believe in'?" He replied, "Sister, if thee had a coat of feathers as white as snow, and a pair of wings as shining as Gabriel's, somebody would be found somewhere on the footstool with so bad a case of color blindness as to shoot thee for a blackbird."

868. Hearers Only

An auditor is one who sits down with the other students, and has the same advantages of learning, but does not have the same responsibilities. When examinations are given, he does not have to take them. He is just an auditor. He may have listened very carefully and have greatly benefited from what he has heard, but he does not have to be checked by his professor. He doesn't have to hand in any term papers or theses. He feels very free when he sees the other duly registered students studying hard while he can take it easy. But the day of graduation comes, and you know what happens then. The one

who sat for the examination and had responsibilities as well as duties receives a diploma, a degree, and can be a practicing lawyer, teacher, doctor, businessman, etc. The auditor, however, can have nothing at all, except possibly a certificate showing that he had been physically present in class while the professor gave the lectures on a certain subject.

869. Blinded by Sin

Isn't light self-revealing? Do we need to stand out in the street and shout to those who pass by, "That's the sun," as we point to it in all its brightness? The sun is self-revealing in the same sense that Jesus Christ was and is the Light of the world. The fact that John the Baptist came to give his witness about the Light did not in any way steal from it the power to reveal itself. The necessity for the human testimony of the Baptist is a clear indication of the complete depravity of man, his inability to comprehend that which is spiritual. His mind and heart have been so darkened by sin that, seeing the Light, he does not recognize it as the Light. We must also remember what men and women actually saw down here on earth was a human Jesus. Their darkened vision could not see anything superhuman in Him. It was necessary for someone like John the Baptist to tell them that this One who walked with them and who ate with them was the Light.

870. God a Necessity

During the French Revolution, Robespierre, himself an inhuman monster, quickly saw that the renunciation of religion would soon bring about the dissolution of all society. He thereupon began to speak in favor of religion, though he admitted that he had been an indifferent Catholic. He ended his first speech in that direction with the words, "If God did not exist, it would be necessary to invent Him." But God has to reveal Himself to man in order for man to know Him fully. He has promised to do this through His Word.

871. Sin Blinds

A little boy who had been born blind underwent an operation to restore his sight. The light was let in slowly. Then one day his mother led him out of doors and uncovered his eyes, and for the first time he saw the sky and earth. "O Mother!" he cried, "Why didn't you tell me it was so beautiful?" She burst into tears and said, "I tried to tell you, dear, but you could not understand me." Sinful man is also blind to the splendor and the glory of the light of the gospel. The only way he can comprehend it is to let the light in, through the enabling of the Holy Spirit.

872. Hidden Treasure

Two men were sent to check a rumor that iron lay beneath the surface of a certain piece of ground. One, a scientist and mineralogist, conscious of his own limitations, took along some instruments. The other, a buoyant, self-confident individual, said, "I believe what I can see; and what I can't see I won't believe." He walked rapidly over the field and said, "Iron? Nonsense! I see no iron; there is no iron here." And that is what he stated in his report. The other man did not trust his eye at all but looked at his instruments. The needle on one pointed to the fact that a rich deposit of iron did lie beneath the earth's surface. As he made his report he said, "My eye couldn't see it, but my magnet discerned it." As the eye cannot see minerals hidden in the earth, so it cannot see what is in the heart of God toward man. Man can look upon the crucified Christ and fail to see God's plan of redemption.

Undiscernment

873. Differing Viewpoints

Not all people can see God in the various manifestations of life. Two men looking at the same person may make two dissimilar observations; they may form two varying opinions, and their judgments will reflect their differing viewpoints. When Thomas Edison was a young man in school in Ohio, his teacher said he'd never amount to anything because, seemingly, he could learn only science and mathematics. He couldn't pass his other subjects because he wasn't interested in them. The poor fellow nearly despaired when his teacher, at wit's end, recommended his expulsion. He knew he was slow in English and history, but he was sure he *was* going to amount to something in spite of it. This young man, as everybody now knows, was a genius, an electrical wizard, a pioneer inventor who helped make America's standard of living what it is today.

874. He Didn't See Snakes

"I will never forget my first experience in hospital work," said Chief Surgeon Millar of the Central Emergency Hospital in San Francisco. "There was an undergraduate nurse in the detention ward, and we had a very violent case—a man in the worst stage of delirium tremens. I was awakened in the middle of the night by the head nurse who requested me to come at once to the patient. When I got there I found him raving and very violent, with the new nurse scared out of her wits." Then the doctor said, "Why did you let him go so far? I left you some medicine to give him as soon as he got delirious." "Yes, doctor," the nurse replied, "but you told me to give that to him if he saw any more snakes, but this time he was seeing blue dogs with pink tails."

875. Spiritually Color-blind

Just as some color-blind people are not aware of their color blindness, so it is spiritually. Those who are sinful are not always aware of their sinfulness, of their spiritual color blindness. In recent years, the great railroad companies test the vision of their employees by the aid of skilled eye specialists, with the result that from 10-25 percent of those who apply for positions as engineers and signal men are found to be deficient in color judgment. This is certainly a very pertinent illustration of Christ's teaching in Luke chapter eleven. As the managers of railroads heed the cry of the newspapers and the public to beware of color blindness, and are determined that the men who drive their trains shall know the difference between red and green, so the warning of Christ comes to every one of us, "Take heed therefore that the light which is in thee be not darkness" (Luke 11:35).

876. A Blessing Overlooked

A man who owned a small estate sent for an agent and asked him to write an advertisement offering it for sale. When the advertisement was ready, the agent read it to him. "Read that again," said the owner. The agent read it once more. "I don't think I will sell after all," said the man. "I have been looking for an estate like that all my life and did not know that I owned it." Have you praised the Lord for what you now possess on this earth which you wouldn't have if the Lord had not given it to you.

877. Spiritually Bankrupt

Aesop speaks in one of his down-to-earth fables of a goatherd who, having been caught in the mountains in a snowstorm, drove his flock into a large cave for shelter. There he discovered some wild goats who had taken refuge before him. The goatherd was so impressed by the size and looks of these goats, so much more beautiful than his own, that he gave the wild goats all the food he could collect. The storm lasted many days, during which the tame goats died of starvation. When the sun shone again, the wild goats ran out and disappeared in the mountains, leaving the disappointed goatherd to make his way home, a poorer, and a wiser man. So it is with all those who exchange the tried and true teaching of God's Word for the ear-tickling speculations of men.

Unity

878. The Uniting Love of Christ

In a museum, an old white-haired man was standing fascinated before a picture of Christ. After gazing at it for a few moments he murmured to himself, with face all aglow, "Bless Him, I love Him!" A stranger standing near overhead him and said, "Brother, I love Him, too," and clasped his hand. A third caught the sentence and said, "I love Him, too"; soon there stood in front of that picture a little circle of people with hands clasped, utter strangers to one another, but made one by their common love of Christ. On further discussion they found they belonged to different Christian denominations. But this did not disturb their fellowship. Perhaps others belonging to their particular denomination, but not to Christ, could not do what they were doing, stand in awe before Christ and have fellowship with those who possessed the same feeling.

879. What Kind of Christian?

Many people turn denominational adjectives into nouns. Instead of saying, I am a Baptist Christian, a Presbyterian Christian, a Catholic Christian, or an Orthodox Christian, they say, I am a Baptist; I am a Presbyterian; I am a Catholic; I am Orthodox, and so on. This is a distortion of values, for being a Christian is the important thing, and what kind of Christian you call yourself is purely secondary.

880. Cooperation

There were two Christians occupying the same cottage, each bound to keep his own side of the house well thatched. They were sadly divided denominationally, one being a Baptist and the other a Presbyterian. After repeated battles with words, they were not on speaking terms. One day these men were at work on the roof, each thatching his own side, when they met at the top and were forced to look into each other's faces. One of the men took off his cap, and scratching his head said to the other, "Johnnie, you and me, I think, have been very foolish to dispute as we have done concerning Christ's will about our churches, until we have clean forgot His will about ourselves; we have fought so bitterly for what we call the truth, that it has ended in spite. Whatever is wrong, it's perfectly certain that it never can be right to be impolite, unneighborly, unkind—in fact, to hate one another. No, that's the devil's work, not God's! The same thing may be the matter with the church as with this house. You are working on one side, and I am on the other, but if we only do our work well, we will meet at the top at last. Give me your hand, old neighbor!" So they shook hands and were the best of friends ever after.

881. Get Your Heads Together

There is an old legend about a herd of mules that was attacked nightly by a pack of wolves from a nearby forest. When the wolves came, the mules began kicking viciously in all directions. Consequently the mules maimed and injured each other while the agile wolves escaped unharmed. Finally, a wise old mule called the rest together for a conference and made known his plans. That night the wolves came yelping from the forest as usual, but instead of the mules kicking, they all ran and put their heads together in a circle and began kicking outward. The wolves were put to flight, and the mules did no harm to each other. Christians need to get their heads together and kick outward against the forces of iniquity. The world must sometimes wonder whether we who call ourselves Christ's fishermen have any heads to put together.

882. A Future Perfection

Probably you've heard of the group who were supposed to have arrived in heaven and been met by St. Peter. In a beautiful meadow they saw some people assembled and asked Peter who they were. Peter replied, "They are Presbyte-

rians." They walked on a distance to a beautiful brook, and one asked, "Who are the people gathered over there?" And Peter answered, "They are Lutherans." Then they came to a tremendously high wall and one asked, "Whose are the voices we hear behind that wall?" "Shh!" said Peter. "Please be quiet!" Then he whispered the name of that denomination and said, "They think they are the only ones up in this place, and we don't want to disillusion them. If they find out that others have made it up here, too, how will they feel?"

883. Workers Together

As you look outside on a snowy day and admire the beauty of the landscape, you may recall that no two snowflakes have ever been found to be alike. Yet each individual snowflake is only a minute drop of frozen water as it falls to earth. However, many snowflakes together cover the ground and can change the course of things and persons. When you do your best, and join that best with the efforts of other Christians, you will be amazed at what God can do with your combined "bests."

884. Nearer the Center

On a blank leaf of his Bible a man had drawn a circle with several radii converging on the center, which he called "Christ." On the radii were written the names of different denominations of Christians. Underneath were written the words, "The nearer to the center the nearer to one another."

Vengeance

885. No Mercy

The first mate on a certain vessel, yielding to temptation, became drunk for the first time in his life. The captain entered in the ship's log, "Mate drunk today." The mate implored the captain to remove it from the record, saying if the ship's owners saw it he would lose his post, and the captain well knew it was his first offense. But the obdurate captain refused, saying, "This is the fact, and into the log it goes." Some days afterward, the mate was keeping the log. After giving the latitude and longitude, the run for the day, the wind and the sea, he made this entry: "Captain sober today." The indignant captain protested, saying that it would leave an altogether false impression in the minds of the owners of the vessel, as if it were an unusual thing for him to be sober. But the mate answered as the captain had, "This is the fact, and into the log it goes."

886. Vengeance

Many Christians are like the woman who had been bitten by a dog and was advised by her physician to write her last wishes, as she might succumb to hydrophobia. She spent so long with pencil and paper that the doctor finally remarked something about how long the will would be. "Will!" she snorted. "I'm writing a list of the people I'm going to bite!"

Weakness

887. Lost Temper

An aged man went to his physician for an examination. The physician expressed astonishment at his robust vigor in spite of his advanced years. The man explained that he had been compelled to live an out-of-doors life. He then went on to say that when he and his wife were married, they made a compact. When he lost his temper, she was to keep silent. When she lost her temper, he was to go out of doors! This is still better advice: "Enter your closet and seek the Lord in prayer."

888. Wrath Yields to Mercy

The pastor of a large city church was walking down the street one day with set lips and a steely look in his eye. A parishioner greeted him with the question, "How are you today, Pastor?" He waked as from a dream and said, "I am mad!" It was an unusual word for this mild-mannered Christian, but he went on to explain with deep emotion: "I found a widow standing by her goods thrown into the street. She could not pay the month's rent. The landlord turned her out; one of her children is going to die; and that man is a member of the church! I told her to take her things back again. I am on my way to see him now!" Wrath against injustice, hypocrisy, and greed can be found throughout Scripture. But if we are to be guided by the Word of God, our wrath must always yield to mercy when the repentant sinner turns to ask forgiveness.

889. Always an Excuse

Some Christians have the same idea about the commandments of God as a little boy who was playing with his sister. A most unpleasant woman who lived near by had been finding fault with them, and the boy said, "I just hate her!" His little sister, greatly shocked, said, "Oh no! The Bible says we must love everyone." "Oh, well," he remarked, "old Mrs. Blank wasn't born when that was written." In the same way the disobedient Christian always finds an excuse.

890. Stop Shouting

A mother had fallen into the disagreeable habit of yelling at her children. She thought this necessary in order to maintain her authority; then she was confined to bed for a week with severe laryngitis. She could not speak above a whisper and had to run the affairs of her household from her bed. "Do you know," she confessed afterward, "I found that the children were far more well-behaved and good-natured when I could only speak to them in a whisper than when I used to shout at them."

891. *Disturbances Within*

Astronomers once blamed the inaccuracy of the images viewed in their telescopes on atmospheric disturbances. Later investigation revealed that a good deal of the disturbance of telescopic images arises from currents within the telescope itself. But though we cannot altogether eliminate the conditioning of outside influences in our quest for truth, we must attempt to free ourselves as much as possible from the disturbing currents within—the moods, tempers, sympathies, and fears that falsely bias the soul.

Will

892. *The Human Will*

A waitress, a fine Christian woman, works in a restaurant. The tax law states that tips received from customers should be declared as "taxable revenue." But the Christian waitress begins to rationalize: "The others do not declare them; Why should I? If I do, I shall get them in trouble." The element of benevolence enters this situation and a sinful action is justified as one of protection of fellow workers. In reality, however, the non-declaration of tips, altogether or in part, is due to the fact that so much tax has to be paid. What, then, does this Christian waitress think of doing? Do not count the tips but declare a flat sum for each working day. Her will hinders her from reporting her actual earnings. The human will is the hardest horse to tame; it is the hardest part of our personality to subject to the will of God. Sometimes we even want the will of God to appear as our own will.

893. *God's Will, My Will*

A lady had a little gold cross, on the upright part of which the words, "God's will," were engraved. On the crossbar were the words, "My will." At the touch of a spring the cross disappeared and left only a straight beam bearing the words, "God's will." Thus, when our will is lost in God's and we are indeed dead unto sin, it is no longer a cross to follow Christ. We shall no longer complain that we do not get our own selfish way, because we shall not have any. When our will is contrary to God's will, then we have a cross to bear.

Witness

Effective

894. Guided by Conscience

A faithful Christian soldier went to his chaplain for advice. "Last night," he said, "when I knelt by my bed and prayed, the fellows began to ridicule me and throw shoes at me. What should I do?" "Well," said the chaplain, "why don't you stop kneeling down? Just lie down in bed and lift your heart to God in silence and He will hear you." After a few days, the chaplain asked the soldier how he was faring with his evening prayers. "I'll tell you, Reverend. I followed your advice for three nights, but my conscience began to bother me because I was betraying my Lord. So I began to kneel down as I did before." "And what happened?" "I was really amazed. Not a single fellow ridiculed me. Now the fifteen men in my tent kneel down with me, and I pray aloud for all of them."

895. Living As You Teach

A missionary who was speaking to a group of Hindu women was surprised to see one of them get up and walk away. Soon she returned and listened more intently than before. "Why did you leave in the middle of my message?" asked the missionary. "I was so interested in the wonderful things you were saying that I went to ask your servant if you live like you teach. He said you do. So I came back to hear more about Jesus," said the woman.

896. The Missionary Lady

An English traveler in Jerusalem was trying to find someone who could speak both English and Arabic. He heard of an American missionary who lived near by. Stopping an Arab boy who knew little English, he asked him if he could direct him to the missionary's home. The face of the boy lit up, and he said, "You mean the lady who lives next door to God?" If an uncouth street urchin could detect one who walked with God, why cannot we so live that the world can see Jesus in us?

897. Christianity Is Catching!

"What argument of mine led you to Christ?" asked a missionary in Egypt of an educated Mohammedan who was preaching Christ with great zeal and success. The missionary was surprised to receive this answer, "Every argument presented I could refute, at least to my satisfaction. It was your life that convinced me of salvation through Christ."

898. A Good Marital Testimony

Not long ago a Hindu woman was converted chiefly by hearing the Word of God read. She suffered much persecution from her husband. One day a missionary asked her, "When your husband is angry and persecutes you, what do you do?" She replied, "Well, sir, I cook his food better; when he complains, I sweep the floor cleaner; and when he speaks unkindly, I answer him mildly. I try, sir, to show him that when I became a Christian I became a better wife and a better mother."

899. Are You a Good Showcase?

Gutav Dore, the famous artist, once lost his passport while traveling in Europe. When he came to the boundary post between two countries and was asked for his passport, he fumbled about and finally announced, "I have lost it, but it is all right. I'm Dore, the artist. Please let me go in." "Oh, no," said the officer. "We have plenty of people representing themselves as this or that great person! Here is a pencil and paper. Now, if you are Dore the artist, prove it by drawing me a picture." He took the pencil and drew some pictures of a scene in the immediate area. "Now I am perfectly sure you are Dore. No one else could draw like that!" said the officer as he allowed Dore to enter the country. So it is with us. People follow what we do on the stage of life. They look to see if our conduct squares with our profession. Are we drawing the picture of Christ, as it were, or of a different person? What the world wants to see is reality in our actions. It has been said that God has great and wonderful things to display if He finds suitable showcases. Are you a good showcase for Jesus Christ?

900. A Rich Conversion

A certain titled gentleman was converted. He loved the Lord a great deal, but he was not well taught in the Scriptures. He thought that he could continue in some of his worldly engagements and still bear a good testimony. On one occasion some weeks after he gave his heart to the Lord, this man accepted an invitation to a rather worldly party. Upon his arrival, one of the guests greeted him with these words: "I'm so glad to see you and to know that it isn't true." "I beg your pardon," he replied, "but I don't think I quite understand you." "Why, " said the other guest, "rumors were around that you had been converted a few weeks ago; I'm so glad you're here and to know the rumor was unfounded." "But it is true!" the man exclaimed. Hesitating a moment, he added, "I see that you think this party is no place for a Christian to be, and you are right. You will never again see me at such an affair, nor will anyone else."

901. Not Words But Deeds

A young man had gone as a missionary to China. He was filled with love for the people but was unable to master the language. At last, having done his best for two years without success, he felt it his duty to take his resignation to the mission house. When this became known, a delegation of natives, composed of heathen as well as Christians, went to the mission house with the pleas that this man remain. Their argument was this: "He has done us all more good than anyone else in the mission, although he does not understand our language and cannot preach to us."

902. Ability to Carry

There was a man who was saved by grace from strong drink. He was seen one day by the tavern keeper, whom he knew only too well, carrying a sewing machine to his wife. "Come and have a drink," cried the tavern keeper. "It will strengthen you." "No, no," replied the former customer. "I've seen the day when I could not carry a dollar past your door; but since God saved me I can carry a whole sewing machine."

903. What the World Needs

Belonging to Christ should create in us a sense of responsibility. His glory should be our concern. We are His image in the world. An American chaplain in the Civil War asked a wounded soldier, "Would you like me to read you something from the Bible?" The soldier said, "I'm so thirsty, I'd rather have a drink of water." After he had drunk it he said, "Could you put something under my head?" The chap-

lain took off his overcoat, rolled it up, and placed it under the man's head as a pillow. "Now," said the soldier, "if I had something over me. I'm so cold." The chaplain took off his jacket and covered the man. Then the wounded man said, "For God's sake, man, if there's anything in that Book that makes a man do for another what you've done for me, let me hear it!" Isn't that what the world needs today—Christians who exemplify Christ?

904. I Will Be a Christian

A Chinese boy in Singapore found Christ as his Savior and arranged to be baptized shortly after his graduation. But to his surprise he won a scholarship of $500 a year for four years in the Hong Kong University. One of the conditions was, "The winner must be a Confucianist." To a poor student the temptation to defer baptism was great, but he resisted and presented himself for baptism at the appointed time. A friend, a Confucianist, stood next in line for the scholarship, but was so impressed that he refused it, saying, "If Christianity is worth so much to my classmate, it can be worth no less to me. I will be a Christian." He trusted Christ as his Savior and was baptized.

905. Missionaries—Walking Bibles

A good example rings louder than any bell to toll people to church. An African prince, after interpreting the missionary's message, said, "I can't read this Book myself," referring to the Bible, "but I believe the words of it because I have watched the missionaries for two years. They have told me no lies about anything else; so when they tell me this Book is God's Word, I believe it. I believe that Jesus died for me, and I am going to follow this Jesus."

906. Not Easily Provoked

Some sailors who were working on a ship in harbor noticed an elderly man engaged in his business on the pier. One sailor laughingly said to another, "You can't make that old man angry no matter what you do to him." The sailor who was addressed immediately took this as a challenge, and snatching up a bucket of dirty salt water ran up to the old man and dashed its contents all over him. The old man backed away at this surprise attack and said in a mild voice, "Young man, the Savior says, 'Whoso shall offend one of these . . . that believe in me, it were better for him that a millstone were hanged about his neck, and that he were cast into the depths of the sea.' Now, since I am one of these who do believe in Him, will He not consider that you have very much offended me?" The sailor turned away quite ashamed and perplexed at the spirit that the injured Christian exhibited. The picture of the old man wet and miserable looking at him with mingled pity and displeasure stayed with him and led him to go back and ask him to forgive him and pray for him. The elderly Christian was very ready to do both, and not long af-

terward the sailor became a Christian. There is reason to believe that many sinners might be converted from the error of their ways if they were to meet such a spirit, as the sailor did, in every professed Christian whom they might insult or abuse.

907. An Effective Ministry

A girl of another faith than Christianity worked in a store during the holiday season. She met with an accident and was taken to a hospital. There she made the acquaintance of a Christian nurse whose loving ministry and gentle goodness soon won her friendship. One day the girl asked the nurse, "Is it true that you are a Christian?" Upon being answered in the affirmative she replied, "You are so kind and polite and gentle, I didn't think you could be a Christian; but then the only Christians I've met are the Christmas shoppers."

908. The Living Testimony

There was once a merchant who had been a very worldly, godless man. He was finally gloriously converted. On being asked what had been especially the means of his conversion, he replied, "The example of one of my clerks." He went on to say, "This young man was one whose religion was in his life rather than in his tongue. He did not bless God and speak evil of his fellowmen. When I uttered an oath, he never reproved me; but I could see it deeply pained him. When I fell into a fit of anger and behaved in a violent manner, though he spoke no word to that effect, I could see how painful the scene was to him. My respect for him led me to restrain myself in his presence and gradually to break off both these habits. In fact, this man, though he never spoke a word to me on the subject of religion, exercised an influence for good over me wielded by no other human being. To him, under God, I am indebted more than to any other for the hope of eternal life through our Lord Jesus Christ in which I now rejoice."

909. Mind Little Things

I remember at one time I received an invitation from a young preacher to speak in his church. He said, "I remember when you preached at my father's church many years ago. My mother had worked all night, and after dinner, you did the dishes. I'll never forget that. I forgot your sermon, but I haven't forgotten your doing dishes at my mother's home."

910. Goodwill Displayed

A Christian family moving into a new community wanted to keep their lawn well mowed so they might be a good testimony in the neighborhood. However, they mowed the lawn so early in the day they disturbed the neighbors. When this was called to their attention, instead of feeling hurt and offended, they made their apologies and promised to cut the grass at a more reasonable hour. What

might have developed into a neighborhood feud became instead an evidence of their good will.

911. Candidate Accepted

An official of a mission board, who knew it takes more than desire to make a missionary, was appointed to examine a candidate. He told the young man to come to his house at six o'clock in the morning. The young man went at six in the morning to be examined, and the examiner kept him sitting in the room until ten. Then he went down to him and said abruptly, "Can you write your name? Do you know what your name is?" "Yes, sir." He put him through a series of questions of that kind, and then went to the mission board and said, "He will do. I tried his patience for four hours, and he did not break down; I then insulted him, and he did not lose his temper. He will do." If a man answers all abuses with magnanimity, patience, fortitude, and gentleness, you can depend upon it, Christ's love has conquered his heart. His Christianity is vindicated by the very quality of his character.

912. Prove Yourself

In Aesop's fables a traveler was entertaining some men in a tavern with an account of the wonders he had done abroad. "I was once at Rhodes," said he, "and the people of Rhodes, you know, are famous for jumping. Well, I completed a jump there that no other man could equal within a yard. That's a fact, and if we were there I could bring you ten men who would prove it." "What need is there to go to Rhodes for witnesses?" asked one of his hearers. "Just imagine you are there now and show us your leap." Thus Paul intimated to the Corinthians, "I don't have to come to listen to your words. You can prove the quality of your life by what you do, and I'll know it from where I am."

913. I Belong to Christ

"Oh," said a woman to a minister, "do you belong to us?" "Well," said the minister, "who are 'us'? I belong to Christ." Then, seeing that this explanation still did not satisfy her, he continued, "I like the Augustinian creed: 'A whole Christ for my salvation, the whole Bible for my study, the whole Church for my fellowship, and the whole world for my parish, that I may be a true Christian and not a sectarian.' "

914. A Generous Concession

A man bought a field next to a farmer who had been engaged in a long-standing dispute with the former owner about the exact boundary line between this field and his own property. When the new owner saw the farmer near the fence one day, he greeted him with the words, "I'm your new neighbor; and I would like to talk to you about the boundary line between our properties." The farmer assumed a belligerent attitude and said, "What about it?" "How much of this field do you claim as belonging to you?" asked the new owner who was a Christian. "I claim that your fence is a good two feet over on my property," replied the farmer. "Well, then, I want you to reset the fence four feet back on my side," said the Christian. This completely took the fight out of the farmer and was the beginning of a new spirit of concession on his part also.

915. Like Jesus

A little girl in a Chinese village watched a missionary as he went about the Master's work. She saw him go to the homes where there were sickness, death, and sorrow, and she watched him as he moved about the village, though she never heard him speak in public. One day she went to another village and followed some girls into a mission school. There she heard a lady talking to them, in Chinese, about someone to whom little children came. One of the little girls asked the visitor, "Do you know who it was?" "Yes," she replied, "she was talking about the missionary who lives in our village." She had never heard about Jesus Christ, and when the teacher described the beautiful life of Jesus Christ, she thought she was describing the missionary.

916. A Real Conversion

Two little children, a boy and a girl, who played together a great deal, received Christ and were converted. One day the boy came to his mother and said, "Mother, I know that Emma is a Christian." "What makes you think so, dear?"

"Because she plays like a Christian. If you take everything she's got, she doesn't get mad. Before, she was selfish, and if she didn't have everything her own way she would say, 'I won't play with you; you are a mean little boy.' " That's what the world sees, the result of our possessing part of the fullness of God. If we have God, then we must act like Him.

917. Something in Our Faces

Be like the Christian policeman who prayed at prayer meeting, "O Lord, put something in our faces as we walk about, that people in trouble may see and so be led to seek our help." How does your face and mine look to those who may be seeking help?

918. Effective Testimony

The famous English deist, Anthony Collins of the 17th century, met a plain countryman one day while out walking. He asked him where he was going. "To church, sir." "What are you going to do there?" "Worship God." "Is your God a great or a little God?" "He is both, sir." "How can He be both?" "He is so great, sir, that the heaven of heavens cannot contain Him; and so little that He can dwell in my heart." The unbeliever Collins later declared that this simple answer from the countryman had more effect upon his mind than all the volumes which learned doctors had written against him. This simple countryman had indeed the right concept of God, the God of the Bible, who as a spirit is the Creator of all things and yet indwells the heart of His believing creatures in the person of Jesus Christ.

919. An Irresistible Argument

A famous atheist once said, "I can stand all the arguing of Christian apologists, but I have a little servant who is a disciple of Jesus Christ, and her good, pure, honest, truthful life staggers me sometimes." The one irresistible argument for the gospel's power is a regenerated, consecrated life which is a demonstration of the life of Christ. The world may miss seeing the life of God in nature, but they cannot miss seeing it in the lives of those men and women who have the life of Christ. What a wonderful thought to know that we as human beings can become the carriers of the life of God and our lives can become the reflectors of His life.

920. Love Triumphant

It is said that Claude, a man of great piety, was unjustly imprisoned in the Bastille. At the same time a man was imprisoned who was so brutal and ferocious that no one dared approach him. The jailer, recognizing Claude's Christian character, begged him to undertake to humanize this monster. Accordingly, the humble Christian was shut up with this inhuman brute who subjected him to the most barbarous treatment. Through it all Claude's only reply was to exhibit silence, patience, and mildness under attack. His prayers achieved the rest. The monster at length looked into the face of his companion, suddenly threw himself at his feet, and burst into a flood of penitent tears. He became a new creature in Christ, and even when set at liberty he could scarcely be prevailed upon to leave his Christian friend.

921. The Show Window

A country merchant once visited New York. The thing that impressed him most was the magnificent and spotless show windows. On his return home he immediately cleaned up his unused show window and made it so attractive that he was soon doing nearly all the business in his town. Instead of failing in business, as he had at one time feared, he became the richest merchant of his county. The show window of the Christian is most important. It has to be attractive, but it must represent the truth; it must show that which can be produced in the storehouse. One of the hardest things for the Christian to do is to be truthful and honest in his showmanship, to let his tongue represent what is in his heart. Thus the argument of James runs: Now you have stated to the world that you are wise, that you possess wisdom, namely, Jesus Christ and His Spirit. Then show it by your good conduct.

922. Come Clear Out

A converted Chinese gentleman, when in America on a visit, was unfavorably impressed with the little difference he saw between the style of living of many professing Christians and the men and women of the world. Referring to the matter on one occasion he said, making at the same time a large sweep with his arm, "When the disciples of my country come out from the world, they come clear out."

923. A Child's Testimony

A little child asked his father, "Daddy, is Satan bigger than I am?" "Yes, he is," answered the father. "Is he bigger than you, Daddy?" The father replied, "Yes, son, he is bigger than I am." Surprised, the boy blurted out, "Is the devil bigger than Jesus?" "No, not by a long shot, David. Jesus is bigger and stronger." The child thought for a while and said, "Then I'm not afraid of him because I have Jesus in me."

924. The Correct Reading

An atheist, who was also an invalid, sent his little daughter to live with friends who taught her to read. She proudly told her father when she came home, "I have learned to read." "Well," said he, "Let me hear you read that," pointing to a board at the foot of the bed on which he had printed in large letters, "God is nowhere." Carefully she spelled out the words in the way that seemed right to her, "God is now here." The unbelieving father was startled and perplexed, but God blessed that new reading to the salvation of his soul.

925. Proof of Pedigree

Murray McCheyne, that great preacher, said, "The Christian is just a person who makes it easy for others to believe in God." Is it easy for others to believe in God because of your presence among them? And that great scientist Pascal said. "I saw that everything that came to pass in the life of Christ must be repeated in the lives of His followers." And another author said, "Say not that you have royal blood in your veins, say not that you are born of God, if you cannot prove your pedigree by daring to be holy."

926. Class Consciousness

A preacher, one Sunday morning, noticed a man in the congregation in his Sunday best. In the evening that same man was there in working clothes. The preacher afterward spoke to him. "Are you going to work?" "No," was the reply, "but this morning something was said that stirred me to go and seek my brother. I knew he had no Sunday clothes, and I knew he would not come if I put on my Sunday clothes. So I put on my working clothes for him, and here he is."

927. Running from, Not After Sin

A little girl, in the days when the conversion of children was not the subject of as much prayer as now, applied for membership in a Baptist church. "Were you a sinner," asked an old deacon, "before this change of which you now speak?" "Yes, sir," she replied. "Well, are you now a sinner?" "Yes, sir, I feel I am a greater sinner than ever." "Then what change is there in you?" "I don't quite know how to explain it," she said, "but I used to be a sinner running after sin, and now I hope I am a sinner running from sin."

928. Testimony of Long-Suffering

A mean, worldly army sergeant was saved, and this was his testimony to his fellow soldiers: "There is a private in our company who was converted. We gave that fellow an awful time. One night he came in from sentry duty, very tired and wet, and before going to bed he got down to pray. I struck him on the side of the head with my boots, and he just went on with his prayers. Next morning I found my boots beautifully polished by the side of my bed. That was his reply to me. It just broke my heart, and I was saved that day." That is really a testimony of Christian long-suffering.

929. Joy Here and Now

A stranger in St. Louis stopped a policeman one Sunday morning and asked him to recommend a church. He directed him to one at a little distance. "What's the matter with these other churches that I see along the way?" asked the stranger. "Why don't you recommend them?" "To tell the truth," replied the policeman, "I am an unbeliever myself, but people coming out of that church are always happy. They are different. If I ever decided to go to church, that's where I'd go. They've got something there that makes them happy." That something was the gospel of Jesus Christ. You may not be able to fully understand it, but it has the power to give you the joy, peace, and satisfaction of heart that the whole world cannot give.

Ineffective

930. I Work for You

Once a clergyman knelt down by a young woman bowed in prayer who was seeking Christ at a time of revival. Something seemed to worry her. "What is it?" asked the minister kindly. "Have you surrendered your all?" "I have tried," the woman sobbed. "What is the matter, then?" "It's the way Christian people have treated me. I am afraid I shall have to give up my place in the family where I work as a servant. The man is so cross and impatient with me." "Give it up then. God will supply something better," said the minister. "For whom do you work?" The woman raised her bowed head. "For you, sir." "It's our June!" gasped the minister, not having realized who she was until that moment.

931. Not Preserved but Pickled

There was a disagreeable man who always liked to be the first to get up in prayer meeting and repeat his stereotyped testimony, "I praise the Lord for saving me and preserving me." Finally, a brother who knew him a little better than the others indignantly got up and said, "Brother, He didn't preserve you, He pickled you."

932. Two Dogs in Us

As someone has said, "There are two dogs within us; one is white and one is black, and they both try to bark through the same mouth, and the result is confusion." Our blessing of God is consequently not clear-cut and it offends those who hear it rather than attracting them to the God whom we seem to bless.

933. A Poor Representative

When Dr. Will H. Houghton was pastor of Calvary Baptist Church in New York City, a glib-tongued salesman came into his study and offered him some oil stocks that he said would make him a fortune. Dr. Houghton looked at the man and said in substance, "If this stock is as good as you say, why aren't you rich? You come in here in a shabby suit, with shoes run down at the heels, and expect me to believe you represent a going concern? I suggest you get into some line of work that produces representatives who inspire more confidence in their product."

934. Setting an Example

A mother said to her child, "Johnny, you take those marbles back to Willie Jones. You know I have told you about playing marbles for keeps; you think you won them, but that is wrong; you go right back and give them to the boy from whom you took them." "Yes, Mama," said Johnny dutifully, "and shall I take back the painted vase you won at Mrs. Jones' bridge party?"

935. Poor Testimony

A group of teenage girls was discussing a new leader for their Bible class. Their frank comments on the woman in question were enlightening and amusing. One girl said, "If you kids pick Mrs. L— to be our teacher, I'm quitting." "Why, what's wrong with her?" asked several of the group. "Plenty," was the reply. "Remember how I used to go to help her with her housework on Saturdays? Well, she still owes me money and she won't pay. Also, she talks a lot about being a good Christian, and boy, you should hear her say nasty things about some of her neighbors. Honest, kids, I know I shouldn't talk about her, but, please, let's wait until we find a teacher who lives what she teaches us on Sunday."

936. The Unworthy Daughter

There is a tradition that Jonathan Edwards, third president of Princeton and one of America's greatest thinkers, had a daughter with an uncontrollable temper. But, as is often the case, this weakness was not known to the outside world. A worthy young man fell in love with her and sought her hand in marriage. "You can't have her," was the abrupt answer of Jonathan Edwards. "But I love her," the young man replied. "You can't have her,"

said Edwards. "But she loves me," continued the young man. Again Edwards said, "You can't have her." "Why?" asked the young man. "Because she is not worthy of you." "But," he asked, "she is a Christian, is she not?" "Yes, she is a Christian, but the grace of God can live with some people with whom no one else could ever live."

937. Words Are Cheap

A non-Christian lawyer attended a church service and listened incredulously to the testimonies of some who were known to him for their shady deals and failure to meet their honest obligations. "How did you like the testimonies?" a man asked him at the close of the service. He replied, "To a lawyer there is a vast difference between testimony and evidence." Words are cheap, and it is perilously easy to give a fine-sounding testimony for Christ, but quite another matter to demonstrate evidences of God's purifying power in our lives through Christ. "This people honoureth me with their lips, but their heart is far from me" (Mark 7:6).

938. Citizen or Archbishop?

Let us not be like that archbishop who one day was overhead swearing. A peasant who stood by seemed to wonder greatly at his conduct. "I swear," said the archbishop, "not as an archbishop, but as a citizen." "But sir," said the peasant, "when the citizen goes to perdition, what will become of the archbishop?" How will God judge us when we appear before His throne? Will it be for what we said in church while praying or preaching, or what we said to our fellow human beings?

939. Ain't Up to Sample

A Salvation Army captain was preaching in Hyde Park in London when a man in the crowd interrupted him. "We haven't anything against Jesus of Nazareth," he said, "but we have something against you Christians because you ain't up to sample." Living examples of Christ is what the world wants to see in Christians.

940. Christian Soldier on Furlough

Once a professing Christian sold a bale of poor hay to a certain colonel who rebuked him, and the church member whined, "I am a soldier too." "You!" exclaimed the colonel in disgust. "What kind of soldier are you?" "I am a soldier of the cross," said the skinflint with a detestable flourish of the hand. "That may be," said the colonel, "but you've been on a furlough ever since I knew you."

941. Religion of Words

One thing God detests is the religion of words. It was Robert E. Speer who said: "After thirty years of leadership in Christian work, it is my conclusion and conviction that the greatest missionary problem is just the failure of Christian people to live up to their profession."

942. Fewer but Better

Once a soldier was reported to Alexander the Great as having shown great cowardice on a particular occasion. When the soldier appeared before Alexander the Great, he asked him his name. On hearing that it was Alexander, he upbraided him with the dishonor that he had brought on such a name and entreated him either to change his name or act differently. It would be better for the cause of Christ to have fewer Christians, but better ones.

943. God's Honor Needs No Defense

King Olaf of Norway was the bloody foe of heathenism. He reigned twenty five years, the scourge and terror of his own people, and never made a friend. Their maimed bodies, burned homes, and plundered property were a perpetual memorial to his merciless zeal. He called to his aid robbers and vagabonds and enrolled them in his army, requiring only one condition, that they should be baptized in the name of Christ. He had white crosses painted on the shields and helmets of all his soldiers. He gave a battle cry, "Forward, Christian men! Crossmen!" With all this, his last battle was a sad defeat in which he was slain in A.D. 1030. He justified himself and his horrible barbarities by saying, "I had God's honor to defend." The question is, does God's honor really need our defense, a defense that harms others? We can be sure any zeal that harms others is evil, no matter how we try to justify it.

Witnessing

944. *Results of Tract Ministry*

A man was giving out gospel tracts on a steamer. One gentleman whom he approached accepted a tract graciously but said, "I haven't much faith in that kind of work." The Christian worker replied, "It was through a gospel tract given to me twenty years ago that I was converted." Asking for particulars, the gentleman discovered that it was he who had given him the tract! He had ceased to do this because he saw so few results from his efforts. He added, "But by the grace of God I shall start again."

945. *A Fisherman*

During the first and second centuries, the symbol of Christianity was the fish. A present-day Christian decided that a fishhook would be the proper emblem for a soul-winner to use for winning people to Christ, so he had a little golden fishhook made to be worn on the lapel of his coat. When people asked him what it meant, he told them that he was a fisher of men. A little newsboy from whom he bought a paper one day said to him, "Mister, do you belong to a fishing club?" "Yes, I do," said the Christian, "and I think fishing is pretty nice, don't you?" "Oh yes," the little fellow replied, "Do you ever catch any big ones?" "I have caught 250 pounders," replied the man. "Go on!" said the lad incredulously. "Yes," said the Christian, "I have caught a 250-pound fish." "Those sure are big," marveled the boy. Then leaning over, the Christian said, "Sonny, to tell you the truth, I would rather catch small fish than big ones." He exclaimed. "No!" "Yes, about your size." The little boy looked down at himself as if he were thinking, "I am not so small." Then the Christian told him that he was a fisher of men, seeking to win souls, and that if he would believe on the Lord Jesus Christ he would be saved. The newsboy took him at his word and came to Christ. Here was a fisherman for Christ who used a gold fishhook on his lapel to catch souls with. You may have some other kind of hook. It makes no difference as long as you catch fish.

946. *The Convincing Witness*

A man traveling along a dark road one stormy night met a man coming from the opposite direction who said to him in a hesitant manner, "I think maybe the bridge is out. At least I heard something to that effect." The traveler was not impressed and decided to proceed. A little farther on a man came rushing out of the dark to him and said, "Stop! Don't go any farther. The bridge is out!" So passionately convincing were his tones that the traveler turned back, and his life was saved. That is how we are to witness, with passion and conviction.

947. Thank You, John

When John Broadus was sixteen he accepted Christ as his Savior and at once began to introduce others to his new-found Friend. His first convert was a school friend. These two lived most of their lives in the same city, Broadus a professor in the university, the other a truck-driver. Broadus said that whenever they met during all those years his friend touched his cap as they passed and said, "Thank you, John, thank you." "I know just what he will say when I meet him coming down the golden street of heaven," said Broadus. "It will be just what he said this morning, 'Thank you, John, thank you.' "

948. A Witness Who Came Too Late

Far up the Amazon River, a Baptist missionary was using a flannelgraph to aid her in telling a group of school children about Jesus. As she talked, an elderly man with stooped shoulders and gray hair joined the children. He listened with rapt attention as the missionary told the story of God's grace as it is revealed in Christ. After the children were dismissed, the old man came up to the missionary with this question: "May I ask, Madam, if this interesting and intriguing story is true?" "Of course," the missionary said, "it is in the Word of God." With countenance and voice revealing his doubt, the old gentleman said, "This is the first time in my life that I have ever heard that one must give his life to Jesus to have forgiveness from sin and to have life with God forever." Then with a note of finality he concluded, "This story cannot be true or else someone would have come before now to tell it. I am an old man. My parents lived their lives and died without ever having heard this message. It cannot be true or someone would have come sooner." Although she tried hard, the missionary could not convince the old gentleman of this truth from God's Word. Turning to make his way back into the darkness of the jungle and the darkness of sin, he kept repeating the words, "It cannot be true; it cannot be true, or someone would have come sooner."

949. The Christian's Walk

St. Francis said one day to one of the young monks, "Let us go down into the town and preach." They passed through the streets and returned to the monastery without having said a word. "You have forgotten, father," said the young man, "that we went down to the town to preach." "My son," Francis replied, "we have preached. We were preaching as we walked. We have been seen by many: our behavior has been noticed; it was thus that we preached. It is no use, my son, to walk anywhere to preach unless we preach everywhere as we walk." "Wherefore, seeing we are compassed about by so great a cloud of witnesses, let us play our part nobly, looking unto Jesus, the Author and Finisher of our faith" (Heb. 12:1).

950. Not Ashamed of Christ

A young man got up to give his testimony for Christ in an open air meeting. Not being accustomed to speaking in public, he stammered a good deal at first. An atheist who came by shouted at him, "You ought to be ashamed of yourself standing and talking like that!" "You're right," the young man replied. "I am ashamed of myself, but I'm not ashamed of Christ."

951. Dedicated Soul-Winner

Melvin Harper is manager of an eight-thousand-acre buckeye ranch and rice farm near Bay City, Texas. "Lord, send me cowboys who aren't Christians," is his daily prayer. Why? Because encouraging cowboys and youngsters to live for Christ is a kind of divine calling for the man who was the nation's top bronco buster and steer rider for more than ten years. Through the personal interest of a pastor who began visiting Harper at the ranch so he could learn to ride and handle cattle, the veteran rodeo performer started attending church regularly and finally made his decision for Christ. Soon he began teaching a

class of boys, but he doubts that he was doing much witnessing for Christ.

A new pastor came to the church, so one day the rugged ranch manager went by to see him. Their conversation soon turned to religion. Melvin asked his new pastor, "Do you believe in the Lord?" After receiving a quick and affirmative answer, Melvin continued, "Then if me and you prayed to God, believed in Christ, and asked for something, would we get it?" The prayer that followed is one which Pastor Eaves will never forget. Melvin and his pastor prayed that God would let him become a soul-winner.

Melvin didn't sleep much that night. At four o'clock in the morning he was fully dressed and on his way to the home of a lost friend. He arrived before daylight and prayed as he waited in a pick-up truck for the lights to come on in the house. The friend was won to Christ; that was only the beginning. Melvin's pastor estimates that he has already won more than fifty people to the Lord. Five cowboys at the ranch have become Christians, and in his Sunday school class of thirteen-year-old boys, twenty-four have accepted Christ in one year.

When asked about the greatest thrill of his life, Melvin told about the year when he was the only rider to stay mounted on the nation's wildest and best bucking rodeo horse in Madison Square Garden and in Houston. "But," said Melvin, "this kind of thrill doesn't compare with winning a boy, his parents, and a cowhand to Christ."

952. A Responsible Position

A young man, a skilled mechanic, was driving a visiting clergyman from his home town, fifty miles across the country, to another city. En route, they passed a huge factory consisting of perhaps twenty buildings scattered over several hundred acres. "Do you see that red brick building over there behind this gray stone one?" the mechanic asked. "I work on the second floor on the south side. There are seventy-four of us in that department, and as far as I know, I am the only one in all that crowd who ever goes to church or tries to live a Christian life. Sometimes I have to remind myself that, as far as that department is concerned, I am all there is of the Christian Church. If I don't do good work, then the Church has failed as far as those men are concerned. If I can't be relied upon, then the Church is undependable. If I am careless, then some poor unfortunate soul may have to pay for the Church's carelessness. It is pretty serious business being the Church in the midst of seventy-four other people."

953. Win Them One by One

When Paul went to Rome, every morning a new soldier of the Praetorian guard was chained to him, until each Praetorian guardsman had Paul under his custody. People might have said, "What a pity that a powerful preacher like Paul should have an audience of only one man a day, and a different one every day at that." But Paul could say, "God has enabled me to preach the gospel to the whole Praetorian guard." Who knows how much the conversion of pagans in Rome may be attributed to Paul's being chained to the soldiers of the Praetorian guard?

954. Joy of a Soul-Winner

Charles H. Spurgeon said, "Even if I were utterly selfish and had no care for anything but my own happiness, I would choose if I might, under God, to be a soul winner; for never did I know perfect, overflowing, unutterable happiness of the purest and most ennobling order till I first heard of one who had sought and found the Savior through my means.

955. Fishing for Men

In the business of fishing for men, it is not one's skill or fine equipment that produces results; it is the power of the Holy Spirit. A fisherman who had all the equipment that the best sporting goods store could sell him was having no success. Seeing a country lad with a stick and a bent pin for a hook, he smiled condescendingly, then did a double take. On the bank beside the boy lay a fine string of trout. "How is it that I can't catch any?" the man inquired. "Because you don't keep yourself out of sight," the boy replied. That's the secret of fishing for men as well as trout. Preach Christ and Him crucified, and send the people away talking about Him instead of praising you.

956. Common Sense in Witnessing

The man who charges up to a perfect stranger and demands, "Are you saved?" may indeed be zealous for the Lord, but he shows very little understanding or love for his fellowman. His tactless approach indicates that he has no real interest in the man as a person, but only as a potential candidate for conversion, an object to witness to. Common sense is essential even in witnessing. Remember this. You should witness not for the sake of witnessing but for the purpose of winning souls to Christ. As a fisher of men you must exercise judgment in casting the net. Or, to change the simile, you must hold your fire until you see the target. Firing your rifle into the air will not accomplish anything. Let this be the judgment you exercise as a steward of the higher truths of life.

957. Two Lights Are Shining Now

A woman who came to know Christ as her Savior returned home full of joy—the unique gladness that overflows the heart of a repentant sinner. After a few weeks, she expressed a desire to leave the community in which she lived because it was so sinful. When her pastor heard this, he said with some severity, "How would you like it if the city removed all the lights from the dirty, dangerous streets and left lights only in the good neighborhoods where no crimes are committed? Didn't Christ say, 'Ye are the light of the world'?" (Matt. 5:14). The woman accepted the rebuke, and some time later said to her pastor, "Now there are two lights that shine in our street." She had led a soul to Christ.

958. The Reason for Happiness

In one of his books, Archdeacon Wilson tells a significant story. Some of the best and ablest of the students at a women's Christian college started a class to teach the poorest men in a neglected suburb. They were fired by the noblest impulse— to give themselves to work for their unfortunate brothers. After some months of teaching elementary subjects, they asked the men whether there was anything in particular they wanted to hear more about. There was silence, and then a low whisper was heard from among them. One of the women went up to find out who had spoken. "What was it you wished especially to hear about?" she asked. "Could you tell us something about the Lord Jesus Christ?" asked one of the men. These men, as they looked upon these college students, did not covet their money, their education or their social position, but longed for that which made them what they were, Jesus Christ. This is what the world should be impelled to crave as they look upon us—not the things about us, or the lack of them, as the cause of our happiness—but rather the Lord Jesus Christ.

959. What Will Hell Be Like?

There was an old Scotch preacher who was passing a glass factory just before going to church to preach. As a door was ajar, and it was some time till the service, he stepped inside. One of the large furnaces had just been opened. He gazed into the white, blue, and purple mass of liquid flame until it nearly seared his face. As he turned away unaware of anyone being present, he exclaimed, "Oh, man, what will hell be like!" A stoker standing in the shadow heard him. Several nights later at the church a man came up to him. "You don't know me, but the other night when you stepped into the furnace room I heard what you said. Every time I have opened that furnace since then, the words have rung in my mind, 'What will hell be like!' I have come tonight to find out the way of salvation so that I will not have to find out what hell is like." God grant that our witness may lead many others to do the same.

960. Luminous Christians

The best argument for Christianity is a consistent Christian life. There is no argument against the silent eloquence of holiness. Actually, a lighthouse building would be dangerous but for the light it sheds abroad, and so it is with us. We may be lighthouses without light. Ships can break themselves on the rock. It is not merely what we say, or what we do, but what we are that matters. That is the witness that is convincing. The greatest thing about us is often our unconscious influence. Second Corinthians 4:11 says, "that the life also of Jesus might be made manifest in our mortal flesh." "Manifest" is a word meaning "brilliantly seen." We accomplish more by our radiations than by our exhortations. May God make us luminous Christians. That's what the light of Christ does for us. Have you ever put a candle within an alabaster or onyx vase? This is commonly done in Egypt. When a light is put inside, the whole thing becomes luminous. That's exactly what happens when Jesus Christ comes into our hearts. We become bright, luminous. Other people can find their way to God through the light we shed abroad.

961. Outspoken Witness

Dwight L. Moody once saw a man freezing to death on the street in Chicago. Moody could not just talk this man into warmth. He pounded him with his fist and got him really angry. The man began to pound back and then got up and ran after Moody. That got his blood circulating and saved his life. Our loud and outspoken witnessing may make people angry, but at least it may awaken them from their spiritual stupor.

962. Facing Death with Courage

Even today, in this so-called advanced state of civilization, we hear of brave soldiers of the cross who lay their lives on the line when they bear a fearless testimony for Christ. Dear personal friends of mine, Costas Makris and his wife Alki, were Greek missionaries to Indonesia. As Costas labored in the jungles, more and more natives were converted and then baptized. The chief became so disturbed about his people turning to Christ, especially the young people, that he decided to do away with Costas. He lined up his spearmen in front of this dedicated young missionary. In the distance Costas' wife and three small sons stood watching their husband and father about to be executed for the cause of Christ. How would you feel in their place? But the face of this missionary shone with a heavenly glory that puzzled these savage people. How could a man face death with a smile? Of course, his wife and many others must have been praying. As the men lifted their spears for the kill, the chief called out "Stop!" He walked up to Costas, embraced him, and told him that a man who could face death with such courage and with such a smile on his face had something that they themselves needed.

963. The World Needs Light

Exactly what does the Lord mean by "mourning," as we find it in the second Beatitude? (Matt. 5:4) It is not just shedding tears or inflicting physical harm on ourselves. Church history tells us of a group of men called the Anchorites who lived in the fourth century. They dwelt in solitude, fasted, and injured their bodies. The nearer they could bring themselves to the level of the animals the better pleased they were. One sect of Anchorites actually grazed with the common herds in the fields of Mesopotamia, and they were hence called *boskoi,* or "shepherds." They acquired a great reputation for holiness because of their mournful attitude toward life. One of the most famous of these monks was Simeon Stylites (395–451A.D.), so called from his standing for years on the top of a column sixty feet high until his muscles became rigid. Some of these hermits hung weights on their bodies; others kept themselves in cages; all endeavored to make themselves holy through being miserable. The motive of many of these men may have been truly honorable, a desire to escape from the vices of the great cities. But the greater the corruption of society, the more need for holy men and women to live in that society. The world can only become darker by the withdrawing of its lights and more corrupt through the removing of the salt scattered over it.

964. Opportunities

A businessman on his way to prayer meeting saw a stranger looking in the door of the church. He invited him to come inside with him. "All right," said the stranger. That was the beginning of a Christian life for him and his family. He afterward told the man who invited him, "I lived in the city for seven years before I met you. No one had ever asked me to go to church. I wasn't here three days before the grocer, the dairy man, the insurance man, and the politician called on me. You are the first one to invite me to church." And it took seven years! Don't wait to pick and choose among the souls of men, but consider anybody you meet as God's field for you to work in.

965. There Is More!

A young man on a visit to Washington went into the National Museum. On one of the cabinets was a label with these words: "The body of a man weighing 154 pounds." "Where is the man?" asked the young man. No one answered him. In the cabinet were two jars of water, along with other jars containing phosphate of lime, carbonate of lime, potassium, sodium, and other chemicals. Another section held a row of clear glass jars filled with gases—hydrogen, oxygen, and nitrogen. The materials in those cabinets were shown in the exact proportions combined in an ordinary man. After looking at the assortment for some time in silence, the young man said, "And that is what I am made of? That is all that goes to make me?" "That is all," said a bystander smiling, and walked on. But the young man did not smile. "If that is all that is needed," said he, "so much lime, so much gas, so much water, we should be exactly alike." There is something more which they cannot put into cabinets. God made us body, soul, and spirit. The soul and spirit cannot be put into bottles.

966. It Takes Only One

There is an inscription on a highway plaque in a small Minnesota town which reads, "On September 1, 1894, a forest fire swept over this area and 450 people lost their lives." As a person reads this sign, he cannot help asking himself, "What do you suppose started that fire?" Along the highways throughout our national forests we see signs urging tourists to be careful with fires. Each has a stern warning that a single match carelessly thrown away can start a conflagration. One match seems insignificant, but think of its tremendous potential. One Christian can be a radiant witness for his Master if he will only resolve to do so and dedicate his life to soul-winning.

967. God's "Helper"

Let us remember that wisdom never imposes itself, but it woos the hearts of others. It is true that we are anxious to help God accomplish His work in the hearts of people, but sometimes we are like the little girl who, after being out for a while, was asked by her mother where she had been. She said, "In the garden, Mother." "What were you doing in the garden?" "I was helping God," the child replied. She explained that she had found a rose almost blossomed and had "blossomed" it. She had only ruined the rose.

Works and Service

968. I'll Take the Job

On a Friday morning an eager young man from Stanford University stood before Louis Janin seeking part-time employment. "All I need right now," said Janin, "is a typist." "I'll take the job," said the young man, "but I can't come back until next Tuesday." On Tuesday he reported for duty. "Why couldn't you come back before today?" Janin wanted to know. "Because I had to rent a typewriter and learn to use it," was the unexpected answer. That quickly-prepared typist was Herbert Hoover. Do you know of a place where there is almost no witness for Christ at all? Learn the job that will take you there.

969. No Idler

King Antigonus, when he had not seen Cleanthes, the philosopher, for a long time, said to him, "Do you continue to grind (referring to the occupation by which he supported himself)?" "Yes, sir," replied the philosopher, "I still grind; that I do to gain my living, and not to depart from philosophy."

970. Joy in Being Useful

A discouraged young doctor in one of our large cities was visited by his father who came from a rural district. "Well, son," he asked, "How are you getting along?" "I'm not getting along at all," was the reply. The old man's countenance fell, but he spoke courage and patience and hope. Later in the day he went with his son to the free dispensary. He sat in silence while twenty-five poor unfortunates received help. When the door had closed upon the last one, the old man burst out, "I thought you told me you were doing nothing. Why, if I had helped out twenty-five people in a month, I would thank God that my life counted for something." "There isn't any money in it, though," objected the son. "Money!" the old man shouted. "What is money compared with being useful to your fellow men?" How true! Mercifulness carries within it its own reward and joy.

971. The Sympathetic Jewel

A man visited Tiffany's jewelry store in New York City. He was shown a magnificent diamond with its gleaming yellow light and many other splendid stones. But he observed one stone that was perfectly lusterless and said, "That has no beauty about it at all." The friend who was with him put the stone in the hollow of his hand and held it there for a few minutes. When he opened it, the man said, "What a surprise! There is not a place on it the size of a pinhead that does not gleam with the splendor of the rainbow. What did you do with it?" His friend answered, "This is an opal. It is what we call the sympathetic jewel. It only needs contact with the human hand to bring out its wonderful beauty." How many lives there are that need only the warm touch of human sympathy to make them gleam with opalescent splendor.

972. Raising the Bell

The story is told of a heavy bronze bell that had sunk into a river in China. The efforts of various engineers to raise it had been of no avail. At last a clever native priest asked permission to make the attempt on the condition that the bell should be given to his temple. He then had his assistants gather an immense number of bamboo rods. These are hollow, light, and practically unsinkable. They were taken down by divers, one by one, and fastened to the bell. After many thousands of them had been thus fastened, it was noticed that the bell began to move, and, when the last one had been added, the buoyancy of the accumulated rods was so great that they actually lifted the enormous mass of bronze to the surface. You may think your bamboo rod is too small and light to make any difference, but it is necessary in God's sight to help in lifting souls to God and to lend strength to the others.

973. Seeing through God's Eyes

On one occasion a prime minister of France summoned an eminent surgeon to perform a very serious operation upon him. "You must not expect to treat me in the same rough manner that you treat the poor miserable wretches at your hospital," said the prime minister. "Sir," replied the surgeon with great dignity, "every one of those miserable wretches, as you are pleased to call them, is a prime minister in my eyes." How important it is for us to realize that the soul of a rich, famous, or highly educated person is not more precious in the sight of God than that of an ignorant beggar. We are all God's field. There isn't a soul on earth to whom we ought to give nothing but our best in cultivating it and making it what God originally meant it to be. Let us look upon the whole of humanity as God's own field deserving our best service.

974. Help Dispel the Darkness

An Australian native preacher went to a little church in the bush to preach. It was dusk when he arrived, the place was without light, and he wondered what to do about it. Presently, he saw twinkling lights moving about through the bush. His congregation was arriving. Each person carried a hurricane lamp, and as they came in they placed their lamps upon a shelf around the chapel wall. Soon the whole place was flooded with light. Each had contributed light that had dispelled the darkness. Your share is needed in a world which desperately needs the illumination of the gospel.

975. A Higher Honor

When an important building was about to be erected, a certain artist begged to be permitted to make one of the doors. If this could not be permitted, he asked that he might make one little panel of one of the doors. Or if this, too, were denied him, he craved that he might at least be permitted to hold the brushes for the artist to whom the honor of doing work should be awarded. If so small a part in a work of earth were esteemed so high a privilege, it is a far higher honor to have even the least share with Christ in His great work of human redemption.

976. Living for Others

If you were to visit Paris, you could see the statues of two men, both named Louis. The first is of Louis XIV, France's absolute monarch, who is remembered today chiefly for his exclamation, "I am the State." He represents one of the supreme achievements of greatness through power. His philosophy of life was that the whole nation and the world, insofar as he could compel it, should serve him. A few blocks away is a less pretentious statue. There is no uniform on this figure carved in stone, no badge of office, no sword, no

crown. It is a memorial to Louis Pasteur, the servant of humanity and servant of God. His life of unselfish, devoted research conferred immeasurable benefits upon all humanity in the years to come through overcoming disease and suffering. The statue of the monarch is nothing more than a piece of sculpture; the statue of Pasteur is a shrine where pilgrims from all over the world pay grateful homage. It is the uncrowned servant of mankind who wears the real crown of men's love and honor. As you look back, would you rather be remembered as Louis XIV who became supreme ruler of France and now has just a statue to commemorate him or Louis Pasteur who is now crowned as an apostle of mercy? God's Word enjoins us not to be affected by the glamor of the moment but rather by the judgment of eternity.

977. Good Service Required

A boy who applied for work was told by the manager he did not think they had enough work to keep another boy employed. The boy said, "But I am sure, sir, that you must have enough work to hire me. You don't know what a little amount of work it takes to keep me busy." Many so-called disciples are like this boy. They want to follow Jesus, not to see how much they can do for Him, but how little. To such the Lord never says, "Follow me." Any who enter Christian service for the sake of having an easy time will be disappointed. Christ is a busy Commander of busy soldiers.

978. Not for Money, for Christ

Is our first interest in life the accumulation of wealth, or are we like that Burmese boatman who, when asked by a missionary whether he was willing to preach the Gospel to his fellow countrymen at only one-fourth of the salary he was now getting, said to the missionary, "I will not go for that small pay, but I will go for Christ."

979. A Life of Service

A certain family had two sons. The older said he must make a name for his family, so turned his face toward Parliament and fame. The younger decided to give his life to the service of Christ and turned his face toward China and duty. He was Hudson Taylor, the missionary, who died beloved and known on every continent. "But," someone wrote, "when I looked in the encyclopedia to see what the other son had done, I found these words, 'the brother of Hudson Taylor.'" It may be that some were inclined to ridicule him when he went to the mission field, but in the end, he was respected and admired. His mercifulness had not been in vain, even as far as the world was concerned. But the merciful also receive recognition and reward from God Himself. This takes place both in this world and, in its full measure, in the world to come.

980. Mansion or Cottage

A rich woman dreamed that she went to heaven and saw there a mansion being built. "Who is that for?" she asked of the guide. "For your gardener." "But he lives in the tiniest cottage on earth with barely room enough for his family. He might live better if he did not give so much to the miserable, poor folk." Farther on she saw a tiny cottage being built. "And who is that for?" she asked. "That is for you." "But I have lived in a mansion on earth. I would not know how to live in a cottage." The words she heard in reply were full of meaning: "The Master Builder is doing His best with the material that is being sent up."

981. The Master and the Violin

A wealthy Englishman had in his valuable collection a rare violin which Fritz Kreisler, the celebrated virtuoso, greatly longed to possess. When the owner persisted in refusing to part with it, Kreisler begged permission to play it just once. That was granted. With trembling hands the artist tuned the instrument and then played. He played as only genius can play. He poured his heart into his music. The Englishman stood as one transfixed until the playing had ceased, and he did not speak until Kreisler had tenderly returned the instrument to the antique box, as gently a mother puts her baby to bed. "Take the violin," he burst out. "It is yours. I have no right to keep it. It ought to belong to the man who can play it as you did." That was odd reasoning, and yet it has something compellingly illustrative of the attitude that Paul wanted to arouse in the Corinthians who were made rich in Christ (1 Cor. 1:5). In a sense, ought not an instrument belong to the master who can draw the finest music from it? Ought not your life and mine belong to the Master who can draw the noblest harmonies from them?

982. Tried by Fire

Pompeii in Italy and St. Pierre in Martinique can both teach us a lesson. On both of these, fire caused by a volcano brought unprecedented destruction. The museums that contain relics of these catastrophes display nothing that was made of wood. All that survived the fire were metallic objects. In Pompeii, pitchers, bowls, jewelry, and other ornaments survived the fire because they were composed of gold, silver, and precious stones. But no remains of wood, hay, and stubble have ever been discovered, for these things were completely destroyed in the heat of the catastrophe.

983. A True Servant

Someone asked an elderly Scotswoman what she thought of Robert Murray McCheyne's preaching. She hesitated for a moment, then replied, "He preaches as if he was a-dying to have you saved." Is that our spirit? Those who watch us will know. How appropriate was Spurgeon's advice to a young minister who complained of the smallness of his congregation: "It is as large a one as you will want to give

account for in the Day of Judgment." The first thing others should discern in us, Paul says, is that we are servants of Christ—subservient, obedient to Him; that He is Master and we listen to what He says and do what He commands.

984. Losing the Bonus

Suppose a wealthy merchant were to charter a ship to go to some distant country and bring back a valuable cargo. To encourage speed and faithfulness, the merchant offers a bonus to officers and crew if they bring the ship home by a certain date with the cargo intact. The ship arrives at the foreign port, and the cargo is placed on board. But unfortunately a quantity of whiskey is also taken on board, and on the way the back the officers and men indulge in it too freely. They drive the ship upon the rocks, with the result that the cargo is lost. They send out an SOS, and men with life-saving equipment put out from a nearby port and save them. They are thus saved from death, but they have *lost the bonus* they might have earned. Unrewarded, and with the loss of all their possessions, they return to their home port at the expense of others. Likewise, some souls escape hell by the skin of their teeth, but they have lost their reward.

985. Poor Service

A preacher went to see a dying old man who was very anxious about his soul. After a few visits by the preacher, the truth dawned upon him, and through repentance and faith he experienced the joy of forgiveness and the assurance of eternal life. Just before he died, he said to the preacher with obvious regrets, "I feel such a sneak because I've served Satan all my life and only now at the end have I yielded my heart to God." His conscience told him it was a mean, despicable way to accept and serve his Master and Redeemer.

986. In Partnership with God

A gardener expressed his idea of a co-worker: "As I work in the garden with the flowers and vegetables I feel that I am having a share in creation." And when a mother says to a little child who carries some small item into another room for her, "You are helping me," what stature it gives to that child and what a sense of dignity and place in life's affairs. This ought to take away any sense of the worthlessness of the countless small tasks you perform day by day. Look beyond the temporal and limited as you work in partnership with God. Your attitude will determine your sense of satisfaction with your task.

987. Singing in the Bishop's Choir

One day at Perth, England, Bishop Wilkinson noticed a thin-faced boy looking at him intently. He went up to him and asked if the boy wished to speak to him. "No, sir," said the lad, "only I sing in the same choir as you are in." The Bishop's friends laughed at the boy's idea of

his association with the Bishop in the church, but the Bishop didn't laugh. It was precisely that spirit of partnership in God's work that he wished to encourage. Similarly what a wonderful sense of satisfaction a Christian has when he can look at an infinite and eternal God and say, "Lord, I am your co-worker." That is the most rewarding and unique privilege we can have.

988. Fellow Laborers

Visit a factory where thousands of persons are employed. There is the manager sitting in his central office where he directs all the operations of the factory. Everyone is doing his or her separate job. But they are all fellow laborers with the manager; they are all necessary. Not one could do without the other. If one does his work badly the whole organization suffers. If one does his work well they all benefit. Some feel they have important work, some less important. But there isn't one who is unimportant in the eyes of that man who is sitting in the general manager's office.

989. The Wealthy Partner

A famous journalist abandoned a lucrative position for reasons of conscience. A friend asked, "Can you afford to do this?" "Well," said the journalist, "you see, I have a very wealthy partner." "Who is he?" asked the friend in surprise. "God Almighty," was the reply. A man who is in partnership with God can afford to lose his own independence, to surrender it to the interests of the Kingdom of God, to accept the Divine dictates, because the wisdom and spiritual resources of the heavenly Father are at his disposal.

990. Jewels

The Koh-I-Noor diamond, when it came into the Queen of England's possession, was a misshapen lump. It was necessary to have its corners cut off and its sides reduced to symmetry. No unskillful hand was permitted to touch it. Men of science were summoned to consider its nature and capacities. They examined the form of its crystals and the consistency of its parts. They considered the direction of the grain and the side on which it would bear pressure. With their instructions, the jewel was placed in the hands of an experienced lapidary, and by long, patient, careful labor its sides were ground down to the desired proportions. The gem was hard and needed a heavy pressure. It was precious and needed every precaution that science and skill could suggest to get it cut and polished into shape without cracking it in the process. The effort was successful. The hard diamond was fashioned into forms of beauty and yet sustained no damage by the greatness of the pressure to which it was subjected. "Jewels, bright jewels," in the form of spiritual children were the heritage God gave to Paul, as a spiritual father. God may permit us to play the same role as spiritual parents to our children, or to the children of God in the

Church. Let us recognize in either case that children are unshapely and need to be polished; they are hard and cannot be reduced to symmetry without firm handling; they are brittle, and so liable to be permanently damaged by the wrong kind of pressure; but they are stones of peculiar preciousness and, if they are successfully polished, they will shine as stars for ever and ever, giving off the glory they reflect from the Son of Righteousness.

991. Seek God's Blessing Daily

When Sir James Thornhill painted the cupola of that world-famous structure, St. Paul's Cathedral, in London, he was obliged to work while standing on a swinging scaffold far above the pavement. One day, when he had finished a detail on which he had spent days of painstaking effort, he paused to evaluate his work. So well had he succeeded in his task that he was lost in wonder and admiration. As he stood there gazing at the structure, he began to move backward to get a better view, forgetting where he was. Another artist, becoming suddenly aware that one more backward step would mean a fatal fall, made a sweeping stroke across the picture with his brush. The shocked artist rushed forward, crying out in anger and dismay; but when his companion explained his strange action, Thornhill burst into expressions of gratitude.

This is an excellent illustration of how God blesses the material things in our lives and why we should ask Him to bless them. There are two possible outcomes: Either our plans will turn out as we hoped or they will fail. Having asked God to bless, we ask Him to be a partner. Only if that is our attitude shall we have the grace to praise God whatever the outcome may be. If we succeed, we shall give Him all the credit. If we fail, we shall take it that He has something different in mind for us.

992. The Wise Pastor

A man who was greatly troubled came to his pastor because he said in all his good deeds he detected a mixture of selfish motives. "Should I stop doing these things," he asked in perplexity, "since I find some self-gratification in all of them?" The wise pastor assured him while we are in the flesh we shall always suffer the humiliation of knowing that nothing about us is perfect, even our motives. It is a matter of committing ourselves to God to love and serve Him in all that we do; and if the by-product of our actions is joy and satisfaction, there is nothing wrong in that.

993. The Two Builders

Paul envisions two builders on the one foundation, Jesus Christ. The one builds a palace, the other a shack. No doubt in Corinth, as in other ancient cities, side by side with the temples shining in marble and brass were the huts of the poor and the slaves, built of flimsy materials such as Paul mentions. He envisions a sudden flame playing around these buildings, the fire of the Lord coming to judgment. The marble gleams whiter, the silver, gold and jewels more resplendently, while the tongues of light leap about the palace. But the straw hut goes up in a flare. The two builders stand before God, the ultimate Paymaster. The one man gets wages for work that lasts; the other gets no pay for what perishes.

994. A Cup of Cold Water

Have you understood what is really involved in the "cup of cold water," as Matthew 10:42 calls it? There is more to it than appears on the surface. In Eastern lands the water is drawn up from a well in the court or fetched from a distance. The housewife brings in a supply in the morning and lets it stand ready for use. As the day goes on the water gets warm. It would be easy for her to give a cup of this water to a thirsty friend or stranger, but a "cup of cold water" implies the kindly thought that would lead her to take the trouble to draw it or fetch it straight from the well, perhaps in the heat of the day. So often we give what amounts to tepid water to save ourselves extra work. But I believe it is the "cup of cold water" that shall in no wise lose its reward. The principle would seem to be that going out of our way, making sacrifices to help the poor, will have a sure reward.

995. Someone Forgot

A hungry, scantily clothed little boy was crying pathetically. "I'm cold, I'm hungry!" he whimpered. A stranger approached him and asked, "Do you believe that God can take care of you?" "Yes," replied the starving little boy with assurance. "Why, then does He not send someone to bring you warm clothing and some food?" "I know, sir, that He asked someone to do it, but I guess this somebody has forgotten it."

996. Motive for Work

An Egyptian architect was commissioned by one of the Pharaohs to build a lighthouse at the mouth of the Nile. On a piece of rock that was duly selected, Cnidus, the architect, erected a fine edifice. Engraved upon the cement covering the outside of the lighthouse was the name Pharaoh. In a few years the effect of wind and rain had worn the cement away and Pharaoh's name had vanished. Then it was discovered that the wily Cnidus had engraved his own name in the masonry beneath. Even Christian work may be done outwardly for the glory of God; but, when the underlying motive is laid bare, our own glory often turns out to be the real aim.

997. Works That Bear Fruit

A farmer was showing his fine orchard to a friend who admired its neat and regular appearance. "But," said the friend, pointing to a peculiarly shaped tree, "if that were my tree I'd root it up in order to preserve the uniformity of the orchard." The farmer smiled and said that he was more interested in the fruit than in the form. "This tree," he said, "has yielded me more fruit than any of those trees that conform to a more regular pattern." Sometimes Christian workers may become so accustomed to doing things in what they consider the traditional or time-honored way that they forget to evaluate its productiveness.

998. Compassion or Convenience

"Aunt Mary was very kind to stay with you this afternoon," said a mother to the small convalescent whom she had left in care of a relative, and whose wearied little face an hour later did not speak well for the success of the experiment. "I hope you are not overly tired when she was trying so hard to amuse you." "She wasn't; she just wanted to amuse herself reading a book of hers to me when I wanted to play puzzles," was the truthful reply.

999. Big Salary—Small Job

A brilliant young man with a magnetic personality went out to the mission field. His salary was just a pittance. A large commercial firm was so eager to obtain his services that they offered him ten times his salary, but he refused. They offered to make it even larger if he would accept. "Oh, the salary is big enough," he told them, "but the job isn't!"

1000. Doing Versus Talking

A converted cowboy put it very well when he said, "Lots of folks that would really like to do right think that serving the Lord only means shouting themselves hoarse praising His name. Now I'll tell you how I look at that. I am working for Jim here. Now if I would do nothing but sit around the house telling what a good fellow Jim is and singing songs to him, I would not suit Jim. But when I buckle on my straps and hustle among the hills and see that Jim's herd is all right, not suffering for water and feed, or being driven off the range and branded by cow thieves, then I am serving Jim as he wants to be served." Let that be our philosophy, too, when the temptation is to talk instead of serving the Lord.

1001. Earthly Body Expendable

We thrill to Nathan Hale's patriotic declaration, "I only regret that I have but one life to lose for my country," yet all too often we make some slight infirmity of the body our excuse for not serving the Lord. We contemplate with awe the inspiring poems of Martha Snell Nicholson, so crippled by arthritis that she was bedridden for years and seldom drew a pain-free breath. Yet her writings are fragrant with praise of her Savior. Her secret? She "endured, as seeing him who is invisible" (Heb. 11:27). Through her poems and example she brought encouragement to thousands.

1002. Loyalty Reciprocated

Queen Elizabeth once sent an ambassador far away on important and difficult business. He objected, saying to the queen, "But what will become of my business and my family?" The queen replied, "You take care of my business and I will take care of yours." He went. In this he showed more faith than Christians who are unwilling to trust God's care for business and family. How many vacancies on the mission field exist because of such a lack of faith or unwillingness to serve the Lord.

1003. First Be Reconciled to Your Brother

There were two brothers who had a quarrel and thereafter refused to speak to each other. The mother did all she could to reconcile them but to no avail. It greatly distressed her and robbed her of peace and happiness. One of the brothers saw how badly his mother felt. Hoping to please her, he brought her a fine gift. She refused it. "I don't want any gift," she said, "until you have become reconciled to your brother."

Worldliness

1004. Avoid Contamination

If a cube of lead is placed on a cube of gold, the two metals slowly but inevitably begin to penetrate each other. In the same manner we tend to imbibe the spirit, to share the opinions, to partake of the qualities of our intimate associates. Though we may believe that our gold will enrich their lead, the opposite is far more likely to prove true—their lead will debase our gold. That is why the Psalmist said, "Depart from me, ye evil doers, that I may keep the commandments of my God" (Ps. 119:115).

1005. Church Tramps

A young man left the church of his parents for another church. Someone asked, "What was the matter with the church you left?" "Nothing," he answered, "except they do a lot more for a fellow at the church where I'm going. They give you a splendid present at Christmas, a social with refreshments once a month, and a chance to get in with folk who can help you socially." That was his idea of the mission of the Church. It was not long, however, before he changed churches again. The same man asked him why. "Oh, they did not re-elect me president of the social league of the church, and I won't stand for being slighted." That

is what Paul would call a carnal Christian.

1006. Following Dual Paths

Kapitango Kusita, an evangelist overseer of an African Church, was talking about following the "white" path, and the "white" path only. It was night, and a crowd of natives sat around the campfire. A native dog passed between the fire and the listeners. "Look at that dog! How many legs has it?" asked the preacher. "Four," came the reply. "Yes, four indeed," retorted Kapitango, "but have you ever seen the four legs of a dog trying to follow more than one path at a time? No, no! The four all go together; yet people with only two legs try to follow two paths: Christ and the world, God and mammon."

1007. The White Dress

A group of young people were about to explore a coal mine. One of the girls was wearing a white dress. A friend urged her to go home and change. Not liking the interference, she turned to the guide who was to conduct them and asked, "Can't I wear a white dress to go into the mine?" "Yes, ma'am," was his reply. "There's nothing to keep you from wearing a white dress down into the mine, but there'll be plenty to keep you from wearing one back."

General Index

lunch, 586
Luther, Martin, 174, 602, 603, 684,
 688, 691, 828
lying, 613, 820, 823, 824
Macartney, Clarence Edward, 303
Macedonia, 447
Maclaren, Alexander, 36, 425
MacLaren, Ian, 475
magnet, 730
Makris, Costas, 962
man, 47
 dying, 985
 English, 981
 rich, 286
 subject, 192
manager, 988
manliness, Christian, 120
mansion, 980
Manton, Thomas, 539, 742
manufacturer, 273
marble, 50, 297
marriage, 411
Martin of Tours, 135
martyrs, 159, 505
Martyr, Justin, 671
Mary, 392, 652
master, gracious, 290
masterpiece, 50
material
 substance, 182
 things, 991
Matheson, George, 57, 450
Mayo, Dr., 558
McCheyne, Robert Murray, 925, 983
McKinley, James, 139
mechanic, 256
mediator, one, 66
meekness, 12, **455–460,** 751, 898,
 911
 fruit of, 457
 of wisdom, 460
Melbourne, Lord, 532
merchant, 408, 442, 446, 531, 563,
 741, 770, 908, 921, 984
merciful, 322
Merrill, Dr. S. M., 207
message from God, 54
messenger, preacher, 520

metal object, 982
Meyer, F. B., 383, 410
Michelangelo, 50, 185, 384, 636, 642
Miller, Peter, 339
mind, 42
 child's, 439
 intelligent, 331
 limited, 432
miner, 620
minister, 51, 63, 97, 112, 155, 313
 gospel, 527
 ill, 522
 prime, 973
ministry, high calling, 525
miracles, 20
mirror, 41, 149, 438, 462
miser, 462
misjudged, 153
missionary, 33, 49, 56, 74, 86, 117,
 126, 128, 221, 445, 455, 457,
 475, 486, 500, 606, 666, 669,
 676, 753, 789, 793, 794, 835,
 864, 895, 896, 897, 901, 905,
 911, 915, 941, 948, 962, 999
 from India, 576
 medical, 371, 492
 misjudged, 579
 society, 116
 teacher, 124
missions, 99, 119, 120
 need for, 360, 713
misuse of Scripture, 22
Mohammed, 617
Mohammedan, 897
monastery, 480
money, 153, 221, 228, 230, 237,
 247, 264, 286, 342, 408, 418,
 442, 444, 446, **461–472,** 449,
 495, 599, 627, 657, 706, 712,
 741, 757, 773, 778, 815, 836,
 837, 841, 904, 940, 999
 love of, 574, 970
monk, 820
Montrose, Marquis of, 159
Moody, Dwight L., 146, 170, 378,
 408, 440, 595, 621, 627, 648,
 681, 682, 828, 961
Moody-Whittle, Mrs. May, 378

(*preacher, cont.*)
  wise, 992
  young, 127, 710, 718, 909
preaching, 48, 256, 369, 380, 513,
    530–557, 670, 895, 949, 955
precious, 26
predicted, 27
prejudice, 96, 605
prepared, 424
preparedness, 695, 697, 699
presence
  God's, 25
  invisible, 70
presumption, 729
pride, 217, 333, 381, 386, 468, 470,
    476, 508, 521, 539, **558–570,**
    594, 633, 700, 714, 717, 746,
    761, 851, 912
priest, 972
prince, 55
  Persian, 577
princess, 118
principle, Christian, 8
priorities, 123, 261, 263, 265, 469,
    499, **571–590,** 574, 581, 592,
    618, 712, 741, 948, 1005
prison, 21, 443, 745, 747, 762, 920,
    953
prisoner, 21, 23, 571
privilege, 7, 975
procrastination, 646, 655
profession, 406
professor, 615
  Greek, 578
  of theology, 40
promise, 20
  God's, 275
property, devil's, 92
proud, 126
proved, 275
public opinion, 764, 767, 772, 773
publican, 608
Puerto Rico, 49
punishment, 207, 736, 824
purity, 199, 207, 211, 241, 345,
    591–593, 785, 798, 1004
pursue, 11

Quaker, 31, 848, 867
quality, 483
  tasting, 583
quarreling, 18, 481, 486, 1003
Queen of Sheba, 790
question, 295, 511
  difficult, 43, 299
quotes, 594–603

rabbi, 43, 305, 462
rabies, 886
radiance, 39
radio, 367, 658, 951
railroad, 875
Raleigh, Sir Walter, 282
rarity, 524
rascal, 294
rays, sun's, 39
real estate, 876
realism, 708
reason, 9, 201, 229
rebirth, 668
recognize, 44
reconciled, 1003
recreation, 270
reformer, social, 56
regeneration, 654
rejected, not, 297
relationship, 15
  husband/wife, 22
religion, 609, 765, 790, 870
remembered, 976
repentance, 227, 547, 624,
    604–613, 631, 641, 654, 674,
    679, 692, 812, 836, 843, 845,
    858, 880, 920, 927, 928
reporter, 139
reproof, 334
rescue mission, 670
resources, available, 84
responsibility, 702
restaurant, 892
resurrection, 57, 167, 168, 171, 172,
    173, 175, 270, **614–617,** 835
revealed, 279, 324
revelation, 28
revival, 504
reward, lost, 984

Scripture Index

Romans

1:9 — 501
1:16 — 859, 950
1:19, 20 — 202, 712
1:20 — 838
2:1 — 154
2:20, 21 — 934
3:4 — 207
3:10, 23 — 739
3:22 — 241
3:22, 23 — 717
4:12 — 311
4:20, 21 — 275
5:3 — 793
5:4, 5 — 258
5:8 — 620
5:9 — 632
5:13 — 736
6:23 — 280
6:24 — 124
7:7, 13 — 30
7:17–19 — 754
7:18 — 181
7:19 — 932
7:23 — 891
7:25 — 674
8:3, 4 — 899
8:18 — 787
8:24 — 71
8:28 — 329, 332, 333, 991
8:37 — 809
8:37–39 — 807
8:38, 39 — 314
9:13 — 313
9:15 — 296
9:20, 21 — 640, 802
10:1 — 129
10:10 — 243
10:12 — 628
10:42 — 311
11:33 — 303, 308, 328
12:1, 2 — 124
12:10 — 137
12:16 — 926
12:18 — 486
13:1–14 — 29
13:1, 2 — 187
13:14 — 725
14:1 — 101
14:10 — 321, 774
14:12 — 174
14:16 — 907
15:1 — 138

1 Corinthians

1:5 — 981
1:10 — 105
1:12, 13 — 879
1:18 — 859
1:23 — 623
1:23, 24 — 710
1:26, 27 — 846
1:27 — 578, 850
2:1 — 370
2:1, 2 — 541, 955
2:3 — 518
2:7 — 267, 302
2:9 — 433
2:10, 11 — 436
2:12 — 68, 650
2:14 — 25, 201, 853
3:3 — 98, 1004
3:9 — 25, 99, 973, 986, 987
3:10 — 993
3:10, 11 — 107
3:11 — 36, 37
3:12–15 — 837
3:13 — 982
3:14, 15 — 980, 982
3:15 — 984
3:16 — 365
4:2 — 983
4:3, 4 — 764
4:6 — 560
4:7 — 381
4:12 — 969
4:16, 18, 19 — 720
5:10 — 199
6:13 — 237
6:19 — 365
7:16 — 898
10:13 — 805
12:12 — 150
12:14 — 106
12:21 — 104
12:22, 23 — 988
12:25 — 93, 101
12:27 — 248
13:4 — 217
13:11 — 348
13:12 — 156, 438, 583
13:13 — 208
14:20 — 325
15:2 — 632
15:10 — 298
15:19–22 — 854
15:29 — 121
15:35 — 167
15:36 — 173, 176
15:36–38 — 162, 168
15:37 — 166
15:37, 38 — 615
15:40 — 614
15:42 — 161
15:50 — 172
15:52 — 109
15:53–55 — 157
15:57 — 811

2 Corinthians

1:3, 4 — 136, 971
1:12 — 513
3:2, 3 — 912
3:12 — 534, 551
3:14–16 — 772
4:6 — 57
4:7 — 539
4:8–10 — 911
4:11 — 960
5:12, 13 — 996
5:13 — 767
5:17 — 662, 663, 669
6:2 — 645
6:3, 4 — 522
6:4 — 143
6:10 — 144
6:17 — 922
7:10 — 985
8:9 — 672
8:11 — 244
9:7 — 188